THE FUTURES OF CRIMINOLOGY

edited by

David Nelken

SAGE Publications
London · Thousand Oaks · New Delhi

For Mical

Editorial arrangement, Introduction, and Chapters 1, 10 ©
David Nelken 1994
Chapter 2 © Massimo Pavarini 1994; English translation ©
David Nelken 1994
Chapter 3 © Stanley Cohen 1994
Chapter 4 © Richard Ericson and Kevin Carriere 1994
Chapter 5 © Stuart Henry and Dragan Milovanovic 1994
Chapter 6 © Wayne Morrison 1994
Chapter 7 © Alison Young and Peter Rush 1994
Chapter 8 © Malcolm Feeley and Jonathan Simon 1994
Chapter 9 © Dario Melossi

First published 1994

 SAGE Publications Ltd
6 Bonhill Street
London EC2A 4PU

SAGE Publications Inc
2455 Teller Road
Thousand Oaks, California 91320

SAGE Publications India Pvt Ltd
32, M-Block Market
Greater Kailash - I
New Delhi 110 048

British Library Cataloguing in Publication data

A catalogue record for this book is available from the British
Library.

ISBN 0 8039 8714 5
ISBN 0 8039 8715 3 (pbk)

Library of Congress catalog card number 94–067239

Typeset by Type Study, Scarborough
Printed in Great Britain by Redwood Books, Trowbridge,
Wiltshire

Contents

Notes on Contributors

Kevin Carriere is a PhD candidate in sociology and a junior fellow in criminology at the University of Toronto, Canada. He has published in the areas of community policing, penology and criminological theory.

Stanley Cohen is Professor of Criminology at the Hebrew University, Jerusalem, Israel. His books include *Folk Devils and Moral Panics* (1972), *Visions of Social Control* (1985) and *Against Criminology* (1988). He is currently doing research on information about human rights violations.

Richard Ericson is Principal of Green College and Professor of Law, Sociology and Anthropology, University of British Columbia. His recent books include *Visualising Deviance* (1987), *Negotiating Control* (1989) and *Representing Order* (1991) (co-authored with Pat Baranek and Janet Chan) and *The Culture and Power of Knowledge* (1992) (co-edited with Nico Stehr). His current research interests include law and communication, risk society theory, mass media and crime and policing.

Malcolm Feeley is Professor of Law in the Jurisprudence and Social Policy Program at the University of California at Berkeley. During 1992–94 he was a visiting professor at the Institute of Criminology and Fellow at the Institute of Advanced Studies at the Hebrew University. He received his PhD in political science in 1969 and has taught at NYU, Yale and Wisconsin, before moving to Berkeley in 1983. Two of his books, *The Process is the Punishment* (1974) and *Court Reform on Trial* (1983) received awards from the American Bar Association.

Stuart Henry is Professor of Criminology in the Department of Sociology, Anthropology and Criminology at Eastern Michigan University. He has published ten books and over fifty articles on aspects of crime, deviance and informal social control. His books include *The Hidden Economy* (1978); *Private Justice* (1983) and with Erdwin 'Bud' Pfuhl, *The Deviance Process* (1993). His latest book, *Criminological Theory* (1994), co-authored with Werner Einstadter, analyses the fundamental assumptions of theorists in thinking about crime.

Dario Melossi is Associate Professor of Sociology at the University of California at Davis and Associate Professor of 'Sociologia Criminale' at the Faculty of Law of the University of Bologna. His most recent publications are *The State of Social Control: A Sociological Study of Concepts of State and Social Control in the Making of Democracy* (1990); 'Weak leviathan and strong democracy, or two styles of social control', forthcoming in *International Journal of Contemporary Sociology* (1994) and 'Gazette of morality and social whip: Punishment, hegemony and the case of the USA, 1970–92', *Social and Legal Studies*, 1993.

Dragan Milovanovic teaches in the Department of Criminal Justice at Northeastern Illinois University in Chicago. He was recently Visiting Fellow at the University of New England (Australia). He has published several books and numerous articles on ideology and law. His most recent book is *Postmodern Law and Disorder: Psychoanalytic Semiotics, Chaos and Juridic Exegeses* (1992). In his current research Dr Milovanovic is developing a constitutive theory of law, incorporating semiotics and addressing the question of agency in relation to law and ideology.

Wayne Morrison teaches criminology and jurisprudence in the Faculty of Law at Queen Mary and Westfield College. His research interests are in the areas of Legal Theory and Criminology and he is currently working on a book reading jurisprudence in the changing contexts of modernity and an undergraduate text in criminology for law students.

David Nelken is Professor of Sociology and Head of the Department of Social Change, Legal Institutions and Communication, University of Macerata (Italy) and Visiting Professor of Law (Criminology) at University College, London. He is on the Editorial Board of journals in Britain, Italy and the United States. His writing focuses on the connections between legal theory, social theory and criminology and he was given a distinguished scholar award by the American Sociological Association for his book *The Limits of the Legal Process* (1983).

Massimo Pavarini is Professor of Prison Law in the Law Faculty of Bologna, Italy. He is co-author with Dario Melossi of *The Prison and the Factory* (1981). He is also the author of *Introduzione alla Criminologia* (1980) and editor of the volumes *I segni di Caino: La rappresentanza delle devianza nelle communicazioni di massa* (1985) and *Potere giudiziario, enti locali e giustizia minorile* (1985).

Peter Rush is a lecturer in the Department of Law, University of Lancaster. He is the author of *Beyond the Edge* (1985) an ethnography of juvenile delinquency and victimisation; and has also written on the phenomenology of legal education, theories of narrative in the law of evidence and the history of criminal justice. He has co-edited *Criminal Legal Practices* (in press) and is the author of *Trials of Sex* (in press), a study of the socio-legal construction of sexual difference.

Jonathan Simon is Associate Professor at the University of Miami School of Law where he teaches criminal procedure and law and social theory. He received his JD and PhD from the University of California at Berkeley and has taught at Berkeley and the University of Michigan. He is the co-author (with M. Feeley) of 'The new penology' published in *Criminology* (1992) and the author of several articles on risk and crime published in *Law and Society Review*, *Law and Social Inquiry*, *The Socialist Review*, and elsewhere, as well as the book, *Poor Discipline: Parole and the Social Control of the Underclass: 1890–1900* (1993).

Alison Young is a lecturer in the Department of Law, University of Lancaster. She is the author of *Femininity in Dissent* (1990), a study of the press coverage of the Greenham Common protest and numerous articles on femininity, criminality and legal discourse. Her forthcoming book *Post-modern Criminology* (1995) analyses narratives of community, disease, femininity and race in discourses of criminal law and criminology. Her current research relates to the role of law in the regulation of representation of biotechnology and reproduction.

Introduction

David Nelken

The purpose behind this book, as set out in the outline sent to prospective contributors, derived from the sense that recent criminology (and in particular English Language criminology) seemed to have produced little new in the way of theoretical thinking and, what was worse, had failed to take stock of new developments elsewhere. As a means of examining and perhaps remedying this situation, a number of scholars, chosen from among those doing work in theoretical criminology, were asked to reflect on the relationship between theoretical developments in other fields and their own thinking about crime and crime control.[1]

In itself this worry about criminology getting out of touch is not new. Criminology – the disciplined study of crime and crime control – has regularly been accused of turning into an overly practical policy science obliged – when necessary – to obtain its intellectual credibility from other sources. In the past it was assumed that the answer to criminology's tendency to slip into technique was to try to relate it more closely to one or other of the master disciplines, whether sociology or psychology, law or medicine, from which it could draw its concepts and theories. Alternatively (or in addition), the solution advocated was a sharper politicisation of the subject designed to make clearer the biases and consequences of the allegedly technical policy considerations which guided its interventions. Now, however, it may not be sufficient just to think in terms of updating the subject by importing the latest theories and findings from sociology or some other master discipline. Under the banners of post-positivism and post-modernism current intellectual work is challenging the very concepts of discipline and progress. Similarly, political strategies of reform or struggle, whether social democratic or Marxist in inspiration, are seen as irremediably bound up with so-called 'meta-narratives' of social progress, when what is to be preferred is a more limited, local and ironicising style of argument and intervention. In a sense, therefore, what has come to be at stake is the very future of criminology, and not just of any particular approach within it. If, as Gouldner (1973) explained, *The New Criminology* succeeded in making criminology intellectually (and not only professionally) respectable by linking it to the wider concerns of social theory, the challenge now faced by those writing criminology is how to assess its ambitions in relation to trends which contrive its fragmentation and threaten its pretensions.

This account may seem a little exaggerated. Has criminology really failed to keep up with intellectual developments elsewhere? Certainly there is good theoretically-informed work still being done. But this mainly seems to involve the elaboration, reassessment or synthesis of past theorising about the causes of crime (Braithwaite, 1989; Roshier, 1989). There are valuable descriptions of particular types of crime and the best ways of dealing with them, as well as much needed studies of neglected (or repressed) topics such as gender and crime, race and crime or, very recently, crime and masculinity. There is also some good historical and comparative work. However, most of the energy, in English language criminology at least, seems to be directed to the study of criminal justice and the pursuit of crime prevention more generally (in large part because this is where government research funding is most generous). Such research does not necessarily support the status quo; it can be and often is critical of the practice of those involved in criminal justice, whether police, prosecutors or judges, and sceptical towards the intention or the outcomes of government initiatives. But it is doubtful whether it can provide an appropriate starting point for reviving criminological theorising. Even those who see themselves as radical or critical criminologists, for political as much as theoretical reasons, now concentrate mainly on being 'realistic' about the factors shaping local level criminal victimisation (putting more utopian strains of critical work such as abolitionists or unreconstructed Marxists on the defensive). With some important exceptions – the rethinking in penology stimulated by the writings of Foucault, the debates over law and criminology within feminism, some recent work on crime in the media – little attention has yet been given to the theoretically daring work which is being done in disciplines such as linguistics, semiotics, cultural studies, social theory or anthropology or even in closely related subdisciplines such as sociology of law, or intellectual movements such as critical legal studies. Far from pioneering in these fields few scholars writing as criminologists have even tried to face the possible relevance for their subject of contemporary debates such as those concerning deconstruction or philosophical pragmatism.

Despite its concern over the future of criminology this is not a book of futurology. It offers glimpses of the possible futures of the discipline both as may be shaped by developments in society and by changes in the self-understanding of the scientific and humanistic disciplines. But whether criminology is or should be necessarily affected by such wider developments is itself controversial. In any case, if futurology were the aim, the safest prediction of the immediate future of the discipline (as in the prediction of recidivism) would be that it would see more of the same sort of work which currently represents the mainstream. Outside of feminism, for example, the attempt to produce a postmodern criminology has still hardly begun. Many, but by no means all, of the contributors in this volume think it important to face this challenge, but, as I argue in Chapter 1, it should not be assumed that this is the only or even the best future for criminology.

The different chapters in this book thus each stand as independent contributions to an agenda for theoretical criminology. But they do also converge on a number of overlapping themes. In particular, the book has been organised around the following topics: the attempt to offer a critical survey of the theoretical accomplishments of the field and their viability for the future; the encounter with new ways of thinking such as postmodernism; and proposals intended to change our ways of analysing current developments in crime and crime control, with particular reference to the new light which can be thrown through the use of comparative perspectives.

The first chapter asks what it means to say that criminology needs to be reflexive, and examines the potential and limits of a movement from social constructionism to reflexivity. This chapter also seeks to bring out some of the points of agreement and disagreement in the other contributions to this book and provide one context for 'reading' their implications. The next three chapters all offer various efforts at a stock-taking of the literature. In Chapter 2 Massimo Pavarini raises some fundamental questions which set the agenda for later chapters: whether criminology is worth saving, how its 'gaze' has been and could be extended, and its applicability in practical interventions. Stanley Cohen starts Chapter 3 with a characteristically succinct review of the theoretical resources of critical criminology and then questions how far these may be relevant in the different circumstances of countries undergoing transitions to democracy. In Chapter 4 Richard Ericson and Kevin Carriere analyse what they call 'the fragmentation of criminology', consider its causes, and discuss whether or not this should be regarded as a problem.

While the proliferation of incommensurable discourses and practices can already be considered a feature of postmodernity (which Ericson and Carriere see no possibility nor need of resisting), the three chapters which follow are even more explicit in seeking to address the encounter between criminology and postmodernism. In Chapter 5 Stuart Henry and Dragan Milovanovic examine how postmodern theorising can be used in deconstructing and reconstructing our notion of crime so as to develop what they call a substitute discourse.

In Chapter 6, on the other hand, Wayne Morrison stresses the negative features of postmodernism. He evokes the melancholy of postmodernist hopes and fears, focuses on the difficulties of avoiding an exclusionary response to the problems seen to be represented by 'the underclass', and calls for a return to the type of theorising characteristic of modernism. Chapter 7, the third of these encounters with postmodernism, is entitled 'The Law of Victimage'. In their chapter, Alison Young and Peter Rush offer a reading of legal and criminological discourses about the victims of crime which pays special attention to the way the use of descriptions and metaphors can suppress voices. In particular they attempt to show how Left Realist writing about the victims of crime, for all its purported 'realism', is unable to present the reality of certain types of victimisation.

The final three chapters each offer accounts of current techniques of crime control enriched by the insights provided by historical and comparative perspectives. Malcolm Feeley and Jonathan Simon (Chapter 8) seek to describe the emerging form of what they call 'actuarial justice' which they see as a reflection of the central importance now being assumed by the concept of risk in criminal justice. Like Morrison they too link this to the existence of a permanent 'underclass', as well as to a failure of the courts to challenge this new type of discourse. While their analysis is based mainly on developments in the United States they conclude by describing the methods used to control the *intifada* Palestinian rebellion in Israel as an analogy of the type of policing that is likely to develop wherever the target of control is an underclass which the larger society makes no attempt to integrate. The last two chapters, by Dario Melossi (Chapter 9) and by David Nelken (Chapter 10), each concentrate on the future of comparative criminology and its potential contribution to criminological theorising more generally. Dario Melossi asks how different cultural settings affect the relationship between crime and politics and contrasts the very different ways elites in the United States and in Italy use their control over crime as a political resource. David Nelken, in the concluding chapter, offers an assessment of the special difficulties and possible ways forward in comparative criminology and puts forward a framework for exploring the relationship between crime, criminal justice and different types of trust.

It would be both rash and arbitrary to pick out any particular issue of the many discussed in these chapters as the key to the future development of criminology. But there are perhaps three topics which could be particularly suitable for raising the level of theoretical discussion in criminology. These have to do with the construction of 'the other'; the perception and control of 'risk'; and the problem of reflexivity. Each of these themes, which relate both to developments in crime and criminal justice and to changes in the way of studying them, could map out in their own right a set of indications for the future of criminology. This concern with difference and 'the other' is already a constant preoccupation in postmodernist writing, both in feminism and in comparative work deriving from anthropology, and could provide an important focus for attention especially where the figures of the other, the stranger and the criminal become intertwined. Similarly, there is much to be learned about risk as both object and methodology of new techniques of social control. We could ask how it plays a different role in responding to the (mal)practices of different sections of society and how it relates to the level and types of trust in society. Finally, reflection in and on criminology as a discipline could contribute greatly to our understanding of reflexivity. This could be examined not only as an aspect of 'civilisation' and self-control, in particular in the management of social and personal life in late modernity, but also as regards the degree of reflexivity possible and desirable in intellectual disciplines and social reforms.

At the same time, without any pretensions to building an all-encompassing social theory out of the particular concerns of criminology, it could also be interesting to look for intersections between these three issues and the way they form a complex whole. To take just one example of their interconnection: current preoccupation with the underclass conjures up the problem of the non-integral 'other' without sufficient stake in the social order to have the normal incentives which make for conformity. Unlike the earlier crimino-legal projects of Classicism and Positivism, however, there seems increasingly to be a tendency to treat these outsiders as a risk to be policed in a way which does not require them to learn how to act reflexively.

Any discussion of the changing boundaries of criminology, and, still more, any suggestion of putting its future in doubt, quickly, and perhaps inevitably, gets mixed up with everyday political struggles about who and what should properly be treated as criminal in any such redrawing of boundaries. But the 'obviousness' of criminal law offers too easy a justification of criminology. Recent British criminology rightly stresses the need for a subject which can help in tackling the problems posed by everyday criminal victimisation. But it is less evident that the present techniques of the criminal law are really the right solution. In Italy – the birthplace of both major schools of criminology – the need for the subject would seem even more beyond discussion. Having passed only recently through a succession of Mafia/terrorist bombings the country now forms a collective audience watching televised corruption trials of former political and business leaders in the hope that the application of the criminal law will help bring about a 'legal revolution' (Nelken, forthcoming). But the special role Italy has played in the creation of criminology, from Beccaria onwards, may actually reflect the extent to which it has relied *too* much on criminal law to solve its political problems. Both in Britain and in Italy (and not only these countries) criminal law may be becoming the first rather than the last line of social defence. Whatever encouragement all this may provide to those betting on the futures of this subject, it is a sign that something has gone badly wrong with public life when we have to look to criminology to provide recipes for social peace or political order.

Note

1 The contributors, who were drawn from scholars working in the broad area of sociological criminology, come from a number of countries and included a number who have had experience in living and working within more than one type of criminal justice system. Needless to say, however, the topics covered do not do justice to the potential range of approaches in criminology but reflect rather the contingencies of putting together this type of collection. At various points attempts were also made to obtain contributions on: feminist criminologies, crime and regulation, crime and technology, historical criminology, anthropology, and penology.

Research for this book benefited from the Italian Ministry for the Universities 40% fund.

References

Braithwaite, J. (1989) *Crime, Shame and Reintegration*. Cambridge: Cambridge University Press.

Gouldner, A. (1973) Preface in I. Taylor, P. Walton and J. Young (eds), *The New Criminology*. London: Routledge and Kegan Paul.

Nelken, D. (forthcoming) 'A legal revolution? The judges and tangentopoly', in S. Gundle and S. Parker (eds), *The Italian Republic: from the Collapse of Communism to the Rise of Berlvsconi*. London: Routledge.

Roshier, B. (1989) *Controlling Crime*, Milton Keynes: Open University Press.

1

Reflexive Criminology?

David Nelken

The postmodern habitat is indeed an incessant flow of reflexivity; the sociality responsible for all its structured yet fugitive forms, their inter-action and their succession, is a discursive activity, an activity of interpre-tation and reinterpretation, fed back into the interpreted condition only to trigger off further interpretative efforts.

(Bauman, 1992: 204)

From social constructionism to reflexivity

What has happened to criminological theorising? In particular, why, with the major exception of feminist writing, is there such unwillingness to engage with current intellectual debates over the way social developments have affected the possibility of representing reality and telling the truth? One way of interpreting this is as a reluctance to return to the impasse criminology got itself into the last time it tried to follow out the implications of treating crime as a social construction.[1] Social constructionism still inspires a lot of interesting work in sociological criminology, such as that on the handling of crimes within the criminal justice process or, more generally, on the labelling, non-labelling or de-labelling of misbehaviour. But the approach is vulnerable to the charge of theoretical incoherence and practical impotence. Insisting on the social contingencies which shape the definition and processing of crime only leads to the inevitable question – what then is the status of your own claim to describe and influence these processes? The practical implications are no clearer. If social construction is unavoidable what does pointing this out add to a debate on the merits of any particular choice? Is it a peculiar 'virtue' of academic writing to expose the contingency of social constructions or is this rather an activity which theorists can permit themselves only because they are not faced by the constraints of practical and political choices?[2] The political motivation for showing that 'censures' (Sumner, 1990) are socially defined is to offer a critique of the pretence that neutral choices shape criminal law and its implementation. But the corrosive force of insisting that law is no more than a social construction can also undermine objective criticism of its injustices and delegitimate attempts to shape it in supposedly more progressive directions.[3]

It is not surprising, therefore, that an influential trend within English language criminology has set its face against any further epistemological expeditions in search of how things might have been different. It stresses instead the need to be realistic about crime, to recognise the harm it causes and the need to take seriously the concerns of those who are its victims (Mathews and Young, 1992; Young and Mathews, 1992a). The strategy followed by the Left Realists neatly side-steps the contradictions of the social construction approach. Although they have little interest in raising fundamental epistemological doubts about social reality they none the less avoid an uncritical dependence on official definitions of crime by drawing on victim surveys to indicate the presence of alternative and neglected priorities for crime control. The practical and political attractions of this solution, however, are bought at the price of a certain theoretical populism by which public consensus is taken as the measure of intellectual progress (Ruggiero, 1992; Taylor, 1992). Whether or not the criminologist chooses to draw attention to it, he or she has to choose between constructing a personal theoretical object or accepting that of others. There can be no direct access to the crime phenomenon simply by adopting the definitions of actual or potential victims (Michalowski, 1991). Even Realist scholars increasingly talk of entering into a dialogue with the public as the means by which their potentially divergent conceptions of crime can be mediated.

An alternative response to the objections raised to Social Constructionism, as represented by the contributions to this book, is to acknowledge their force but treat them as proof that the approach needs to be taken even further (Pollner, 1991).[4] A radical extension of the social construction approach would apply it to the production of all discourse about crime, including, not least, criminology itself.[5] In this way the paradoxes of trying to be a consistent social constructionist would not be dismissed as the sort of philosophical contradictions which the working social scientist can shrug off as irresolvable and therefore not worth worrying about. Rather they would be taken as a challenge to identify the special features of theoretical production in criminology and the way this relates to the practices of those it describes or seeks to influence. Only when theorising is itself seen as a practical activity, subject to its own constraints, does it become possible to investigate the similarities and differences between this practice and that of the actors whose activities are being described.

What are the resources which criminology could use to become more conscious of its role in the construction of crime? A major contribution is provided, of course, by Foucault's investigations of 'the disciplines', and the large secondary literature that grew up around his work. But the impetus of Foucauldian studies is now diminishing and it seems that criminology is (again) at risk of becoming separated from wider debates in epistemology, the social sciences and the humanities. In so far as criminologists have begun to respond to these developments they have tended to see the issue as one regarding the desirability of building a postmodernist criminology. This issue is likely to become more central given the ever-multiplying literature on postmodernism in the social sciences,[6] but to link the future of theorising in criminology to the outcome of the debate over postmodernism oversimplifies the range of options on offer and risks polarising the field between those willing to embrace and those who continue to reject some of the more extreme positions described as post-modernist (Hunt, 1991). In any case while some of the contributors to this book show varying degrees of sympathy towards the claims and methods of postmodernism none of them evidence the theoretical scepticism or political nihilism which this trend is supposed to encourage. The question on which it seems more appropriate to focus in this introductory chapter therefore is less the issue of postmodernism as such and more the more specific problem of how far criminology can go in trying to understand the constraints and con-sequences of its own constructions of crime – what we could call *the prospects for a reflexive criminology*. While there is some overlap[7] with the debate over postmodernism, this is, at first sight, a much less controversial propo-sition (no one has yet come forward in favour of an unreflexive criminology). But claims that criminology need to be more reflexive do not always refer to the same thing and rarely spell out all the implications of this requirement. Much remains to be clarified about a term which is interpreted, for example, as: first, a way of overcoming the domain assumptions of one's theoretical starting point (Cain, 1990; Young, 1992); second, a defining characteristic of the operations of post (or late) modern society, or of the individuals or sys-tems in it (Luhmann 1982; Giddens 1991; Bauman 1992; Beck 1992); third, a method of giving attention to persuasive tropes in the writing of social sci-ence (Clifford and Marcus, 1986; Woolgar, 1988); fourth, a call for a differ-ent form of social investigation which involves greater collaboration between the researcher and the subjects of research (Steier, 1991); or fifth, the key to a new reflexive method of regulating modern societies by stimu-lating self-regulation (Teubner, 1983, 1988, 1993).

In this chapter I shall argue (referring also to the other contributions in this volume) that the issue of reflexivity can set an agenda for further theor-etical work in criminology. I shall show, as the above illustrations suggest, that this topic can arise in relation to the criminologist's *discipline, context, rhetorical strategies, standpoint* and *practice*. In addition, I shall underline the importance of distinguishing between two ways of thinking about reflex-ivity: the first invites the theorist to be more *reflective* about the point and manner of his or her theorising, the other draws attention to the *recur-siveness* which characterises the way contemporary systems, discourses and agents actually reproduce themselves.[8] These different aspects and mean-ings of reflexivity obviously carry a variety of implications for theorising, re-search and practice; I shall concentrate mainly on the much vexed problem of the extent to which theorising in a reflexive way can be kept from ending up in an unproductive infinite regress.

Criminology's limits

How does criminology define and change its conception of itself? What de-termines its boundaries and how can they be overcome? Must criminology's evolution be conditioned by changes in the world of crime and crime control? Does extending criminology's 'gaze' necessarily mean arguing for more criminal law? Like the other forms of reflexivity to be considered, disciplinary reflexivity can be taken 'too far'. It could, for example, turn criminology into a sort of sociology of knowledge which loses touch with the study of crime.[9] On the other hand, if criminology does not try to understand itself and its own conditions of existence it is unlikely to offer much insight into crime either.

The contributors to this volume offer a range of approaches to these basic questions. Some offer outlines of where criminology or types of criminology could go in the future (Pavarini, Nelken). Others look at the various grids (political, anthropological, deviance theory) which have shaped past examinations of the problem of criminality, and query the applicability of these bodies of theorising when transferred to other societies (Cohen). Some consideration is given to the possibility of renewing criminology by reviving older approaches such as the labelling perspective (Melossi, Henry and Milovanovic). There are contrasting attempts to describe, deplore or deploy features of postmodern criminology (Ericson and Carriere; Henry and Milovanovic; Morrison; Young and Rush).

Criminology has been attacked both for having too narrow limits and for not knowing what its limits are. Arising at a time when the lines separating political, practical and intellectual projects were perhaps more blurred than now (Foucault, 1977, Garland, 1985), controversy in criminology is as likely to reflect changes in political viewpoint as theoretical debate for its own sake, as can be seen from the self-descriptions of approaches such as critical or peacemaking criminology (Maclean and Milovanovic, 1991; Pepinsky and Quinney, 1991). The discipline thus embraces an uneasy mixture of explanatory, descriptive, political and normative concerns, and ranges well beyond the social sciences into the realms of law and medicine, philosophy and social theory, policy science and politics.[10] Subjected to the requirements of effective crime prevention and control set by everyday practical politics, it nonetheless inspires normative blueprints (Braithwaite and Pettit, 1990), utopian visions (Haan, 1990) or dystopian forebodings (Christie, 1993).

The mainstream (particularly American) approach to the discipline tries to maintain the subject within the limits inherited from the classical and positivist approaches to understanding crime and criminality. There seems good support, for example, for the recently reelaborated thesis that crimes are most likely to be committed by those who also behave recklessly in other spheres of social life – provided that appropriate opportunities present themselves (Gottfredson and Hirschi, 1990; Gramsick et al., 1993).[11] But such conclusions are reached by a form of theorising which deliberately sets out to produce universally valid propositions about crime at the expense of being unreflexive about the social and cultural context which shapes its meaning and control.[12] (Likewise its role for the criminologist is one which keeps him or her as far as is possible out of the frame of the data to be explained.) This approach to theory may work well enough for enumerating those factors which characterise those likely to end up being processed as criminals. But little progress can be made in understanding crime unless a more reflexive approach is adopted which highlights how crime itself is defined. Given the reciprocal relationship between crime and punishment many of the findings of criminology can equally well be deduced from the nature of law and law enforcement.[13] Some of the most influential recent contributions to criminology therefore review the evidence concerning both the causes and the reaction to crime hoping thereby to demonstrate the case for specific strategies of crime control such as 'reintegrative shaming' (Braithwaite, 1989). But here too given the contextual form and meaning of punishment the plausibility of such proposals depends on a wider analysis of historical and cultural differences in the link between systems of punishment and social structure. To investigate these matters means that criminology has to cope with an almost unlimited range of potentially relevant disciplines from which it does or could borrow concepts and methods.

Following the initial predominance of subjects such as law, social statistics, political theory, medicine and psychoanalysis (as well as less presentable 'disciplines' such as eugenics) a series of different social sciences have since been the dominant influences – at least in English language criminology. Psychology continues to provide the main resources for positivist investigations of individual differences in criminality. In the academic environment, sociology has been especially important, perhaps because of its pre-eminent role within American criminology. Yet disciplinary boundaries are increasingly becoming meaningless in criminology, as elsewhere (Ericson and Carriere in this volume). Thinkers who have recently had an important influence within criminology such as Michel Foucault or Norbert Elias transcend or reshape academic territories. Original and sometimes controversial uses of history (Garland, 1990), psychology (Katz, 1988; Turk, 1989), anthropology (Feldman, 1991) and economics (Gambetta, 1992), are at the cutting edge of innovation. Stimulating ideas are also being borrowed from psychoanalytic, feminist or postmodern writings – though it may be some time before they find acceptance in the major criminological journals. Work based on the theories of Lacan, such as his ideas about desire and the process of subjectivisation, are giving a new psychoanalytic twist to theories and interpretations of crime.[14] Similarly, Baudrillard's descriptions of the role of the media and consumption in constructing the virtual reality of contemporary society may be instructive (Poster, 1988; Gane, 1991a, 1991b).[15] Some of his more recent disquisitions on the forms of rules and the seduction of law breaking[16] may be particularly relevant, not least by suggesting the limits of a criminology which is tied to the legal gaze (Baudrillard, 1990a, 1990b).[17] It is interesting for our purposes that reflexivity is an important element in the thought of many of these writers.

Thus the diversity of intellectual resources on which criminology can draw can be seen as either a blessing or a curse. For some, criminology, too often, comes to serve merely as a repository for ideas torn out from other fields and applied without respect to their original sense (Cerretti, 1992; Pitch, 1992b). It is argued that the subject can only develop systematically if it follows a coherent discipline or subdiscipline such as sociology (Hagan, 1988) or 'the sociology of deviance' (Downes and Rock, 1982). Alternatively, the plea is that criminology's boundaries should be redefined inductively: Shearing, for example, would like its focus to be shifted from crime to 'guaranteed ordering' so as to accommodate the fact that following up phenomena such as the rise of private policing involves going outside the strict territory of criminology (Shearing, 1990a, 1990b). For other writers the main problem for criminology to overcome is the partiality of the different perspectives on crime which it has inherited: to master its object it must ensure that its gaze manages to take in all the aspects of criminal events – offence, offender, victim, and wider context (Taylor et al., 1973; Young, 1992). Like penal politics, however, criminological theory tends to oscillate between giving its attention to one or other of these.

On the other hand, there are those who insist that criminology is 'the richest of the social sciences' (Cohen, 1990b). Sociology (a major player in criminology) is claimed to be the most reflexive of disciplines because of its distinctive ability to apply its questions also to itself; this makes it peculiarly suited to reveal the constraints of other discourses such as law (Cotterrell, 1986).[18] The weakness and indefensibility of criminology's disciplinary boundaries can even be seen as a positive advantage. It obliges criminologists to go beyond any narrow definition of their subject (Hunt, 1990) or, as we might put it in terms of the present argument, it makes criminology more reflexive about its concepts and claims (Pavarini in this volume).[19] In practice, however, it is difficult to know how far to take this sort of reflexivity. It is true that criminology has certainly both promoted and benefited from related areas of study.[20] Yet to actually prescribe this as a necessary part of disciplinary advance would lead to an odd sort of horizontal infinite regress in which each discipline or subdiscipline is told to look elsewhere for inspiration.

In addition to looking elsewhere for insights it would therefore seem appropriate for criminology to examine the way it makes use of these other disciplines. But can criminology be brought to see its own way of seeing? A lot depends on whether there is a specifically criminological perspective. In Burke's dramaturgical sociology (1989) we are reminded that every way of seeing is always also a way of non-seeing. For Luhmann (1982, 1988), subsystems such as law, economics or politics cannot interrogate the basic distinctions which provide the basis for their operations. As he might put it, the distinction between criminal and non-criminal is itself neither criminal nor non-criminal. The question of limits has become a crucial issue in feminist attitudes to criminology. Some feminists see their contribution as transgressing the boundaries of criminology (Cain, 1989). But others have gone on to argue that the subject must actually be abandoned because 'the one thing that criminology cannot do is to deconstruct crime' (Smart,

1990: 77). While one response to this challenge has been to dismiss it as a 'boundary dispute' between criminology and sociology (Young, 1992) the question of what (other than legal definitions) holds the category of crime together will continue to be a difficult issue.

A major constraint on the ability of criminology to set its own limits is the way it is conditioned by legal definitions of the phenomena it investigates.[21] Criminologists join in debates over what sorts of behaviour should or should not count as crime, (for example, 'victimless' crimes, corporate crime or domestic assaults), or what constitute proper heads of culpability (such as the definition of consent in rape, provocation in homicide, or the criminal responsibility of corporations). They demonstrate (and instantiate) the proposition that what ends up being treated as crime depends in practice on political and professional interests and available institutional resources. But where they have attempted to substitute non-legal definitions of crime as the starting point of their discipline (as with early positivist writers or in some of the arguments over white-collar crime) they have met with scarce success.

Because of its difficulty in establishing its own definition of crime criminology easily ends up depending on as well as reinforcing common sense. To be reflexive about the discipline therefore requires us to examine how criminological discourse influences stereotypes of crime and criminality (see Henry and Milovanovic, and Young and Rush, in this volume). Talking about crime as dispute sets the stage for mediation; treating it as illness authorises the professionals of rehabilitation to follow their approach to punishment; identifying it as a social disease makes it appropriate to rely on social engineering to alleviate the problem by appropriate prophylactic measures. The 'abolitionist' approach to crime and punishment, which aimed to substitute criminal with civil and administrative remedies, was well aware of the importance of language (as in Hulsman's plea for the use of the expression 'regrettable acts'). More recently, however, many criminologists (and not only Left Realists) have abandoned their earlier sympathy for non-intervention and abolitionism in order to urge sterner action against crimes against women, corporate misbehaviour, environmental damage, state crimes, war crimes and crimes against human rights. Sometimes these calls for criminalisation are strangely forgetful of earlier reservations about the efficacy of the criminal sanction (Cohen, 1988: 235–77). But it is not always clear when attempts to broaden criminology's gaze are intended to lead to the extension of criminal law.[22] While social movements often see this as symbolically important, the criminologist could have in mind a variety of administrative, therapeutic, conciliatory, private, or other forms of conflict resolution.[23] But unless these alternatives are spelled out it will be difficult to change the social meaning of crime even if its definition is changed so as to become, for example, the 'violent refusal of democratic behaviour' (Pepinsky, 1991) or 'the power to deny others their humanness to make a difference' (Henry and Milovanovic in this volume). The problem with so-called efforts to 'decriminalise criminology', while simultaneously campaigning for the extension of the criminal label to new forms of injury, is that the intelligibility of the crime label is parasitic on its common-sense meaning, which therefore, tends to be reinforced even as it is being attacked.

The context changes

Whatever stand we take on criminology's future prospects, if we are to understand why reflexivity has lately become such a preoccupation we will need to place developments within the discipline in a wider context of social change. What are the relationships between criminology and the society it seeks to understand? How are we to theorise its own reflexivity in relation to that of the phenomena it seeks to interpret?

The contributors to this volume highlight a number of ways in which criminology interacts with its environment, underlining the cultural embeddedness of ideas about crime (Nelken, Cohen, Melossi) and the way criminological thinking changes over time as a consequence of wider intellectual and social movements (Pavarini, Ericson and Carriere, Morrison, Young and Rush); as for example the paradigm shift connected with the rise of insurance (Feeley and Simon). Almost any widespread social or technological change has implications for patterns of crime and social control. Some transformations, such as the steady rise in the number of organisations as holders of resources and as social actors, are reflected in crime patterns in a relatively straightforward manner. Thus criminal statistics show organisations increasingly figuring as victims (Heiland et al., 1992) and a continual growth in the number of crimes which involve access to organisations – the so-called 'crimes of the middle-class' (Weisburd et al., 1991). Likewise, the growth of the so-called 'underclass' of marginalised population of permanently unemployed will have effects on strategies of crime control (Dahrendorf, 1985; Feeley and Simon, Morrison, in this volume). At the other end of the scale 'crimes of the upperworld' (and organised crimes) are intimately linked to changes in international finance such as the development of the so-called 'casino economy' in the 1980s (Calavita and Pontell, 1992), as well as to shifts in political and economic frontiers and patterns of international trade (Passas and Nelken, 1993; Van Duyne, 1993).

On the other hand, we should not be too quick to see the social context as necessarily determinative (Nelken, 1990a). Developments in crime and criminal justice do not always mirror wider changes,[24] just as trends in criminal justice do not necessarily follow those in crime (but may even create them). Criminal justice may relate in oppositional ways to wider developments as in the supposed inverse relationship between formal and informal control (Black, 1976); procedures modelled on criminal law may offer anachronistic cover to the rise of administrative regulation (Nelken, 1982). The search for cause and effect may often be fruitless; criminal justice and social life are in many respects mutually 'constitutive' (Gordon, 1984) forming part of common social and cultural patterns such as those described by Foucault or Elias (Garland, 1990).

It is increasingly being argued that current developments in Western societies form a package variously identified as *high, late* or *post* modernity (the label varies more than the phenomena pointed to as evidence of such changes).[25] Some of this discussion has become conceptually complex: this is not the place to examine differences between the various attempts to specify what distinguishes the present period from the earlier stages of modernity, still less to enter into finer contrasts between postmodern, postmodernism and postmodernity (Hudson, 1986). A rough distinction must be made however, between what, for simplicity's sake, can be called *the sociology of postmodernity*, which remains faithful to sociology's classical ambitions of description and explanation of social reality and, on the other hand, *postmodern sociology*, which seeks to question this project. As will be seen, however, the distinction is not always that easy to maintain.

Sociologists of the postmodern point to a number of features which could be relevant to criminologists. Important starting points for investigation can be found in topics as varied as how changes in time and space in the modern city are affecting work and identity (Harvey, 1989; Giddens, 1990, 1991; Bauman, 1992; Smart, 1992); or discussions of the growth of the information society (Poster, 1990), its potential for surveillance and its use of spectacle. Some attempts have already been made to draw future-present accounts of social regulation in the modern city (Davis, 1990; Pfohl, 1992; Stanley, 1993a, 1993b). Especially interesting for our purposes is the way so many of these authors agree on characterising present-day society as one which is becoming ever more reflexive both at the level of how the social system behaves and how the individual conducts him- or herself. Not surprisingly, however, there are important differences in the way they envisage such reflexivity. Beck, a leading theorist of what he calls *Risk Society* (1992), for example, devotes a third of his book to 'reflexive modernisation', describing how risk assessment has become a method of 'colonising the future' in the face of society's self-inflicted risks. His aim (in the spirit of Habermas) is to increase political and public control over risky technological developments. Luhmann (1982), on the other hand, goes to great lengths to underline the need for different subsystems to keep to their functions and their own ways of handling social complexity in order to avoid what he calls the 'de-differentiation' of society.

The work of Giddens offers a series of valuable discussions about what is happening to the individual in high modernity which emphasise self-monitoring, 'life as a project', and 'the reflexive organisation of the self'. Basing himself on a fundamentally Foucauldian conception of the modern invention and handling of deviance (Giddens, 1991: 160ff.) he also interprets contemporary disorders such as anorexia as 'the reflexive deviance of the body' (Giddens, 1991: 103–8). Among other ideas of interest to criminology (Bottoms, 1993) there should be noted Giddens' attempt to bring the study of the emotions back within the remit of sociology, as when

he points to 'dilemmas of the self', such as powerlessness versus appropri-
ation, authority versus uncertainty, or personalised versus commodified
experience (Giddens, 1991: 187–201). Giddens' arguments are thus a
further illustration of the way reflexivity can serve as a topic *for* criminology
as well as a way of *doing* criminology.

The line between the sociology of the postmodern and postmodern
sociology cannot be drawn too sharply, however.[26] What we take to be a
given context is itself constructed through our discourses and so changes as
these do. Moreover, as Bauman (cited in the introductory quotation, see
p. 7) suggests, if reflexivity is part of the context of what is to be explained it
must also apply to the changing nature of our discourses and the character of
our explanations. Criminology, for example, is bound to be affected by the
multiplying of heterogeneous and incommensurable expertises (Carty and
Mair, 1990; Ericson and Carriere in this volume). Will criminologists
become mere 'experts' – judged by their ability to improve 'performance'
(Lyotard, 1984; Bennington, 1988) or otherwise be supplanted by management scientists or information systems specialists? Do they have to give up
their claim to represent a universal class – having been demoted from
'legislators' to 'interpreters' capable of only local and defensive interventions (Bauman, 1987)? Or can they resist these developments in the
name of a new universal class of 'the victim' (see Young and Rush in this
volume; cf. Walklate, 1989). How else is criminology likely to be transformed as part of high or postmodernity? Is it one of those disciplines which
ensure their own survival on the basis of a never fulfilled claim to reduce risk
(Beck, 1992)? Given its ties to criminal law and the awesome responsibilities
of punishment, can it deal with the postmodern decentring of the individual
subject (Romano, 1988; Carty, 1990) or arguments which revel in indeter-
minacy? Does it have some special role in resisting these intellectual
fashions? Or have criminal law and criminology long ago reached a division
of labour for which the establishment of legal responsibility has only a loose
relationship with reigning philosophic and scientific viewpoints (Smith,
1981; Nelken, 1987, 1990b; Smith and Wynne, 1989).

Placing criminology in context thus leads on almost inevitably to the issue
of the desirability and prospects of a postmodern criminology.[27] If criminology is to be seen as an exemplar of modernism (Morrison in this volume)
it is one characterised by both the best and worst of its features. Both
classicism and positivism were (leading) contributors to the 'meta-narrative'
of 'progress', confident in their ability to reduce crime, despite their
differences over strategies of regulation. At the same time criminology has
always exhibited modernity's typical sort of blindness, or tendencies to
exclusion and manipulation, when dealing with other races or women
(Smart, 1989, 1990; Fitzpatrick, 1992); and it has often been prominent in
finding scientific reasons to devalue 'the other'. This legacy helps explain the
ambivalence of criminology's response to the critique of modernity presented by postmodernism (reflected also in the contributions to this
collection).

One reaction to the challenge of postmodern sociology is to argue that criminology has already been through this phase (Cohen, 1990a),[28] or that in any case this is just the sort of theorising it does not need (cf. Morrison in this volume). Apart from a dislike of the apparent lack of methodological protocols, and what is seen as a flight from context to text,[29] there is a generalised fear of the nihilistic or other undesirable political consequences of this form of theorising. The techniques of textual deconstruction in particular are seen as leading to an infinite regress which destabilises meaning without offering anything in its place. Even critical criminology, whether in its search for new forms of criminality or in its rediscovery of street crime, would seem to have little use for the epistemologies of postmodernism. In a field of public policy as sensitive as this, it seems more important to find means to check the reality of our representations rather than put in doubt representationalism itself. The politics behind the recent turn to Left Realism, for example, could not be more opposed to the claims of some postmodern writers about hyperreality. Fears of crime are declared to be in large part realistic and criminology must find a serious response to them. There is understandable suspicion shown towards arguments which suggest there is anything unreal about economic crashes or wars (Norris, 1990) in so far as this could be taken to deny pain and suffering. In reply to the loss of 'foundational certainties', criminology offers the liminal figure of 'the suffering victim' (Young and Rush in this volume).

But, on the other hand, at least some of this caution seems misplaced. When less extreme language is used we can readily see the importance of asking how much of what we believe nowadays is a 'virtual reality' produced by and for the media.[30] As the Realists have discovered, it is not easy to resolve the question of how far crime prevention measures should be based on (media shaped) fears of victimisation (Sparks, 1992a, 1992b). Even the extreme lengths to which Baudrillard takes his arguments may be salutary as we try to grasp the level to which human behaviour can sink, as in the commercial marketing, in Europe and the United States, of videos of the ethnic rapes presently taking place in Bosnia. Similarly, only the most superficial reading of authors such as Lyotard (the inventor of the term 'postmodernism') or Derrida (the father of deconstruction) could take them to be celebrating nihilism.[31] Nor is it difficult to detect the transcendent concern for justice which runs through their interrogations of the effects of discourse under postmodern conditions (whether or not this is consistent with their supposedly sceptical theoretical positions).[32] Like most innovative forms of theorising the interest lies in seeing the sense of new ways of posing issues more than in endorsing the conclusions which are said to follow. To take just one example: criminologists who are presently trying to come to terms with the spread and 'forgetting' of State Crimes and other criminal violations of human rights (Cohen, 1993), have much to gain by listening to Lyotard searching for ways of finding persuasive discourse about Auschwitz, in the face of those who deny it happened (Lyotard, 1988; Benjamin, 1989: 360–93), or Derrida and others trying to demonstrate the violence inflicted by law[33] (Cover, 1986; Derrida, 1990; Sarat and Kearns, 1991; Resta, 1992; Douzinas and Goodrich, 1993).

There is then also a more positive response to postmodernism. By learning to live with its shaky foundations criminology does indeed anticipate typically postmodern forms of 'weak thinking' (Pavarini, Ericson and Carriere in this volume). Similarly, some forms of critical criminology have much to gain from exploiting postmodern techniques of reading and writing in order to examine the suppressed voices of those on the margin (in ways rather different from those employed earlier by sociologists of deviance). Feminist criminologists influenced by Critical Legal Studies have already done much to exploit this potential. As much as the supposed substantive implications (or lack of implications) of postmodernism, the issue for criminology therefore turns on the advantages and disadvantages of taking up its unfamiliar styles and methods of argument.

Rhetorical answers

The postmodern focus on the way texts persuade is likely to increase interest in exploring the significance of differences in criminological style in different historical periods and in different cultures (as well as the impressive persistence of positivism). It may also have the consequence of sensitising those presently writing about crime to give more careful attention to their own creations; as Garland argues, 'it is time for criminologists to become conscious of how their texts represent offenders' (Garland, 1992). But will a focus on 'writing' and the structure of criminological arguments go too far in shifting attention from crime to criminology or is it just what criminology needs in its search for reflexivity?

A number of issues can be raised under the heading of what could be called rhetorical reflexivity. How does, and how should, criminological argument relate to the techniques of description and persuasion used by those (police, prosecutors, judges, journalists, offenders, other criminologists etc.) whose communications they analyse and often criticise? What, if anything, makes it superior? Are some forms of writing more reflexive than others? Is there a limit to the extent to which it is practical or desirable to reveal the props of production which make accounts convincing? The attempt to tackle these questions is reshaping fields as varied as anthropology, psychology and the sociology of science, and could well be the terrain most suitable for those trying to take theorising about deviance beyond Social Constructionism.[34] Some of those most stung by criticisms of that approach have indeed made a bold start with new forms of reflexive writing (see Pfohl, 1992). But others may be reluctant to experiment with ways of putting representation and reference in doubt because of an understandable fear that it could degenerate into no more than academic indulgence.

The dangers of regress in attempts to take this type of writing to the limit are real enough. Trying to make persuasive tropes transparent by including competing voices or dialogues (Pinch and Pinch, 1988) can make texts artificial and even unreadable (Latour, 1988). Drawing attention to the tricks used to make arguments convincing does not provide any more warrant for believability. It can easily be dismissed as just another trope which conceals rather than reveals the process by which it was itself constructed. The attempt to accompany an argument with its own commentary is thus neither necessary or sufficient (the reader must always exercise caution over what he or she believes); rather it represents the production of a guarantee which cannot itself be relied on. If it is impossible to arrive at a transparent meta-theory,[35] a 'false' appearance of dialogue may even displace attention from what would otherwise be more worthy of debate. At the most it may be reasonable to ask of a text that it be self-exemplifying (what Latour calls 'infra' rather than 'meta' reflexivity) of its own argumentative protocols.[36]

The best way of responding to these objections is to appreciate the wide range of ways of examining rhetorical structures which do not necessarily involve applying the techniques of deconstruction (with their possibly suicidal consequences). At one extreme some ways of studying texts, such as the work produced by communication and media studies or some versions of semiotics, are easily compatible with mainstream sociological criminology, which has itself become increasingly interested in media presentations of crime (see, for example, Carey, 1988; Fiske, 1990; Ericson, 1991; Ericson et al., 1991).[37] At the other end of the continuum, literary and sociological sensibilities do become blurred as social science rediscovers its kinship with the humanities and becomes reconciled to telling 'sociological fictions' (Game, 1991).[38] But there are also many ways of 'reading' and criticising texts which stand between these alternatives.[39] What has been called 'the interpretive turn' in the social sciences (Rabinow and Sullivan, 1979) by now embraces, inter alia, the return to hermeneutics (Gadamer, 1979; Thompson, 1981; Ricour, 1986; Valdes, 1991); discourse analysis in social psychology (Potter and Wetherell, 1987; Potter, 1988) the new anthropology (Clifford and Marcus, 1986; Marcus and Fischer, 1986; Clifford, 1988); social and critical semiotics (Goodrich, 1986, 1987, 1990; Hodge and Kress, 1988; Manning, 1988, 1991); the study of 'narrativity' (Jackson, 1989; Douzinas et al., 1991; Mumby, 1993); encounters between legal, social and literary theory, in Critical Legal Studies (*Stanford Law Review*, 1984) and the field of law and literature (for example White, 1985a, 1985b, 1990; Weisberg, 1992), as well as arguments by philosophical pragmatists aimed at showing how discourses construct their own objects (Rorty, 1982, 1989). The issue of reflexivity is certainly taken seriously by these approaches but it is treated as something which enables rather than disables theorising.[40]

The possibilities for criminology which are opened up by these developments are well evidenced in some of the most exciting recent contributions to our field. The type of question posed is no longer, for example, to what extent does punishment succeed in reducing crime, but, rather, how can we read punishment as an expression of culture (Garland, 1990)? In place of

seeking to show whether violence on television produces copy-cat crime, the
enquiry shifts to one concerned with what it means to talk about rational
fears of victimisation and television's role in this (Sparks, 1992a). The
problem to be resolved is not simply what are 'the causes' of political
criminality? Instead, with a concreteness which derives from ethnography,
oral history and close textual analysis, studies set out to elucidate the social
and criminological meaning of the local and particular. The Greenham
Common peace protest can be illuminated by showing how existence on the
feminine edge of sexual difference becomes operationalised as a means to
censure, condemn and control (Young, 1990). Methods are found to map
the cultural construction of violence, body and history in urban Northern
Ireland (Feldman, 1991). Connections are drawn between bad politics and
bad theatre in the kidnapping of Aldo Moro by the Italian red brigade
(*brigate rosse*) (Wagner-Pacifici, 1986).

   The Moro Morality Play (Wagner-Pacifici, 1986), for instance, sets out to
provide a case study of how political reality is constructed and the way the
citizens of mass media(ted) society come to know about events. The issue of
reflexivity arises in a number of guises; in describing the theatrical
self-consciousness among the participants in this social drama; in the liminal
quality of Moro's kidnapping as a moment for social reflection; in explaining
how the discrediting of certain versions of what was happening had a
reflexive influence on the event itself which could no longer be 'moved' in
certain directions;[41] and in the methodological problems of 'interpreting
interpretations' (and presenting 'a theory of the third order'). This
'ethnography of the text' cuts across the boundaries between anthropology,
hermeneutics, and genre-criticism. But its rich account of the aesthetic
dimensions of politics is never allowed to collapse into itself.

   Various forms of rhetorical reflexivity are also illustrated in the contributions to this collection. Melossi examines changes in crime rhetoric in
relation to the notion of 'normal crime', but, like Nelken's interpretation of
cultural differences in types of trust, he touches on but does not really
develop the theme of the relationship between language and reality. Some
of the other contributions, however, do seek to expose the 'linguistic
injuries' inflicted by theorising itself (Goodrich, 1990). Henry and Milovanovic set out a programme intended to unsettle the master narratives of
criminology which they describe as reality-claiming discourses which
hegemonise discussions of crime by police and politicians – and criminologists. Their stated goal is to loosen the cultural bonds which tie down
linguistic signifiers so as to construct a replacement discourse about crime.
Young and Rush go even further in trying to show how alternative
discourses are repressed. They conduct a polemical deconstructive 'reading'
of samples of judicial and (Realist) criminological writing so as to show how
their 'deeply embedded rhetorical structures' direct the argument and
constrain what is said and sayable. The exploration of how arguments work
as metaphors and metaphors function as arguments is certainly of particular
relevance to a subject in which 'metaphorical truths' (Cooper, 1986;

Ricoeur, 1986), such as talk of 'the war against crime', carry such significance. Legal texts produced by judges, lawyers, prosecutors and others involved in the criminal justice process can provide important and unexpected insights into the relationship between crime and control (for example, Alldridge, 1993)[42] which criminologists would be unwise to neglect. While there is always the risk of taking Derrida's claim that 'there is nothing outside the text' too literally, much of criminal justice can be illuminated in terms of communications, signs and spectacles.[43] More controversial is the attempt to apply rhetorical and aesthetic styles of interpretation to examples of sociological and criminological writing (Young and Rush in this volume).[44] This is bound to have an unsettling effect on the normal proprieties of intellectual debate in as much as this gains its normal sense from the effort to distinguish between 'knowing' and 'persuading' (Bobbio, 1993).[45] It is all too easy to demonstrate the principle that persuasive tropes are as essential to criminological as they are to other arguments.[46] However, criminologists (unlike, say, police or probation officers) are likely to answer back to substantive interpretations of their texts, especially if claims are made not just concerning what authors are alleged to have said but what their discourse obliges them to mean. It will be difficult for interpreters to avoid employing in the course of their interpretive work the same persuasive methods which they identify in a given text: for example by 'silencing' those interpreted, implying superior access to reality, or using the accusatorial tone even when responsibility is not intended.[47] The justifiable temptation to expose such apparent contradictions may make it too easy for those interpreted to refuse to accept that they can ever mean what they do not say.

For this and other reasons there is still little agreement on the appropriate methodological protocols for conducting and verifying investigations of rhetorical structures. How far is the appropriateness of an ironic or surrealistic account of crime control (for example, Weait, 1992) to be judged by aesthetic criteria? How is the validity of Lacanian-inspired psychoanalytic interpretations of notorious criminal cases to be decided? What makes a deconstruction a success? Whatever answers are offered to these questions will tend to undermine criminology's pretensions to representing itself as a distanced form of scientific knowledge.[48] Giving more attention to the aesthetic dimension of argument, instead of delegitimising criminology, however, could bring it nearer to those disciplines (such as law) whose communications gain in credibility by not being restricted to a community of experts.[49] Much, therefore, depends on which audiences criminological arguments are intended to persuade and what these audiences expect from criminology.

The standpoint matters

The question of standpoint and audience, crucial as it was to the ancient tradition of rhetoric, has therefore again become central to the social sciences. Who is doing criminology, for whose interests, and for which publics? (Is 'The Criminologist' a white, male, heterosexual, middle-class English speaker? What can be done about this?) Can and should criminological topics be examined from the standpoint of the whole society, from that of a specific group such as women or an oppressed class, or from within a still more restricted local setting? What is it that entitles the researcher to claim a privileged standpoint?

These issues affect the way research is organised and conducted. The choice whether to examine crime from the point of view of the offender, victim, potential victim or controllers, for example, is never innocent of consequences.[50] If we take seriously the idea that knowledge is a cultural construction and that people co-produce rather than simply discover the worlds of their research it may be both right and essential to draw the subjects of our investigations into the research process, especially where the project is supposedly for their benefit (Steier, 1991). The studies organised by Carlen into the social worlds of women criminals and prisoners are excellent examples of this sort of initiative (Carlen, 1983, 1985, 1988) though Carlen (1992) is careful to stress that there is a necessary limit as to how far the subjects of research can be made 'to speak for themselves'.

The importance of standpoint is highlighted in a number of chapters in this collection. Pavarini suggests that recent progress in criminology has come more from changing the standpoint adopted than from inventing new concepts or discovering new facts. Cohen tries to see how far a change in political context changes the sense of criminological argument. Young and Rush describe the complicated standpoint, involving both reverence and revulsion, which may be taken towards a group such as women victims. The chapters by Feeley and Simon, Melossi, and Nelken (Chapter 10) all try to use comparative perspectives to throw new light on otherwise taken for granted cultural standpoints.

On the other hand, as with the previous examples of reflexivity, there are certainly limits to our ability to take into account the influence of our identity, interests and cultural values in the way we formulate our questions.[51] Habermas' attempt to pose transcendent regulative ideals to show us the way to overcome our present standpoint has been criticised as necessarily arising from and appealing to the very cultural biases that it wishes to transcend (Gadamer, 1979; Geuss, 1981). Beyond a given point, open declarations of partiality, bias and relativism threaten not only to antagonise potential audiences but also to undermine the persuasive force of any description or argument being put forward. Much the same applies to efforts to democratise the research process. The collaborative stance of ethnographers may come up against the obstacle that the subjects of our research may not know (or want to know) the answers to our questions (Hammersly, 1992). Both the larger public and offenders themselves frequently have conventional views about crime which criminologists want to challenge rather than endorse. Consumer-led research can be self-defeating if the criminologist is being asked for an intervention precisely on the basis of his or her unique skills or knowledge (Gelsthorpe, 1990).

But if the subjects of our theorising are not, or cannot be, included in the process of research itself, it becomes all the more important to give attention to the way we 'represent the other'. The encounter with those whose behaviour, culture or beliefs is strange to us has to tread the difficult line between stereotyping the other as inherently different or insisting on their similarity to ourselves to the point of repressive assimilation. Criminologists (such as feminist theorists, sociologists of deviance and of mental and physical disability; those doing work on sexual, racial and ethnic difference; or those conducting comparative studies) may have a particular contribution to make in finding new ways to incorporate 'outsiders voices' (Minow, 1991). Something may also be learned from attempts by philosophers such as Levinas to theorise ways of relating to the 'other' which are not based simply on reciprocal recognition of rights (Certeau, 1986: xiv; Hand, 1989: 37–59).

The issue of standpoint plays a double role in academic argument. It is common to reduce and often delegitimate other people's ideas and values by reducing them to the interested standpoint from which they are produced. The sociological truism that viewpoints vary with class and other social location[52] can also be applied to criminologists or sociologists (as argued by Wright-Mills, 1945; Pitch, 1986; Callinicoss, 1989). But, on the other hand, a specific standpoint can also be seen as the basis of a superior epistemology or politics. Mannheim (1960), for example, thought that it was the marginal social location of the intelligentsia which gave them some hope of escaping from ideology. Cain (1990) sees it as a strength of (reflexive) criminology that the question of standpoint cannot easily be avoided because this keeps alive the idea that there are two sides to every knowledge. Deciding 'whose side you are on' is certainly a question hard to avoid in a field which deals so much with the labelling of 'outsiders' (Becker, 1967). The most bitter debates within such a politicised discipline as criminology tend to be over whether a particular approach should be considered as standing for or against those in power, to the right or left (and what counts as such), for or against the interests of women; for or against that of minorities and so on (Stenson and Cowell 1992). Likewise what were mounted as theoretical attacks on 'correctionalism' or 'positivism' can be reinterpreted as mainly arguments about standpoints.[53] A correctionalist stance may become acceptable, indeed the only realistic approach, if adopted in the interests of working class victims of crime.

Some types of criminological theorising are particularly likely to reflect on their own standpoint as well as that of others. Feminist writers were able to rethink the criminality of women by arguing by showing how the question used to be examined only in terms of their relative conformity compared with men (it will be interesting to see how the new criminology of masculinity responds). Writers within feminist criminology and jurisprudence are continuing to debate important issues such as whether there is a

peculiarly feminist viewpoint, whether it should be privileged, and whether
'good work' has criteria which transcend such a criterion (Gelsthorpe, 1990;
Kerruish, 1991; Carlen, 1992; Pitch, 1992a). Cain has recently defended a
strong version of what she calls standpoint feminism, (to be distinguished for
example from feminist empiricism and postmodern feminism), which places
considerable stress on the importance of reflexivity (Cain, 1990). For her the
theorist must be personally reflexive about the site from which she is
speaking and theory is seen as superior to common sense precisely by virtue
of such reflexivity. It is essential to connect one's theorising with the
researched population and with those for whom the research is being
conducted. Feminist research will therefore be linked, however loosely, to
the goals of feminism as a social movement. While she does not assume that
only women can do feminist let alone other types of standpoint research,
Cain does think women have particular advantages which help them see and
overcome false dichotomies in social explanation.

Another area where standpoint is crucial is in comparative work.[54] The
possibilities and advantages of overcoming the limitations of culturally
shaped standpoints is the major challenge facing those pursuing comparative
work on crime and criminal justice. The dangers of criminological imperialism – and not only the influence of American-style positivist criminology –
are real enough (see Nelken, Chapter 10 in this volume). Comparative work
should provide some defence against ethnocentrism not only by revealing
that there are differences in conceptions of crime and responses to crime[55]
but also how culture shapes the discipline of criminology itself (Melossi,
1990; Cohen in this volume).[56] On the other hand, such work also has its
limits; it is often said, for example, that taking the question of cultural
difference too seriously ends up in relativism (Beirne, 1983). Yet there is
much which can be said about the way culture shapes the way crime
problems are posed, as well as what count as satisfactory 'solutions', without
necessarily endorsing either cognitive or moral relativism. There is an
inescapable dialectic between the search for difference and the presumption
of similarity (Nelken, Chapter 10 in this volume). If it is impossible ever to
aspire to a full understanding of another society one of the main advantages
of trying to gain it may be to learn more about what is taken for granted in
the criminologist's own society. These issues need to be faced even in
comparative work geared to practical purposes such as learning how to
reduce crime. A reflexive approach to comparative study suggests that a
society's solutions to its crime problems tend to reproduce these problems
precisely because the solution comes out of the same culture – on the other
hand, paradoxically, any proposed solutions which do not reflect the culture
are likely for that very reason not to find favour (or else are swiftly
'domesticated').

The issue of standpoint can provide the nexus between theorising and
practical action. Both the discussions of feminist and comparative work
suggest that if our theorising is intended to have policy implications or
otherwise gain political support it will have to take account of specific

alliances and relate to a given cultural context. To some extent this practical interest is already built into the subject. Criminology, like the other cultural sciences, produces 'local knowledge' (Geertz, 1983); the cultural sciences cannot stand outside their culture even if they wanted to. What is more problematic, however, is how far a deliberate effort should be made to shape theorising in the direction of particular practical interventions. Criminology has seen more than a few examples of action-research dedicated to producing desired change without its interventions being misappropriated for other purposes (see, for example, Mathiesen, 1980). But the extent to which theory should be subordinated to this goal depends on recognising in what way the standpoint of theorising can be distinguished, if at all, from that of practice or politics.

Theorising as a practice

Is there then a special theoretical standpoint? How does and should criminological theorising relate to the practical considerations of those who make policy or play roles in the criminal process – or to the political projects of those who seek to challenge this process? Consideration of these questions requires us, by way of conclusion, to examine some of the ways a concern with reflexivity could lead to a reassessment of the relationship between theorising, politics and practice.

Even though the chapters in this volume do not focus on policy questions their theoretical arguments do have broad implications for practice. Melossi, for instance, warns that advocacy of violent solutions to inter-national conflicts helps shape an internal culture which finds expression in violent crime. Feeley and Simon imply that the American courts should be more robust in limiting the spread of actuarial justice. Nelken claims that building distrust into the procedures of criminal justice can prove counter-productive. But, for other contributors, the relationship between theorising and practical politics is itself posed as the problem. Morrison is worried about the practical implications of some postmodern theorising. Pavarini and, to some extent, Ericson and Carriere, suggest that practical impli-cations need not necessarily be uppermost in the considerations of the theorist. Henry and Milovanovic (as also Young and Rush) treat theory as an intrinsic part of criminal justice practice. Because of their concern that even critical theorising may end up reproducing the repressive effects of control talk they recommend a 'transpraxis' intended to lead to 'reflexive reconceptualization' so as to build an alternative framing of narrative events.

According to a still common view of criminology as a type of applied or policy science, the relationship between theory and practice is that between basic theory and its application. Legitimised by its promise to study and help solve the 'social problem' of crime, its remit is to establish the individual and social causes of crime, to clarify the existence or otherwise of criminal careers, and suggest and evaluate programmes of crime prevention and control. This so-called 'correctionalist' assumption has been attacked by sociologists for impairing our ability to 'appreciate' the complex and ambiguous meanings and outcomes of deviance. In turn this alternative vision of criminology has come in for the opposite criticism (put by Left Realist criminologists) which alleges that it is politically misguided and impractically utopian. For these authors the test of good theory is precisely its political implications or practical outcome.

But this way of posing the problem of how to relate theory and practice is itself being rewritten. According to Foucault (1977), for example, criminology is inevitably a form of 'knowledge-power' inherently connected to penal practice.[57] Instead of asking how knowledge can produce certain outcomes he advises us to examine how power produces types of knowledge. This approach can be applied also to struggles among criminologists (Stenson, 1992: 11–17). But it is more difficult to see the type of interventions which would be indicated by a Foucauldian approach which defines power as enabling as well as repressive.[58] In general, in the light of recent work in social theory, drawing practical or political conclusions from theoretical work, never easy at the best of times, has become much more difficult:[59] choices still have to be made but are not warrantable as they once were (Cornell, 1992). As we have seen, the postmodern rejection of programmatic political or practical guides to action rests on a suspicion of meta-theory and meta-logics which undermines the theoretical warrant for broad political projects and social interventions and leads to the privileging of highly specific local narratives. How then would a focus on reflexivity affect the way criminologists argue about the problem of theory and practice?

On the one hand, reflexivity may also form part of a continuing commitment to the modernist project. Cain, for example, regards it as an essential element of her conception of theorising as political praxis. 'Good knowledge' can only be achieved following certain guidelines and alliances, must be assessable by others, and will fall to be judged eventually by its political effects (Cain, 1990). Other writers who have been dismissive of postmodern tendencies, likewise place reflexivity at the centre of an approach to critical theorising which insists on its potential for leading towards social progress (Habermas, 1987). But even those who are more sympathetic to the anti-foundationalist claims of postmodernist writers find in reflexivity a new measure for ensuring academic accountability (just as accountability may itself be seen as a form of reflexivity). If scholars cannot rely on theory to legitimise anything more than local and defensive interventions they can at least be held responsible for their own theoretical productions. And it is exactly the force of the arguments against representationalism and foundationalism which obliges the writer to use reflexivity as a substitute for the yardstick of descriptive accuracy.

Of greater interest, however, is the way a focus on reflexivity helps in working out the implications of treating theory as itself a practice. One common view of theory assumes that its capacity to know 'better' than practitioners, and to clarify or guide practice, is the result of its being able to conduct 'mental experiments' (or monitor practical activities) without being subject to the limitations of a given practical context. Certainly there are some intellectual gains which accrue to the theorist because of the differences in vantage point, knowledge or time for reflection as compared with social actors. Theorising's freedom from practical constraints is also what gives it its potential to undermine official claims and legitimations about crime and its control. But theoretical work can also misconstrue the practices it seeks to understand or influence precisely because it exaggerates the degree, or mistakes the kind, of reflexivity which is or could be possessed by practical actors. This is especially likely if theoretical accounts fail to elucidate the very 'constraints' (Nelken, 1985), such as the lack of foreknowledge, limited perspective and circumscribed roles, which provide the sense to 'practical logic' and shape its capacity to appropriate theoretical suggestions (Bourdieu, 1990; Harker et al., 1990).

The problem of how to go from theory to practice is therefore not limited to the familiar charge, so often justly levelled at criminologists, that practical concerns can encroach on scholarly autonomy and distort theoretical work. Theorising may in many ways also be unsuited to understanding and guiding practice. In a much quoted passage Cohen (1990a: 10–11) points to the difficulties in reconciling the demands of what he calls criminology's 'jealous gods'. He argues that the different tasks of theorising for its own sake, offering guidance for political interventions and practical policy-making, and deciding on humanitarian intervention on an individual case-by-case basis, may sometimes enter into conflict and that they therefore need to be guided by different requirements. There is an unresolvable tension, for instance, between the necessarily distanced attitude of doubt, irony and scepticism characteristic of intellectual life and the commitment required by participating in practical interventions, where it is necessary to act on the basis of 'moral pragmatism' (Cohen, 1985, 1990a) without being able to forecast many of the effects of our actions.[60]

Young (1992) has since responded to Cohen's argument that it is impossible to separate theory from practice, that external conditions inevitably inspire or condition developments in theorising, and that practice requires theory and theory learns from practice. He also challenges Cohen's descriptions of theory and practice, suggesting for example that bureaucrats may be more sceptical and theorists more confident than in his argument. For reasons of theoretical growth and not just practical commitment criminologists are urged not to stay cocooned in academic or political isolation. The right approach must be to continue to try to integrate theory and practice rather than live with their contradictions. On the other hand, while they applaud many of the political initiatives initiated by Left Realists in the realm of crime prevention,[61] Cohen (1988, 1990a), Carlen (1992), and Pavarini (this volume), none the less differ from Left Realists over this attempt to unite theory and practice or judge the value of theorising only in terms of its practical achievements (or vice versa). Carlen (1992: 60) has talked of 'the theoretical bad faith which results from attempting to fashion a

theory in the service of politics'[62] and others have illustrated the consequences to which this can lead. But if this significant debate is to be taken
further we also need to understand why theorising itself is not always able to
yield adequate or unequivocal guidance for the making of practical choices
and why it may even misrepresent the way such choices are or must be taken.

But is it possible to theorise this limit to theory? Does a theory of its limits
allow us to know the limits of theory, or does the limitation of theorising lie
precisely here? In so far as it is possible to find an answer to such paradoxical
questions the route would seem to lie through theoretical work becoming
more reflexive about the constraints of its own production – such as the
contexts, incentives and style requirements of academic life – and the way
this affects its possibilities of shaping (other) practices which have their own
reflexive constraints.

Rather than being able to legislate a relationship between theory and
practice we need to explore the possible interconnections between these
different activities. All practical activities – as shown in the classical accounts
of everyday life by writers such as Goffman or Garfinkel – may be seen as
resting on some implicit theoretical underpinning, and the necessity of
self-monitoring is, as we have seen, said to be increasing under the influence
of current social changes. Reflexivity as such cannot therefore be seen as a
special feature of theoretical work as compared with practical activity.
Social scientists operate with a second- or even third-order (Shotter, 1993)
reflexivity which they use to try to unpack the reflexivity of everyday life.
But this means that their accounts and recommendations can have only an
unpredictable and ironic influence and effect on politics and practice. While
they will sometimes end up becoming self-fulfilling prophecies, the reflexivity of practical actors (ranging from politicians to those working within the
criminal justice system) also means that they can and often will anticipate
and out-manoeuvre the theoretical intentions of reforming laws and
projects.

To argue that theorising is (also) a practice does not mean that all
practices are the same but it does mean moving from abstract definition to
exploration of the ways different activities combine thinking and making
choices. Some of the practices which interest the criminologist are themselves relatively 'academic' (for example, judicial reasoning, lawyers'
arguments or political ideologies) and some of these actors are at least as
reflexive as criminologists about their tasks (Carter, 1992). On the other
hand, criminologists do not confine themselves to producing rather than
applying knowledge (Carlen, 1992) and the theoretical techniques available
to them include a variety of 'praxiologies' in which pragmatic considerations
are uppermost.[63] To make further progress it could also be useful to put
Cohen's arguments about the differences between theory and practice to the
test. We will need to examine when and why theoretical practice differs from
practical or political activities in time pressures, the requirement of finality
and clear-cut solutions (or alternatively the cultivation of deliberate
ambiguity), in room for manoeuvre, in the need to satisfy superiors or

special interests, in the importance of persuading given audiences, in the importance given to legitimising institutions and so on (Nelken, 1987, 1990b). The challenge is to see how the contexts of decision – the 'rational choices' of some criminals; the caution of the civil servant caught between the limitations of legal precedent and political feasibility; the phenomenology of the judge responding to the need to 'do something' about the recidivist; the journalist poised between reflecting and making the news; the politician seeking a policy (or slogan) that will appeal to as many people as possible – shape the process of reflexive practice. These micro-contexts (themselves of course the site of larger social changes) may help explain why theoretical explanations are so often thought to be unconvincing or unworkable when brought to the notice of those engaged in practice. It may even be possible to explain why practitioners often have little interest in explanation as such – as Latour puts it, those engaged in a practical activity are usually satisfied with what he calls 'weak accounts': the need for explanation depends precisely on being outside a context and seeking 'to act at a distance' (Latour, 1988: 159–61).

What follows from these considerations concerning the difficulties of uniting theory and practice? At the extreme it has recently been argued that there is little point in calling upon abstract 'theoretical' arguments to guide or justify a given practical choice. The success of any move within a practice depends on criteria internal to the practice: good moves are defined by practitioners in the course of the game itself (Fish, 1980, 1989). As against this a strong plea has been made for the importance of sticking to theoretical principles which transcend those of one's interpretive community and the situationally accepted moves of a given practice (Weisberg, 1992: 167–75). The claim here seems to be that it is the belief that theorising makes a difference which itself can make the difference. The need to stand firm on theoretical principles despite the pressures of everyday practice is no less essential in the politics and practice of crime control – but it is the theoretically reflective practitioner rather than the theorist who carries the main burden. There is less to be said for the tendency of theorising to attempt to reconstruct practical activities in its own image, as in the otherwise laudable suggestion that the criminal process should be open at every one of its stages to alternative accounts of the crime events being tried (Henry and Milovanovic in this volume).[64] Nor are the limits of criminal justice practice just a matter of time and other pressures. An influential recent line of legal and social theorising has paid particular attention to the way each form of knowing and acting in the world reinterprets others in the course of reproducing its own operations (Teubner, 1988, 1989, 1993; King and Piper, 1990). The claim made is that law can regulate social life only by regulating its own elements (including its own images of society and of other disciplines). This approach can be used to provide original insights into the reflexive limits of policy-making and law reform even if the positive policy implications which are being drawn from such theoretical discussions, such as the necessity to develop forms of 'reflexive law' or 'autopoietic law', remain highly controversial.

Reflexive criminology is less the name of a new theoretical approach to criminology than a way of restating what is involved in the practice of theorising. It may help pose new questions, draw attention to unnoticed continuities between texts and contexts, and inspire different ways of carrying out and writing up research. One awkward issue (at least) remains. How much reflexivity, we can ask, is enough reflexivity? It is enough to pose this question to see that there is no way to lay down a solution in advance when talking of a heuristic strategy. But we should at least note that the way this problem is handled will depend on the conception of reflexivity employed. If reflexivity is interpreted as a call to constant self-reflection we could perhaps define too little reflexivity as that which leaves the sources of a discipline's concepts and assumptions unexamined, while too much would characterise a process by which it gets caught up in internally referring academic debates and responds solely to their logic. On this view it would be conceded that the theorist cannot (and may not want to) actually 'escape' from the limits of discourse, context, culture, writing, standpoint or theorising as a specific type of practice. But progress would be measured by the ability of the theorist 'to place him- or herself in the frame'. Conceptualising reflexivity in terms of the recursiveness inherent in the self-referential character of social structures and discourses, on the other hand, would lead to a concern with how to appreciate and respect such limits rather than how to overcome them. For this approach, knowing the theory of your own behaviour, or the code of a given discourse, does not release you from its constrictions (Luhmann, 1990: 16). 'Misrecognition' or 'misreading' may in some cases even be essential to the success of a given social practice such as law (Santos, 1987; Teubner, 1988, 1989).

In one way or another, then, the issue of reflexivity is central to many of the important developments in current theorising. A valuable recent attempt to build a 'non-foundationalist radical theory', for example, relies on the notion of reflexivity as the key to an approach which does not make the truth claims foundational to modernist social science, and which allows a trade off to be made between 'being in touch with the worlds of those studied or opening up new ones' (Crook, 1991: 201–6). Faced with the gravity of injury and suffering it is natural to underwrite the reality of those in pain and endorse the modernist project of describing and reforming the conditions which allow it to occur. But a sign of criminology's commitment to social change must also be the seriousness with which it faces up to challenges to its ways of theorising.

Notes

1 How much importance should be given to this (or any other) theoretical problem in explaining the evolution of a discipline is of course controversial. It was certainly much debated in the closely related field of 'social problems'. Writers who attempted to construct 'privileged' accounts of the construction of social problems which revealed their 'true' origin and characteristics were accused of 'ontological gerrymandering' (Woolgar and Pawluch, 1985).

There are instructive differences as well as similarities between this debate and that in the sociology of knowledge concerning the unresolved epistemological status of social (scientific) studies of science (see Woolgar, 1988).

2 McConville et al.'s (1991) study of the social construction of crime in the criminal process, despite being widely praised, was accused by some reviewers of selecting its data in the same partial way as that of the subjects of its research (policemen and prosecutors) whose actions it criticised. But none of these reviewers discussed whether the criteria that apply to the selectivity exercised by an author are or should be the same as those applying to officials carrying out their legal duties.

3 This may be a latent weakness of Lacey et al.'s (1990) pioneering effort to place criminal law 'in context'.

4 The tragedy of Narcissus, it has been argued, was not the consequence so much of his being self-obsessed as of his not being *conscious* of being self-obsessed (Steier, 1991: 7).

5 Ditton's provocative thesis (Ditton, 1979) that crime is an artefact of its own control, leaves untouched the problem of the artefactual nature of his and others' accounts of crime events.

6 Hassard and Parker (1993) offer a balanced set of papers which assess the arguments for and against postmodernist approaches in the sociology of organisations. This is of particular value to criminologists because of its consideration of postmodern ideas in the context of empirical research as well as because of criminology's current preoccupation with the activities of criminal justice organisations.

7 Hassard (1993) distils the issues raised by postmodernism as representation, reflexivity, writing, difference, and decentring the subject.

8 This distinction can also be linked to the wider debate in social theory between Habermas and Luhmann concerning the degree to which theoretical reflection is able to transform the structures which reproduce meaning in society (see, for example, Holub, 1991).

9 Strictly speaking, though, if we accept the philosophic definition of reflexivity as the untenability of drawing a distinction between doing meta-theory (theorising about theory) and theorising itself (Lawson, 1982), writing *about* criminology will also count as a contribution *to* the subject.

10 Most textbook discussions of criminology as an interdisciplinary enquiry use definitions of the 'disciplines' which are premised on a positivist epistemology. When the term is extended to cover normative enquiries, including law, the question of interdisciplinarity is complicated by fundamental differences in the character and functioning of theoretical and practical reasoning (Ost and Van der Kerchove, 1987; Nelken, 1991).

11 The theory is least helpful for explaining those kind of crimes where, as the authors note, self-control is necessary for acquiring the position to engage in or organise offending (and control theory in general underestimates the importance of norm-following, whether social or group norms, in shaping crime).

12 Their argument seems much less relevant in Italy, for instance, where public concern concentrates more on white-collar crime, organised and political crime than on juvenile delinquency or street crime.

13 One of the virtues of the Classical school was that it avoided a separation between the causes of crime and the role of the state (Roshier, 1989). Gottfredson and Hirschi's argument could equally well be deduced from the fact that legal and other rules usually require people to take the longer route to satisfy their interests. They see tautology as in any case a strength of their type of theorising (Hirschi and Gottfredson, 1993).

14 Contrast the way Lacan is used as an ingredient in postmodern theorising by Henry and Milovanovic, in this volume, and in Milovanovic (1991), with Salecl's (1993) Lacan-inspired analyses of otherwise inexplicable crimes and illuminating interpretations of the difference between serial and mass murderers.

15 According to Kennedy (1992), John Hinckley's attempted assassination of President Reagan was influenced by a film which was itself based partly on the true story of a previous assassination attempt. Kennedy's discussion of the genesis and trial of this offence provides a fascinating analysis of the legal and criminological implications when 'real life meets reel life'.

16 'We owe the rules only a token fidelity and do not feel we have to transgress them, as is the case with the law' (Baudrillard, 1990a: 137).

17 'Law is in an increasingly incongruous position: it vainly attempts to isolate the real in an era in which reality is becoming rapidly indistinguishable from its fictional representations' (Baudrillard, 1990a: 28).

18 But this assumes that these other discourses work in the same way, otherwise it would be more correct to say that sociology only highlights the sociologically relevant features of other discourses (Nelken, 1990b, 1991).

19 Cf. Latour, who says of the sociology of science, 'if the work in our domain ends up generating a specific, distinct field of scholarship – defined as such perhaps in curricula, it means all our work has been by definition unreflexive' (Latour, 1988: 175).

20 The reciprocal relationship between criminology and sociology of law (with which I am most familiar) has been a particularly fruitful one, though even here the contacts are intermittent. Few of the ever popular evaluation studies of penal initiatives refer to the extensive body of research on the implementation of laws and regulations, or to the theoretical problems associated with such work (Nelken, 1981, 1983). Nor have criminologists so far shown much interest in recent significant changes in the explanatory frameworks found persuasive in this field (Nelken, 1986, 1988).

21 But it is less often noticed that, if criminology is tied to criminal law, the rules of law are in turn reflexively shaped by perceived types of prevalent crimes and their assumed motives (see, for example, Horder, 1992).

22 Pavarani (in this volume), for example, points to the organised crime elements that, in Italy, lie behind the phenomenon of unwelcome offers to wash car windscreens. But he should not be assumed to be arguing for the criminalisation of this activity.

23 It is the criminal justice system which can be seen as marginal among the array of possible responses to deviance and crime (Nelken, 1989).

24 Thus, while the rise of 'actuarial justice' may be connected to the growth of insurance (Feeley and Simon, this volume), whether and how it is used in the sphere of criminal justice will depend on its relationship to wider processes of 'normalisation' (Ewald, 1991), and the different tactics perceived as appropriate to regulate ordinary citizens as compared with the marginalised underclass who are presumed to lie beyond the range of society's normal signals, incentives and deterrents.

25 For introductions to what is becoming an abundant – but sometimes repetitive – literature, see Featherstone (1988); Lash (1990); Crook et al. (1991); Smart (1992). For a neo-Marxist but not unsympathetic analysis see Harvey (1989); for a highly critical perspective see Callinicos (1989).

26 There are ingenious attempts by sociologists of the postmodern to make use of this overlap. Reiner, for example, in describing the challenges faced by the police in Britain draws on postmodern accounts of the decline of meta-narratives to argue that the police must therefore make their claims to legitimacy much more concrete and modest so as to recognise that they 'are providers of a mundane public service not sacred totems of national pride' (Reiner, 1993: 781).

27 This way of posing the issue covers (or confuses) a number of questions, for example: Is criminology (still) part of the modernist project? What has criminology to do with postmodernism (or with deconstruction)? Has it already been through it? Can it avoid being affected by it? Is it capable of making the transition?

28 Examples cited include Matza's ironic and reflexive accounts of criminological 'explanations' (especially in *Becoming Deviant*, Cicourel's analyses of police and probation reports, Douglas' critique of sociologists' reliance on (criminal) statistics, and, in general, work inspired by ethnomethodology and phenomenology (Cohen, 1990a: 11). Cohen argues that the criticisms of the positivist criminological mainstream by sociologists of deviance have considerable similarities to deconstructionism and suffer from the same meta-problems of essentialism, idealism and negative scepticism. But to point out meta-problems assumes the possibility of meta-theorising!

29 Just as we cannot explain changes in a social context as if this was the same as interpreting

a text, so the power of a text cannot be analysed in the same way as the effects of other social forces.

30 The contrast drawn by the Left Realists between crime as a media panic and crime as 'an event with consequences' demands an unnecessary choice between these alternatives.

31 It was Derrida who defended Reason in a famous debate with Foucault in which the latter tried to collapse the difference between rationality and irrationality (see Boyne, 1990: 123–66).

32 Criminologists influenced by postmodernism could best be classified as what Rosenau (1992) calls 'affirmative sceptics' rather than negative sceptics. Thus Henry and Milovanovic (1993: 12) claim to be using 'a pragmatic and situated deconstruction' so as to advance the case for a peacemaking criminology. Likewise, Alison Young (1990: 164–5) pleads for 'strong' scepticism – 'an act of both refusal and demand'.

33 Norris, who is far from uncritical of postmodernism, argues that Derridean techniques can be used to resist the force of bureaucratic language (Norris, 1990: 134–64).

34 The precedents here include the influence of ethnomethodology (Cicourel, 1976; Nelken, 1983); accounts of 'official discourse' (Burton and Carlen, 1979), and discussions of 'control talk' (Cohen, 1985).

35 Latour (1988) claims that reflexive writing is caught between trying to say everything – to overcome absence', as illustrated by ethnomethodology, and trying not to say anything – 'to escape from presence', which he identifies with deconstruction.

36 See, for example, the story of the stories of 'the postmodern transition' as told by de Sousa Santos (Santos, 1991).

37 Some criminology texts draw a clear line between social science accounts and fictional accounts of crime by discussing them in separate chapters (Bessette, 1982; Reiner, 1985).

38 Which is not to assume that the approaches to literary criticism are limited to the techniques of deconstruction (see, for example, Newton, 1990).

39 There are naturally also important differences among these approaches, and evolving debates within them, which a criminology trying to examine its role in constructing constructions of crime would eventually need to face (see, for example, Nencel and Pels, 1991). The new anthropology, for example, presents itself as a critique of the neglect of writing in Geertz's interpretive approach to cultural anthropology, just as there are sharp divisions between different schools of semiotics. Some scholars also complain that deconstructionists have distorted the historical message of rhetoric (Vickers, 1988).

40 Discourse analysis in social psychology, for example, tries to turn reflexivity into a resource. Because talk is about the world, but is also part of it, any points made must apply also to oneself (Potter and Wetherell, 1987: 183).

41 Cf. also Feldman: 'The event is not what happens, it is what can be narrated' (Feldman, 1991: 2). Feldman's study concerns the effect of situated practices in constructing political agency in 'late modernity' and in particular the way such agency is 'predicated on self-reflexive, interpretive framings of power'. It describes how narratives move action by allowing the 'erection of authorising centres – from out of dispersed, regional and enclosed spaces of violent exchange' (Feldman, 1991: 1–2).

42 'A crime based on the threat to reveal (sexual) truth reveals truth about the institutions of law' (Alldridge, 1993: 387).

43 In the sociology of organisations, P. Thompson (1993) has raised the objection that techniques which are apposite for studying texts are not necessarily suitable for studying organisations. On the other hand, Jeffcut (1993) and Linstead (1993) show that the idea of 'organisations as multi authored texts' can be put to good use.

44 For other relevant examples of textual 'readings' see, for example, Atkinson (1990: 139–44), discussing studies in the sociology of crime, Brown (1987: 122–32) discussing total institutions as texts and Dant (1991: 207–28).

45 For this and other reasons Habermas (1987) is sweeping in his dismissal of many postmodern theorists. But he has been well criticised for failing to recognise that the question of how arguments persuade cannot be easily separated from that of the truth of their substance (Rasmussen, 1990).

46 Left Realists such as Jock Young are particularly prone to rhetorical flourishes. As with

earlier statements of the credo, for example Young's manifesto for Realism (1991) establishes the persuasiveness of its 'correct' theory by polarising competitors into 'administrative criminology' and 'left idealism', each guilty in their turn of overemphasising either the objective or the subjective aspects of criminal behaviour. Yet the Realist theorist then feels entitled to classify both the objective and subjective (mistaken) moments of the offender's understanding of the world according to an attributed (political) logic which leaves no room for empirical exploration of the agent's actual motives. Crime is said to arise because individuals and groups 'see through the deception and inequality of the world' but that they then make the mistake of seeking the solution in criminal instead of political action (left idealists are accused of the same confusion between crime and politics). 'Crime is therefore, in its impact largely antisocial but in its origin profoundly social . . . it is the person well socialised into our culture who is the criminal' (Young, 1991: 10). Despite its recycling of anomie theory, this is rather a rash generalisation – given that crime may also have anti-social origins and (pro)social impact. But what is more interesting is the way the word 'social' is used in two different senses, one descriptive and the other evaluative (otherwise why not recognise that an anti-social act may still be profoundly social), so that it is tempting to see the play on the word 'social' carrying the argument along almost beside itself. More recently (1992b: 16) Young and Mathews conclude their reply to their critics by arguing that the alternative to their views 'is unreal about social reality and unrealistic about real politics'.

47 Claims about what is unpresentable in a given discourse can also turn subtly into what is an essentially structuralist (rather than poststructuralist) argument about the *necessary* limits of discourse.

48 The image of science being undermined may be that of the 'ordinary person' rather than that of those philosophers of science (Zolo, 1989) or pragmatic philosophers (Rorty, 1982) who see the process of proof as itself inevitably reflexive and persuasive.

49 'Legal authority, then, rests on the ability of legal narratives to reside simultaneously in the normative universes of legal and nonlegal worlds' (Scheppele, 1991: 65). Boyd White (1985a, 1985b, 1990) returns frequently to the example of criminal law and its (criminologically influenced) complex justifications of punishment as his central case of bureaucratic language being unable to carry normative conviction.

50 Who is identified with also plays a crucial role in the process of judicial reasoning and justification, as can be illustrated from the arguments of Lord Simon and Lord Hailsham in the controversial case of 'mistake' over consent of *D. P. P.* v *Morgan* 1976 A.C. 182 (Duncan, 1994). For a discussion of the way Lord Scarman positioned himself between police and the black community in the Brixton enquiry see Goodrich (1986: 204–6).

51 This is sometimes an exercise better left to others. For this and other reasons I have not tried to make this chapter self-exemplifying.

52 But criminology has so far failed to follow up the stimulating work of so-called 'cultural theorists' (Thompson et al., 1990) who try to show how the construction of social problems and risks and social reactions to deviance can be related to membership in more or less tightly bound or regulated groups.

53 The periodic crises over standpoints within academic disciplines and movements are themselves of theoretical interest as in the way the third 'generation' of feminism have started to ask 'who are the "we" we are fighting for?' (Daly, 1993).

54 Historical investigations ('the past is another country') can also provide the culture shock which comes from being obliged to change all normal points of reference.

55 See the subtle comparison of violence in the United States and Norway in Pepinsky (1991: Ch. 2).

56 In Italy, for example, there is no recognisable discipline concerned with empirical studies of the everyday processes of criminal justice such as the exercise of police discretion; nor much reference to categories such as 'crime control' versus 'due process' (Ferrajoli, 1988; Nelken, 1993). On the other hand, in Italy, and civil law countries in general, it is impossible to think of the problem of criminal justice without reference to the state, whereas in English-language criminology it is common to lament the 'false dichotomy' between the study of the state and of everyday decision-making in the criminal process (McBarnet, 1978).

57 Obviously there are many types of criminology and a variety of sites at which it is practised. So Garland (1992) is right to reply to Foucault that much of the criminology produced in the universities (unlike the prison) is structured by academic constraints rather than those of knowing and classifying individual offenders. But it should not be assumed that university departments on the European continent give criminology the sociological slant we have got used to in English speaking countries (see, for example, Pavarini in this volume). In any case what both sites may have in common is what Foucault saw as an interest in coming to know ourselves by knowing criminals.

58 It remains controversial whether this should be interpreted as intellectual rigour or as a failure of political nerve (Waltzer, 1986; Dews, 1987: 67 ff.; Culler, 1989: 66–8).

59 Some of the most forthright proponents of autopoeisis and similar systems approaches, for example, propound theories which appear to leave little scope for human agency but proclaim themselves equally determined defenders of humanistic notions of responsibility (see, for example, Maturana, 1991; Von Forster, 1991).

60 Feeley and Simon (this volume) point out that both liberal and more conservative approaches to penology helped give rise to actuarial justice. But the need to resist this trend which their analysis implies could equally well also have unexpected consequences.

61 Pavarini is in fact developing similar schemes in Bologna and elsewhere.

62 Ruggiero (1992) provides some apt examples of the narrowing effect of the attempt to link criminological theorising to the political project of mobilising consensus for the Labour Party by developing more responsive schemes of crime prevention and policing. The allegedly theoretical contrast drawn between Left Idealists and Left Realists can also be understood as a transposition (with signs reversed) of an older political opposition between reformists and revolutionaries.

63 Norrie (1993: 260) cites Bhaksar's discussion of praxiologies such as utilitarian theory, public choice theory or neo-classical economic theory, in order to argue that criminal law is itself such a technique – geared to explaining and guiding action individualistically while bracketing off historically given social relations.

64 Current critical theorising about criminal law argues that it is 'a combination of practical necessity and intellectual impossibility' (Norrie, 1993). The role of the criminologist is not only to examine critically both parts of that claim but also to appreciate what such a combination offers to the practical flexibility of criminal law's functioning.

References

Alldridge, P. (1993) 'Attempted murder of the soul: Blackmail, privacy and secrets', *Oxford Journal of Legal Studies*, 13: 368.

Atkinson, P. (1990) *The Ethnographic Imagination: Textual Constructions of Reality*. London: Routledge.

Baudrillard, J. (1990a) *Seduction*. London: Macmillan.

Baudrillard, J. (1990b) *La Transparence du Mal*. Paris: Editiones Galileé.

Bauman, Z. (1987) *Legislators and Interpreters*. Cambridge: Polity Press.

Bauman, Z. (1992) *Intimations of Post Modernity*. London: Routledge.

Beck, U. (1992) *Risk Society* (trans. Mark Ritter). London: Sage.

Becker, H. (1967) 'Whose side are we on?', *Social Problems*, 14: 239–47.

Beirne, P. (1983) 'Cultural relativism and comparative criminology', *Contemporary Crises*, 7: 371–91.

Benjamin, A. (ed.) (1989) *The Lyotard Reader*. Oxford: Blackwell.

Bennington, G. (1988) *Lyotard: Writing the Event*. Manchester: Manchester University Press.

Bessette, J.-M. (1982) *Sociologie du crime*. Paris: PUF.

Black, D. (1976) *The Behaviour of Law*. New York: Academic Press.

Bobbio, N. (1993) *Il Dubbio e la scelta: intellettuali e potere nella societa contemporanea*. Rome: La Nuova Italia Scientifica.

Bottoms, A. (1993) 'Recent criminological and social theory . . .', in D. Farrington, R.-J. Sampson and P.-O. Wikstrom (eds), *Integrating Individual and Ecological Aspects of Crime*. Stockholm: BRA Report.

Bourdieu, P. (1990) *The Logic of Practice*. Cambridge: Polity Press.

Boyne, R. (1990) *Foucault and Derrida: The Other Side of Reason*. London: Unwin Hyman.

Braithwaite, J. (1989) *Crime, Shame and Reintegration*. Cambridge: Cambridge University Press.

Braithwaite, J. and Pettit, P. (1990) *Not Just Deserts*. Oxford: Oxford University Press.

Brown, R. H. (1987) *Society as Text: Essays in Rhetoric, Reason and Reality*. Chicago: University of Chicago Press.

Burke, K. (1989) *On Symbols and Society*. Chicago: University of Chicago Press.

Burton, F. and Carlen, P. (1979) *Official Discourse*. London: Routledge and Kegan Paul.

Cain, M. (ed.) (1989) 'Introduction: Feminists transgress criminology', in *Growing up Good: Policing the Behaviour of Girls in Europe*. London: Sage.

Cain, M. (1990) 'Realist philosophy and standpoint epistemologies, or Feminist criminology as a successor science', in L. Gelsthorpe and A. Morris (eds), *Feminist Perspectives in Criminology*. Milton Keynes: Open University Press.

Calavita, K. and Pontell, H. (1992) 'The savings and loans crisis', in M. Ermann and R. Lundman (eds), *Corporate and Governmental Deviance*. Oxford: Oxford University Press.

Callinicoss, A. (1989) *Against Postmodernism*. Cambridge: Polity Press.

Carey, J. (1988) *Communication as Culture*. London: Unwin Hyman.

Carlen, P. (1983) *Women's Imprisonment: A Study in Social Control*. London: Routledge.

Carlen, P. (1985) *Criminal Women: Autobiographical Accounts*. Cambridge: Polity Press.

Carlen, P. (1988) *Women, Law and Poverty*. Milton Keynes: Open University Press.

Carlen, P. (1992) 'Criminal women and criminal justice: the limits to, and potential of, feminist and left realist perspectives', in R. Mathews and J. Young (eds), *Issues in Realist Criminology*. London: Sage.

Carter, L. H. (1992) 'How trial judges talk', in G. Leyh (ed.), *Legal Hermeneutics*. Berkeley: University of California Press.

Carty, A. (ed.) (1990) *Post-modern Law: Enlightenment Revolution and the Death of Man*. Edinburgh: Edinburgh University Press.

Carty, A. and Mair, J. (1990) 'Some post-modern perspectives on law and society', *Journal of Law and Society*, 17: 1.

Cerretti, A. (1992) *L'Orizzonte Artificiale: Problemi Epistemologici della Criminologia*. Padova: Cedam.

Certeau, M. de (1986) *Heterologies: Discourse on the Other* (trans. B. Massum). Manchester: Manchester University Press.

Christie, N. (1993) *Crime Control as Industry*. London: Routledge.

Cicourel, A. (1976) *The Social Organisation of Juvenile Justice* (2nd edn). New York: Wiley.

Clifford, J. (1988) *The Predicament of Culture: Twentieth Century Ethnography, Literature and Art*. Cambridge, MA: Harvard University Press.

Clifford, J. and Marcus, G. (1986) *Writing Culture: The Poetics and Politics of Ethnography*. Berkeley: University of California Press.

Cohen, S. (1985) *Visions of Social Control*. Cambridge: Polity Press.

Cohen, S. (1988) *Against Criminology*. New Brunswick, NJ: Transaction Books.

Cohen, S. (1990a) 'Intellectual scepticism and political commitment: the case of radical criminology', Bonger Lecture, Amsterdam Universiteit.

Cohen, S. (1990b) 'Preface' to W. de Haan, *The Politics of Redress: Crime, Punishment and Penal Abolition*. London: Unwin Hyman.

Cohen, S. (1993) 'Crimes of the state: accountability, lustration and the policing of the past', Paper presented to the British Criminology Conference at Cardiff, 28–31 July.

Cooper, D. (1986) *Metaphor*. Oxford: Blackwell.

Cornell, D. (1992) *The Philosophy of the Limit*. London: Routledge.

Cotterrell, R. (1986) 'Law and sociology', *Journal of Law and Society*, 13: 9.

Cover, R. (1986) 'Violence and the word', *Yale Law Journal*, 95: 1601.

Crook, S. (1991) *Modern Radicalism and its Aftermath*. London: Routledge.

Crook, S., Pakulski, J. and Waters, M. (1991) *Post-Modernization*. London: Sage.

Culler, J. (1989) *Framing the Sign: Criticism and its Institutions*. Oxford: Blackwell.

Dahrendorf, R. (1985) *Law and Order*. London: Stevens and Sons.

Daly, K. (1993) 'Representing criminalised women', Paper presented at the British Criminology Conference at Cardiff, 28–31 July.

Dant, T. (1991) *Knowledge, Ideology and Discourse*. London: Routledge.

Davis, M. (1990) *City of Quartz*. London: Verso.

Derrida, J. (1990) 'Force of law: the mystical foundations of authority', *Cardozo Law Review*, 11: 919.

Dews, P. (1987) *Logics of Disintegration*. London: Verso.

Ditton, J. (1979) *Contrology: Beyond the New Criminology*. London: Macmillan.

Douzinas, C. and Goodrich, P. (eds) (1993) *Law and Critique: Special issue on Violence*, 4(2).

Douzinas, C. and Warrington, R. with McVeigh, S. (1991) *Postmodern Jurisprudence*. London: Routledge.

Downes, D. and Rock, P. (1982) *Understanding Deviance*. Oxford: Clarendon Press.

Duncan, S. (1994) 'Law as literature: deconstructing the legal text', *Law and Critique*, 5: 5–29.

Ericson, R. (1991) 'Mass media, crime, law and justice', *British Journal of Criminology*, 31: 219–49.

Ericson, R., Baranak, P. and Chan, J. (1991) *Reproducing Order*. Milton Keynes: Open University Press.

Ewald, F. (1991) 'Norms, discipline and the law', in R. Post (ed.), *Law and the Order of Culture*. Oxford: California University Press.

Featherstone, M. (1988) *Theory, Culture and Society*, special issue 5: 2–3.

Feldman, A. (1991) *Formations of Violence: the Narrative of Body and Political Terror in Northern Ireland*. Chicago: University of Chicago Press.

Ferrajoli, L. (1988) *Diritto e Ragione*. Rome: Laterza.

Fish, S. (1980) *Is there a Text in this Class? The Authority of Interpretive Communities*. Cambridge, MA: Harvard University Press.

Fish, S. (1989) *Doing What Comes Naturally: Change, Rhetoric and the Practice of Theory in Literature and Legal Studies*. Oxford: Clarendon.

Fiske, J. (1990) *Introduction to Communication Studies* (2nd edn). London: Routledge.

Fitzpatrick, P. (1992) *The Mythology of Modern Law*. London: Routledge.

Foucault, M. (1977) *Discipline and Punish*. London: Penguin.

Gadamer, H. (1979) *Truth and Method* (2nd edn). London: Sheed and Ward.

Gambetta, D. (1992) *The Sicilian Mafia: The Business of Private Protection*. Cambridge, MA: Harvard University Press.

Game, A. (1991) *Undoing the Social: Towards A Deconstructive Sociology*. Milton Keynes: Open University Press.

Gane, M. (1991a) *Baudrillard's Bestiary*. London: Routledge.

Gane, M. (1991b) *Baudrillard: Critical and Fatal Theory*. London: Routledge.

Garland, D. (1985) *Punishment and Welfare: A History of Penal Strategies*. London: Gower.

Garland, D. (1990) *Punishment and Modern Social Theory*. Oxford: Clarendon.

Garland, D. (1992) 'Criminological knowledge and its relations to power: Foucault's genealogy and criminology today', *British Journal of Criminology*, 32(4): 403–22.

Geertz, C. (1983) *Local Knowledge: Further Essays in Interpretive Anthropology*. New York: Basic Books.

Gelsthorpe, L. (1990) 'Feminist methodologies in criminology: old wine in new bottles?' in L. Gelsthorpe and A. Morris (eds), *Feminist Perspectives in Criminology*. Milton Keynes: Open University Press.

Geuss, R. (1981) *The Idea of a Critical Theory*. Cambridge: Cambridge University Press.

Giddens, A. (1990) *Consequences of Modernity*. Cambridge: Polity Press.

Giddens, A. (1991) *Modernity and Self Identity*. Cambridge: Polity Press.

Goodrich, P. (1986) *Reading the Law*. London: Blackwell.

Goodrich, P. (1987) *Legal Discourse*. London: Macmillan.

Goodrich, P. (1990) *Languages of Law*. London: Weidenfeld and Nicolson.

Gordon, R. (1984) 'Critical legal histories', *Stanford Law Review*, 36: 57–127.

Gottfredson, M. and Hirschi, T. (1990) *A General Theory of Crime*. Stanford, CA: Stanford University Press.

Gramsick, H. G., Tittle, C. R., Bursik, R. J. Jr and Arneklev, B. J. (1993) 'Testing the core implications of Gottfredson and Hirschi's general theory of crime', *Journal of Research in Crime and Delinquency*, 30(1): 5–30.

Haan, W. de (1990) *The Politics of Redress: Crime, Punishment and Penal Abolition*. London: Unwin Hyman.

Habermas, J. (1987) *The Philosophical Discourse of Modernity*. Cambridge, MA: MIT Press.

Hagan, J. (1988) *Structural Criminology*. Oxford: Polity Press.

Hammersly, M. (1992) *What's Wrong with Ethnography*. London: Routledge.

Hand, S. (1989) *A Levinas Reader*. Oxford: Blackwell.

Harker, R., Mahar, C. and Wilkes, C. (eds) (1990) *An Introduction to the Work of Pierre Bourdieu*. London: Macmillan.

Harvey, D. (1989) *The Condition of Postmodernity*. Oxford: Blackwell.

Hassard, J. (1993) 'Postmodernism and organizational analysis: an overview', in J. Hassard and M. Parker (eds), *Postmodernism and Organizations*. London: Sage.

Hassard, J. and Parker, M. (eds) (1993) *Postmodernism and Organizations*. London: Sage.

Heiland, H., Shelley, L. and Katoh, H. (eds) (1992) *Crime and Control in Comparative Perspectives*. Berlin and New York: De Gruyter.

Henry, S. and Milovanovic, D. (1993) 'Back to basics: a postmodern redefinition of crime', *Critical Criminologist*, 5(2/3): 1.

Hirschi, T. and Gottfredson, M. (1993) 'Commentary: testing the general theory of crime', *Journal of Research in Crime and Delinquency*, 30(1): 47–55.

Hodge, R. and Kress, G. (1988) *Social Semiotics*. Oxford: Blackwell.

Holub, R. (1991) *Habermas: Critic in the Public Sphere*. London: Routledge.

Horder, J. (1992) *Provocation and Responsibility*. Oxford: Oxford University Press.

Hudson, W. (1986) 'Postmodernity and contemporary social thought', in P. Lassman (ed.), *Politics and Social Theory*. London: Routledge.

Hunt, A. (1990) 'Reply to Shearing', *Canadian Journal of Criminology*, 31: 657–8.

Hunt, A. (1991) 'Postmodernism and critical criminology', in B. D. Maclean and D. Milovanovic (eds), *New Directions in Critical Criminology*. Vancouver: Collective Press.

Jackson, B. (1989) *Law, Fact and Narrative Coherence*. Merseyside: Deborah Charles.

Jeffcutt, P. (1993) 'From interpretation to representation', in J. Hassard and M. Parker (eds), *Postmodernism and Organizations*. London: Sage.

Katz, A. (1988) *Seductions of Crime*. New York: Basic Books.

Kennedy, R. (1992) 'Spectacular evidence: discourses of subjectivity in the trial of John Hinckley', *Law and Critique*, 3(1): 3–28.

Kerruish, V. (1991) *Jurisprudence as Ideology*. London: Routledge.

King, M. and Piper, C. (1990) *How the Law Thinks about Children*. London: Gower.

Lacey, N., Wells, C. and Meure, D. (1990) *Reconstructing Criminal Law*. London: Weidenfeld and Nicolson.

Lash, S. (1990) *The Sociology of Postmodernism*. London: Routledge.

Latour, B. (1988) 'The politics of explanation: an alternative', in S. Woolgar (ed.), *Knowledge and Reflexivity*. London: Sage.

Lawson, H. (1982) *Reflexivity*. Oxford: Oxford University Press.

Linstead, S. (1993) 'Deconstruction in the study of organisations', in J. Hassard and M. Parker (eds), *Postmodernism and Organizations*. London: Sage.

Luhmann, N. (1982) *The Differentiation of Society* (trans. Holmes and Larmore). New York. Columbia University Press.

Luhmann, N. (1988) 'The self regulation of law and its limits', in G. Teubner (ed.), *Autopoietic Law: A New Approach to Law and Society*. Berlin: De Gruyter.

Luhmann, N. (1990) *Essays on Self Reference*. New York: Columbia University Press.

Lyotard, J. (1984) *The Post Modern Condition: A Report on Knowledge*. Manchester: Manchester University Press.

Lyotard, J. (1988) *La Differend*. Manchester: Manchester University Press.

McBarnet, D. (1978) 'False dichotomies in criminal justice research', in J. Baldwin and K. Bottomley (eds), *Criminal Justice: Selected Readings*. Oxford: Martin Robertson.

McConville, M., Sanders, A. and Leng, R. (1991) *Constructing the Case for the Prosecution*. London: Routledge.

Maclean, B. D. and Milovanovic, D. (eds) (1991) *New Directions in Critical Criminology*. Vancouver: Collective Press.

Mannheim, K. (1960) *Ideology and Utopia*. London: Routledge and Kegan Paul.

Manning, P. (1988) *Symbolic Communication: Signifying Calls and the Police Response*. Cambridge, MA: MIT Press.

Manning, P. (1991) 'Critical semiotics', in B. D. Maclean and D. Milovanovic (eds), *New Directions in Critical Criminology*. Vancouver: Collective Press.

Marcus, G. and Fischer, M. (1986) *Anthropology as Cultural Critique*. Chicago: University of Chicago Press.

Mathews, R. and Young, J. (eds) (1992) *Issues in Realist Criminology*. London: Sage.

Mathiesen, T. (1980) *Law, Society and Political Action*. London: Academic Press.

Maturana, H. (1991) 'Science and daily life: the ontology of scientific explanations', in F. Steier (ed.), *Research and Reflexivity*. London: Sage.

Melossi, D. (1990) *The State of Social Control*. Cambridge: Polity Press.

Michalowski, R. (1991) 'Niggers, welfare scum and homeless assholes': the problems of idealism, consciousness and context in Left Realism', in B. D. Maclean and D. Milovanovic (eds), *New Directions in Critical Criminology*. Vancouver: Collective Press.

Milovanovic, D. (1991) 'Critical criminology and the challenge of post-modernism', in B. D. Maclean and D. Milanovic (eds), *New Directions in Critical Criminology*. Vancouver: Collective Press.

Minow, M. (1991) 'Partial justice: law and minorities', in A. Sarat and T. Kearns (eds), *The Fate of Law*. Michigan: Michigan University Press.

Mumby, D. (1993) *Narrative and Social Control: Critical Perspectives*. London: Sage.

Nelken, D. (1981) 'The "gap problem" in the sociology of law: a theoretical review', in *Windsor Yearbook of Access to Justice*: 35–62.

Nelken, D. (1982) 'Is there a crisis in law and legal ideology?', *Journal of Law and Society*, 9: 177–89.

Nelken, D. (1983) *The Limits of the Legal Process: A Study of Landlords, Law and Crime*. London: Academic Press.

Nelken, D. (1985) 'Legislation and its constraints', in A. Podgorecki, C. J. Whelan, and D. Khosla (eds), *Legal Systems and Social Systems*. Beckenham: Croom Helm.

Nelken, D. (1986) 'Beyond the study of "law and society": a review essay', *American Bar Foundation Journal*, 11: 323–38.

Nelken, D. (1987) 'Criminal law and criminal justice: some notes on their irrelation', in Ian Dennis (ed.), *Criminal Law and Justice*. London: Sweet & Maxwell.

Nelken, D. (1988) 'Changing Paradigms in the Sociology of Law', in G. Teubner (ed.), *Autopoietic Law: A New Approach to Law and Society*. Berlin: De Gruyter.

Nelken, D. (ed.) (1989) 'Criminal justice on the margin': Special issue of the *Howard Journal of Criminal Justice*.

Nelken, D. (1990a) 'Alternative logics in criminal justice', in R. Light (ed.), *Public and Private Provisions in Criminal Justice*. Bristol: Bristol Centre for Criminal Justice.

Nelken, D. (1990b) *The Truth about Law's Truth*. E.U.I. Working Paper, Florence: E.U.I. Law Department.

Nelken, D. (1991) 'The loneliness of law's meta-theory', in R. de Lange and K. Raes (eds), *Plural Legalities: Critical Legal Studies in Europe*. Ars Aequi: Holland.

Nelken, D. (1993) 'Le giustificazioni della pena ed i diritti dell'imputato', in L. Gianformaggio (ed.), *Le Ragioni del Garantismo*. Turin: Giappichelli.

Nencel, L. and Pels, P. (1991) *Constructing Knowledge*. London: Sage.

Newton, K. M. (1990) *Interpreting the Text*. Hemel Hempstead: Harvester Wheatsheaf.

Norrie, A. (1993) *Crime, Reason and History*. London: Weidenfeld and Nicolson.

Norris, C. (1990) *What's Wrong with Postmodernism*. Baltimore: Johns Hopkins Press.

Ost, F. and Van de Kerchove, M. (1987) *Jalons Pour une Théorie Critique du Droit*. Bruxelles: Free University.

Passas, N. and Nelken, D. (1993) 'The thin line between legitimate and criminal enterprises: subsidy frauds in the European Community', *Crime, Law and Social Change*, 19: 223–43.

Pepinsky, H. (1991) *The Geometry of Violence and Democracy*. Bloomington: Indiana University Press.

Pepinsky, H. and Quinney, R. (eds) (1991) *Criminology as Peacemaking*. Bloomington: Indiana University Press.

Pfohl, S. (1992) *Death at the Parasite Cafe: Social Science (Fictions) and the Postmodern*. London: Macmillan.

Pinch, T. and Pinch, T. (1988) 'Reservations about the new literary forms, or Why let the Devil have all the good tunes', in S. Woolgar (ed.), *Knowledge and Reflexivity*. London: Sage.

Pitch, T. (1986) 'Viaggio attorno alla Criminologia: Discutendo con i Realisti', *Dei Delitti e delle Pene*, 3: 469–89.

Pitch, T. (1992a) 'A sexual difference approach to the criminal question', *Social and Legal Studies*, I(3): 357–71.

Pitch, T. (1992b) 'Il futuro della Criminologia', *Dei Delitti e delle Pene*, 92/3: 169–73.

Pollner, M. (1991) 'Left of ethnomethodology: the rise and decline of radical reflexivity', *American Sociological Review*, 56(3): 370–81.

Poster, M. (1988) *Jean Baudrillard: Selected Writings*. Oxford: Polity Press.

Poster, M. (1990) *The Mode of Information: Postmodernism and Social Context*. Oxford: Polity Press.

Potter, J. (1988) 'What is reflexive about discourse analysis? the case of reading readings', in S. Woolgar (ed.), *Knowledge and Reflexivity*. London: Sage.

Potter, J. and Wetherell, M. (1987) *Discourse and Social Psychology*. London: Sage.

Rabinow, P. and Sullivan, W. (eds) (1979) *Interpretive Social Science: A Reader*. Berkeley: University of California Press.

Rasmussen, D. M. (1990) *Reading Habermas*. Oxford: Blackwell.

Reiner, R. (1985) *The Politics of the Police*. Brighton: Harvester Wheatsheaf.

Reiner, R. (1993) 'Policing a postmodern society', *Modern Law Review*, 55: 761–81.

Resta, E. (1992) *Saggio su Diritto e Violenza*. Rome: Laterza.

Ricouer, P. (1986) *The Rule of Metaphor*. London: Routledge and Kegan Paul.

Romano, B. (1988) *Soggettività, Diritto e Postmoderno*. Rome: Bulzoni Editore.

Rorty, R. (1982) *Consequences of Pragmatism*. Minneapolis: University of Minnesota Press.

Rorty, R. (1989) *Contingency, Irony and Solidarity*. Cambridge: Cambridge University Press.

Rosenau, P. M. (1992) *Post-Modernism and the Social Sciences: Insights, Inroads and Intrusions*. New Jersey: Princeton University Press.

Roshier, B. (1989) *Controlling Crime*. Milton Keynes: Open University Press.

Ruggiero, V. (1992) 'Realist criminology: a critique', in J. Young and R. Mathews (eds) (1992) *Rethinking Criminology: the Realist Debate*. London: Sage.

Salecl, R. (1993) 'Crime as a mode of subjectivization: Lacan and the law', *Law and Critique*, 4(1): 13–20.

Santos, B. de Sousa (1987) 'Law: a map of misreading', *Journal of Law and Society*, 14: 279.

Santos, B. de Sousa (1991) 'The post modern transition: law and politics', in A. Sarat and T. Kearns (eds), *The Fate of Law*. Michigan: Michigan University Press.

Sarat, A. and Kearns, T. (1991) 'A journey through forgetting: towards a jurisprudence of violence', in A. Sarat and T. Kearns (eds), *The Fate of Law*. Michigan: Michigan University Press.

Scheppele, K. L. (1991) 'Facing facts in legal interpretation', in R. Post (ed.), *Law and the Order of Culture*. Oxford: University of California Press.

Shearing, C. (1990a) 'Decriminalizing criminology: reflections on the literal and tropological meaning of the term', *Canadian Journal of Criminology*, 3: 169–78.

Shearing, C. (1990b) 'Reply to Hunt', *Canadian Journal of Criminology*, 31: 659–60.

Shotter, J. (1993) *The Cultural Politics of Everyday Life*. Milton Keynes: Open University Press.

Smart, B. (1992) *Modern Conditions: Postmodern Controversies*. London: Routledge.

Smart, C. (1989) *Feminism and the Power of Law*. London: Routledge.

Smart, C. (1990) 'Feminist approaches to criminology, or postmodern woman meets atavistic man', in L. Gelsthorpe and A. Morris (eds), *Feminist Perspectives in Criminology*. Milton Keynes: Open University Press.

Smith, R. (1981) *Trial by Medicine*. Edinburgh: Edinburgh University Press.

Smith, R. and Wynne, B. (1989) *Expert Evidence: Interpreting Science in the Law*. London: Routledge.

Sparks, R. (1992a) *Television and the Drama of Crime*. Milton Keynes: Open University Press.

Sparks, R. (1992b) 'Realism and unreason in "Left Realism": some problems in the constitution of the fear of crime', in R. Mathews and J. Young (eds), *Issues in Realist Criminology*. London: Sage.

Stanford Law Review (1984) Special issue on critical legal studies, 36.

Stanley, C. (1993a) 'Repression and resistance: problems of regulation in contemporary urban culture: part 1, "Towards Definition"', *International Journal of Sociology of Law*, 21(1): 23–49.

Stanley, C. (1993b) 'Repression and resistance: problems of regulation in contemporary urban culture: part 2, "Determining Forces"', *International Journal of Sociology of Law* 21(2): 121–45.

Steier, F. (ed.) (1991) *Research and Reflexivity*. London: Sage.

Stenson, K. (1992) 'Making sense of crime control', in K. Stenson and D. Cowell (eds), *The Politics of Crime Control*. London: Sage.

Stenson, K. and Cowell, D. (eds) (1992) *The Politics of Crime Control*. London: Sage.

Sumner, C. (ed.) (1990) *Censure, Politics and Criminal Justice*. Milton Keynes: Open University Press.

Taylor, I. (1992) 'Left Realist criminology and the free market experiment in Britain', in J. Young and R. Mathews (eds), *Rethinking Criminology: the Realist Debate*. London: Sage.

Taylor, I., Walton, P. and Young, J. (1973) *The New Criminology*. London: Routledge and Kegan Paul.

Teubner, G. (1983) 'Substantive and reflexive elements in modern law', *Law and Society Review*, 17: 239.

Teubner, G. (ed.) (1988) *Autopoietic Law: A New Approach to Law and Society*. Berlin: De Gruyter.

Teubner, G. (1989) 'How the law thinks: towards a constructivist epistemology of law', *Law and Society Review*, 23(5): 727–56.

Teubner, G. (1993) *Autopoietic Law*. Oxford: Blackwell.

Thompson, J. (1981) *Critical Hermeneutics*. Cambridge: Cambridge University Press.

Thompson, M., Ellis, R. and Wildasky, A. (1990) *Cultural Theory*. Oxford: Westview.

Thompson, P. (1993) 'Postmodernism: fatal distraction', in J. Hassard and M. Parker (eds), *Postmodernism and Organisations*. London: Sage.

Turk, A. (1989) 'Seductions of criminology: Katz on magical meanness and other distractions', *American Behavioral Scientist*, 33: 180.

Valdes, M. (1991) *A Ricoeur Reader*. New York: Harvester Wheatsheaf.

Van Duyne, P. (1993) 'Organised crime and business crime enterprises in the Netherlands', *Crime, Law and Social Change*, 19: 103–43.

Vickers, B. (1988) *In Defence of Rhetoric*. Oxford: Clarendon.

Von Forster, H. (1991) 'Through the eyes of the other', in F. Steier (ed.), *Research and Reflexivity*. London: Sage.

Wagner-Pacifici, R. E. (1986) *The Moro Morality Play*. Chicago: University of Chicago Press.

Walklate, S. (1989) *Victimology*. London: Unwin Hyman.

Waltzer, M. (1986) 'The politics of Michel Foucault', in D. Couzens-Hoy (ed.), *Foucault A Critical Reader*. Oxford: Blackwell.

Weait, M. (1992) 'Swans reflecting elephants: imagery and the law', *Law and Critique*, 3: 51–67.

Weisberg, R. (1992) *Poethics and other Strategies of Law and Literature*. New York: Columbia University Press.

Weisburd, D., Wheeler, S., Waring, E. and Bode, N. (1991) *Crimes of the Middle Classes*. New Haven, CT: Yale University Press.

White, J. Boyd (1985a) *The Legal Imagination*. Chicago: University of Chicago Press.

White, J. Boyd (1985b) *Heracles' Bow*. Madison: University of Wisconsin Press.

White, J. Boyd (1990) *Justice as Translation*. Chicago: University of Chicago Press.

Woolgar, S. (ed.) (1988) *Knowledge and Reflexivity*. London: Sage.

Woolgar, S. and Pawluch, D. (1985) 'Ontological gerrymandering: the anatomy of social problems explanations', *Social Problems*, 32(3): 214–27.

Wright-Mills, C. (1945) 'The professional ideology of social pathologists', *American Journal of Sociology*, 49: 165–80.

Young, A. (1990) *Feminity in Dissent*. London: Routledge.

Young, J. (1991) 'Ten principles of realism' : Paper presented at the British Criminology Conference at York, 24–7 July.

Young, J. (1992) 'Ten points of realism', in J. Young and R. Mathews (eds), *Rethinking Criminology: The Realist Debate*. London: Sage.

Young, J. and Mathews, R. (eds) (1992a) *Rethinking Criminology: The Realist Debate*. London: Sage.

Young, J. and Mathews, R. (1992b) 'Questioning Left Realism', in R. Mathews and J. Young (eds), *Issues in Realist Criminology*. London: Sage.

Zolo, D. (1989) *Reflexive Epistemology*. Dordrecht: Kluwer.

2

Is Criminology Worth Saving?

Massimo Pavarini

What to take with us?

In his last book, published posthumously as *Six Proposals for the Next Millennium*, Italo Calvino set himself a rather special task. What, he asked, are the virtues of literary achievement in the last millennium, in any language, which would be worth saving for the next? This question is a stimulating one which it would be interesting to apply also to criminology, especially if we recall that, for Calvino, every worthwhile 'virtue' of literature had its corresponding 'vice' which he wanted to see removed once and for all.

Criminology is relatively young as a scientific discipline and has only had academic recognition for little more than a century. It is now facing a situation of crisis of identity so profound that we may have serious doubts about its capacity for survival as presently constituted (see, among the many discussions of this crisis, Melossi, 1983: 447; Chambliss, 1988; Cohen, 1988). What will a future criminology look like? Strictly speaking I cannot really answer that question because in order to decide which ways of talking about crime will be seen in the future as properly criminological I would first have to be able to predict the types of problems of social order which future societies will face. But the gift of prophecy is not one of the 'virtues' of criminology! So it makes no sense to seek to describe the discourse that would be built up in formulating notional solutions to these unknown problems.

On the other hand, even if I cannot know what crime problems the societies of the future may have to deal with, I can be quite certain that any answers formulated will only be able to take as their starting point the available stock of knowledge, or presumed knowledge, about crime. But how is criminology to renew itself to face the challenge of the future? We could think of the development of scientific disciplines in terms of a ship which can only repair damage caused by the perils of navigation using the tools which are already on board or which can be adapted from them; there is no possibility of putting in for refitting at a properly equipped dry dock. Continuing the metaphor, we should also recognise that it is not even possible to take on the voyage all the equipment which could be needed but only that which is absolutely necessary. The issue which I would like to examine in this chapter is, therefore, the following. Which of the findings, methods and approaches so far produced by criminology would I choose to put in the tool-box to be taken on this voyage so that we would be best prepared to encounter the crime problems of the future? These essential, albeit minimal, achievements of the past and the present are what I would call 'criminology's virtues'.

Knowingly dealing in fictions

The object which criminological science seeks to describe – crime and the response to it – is necessarily an artificial one because it is in all senses a product of society's conventions. On this point nowadays most, even if not yet all, scholars are in agreement. This is seen clearly when we remember that modern legal science has to base its punitive interventions on a political a priori; the social contract or the founding constitutional agreement taken to constitute society. This means that we have to recognise explicitly that the punitive response has nothing abstractly 'rational' about it. There is nothing we should consider less 'natural' than punishment or criminal deviance. Any system of crime and punishment is a perfect example of a strictly conventional order.[1]

Very specific reasons forced the penal system, between the eighteenth and the nineteenth centuries, to seek legitimacy by espousing the fiction that crime was a natural and not a conventional phenomenon (Roshier, 1989). This has been well known for some time to those adopting a critical perspective on criminology. It was, for example, basic to the revolution against aetiological explanation in criminology which was launched by one of the major approaches to the sociology of deviance in the mid-1960s (Matza, 1964, 1969). We can say that the historical process which transformed the penal system from one based on adversarial principles ('the justice model') into one based on the goal of integration ('the correctionalist model')[2] reached its extremes in the form, on the one hand, of the so-called 'integrated model of penal science'[3] and, on the other, in the focus on specific deterrence. An important consequence of these developments was to treat criminal deviance as if it were a natural pathology in need of cure. It seems to me sadly true that over the past 20 years we have done little more than repeatedly break down this already open door in order to reveal the shamelessness of criminology's 'big lie' and demonstrate the ideological character of discourses about crime.[4] The banality, for example, of Becker's argument, that a criminal is one who is so defined by others (Becker, 1963), is such as would induce Beccaria to feel only compassion for so-called scientific 'progress'.

And yet – and here we catch one of the paradoxes of critical thinking in criminology – once having revealed the normative fallacy of mistaking prescriptive models and assumptions for descriptions of facts in the world, it actually ended up proposing a new naturalistic vision of criminality in its own right (Hess, 1986: 187–213). I am thinking here in particular of the 'radical abolitionists'[5] who in order to free us from systems of penal law found themselves obliged to describe deviance as something inherently natural and unavoidable. As Luke Hulsman is fond of repeating, 'throughout my life I have never come across "evil" people (in the sense of those freely choosing to do harm whilst being able to behave differently) but only people who were powerless and in need of help' (Hulsman, 1983: 71). But the same could also be said of the type of utilitarian critique of the penal system set out by Nils Christie when he accuses criminal law of having shown itself incapable of really protecting people from crime (Christie, 1981). In fact we could only accept his argument that there is no time or place in which criminal law has succeeded in defeating crime if we were prepared to believe that crime really did exist as a non-normative phenomenon which precedes the process of legal definition. I shall not develop the same point in relation to the Realists, whether they be of the Right,[6] or of the Left (Lea and Young, 1984; Kinsey et al., 1986; Young, 1989). But here too it could be said that for them the social dangerousness of criminal behaviour seems sufficient in itself to confer a sort of natural quality on it (cf. Pitch, 1986: 469–87). What I want to ask rather is whether there is still any point in unmasking the naturalistic fallacy: how many times should we need to demonstrate the normative ambiguity that has dogged criminology since the sneaky fiction of *Homo criminalis* replaced that of *Homo penalis*? I strongly believe that it is time criminology stopped repeating this exercise.

Let me use an example which is particularly relevant to criminologists working in Latin America. In countries which are situated on the 'periphery' of the capitalist world system a coherent position for critical criminology was taken to be a 'criminology of liberation' in the sense theorised by my friend Aniyar de Castro (1987) only a few years ago. Such a criminology sets out to denounce, in no half terms, the obscene mixture of discourses within the model of an integrated penal science. It screams that 'the emperor has no clothes' when behind the socially constructed image of dangerous criminals it is all too easy to see the face of imperialistic power. One example will be sufficient: the drug problem in Latin America is in fact socially constructed in the policy-making councils of hegemonic countries in ways which reflect the economic dependence of countries of the periphery (see, most recently, Kaplan, 1989). So far, then, the analysis offered by the criminology of liberation may be taken as true. Perhaps if anything it is assumed to be too obvious. We can go even further than this. In those political systems in which the hegemony of the few ultimately rests on techniques of repressive terror it is easy to show that the theoretical discourse of criminology plays no more than an ancillary role for the material practices of torture and executions (Del Olmo, 1981). But is there anything else that the criminology of liberation can offer apart from tearing away the mask so as to reveal how criminologists have prostituted their discipline in the service of tyranny? It would seem that it can only invoke a socialist revolution along the lines of that followed by Castro or the Sandinistas. In short: the criminology of liberation aims at freeing criminology from its dependence on the powers that be so as to make it available for the purposes of revolution. But then who does the criminology of liberation *actually* liberate? Only, I suspect, the conscience of the critical criminologist.[7]

It follows from this that recognising the artificiality of the criminological discourse should not be taken to reduce the role of criminology to merely criticising either the penal system or the legitimising functions of criminological discourse itself. Apart from anything else, this task can be fulfilled better by legal and political philosophy than by critical criminology.[8]

On the other hand, this awareness of the conventionality of criminology's object is undoubtedly one of the most precious virtues of productive work in criminology. What it implies is the need to be constantly self-critical of the criminological 'gaze' so as to ask how our object of study is constituted. This is all the more important because this 'gaze' is certainly not limited only by the definitions of crime enshrined in law. I shall try to explain more clearly what I mean by this by drawing on the idea of a limiting 'horizon' and in particular, with reference to criminology, that of an artificial horizon, a felicitous image used as the title of a recent book by Ceretti (1992), who himself borrows it from Gadamer.

> Every present, Gadamer has taught us, has its limits (Gadamer, 1983: 352). The very notion of being situated in time is implicitly based on a particular vantage point which limits our range of vision. Thus the concept of situation and that of horizon are essentially linked together: the concept of horizon refers to that circle which embraces all that can be seen from a certain point of view.[9]

If we apply this idea to criminology it would be more appropriate to speak of an 'artificial horizon'. Reference is being made explicitly to the workings of the

> important navigation instrument in the cockpit of an aeroplane which has the function, when flying with low visibility, of standing in for the actual horizon. The instrument's face shows the pilot a schematic outline of the aeroplane with its longitudinal and side inclinations positioned exactly as they are in reality with respect to the actual horizon; in this way the pilot can directly read off at any moment the plane's angle of pitch and roll. (Ceretti, 1992: 20)

The issue therefore is not to put in doubt the usefulness, or rather, the necessity, of using an 'artificial horizon' as our reference if we wish to be able to navigate safely. The point is rather to decide whether the artificial representations which have guided us so far are still useful for continuing our journey or whether it would be possible to create a different image of criminology by selecting a different artificial horizon, one which would allow us to adopt different perspectives within different limits.

We can be sure of one thing. Up until now criminology has always made use of perspectives taken from other systems in order to constitute artificially its object. It has, first and foremost, relied on the legal framework, but it has also exploited the schemes of thought belonging to other branches of knowledge such as psychology, sociology or anthropology (Pitch, 1989: 39). We can also be relatively certain that the fixed point of the horizon, the limit, as it were, of the criminological viewpoint, was set by an attempt to understand the different, often very different, forms of conflict between capital and labour at the point that these produced breaches of the social order or risked doing so (see Pavarini, 1982). Or to put the same point better, we might say that criminology insisted on reducing all breaches of social disorder to the underlying social conflicts caused by capitalism, (see Melossi, 1980: 277–362). This can readily be seen if we consider the topics with which criminology is most obsessed: poverty, immigration, urbanis-ation, race (focusing on those economically on the margin), youth (as subjects not yet admitted to the labour market), etc. It is because this limit of the horizon is such a constant that the main differences in criminology come through different readings of the political significance of the social struggles produced by capitalism; whether criminologists produce reactionary, con-servative, progressive or revolutionary accounts of them depending mainly on the personal sympathies of the different actors involved.

The question I think we should now face up to is the possibility of defining a new artificial horizon which could include within its range matters which are presently hidden, or which the limits of the current horizon forces us to misinterpret. Let me explain this with two examples. The first is suggested by reflecting on some of the findings which have emerged from feminist criminology in its study of violence against women.[10] Male violence, and in particular sexual violence, against women could be said to be a classical criminological subject, given that such violence has been criminalised by all modern penal systems and therefore is clearly included within the artificial horizon of the criminological discipline. But the gaze through which this specific type of violence was usually interpreted was one which precisely negated its specificity (see Pitch, 1989: 197–201); its causes were to be assimilated to those of violence *as such*. In this way it was treated as the product of ignorance, of poverty, of inadequate education, of alcoholism or, if there was really no other way of understanding the behaviour, it was just put down as a sign of mental disturbance. In short, sexual violence was seen as one of the unfortunate attributes of the same 'poorer classes' who are usually seen as the location of criminality and categorised as yet another of the pathologies which afflicts those on the margins of society.

Over the last few years,[11] however, the formation of the women's movement and women's political activism has changed this situation. In the first place it is women themselves who have changed their perception of the violence they suffer, but in the second place there has been increasing awareness of the fact that male violence against women is found among all levels of class and education (Hamuer and Maynard, 1987; Ventimiglia, 1991, 1992). The lesson is obvious. This phenomenon can no longer be explained in terms of individual or social abnormality and pathology; nor can it be relegated to the circumscribed sphere of multi-problem families.

Scholars writing from the feminist perspective have also demonstrated how men and women differ in their ways of understanding violence against women. This obliges us to search for a different point of view for criminology which will include within its horizon also the existence of gender, and which means thinking in terms of two distinct subjects, male and female, instead of the presupposed viewpoint of 'universal man'. Such a revision of perspective would mean extending our gaze so as to grasp and legitimise a different way of looking at life and the world. It would involve recognising explicitly that

> persistence in privileging the masculine point of view [is] not only a constraint which subordinates women's powers of decision-making and cultural progress in a way that has meant that it is women who have so far paid the price of the ambiguous communication which characterises the relationship between the sexes. [In addition it represents] a cognitive and political limit which has prevented a correct reading of the nature of the problem and of the interventions to deal with it, with the result that scientific work on the problem of violence against women serves as a site which serves to rationalise the strategies of justification and denial of many violent men. (Creazzo, 1992: 13)

Probably still more to the point of my present argument, however, is the fact that the new gaze on women's violence is one which defines a horizon in which new objects of understanding will be able to show themselves while those we already thought we knew about will come to be understood differently.

My second example is suggested by new approaches now being taken to the study of organised crime. In this topic we once again find ourselves dealing with a traditional object of criminology's attention (Sutherland, 1949; Cressey, 1969) one that has always been within criminology's speculative horizon in so far as the illegal conduct attributed to organised criminals has been criminalised everywhere. For a long time in the United States (which was the first country, we should remember, to use the term 'organised crime') criminal policy-makers used the organised crime label only to refer to the phenomenon of the Mafia. At this period, from the 1920s onwards, North American criminological writing struggled with the problem of satisfactory definitions. At first it explained the significance of the organisational aspect of this form of criminality by referring to the entrepreneurial model of an 'anonymous holding'. The organisation had a pre-eminent and independent role with regards to its individual members and exercised rationality in the management of illegal goods and services.[12] Later, and in part this reflected a rethinking of the topic, the definitions of organised crime in the American literature tended to stress the nature of the interconnections between the legal and illegal economy (Chambliss, 1978), as well as to stigmatise the tendency of some firms to dominate the market as monopolies or oligopolies making use where necessary of criminal methods (Pearce, 1976). On these interpretations organised crime is simply turned into an aspect of economic crime.

In the Italian context things are different. The widespread social alarm over this phenomenon, reflected in the way criminal policy is formulated, has meant that the concept of organised crime is constructed almost exclusively on the basis of the 'fearfulness' and 'dangerousness'[13] of the facts of certain crimes, which otherwise have absolutely nothing in common. In other words organised crime here became part of the political–legal lexicon only when certain, often long-standing, forms of criminal behaviours, reached levels in excess of what was socially tolerable. But this means that this type of crime is defined in terms of an external element – the type of social reaction – rather than in terms of any of its intrinsic characteristics.

As these accounts show, those who have contributed to the enormous literature on the subject of organised crime,[14] despite their differences of approach, have all been obliged to understand the organisational aspect of crime as if it was no more than an exaggerated feature of some familiar aspect of criminality. As compared with other forms of crime, organised crime is seen as more dangerous, more structured, more intertwined with legal behaviour, more dependent on political collusion, etc. In this way it seems that the point of view chosen by criminology cannot see 'beyond' its artificial horizon or conceive of matters in any radically different way.

If we turn, on the other hand, to a perspective outside of criminology, such as that of political economy, we gain the possibility of quite another way of grasping the significance of this type of criminality. It suggests how some national economies are supported entirely on processes of accumulation and distribution, which, from a legal point of view, must be considered criminal, and shows us how criminal organisations heavily condition both the economics and politics of many countries or at least of vast areas of their territory (Kaplan, 1989; Tenorio Tagle, 1991). The gross national product of such illegal activities world-wide is not much inferior to and may even exceed that of legal business. Also nowadays, and perhaps especially nowadays, the riches of nations are in large part the result of organised criminality. Italy, unfortunately, offers a particularly suitable vantage point for making such a claim.

This new starting point also enables us to take a further step so as to recognise that the tendency inherent in capitalism which leads to monopoly and oligarchy also applies to that which we define as illegal business activity. The discipline of criminology, even when it claims to have substituted its old concepts with new ones, is perhaps the only sociological perspective still tied to an outdated framework of political economy based on the fiction of the 'free market'; for this science criminals are assumed to be small-scale independent economic actors . . . engaged in free competition! What the alternative perspective based on political economy reveals is quite different. Leaving aside crimes of negligence and opportunistic crimes (there are still some cases of jealous lovers murdering their rivals), in Italy every significant form of crime, and not only economic crime, finds itself increasingly forced towards a structure based on oligopoly or some other form of tight network of collaboration.[15] In other words: nowadays no form of illegal activity which is in any way economically productive can survive outside of an organised criminal network or manage without a symbiotic relationship with the legal economy.

But there are still other insights that we can reach by adopting this alternative perspective. We come to appreciate that this enormous criminal economy not only accumulates enormous capital resources but systematically distributes this wealth for criminal purposes. This is not just for the essential task of corrupting politicians and administrators [16] but also so as to maintain what amounts to a regular army of 'paid employees' who make of crime a job like any other, often for a level of pay which does little more than guarantee them subsistence wages (Hobbs, 1988; Ruggiero, 1992: 95). [17]

Certainly it would be possible to reply in defence of criminologists that they too 'imagined' crime scenarios such as these. But this is precisely the point. All criminology could do was to 'imagine' them, like something whose existence can be intuited but which nevertheless is beyond the cognitive horizon. For criminology they represent unexplored continents marked on the map only by the legend *Hic Sunt Leones*. But if, on the contrary, these scenarios were to be at the centre of our reflections then necessarily all of our way of looking at the question of criminality would assume a different perspective.

These examples, it should be well understood, are only two of the many which could be used to show the need to extend the criminological gaze by using different perspectives and looking in unfamiliar directions. But it is certainly true that adopting a gaze capable of taking in such vast horizons can produce a sense of vertigo; not only must we be conscious of the artificiality of using law to define crime but by moving to these new points of view we can come very close to losing our anchorage in the very notion of criminality itself.

The temptations of suicide

Like all adolescents, criminology too has always hugged to itself the awful desire to end it all, to deny itself any future as a separate discipline. One of the founding fathers of the subject, Enrico Ferri, at the end of his book *Sociologia Criminale*, offered the following dream of how criminology might come to an end

> [Criminology] will dig its own grave because scientific diagnosis and positivist explanation of the causes of criminality . . . will reduce the number of delinquents to an irreducible minimum in the future organisation of society which everyday is emerging more strongly. In such a society the lower requirement for penal justice will be substituted by a higher level of social justice. (Ferri, 1900: 936)

Other authors, certainly less optimistic about the irresistible progress of science and socialism, in asking themselves questions about the epistemo-logical foundations of positivist criminology came to the radical conclusion that no such scientific discipline had ever really come into existence (Michael and Adler, 1933). They pointed to its confused claims to knowledge and to the synthetic quality of the discipline or, rather, to the way it was parasitic on developments in other branches of science. In fact, it can hardly be gainsaid that criminology does regularly prey on and overlap with other disciplines. Each scholar remains relatively free to trace his or her own boundaries for this discipline and no attempt to provide a final authorised ruling on boundary lines has ever gained the unanimous consent of those institutionally and, in particular, academically, recognised as forming the community of criminologists.[18]

One result of all this is a widespread feeling of insecurity about the status of the discipline and a sense of its being in continuing crisis. Any listing of the topics tackled by criminology would reveal the numerous discussions of its alleged crisis. It is no surprise therefore that at the slightest occasion the cry goes up 'criminology is dead'! The strange thing, perhaps, is that it is only criminologists who raise this cry. Yet, it is important to be clear, this permanent state of precariousness and crisis, this recurrent temptation towards suicide, is not necessarily a bad thing. Sometimes, as experience has shown, the very absence of a secure homeland or refuge, under emergency conditions, can itself play a part in ensuring the survival of a people or an individual. By this what I mean is simply that the reason the criminologist finds it relatively easy to 'pack his or her bags' and emigrate elsewhere, to other disciplines, is that there is very little to abandon. This looseness of disciplinary attachment could therefore be considered one of criminology's strengths in facing the future. In my view the challenge of ever-growing social complexity, with the necessity it brings to take decisions without being able to foresee their consequences, could be considered just such an emergency. The 'lightness' of the scientific baggage carried by the criminologist, in a sense even his or her scientific 'irresponsibility', could turn out to be an advantage.[19] In short: the disciplinary weaknesses of the subject make criminology well adapted, as compared with other disciplines, to the need to make partial and tentative responses to the problems it is asked to resolve. It feels less need to arrive at its diagnoses by following rigorous methodological guidelines if only because, from its very beginnings, it has lacked its own unique theoretical paradigm. Criminology has always been, and still is, in the vanguard of what philosophers of the postmodern have called theorising on the basis of a 'weak ontology' (Vattimo and Rovatti, 1983).

I shall try to illustrate the effect this has on my current scientific and professional work. For the past two years I have been heavily engaged in the politics of 'the new crime prevention'.[20] I direct a popularising magazine aimed at providing information about improving security against the criminal deviance which afflicts city life; this is aimed at social and community workers, at volunteers, and at those with political and administrative responsibility at all local levels. In addition I originated, and am presently coordinating, research on social perceptions and panics over crime in the city. In developing projects of crime prevention I seek to convince those who are willing to listen that it is possible to live more securely, and with less fear of crime, by spreading the consciousness of 'new approaches to collective crime prevention' and by getting local communities involved in them. I place my trust in the idea that by activating and increasing social interaction and communication among its members a community can find the resources required to meet its need for security. From the early results of these efforts I feel that this message has been found reasonably convincing.

How should this activity be conceived of in terms of my perspective within criminology? If we leave out of account undeniable differences of political, cultural and institutional context it could certainly be said that in many respects I am working along the lines proposed by the New Realists of the Left, as well as that indicated by some of the abolitionists. But while my practice may seem similar to that which they propose I do not *think* as they do. On the contrary, I am extremely critical of some of their theoretical arguments (Pavarini, 1985: 525–54). More than this; what I contest is the very notion that it is necessary to have a general theory of crime and social control in order to intervene in the effort to alleviate some particular aspect of the crime problem (no-one would ever expect you to resolve the problem once and for all!). Naturally I too have had, and still have, some general ideas about the nature of crime, and it is hardly possible to avoid having some such opinions. But it is just because I have seen my ideas so change over time that I have come to appreciate that such general views are nothing other than provisional conceptualisations with nothing more than heuristic value. They may be useful in explaining some aspects of crime and, by the same token, less helpful in accounting for others. The more such working theories are pitched at a high level of generality the more they dissolve the specificity of any particular aspect of the crime problem. Eventually such theorising can even risk losing contact with the issue of crime itself. What I am arguing, however, is that *for the purposes of theory* this can perhaps be actually considered a positive advantage.

In this way, to return to my own experience nowadays, while I spend my time in constructing practical projects aimed at crime prevention, I continue to be none the less fascinated by the idea that there is no longer any point in seeking to explain crime, or rather, that this question is steadily losing any claim to its own specificity. I too (like Stan Cohen) have my 'visions of social control'. I can imagine that the definition and distribution of criminality becomes nothing other than a 'risk' which accompanies social competition. As an inevitable consequence of the hypertrophy of social control the disciplinary system will progressively lose its original fragmentary character and instead present itself as a total, all-encompassing, system of social protection. From an instrument designed to safeguard the natural order (when the order of the market was believed to be 'natural') the technologies of social control have come to be methods used for reinforcing what is known to be an artificial order.[21]

The question of what counts as crime becomes under these conditions a 'good' or a 'resource' that can be traded. Criminal prohibitions take their place, as Sgubbi explains, 'among the so-called public goods which, according to the neo-corporatist model of social organisation, are the objects of bargaining between public authorities, on the one hand, and organised social groups, on the other' (Sgubbi, 1990: 26). Each individual, in his or her particular situation, is obliged to take part in the game by which advantages and handicaps are handed out by the system of social control. The social bargaining geared to producing the net social distribution of crimes and punishments is carried out in what is by now a neo-contractual context. The strongest actors seek to gain the greatest share of this 'good' by penalising the conduct of other parties while trying to maximise their own immunity, and thereby they make sure that the distribution of punishments will be an unequal one.

However, this emergent system of social control has characteristics which distinguish it strongly from those which precede it . The bargaining which leads to this unequal distribution of penalties only pursues the goal of 'disadvantaging' some activities or social actors as against others. Its function is *not* actually to prevent such activities taking place nor is it to eliminate or re-socialise certain actors. The control system thereby becomes an element *internal* to social conflicts between groups, which the various collective social subjects and groups of organised interests use to support or confirm their contractual and institutional power. The 'artificial distribution' of penalties and immunities which results is an aspect of the overall political distribution of social wealth understood in its widest sense. The allocation of criminality, in short, is a contingent product of social conflicts whose outcome determines who and what is considered criminal. But what distinguishes this as a new situation is that the definition of criminality is not only one that is conventional but that it has lost any specificity: the crime label is only a resource of social exchange with symbolic value, exactly like money. But if this is the case what further sense would criminology have as that discipline specifically dealing with the question of criminality?

A partisan vocation?

According to Stan Cohen it is possible to be a professional criminologist without being obliged to answer the question 'whose side are you on?' (Cohen, 1985:238). If sociologists of religion are not required to put on religious vestments, or to pray to any god, so sociologists of deviance should not be asked to suggest or side with any particular policy towards crime. Or at least, it should not be strictly necessary for them to do so.

Certainly such indifference is only an abstract possibility, in the sense that we can insist on the right not to take sides but, in practice, we may doubt that the criminologist has ever been allowed such a luxury. What I think would be interesting to ask ourselves is whether we should actually want to be given such freedom. Let me be clear about this. I am not concerned here with the unresolved and irresolvable question of whether science can ever be neutral. The 'low' level at which criminology operates has meant, I believe, that it has never even come up against this epistemological conundrum. What I want to claim, much more simply, is that virtually every criminological discourse has been translated into criminal policy, and every form of criminology has its corresponding praxis. I do not believe the same can be said, for example, for each approach to the sociology of religion.

But if criminology has always been so compromised by its practical applications what sense does it make to ask the criminologist 'which side are you on'? I certainly doubt that there is any point to the question when it comes to criminology's actual praxis. That would mean conceding the possibility of an antinomy between freedom and authority in the politics of controlling criminal deviance. And the possibility of such an antinomy has never been permitted.

The fact that the question was ever posed can be attributed to a certain mental laziness that uncritically transferred to criminology and the activities of social control the presence of an 'ambiguity' which more correctly belongs to other types of knowledge and power, such as, for example, psychiatry and other practices concerned with mental health. When it comes to psychiatry it does make sense – or did make sense – to ask to whose mandate the psychiatrist responds. Is the psychiatrist concerned with protection 'for' or 'from' those who are mentally ill? Is it the psychiatrist's role to defend those who are mad from society, or society from those who are mad (Betti and Pavarini, 1984: 163–83)? In fact, whenever the psychiatrist is responsive to the demands of 'protection for' the deviant, this defines the right of freedom from interference (as also rights to health care); on the contrary, whenever the psychiatrist responds to the demand for 'protection from', he or she ends up in the direction of the denial of liberty and therefore becomes involved in repression, in social control – in short the psychiatrist ends up on the side of the authorities.

Historically speaking, however, criminological practice, has never allowed for such ambiguity. It belongs entirely to the camp of those concerned with organising social defences against criminality. In these terms it seems to me that criminology belongs, I would say genetically, only to the side of authority. From this point of view, that which concerns the ends of criminological practice, there is no point in asking about the dichotomy between freedom and authority. The criminologist, on this decisive matter, can only take a stand on one side, because only one side exists.

This can be confirmed even when it is argued that the job of criminology should be to try to reformulate questions asked about social order rather than seek to offer answers to them (Pisapia, 1992: 77). For it is easy to discover that what is socially expected from the criminologist is always to find *answers* to the problem of crime. However hard the criminologist tries to reformulate the questions worth asking about social order he or she is allowed to do so only as a function of the different solutions seen to be offered.

Matters are different, however, if the point of view that concerns us is not so much the *ultimate* aim of all criminological praxis but rather the perceptions which various social actors, including the criminologist, may have of given policies and practices. In a recent important contribution Tamar Pitch (1989: 13 ff.) has clarified for us the way the alternatives of freedom and authority in social control policy-making may also be related to the 'points of view' of the actors involved in the social control process. With this approach, which I would call 'subjective', as compared with the previous objective one, both the ideas of social control and that of deviance become more ambiguous concepts.

The category of social control can then be interpreted in very different, even contradictory, ways. It may be seen as a political question concerning, for example, how to impose, change, or conserve a given social order. In this perspective the relevant interpretive concepts are political and legal – power, domination, state, law, repression – and authority.[22] As a sociological category, however, a variety of other paradigms are relevant to the interpretation of social control. Here the focus is on the motivations of social action, on social integration and socialisation, and these are examined in terms of a consensus model of society in which those who are controlled are not assumed to be standing for any 'alternative' as compared with those who are exercising the power of control.[23]

The first approach to social control, which sees it as a political issue involving social conflict, produces a 'positive' definition of criminal deviance. The deviant is seen as the bringer of innovation, the bearer of a difference which cannot be assimilated. The deviant is therefore in certain respects a political actor, an agent of transformation; often the deviant may even be revolutionary. The second way of conceiving social control, on the other hand, that belonging to consensus sociology, generates a 'negative' definition of the deviant; the deviant is one who suffers because he or she has less than others, not because of any difference. From this it necessarily follows that the deviant must be a pathological case requiring either to be cured or given whatever other treatment is relevant to one in need.

As this suggests, the two academic conceptions of social control and deviance correspond to two opposite points of view which can be taken by the social actors themselves. The first reading, in terms of conflict theory, because it emphasises the authority aspect of the control situation, also for that very reason defines the space of possible freedom from control. The second conception, precisely because it does not see any conflict, is incapable of indicating a space of freedom 'outside' the sphere of control.

The appropriate terminology for translating into subjective perceptions the notions of 'freedom' and 'authority' as polarities in the control of deviance are therefore the alternatives of resistance and acceptance in the deviant's response to the actions of the controllers. These responses are inherently contingent and changing: what I resist today, you may accept tomorrow. Naturally, to this it could be objected that someone who is dragged to the scaffold, or condemned to rot in prison, could hardly perceive the criminal justice system as other than antagonistic. But I wonder whether the same could always be said for the young delinquent to whom the penal system offers a course of professional training or education. Nor should we always assume antagonism on the part, say, of the young drug taker, also involved in criminality, who is punished by being enrolled in a therapeutic programme designed to cure his or her addiction to drugs.

It is only in respect of *this* ambiguity in the subjective perception of social control activities that the criminologist can, and in fact must, decide whose side he or she is on. It is from this starting point, certainly, that we can identify the existence of what has been called an 'administrative criminology'; it is here too where we should look for distinctions between left wing and right wing as well as other alternative positions in criminology. What I have been stressing so far, however, is the total impossibility for the criminologist to choose an 'alternative' position on which to construct a distinctive criminological discourse unless this is tied to the actual subjective perceptions of the social actors caught up in the disciplinary processes of social control. This is not to deny that there have of course been efforts, sometimes praiseworthy and scientifically sophisticated ones, to escape the contingency of such a subjective approach, so as to seek to identify a 'material referent' in the social construction of criminality based only on the repression of objectively harmful conduct. But the truth is that these efforts have produced few appreciable results (Baratta, 1983: 5–13).

It is, therefore, in the sense just outlined that the criminological vocation, when it translates itself into practice, can hardly be anything but partisan. The reservations that may reasonably be entertained with reference to the position taken by the New Realists on the Left, to take only one example, therefore, certainly do not have anything to do with their declared choice to opt for a criminal policy which is intended to protect the 'working classes' from the risks of victimisation and criminalisation. The problem is related rather to the way they are taken to have reproduced a new reification of the nature of criminality (De Leo, 1986: 453–67;Pitch, 1986: 469–89; Ruggiero, 1992: 95–113).

I am therefore prepared to defend as a virtue the taking of sides in criminological praxis, provided, however, that the definition of what counts as deviance and as social control is seen as decisively influenced both by those who have 'the power to define' and also those who have the possibility to 'resist these definitions'. In fact, defining a social process as one of social control, or a given social behaviour as deviant and criminal, is bound to take into account, in the last instance, the level of opposition to such labels and the extent of rejection of the 'naturalness' of such social interventions. The choice whether to criminalise a given social problem, or to control it in some other way, through psychiatry or social security for example, or, more basically still, to deal with it at the stage of primary socialisation, always goes back to the social construction of the problem itself. In this choice a central and decisive consideration is the degree of intransigence that is seen as likely to be displayed by the social actors who are intended to be the target of the particular disciplinary intervention. To make this theoretical point clearer it is enough to think about two extreme and opposite cases of the social construction of deviance. On the one hand, we could take the administratively routinised form of social control used to handle juvenile delinquents. Here the goal of policy is typically that of rehabilitation and assistance. On the other hand, we could contrast the status of political prisoner which is reserved, in some situations, for members of terrorist organisations who have committed crimes and who are known to be particularly intransigent.

In the different perspective I am advocating the question of how much 'freedom' or 'authority' is adopted in the handling of deviance is understandable only 'from the point of view' of those defined as deviant. The process is dialectical: the more resistance is offered and opposed to the activity of control the more 'freedom' to define their own conduct is given to deviants, and vice versa.

Let me demonstrate this with an example. If we consider the social problem of drug addiction, suspended as it is between criminalisation and medicalisation, it is clear that constructing the consumption of illegal drugs as criminal reinforces rather than weakens the tendency of those defined as drug takers to feel themselves opposed to the rest of society. On the other hand, the social construction of drug addiction as a therapeutic problem for which addicts need help inexorably undermines their oppositional stance and hence limits their freedom. But this is true only in the abstract. In practice the 'freedom' which results from each of these responses towards the drug problem depends on the reaction of the deviant. I am thinking here of the young drug addict who actually 'sees' him- or herself as 'sick' and therefore invokes the right to undergo a cure. In sum: if the addict agrees with and hence does not resist a social intervention based on a construction of drug addiction as a health matter the drug addict's freedom is actually better protected by applying for cure than by demanding punishment.

The question which this raises is the following. Can we be certain that the crucial element which determines whether one or other style of social control is more legitimate is the point of view of the person who will undergo the intervention? Is it a convincing argument, for example, to say that the choice to criminalise, rather than medicalise (or hand over to the psychiatrists) a given form of behaviour, is legitimate if the deviant claims 'subjectively' the right to maintain an intransigent opposition towards the actions of the controllers?

The answer is that it is not so straightforward. In the management of deviance in general, and in the praxis of criminology in particular, the question 'whose side to take' is never reducible to a binary logic. The choice is in effect much more complex, and must include reference to all the other social actors involved, both those forming part of the situation defined as problematic and also those engaged in activating the disciplinary response. The range of relevant actors goes from victims and their families to deviants and their families, it extends to the sections of society most exposed to the risks both of victimisation and of criminalisation, and, ultimately, it must include the community as a whole.[24]

Having considered all these 'points of view' the criminologist may well find that some of them may be in conflict and even diametrically opposed (even if this will not always and necessarily be the case). The question will then present itself: whose 'point of view' should be preferred? And the criminologist will have to choose. There is no way out of it.

Notes

The translation from the Italian is by David Nelken.

1 A clear appreciation of the conventional character of the system of social control is the only sure way to argue politically in favour of procedural and other guarantees (that is, libertarian principles) in the criminal justice system. On this terrain the work of Ferrajoli (1989) is incontestable.

2 This is the context in which I would seek to understand the changing arguments used by critical movements in the face of the breakdown of the correctionalist approach to criminal justice in the United States (see for example American Friends Service Committee, 1971; Fogel, 1975; Lipton et al., 1975).

3 For details of the model used to integrate legal and penal science with the social sciences, with reference to Germany in particular, see the penetrating discussion by Baratta (1982: 40–3).

4 The pioneering work in this perspective was certainly that by Taylor et al. (1973). Even if the authors of that successful book are now extremely critical of what they believed, and perhaps were, 20 years ago, I suspect, ironically, that they will pass into the history of criminological thought precisely for what they now seem almost ashamed of.

5 For a bibliographic survey of the work of the abolitionist school see Garcia Mendes (1985: 591–6). In fact it is much smaller in extent than the echo with which it reverberated through the community of easily frightened traditional criminologists thanks to the revolutionary fervour of certain high priests of abolitionist thought.

6 For a strongly critical and highly convincing interpretation of the role of these so-called intellectuals in the Reaganite politics of 'law and order', see Platt and Takagi, (1977: 1–16).

7 It is still more difficult to work out the possible routes of an 'emancipatory' criminological *practice* under these conditions. Personally I have never felt the attraction of arguments which claim that we should see every criminal as someone who is undergoing exploitation, with all that would follow from this judgement. This is not of course because I deny that 90 per cent of the prison population in such countries is in fact composed of 'poor devils', but simply because 99 per cent of those who do *not* finish up in prison are also 'poor devils'. I agree on this point therefore with my friends the Left Realists: certain slogans belong by now to the archaeological remains of romanticising criminology.

8 It is not by chance that within the Italian academic world those who have most contributed to this approach have drawn on disciplines other than that of criminology as such. I am thinking here of the brilliant work of Costa (1974) in legal history, or that of my friend Baratta, in particular in his 1982 volume, which is basically a work of philosophy of law applied to criminology.

9 This and all further quotations from works in Italian have been translated by the translator of this essay.

10 More generally, for a selection of readings in Italian of criminological writing by women on women, see Pitch (1987).

11 For an annotated bibliography of the literature on women, deviance and social control see Faccioli (1983: 239–44).

12 A historical reconstruction of the various interpretive paradigms used in the study of organised crime in American culture can be found in Dwight C. Smith (1991: 135–54).

13 This was precisely the meaning given during the conference on 'Organised crime and emergency legislation', Bologna 7 March 1992 (see *Dei delitti e delle pene*, March 1992).

14 With reference only to recent contributions to the study of the problem of organised crime in Italy see Arlacchi (1983); Catanzaro (1988); Zincani (1989); Falcone (1991, 1992).

15 The Prefect of Bologna, Dr Sica, in private conversation, gave me a vivid illustration of this point. Like many others I regularly end up giving money to the non-European immigrants who offer to wash the windscreen of my car when it is stationary at traffic lights in Bologna. It is something I do more so as not to be bothered any further than out of any genuine pity for them. However, according to Dr Sica, it is certain that at least half of the coins I give them end up in the pockets of the organised criminals who control the racket of 'illegal windscreen washers'. These same criminals also run a large part of the distribution of illegal drugs, again making use

of the forced labour of illegal immigrants. But in order to be economically viable as players in the drugs market, such criminals need to have large supplies of capital at their disposal. Such funds will be provided from the world of illegal economic activities by those specialised in running prostitution rings or in the hijacking of lorry loads or in bank robbery. In turn, criminals specialising in bank robbery will need access to costly technology such as thermic lances and sophisticated weaponry. These can be bought or hired only from those who in practice have a monopoly over the supply of these materials and these same criminals are frequently those engaged in international drugs and arms trading. The enormous profits that are made in this trade are regularly recycled in the banking system and the money, finally laundered 'clean', is then invested in absolutely legal activities. It is in this way that, link after link, the great 'net of the illegal economy' is stitched together and its complicated pattern interwoven with that of the legal economy (for further illustrations see Sica, 1992: 34–9).

16 In terms of the current political situation in Italy the main point to emerge strongly recently is the way corruption is systematically diffused in certain contexts in the form of a sort of 'protectionist agreement' between businessmen and the local politicians who control the area in which their businesses operate and control the flow of favours they require. This 'corrupt environment' generates what can be described as a perverse and illegal re-feudalisation of the relationship between politics and the economy (Della Porta, 1992). But, because these are essentially illegal agreements, both the political parties and the businesses involved have to immerse themselves in a culture of criminality so as to work out the most effective strategies to pursue in the illegal marketplace which conceals the transactions in these economic resources. We may, therefore, safely assume that many of the steps required for the organisation of such protectionist agreements will require the use of structures and services offered by organised crime and, by the same token, that organised criminals will offer themselves as mediators both to politicians and businessmen to help them conclude such agreements (Pavarini, 1992: 9–11).

17 It has been estimated that more than 300,000 people live from trafficking in contraband cigarettes in the Province of Naples alone. But the illegal economy goes well beyond this: thousands of others live by or from prostitution; then there is the army of those who live by providing the opportunity for illegal gambling ('black' lotteries and football pools). Then there is the enormous business of the drugs trade. It has been calculated that the places in Naples where it is possible to acquire illegal drugs 24 hours a day exceed the considerable number of local tobacconists who are the official retail outlets for the state monopoly on the sale of tobacco and salt (Lamberti, 1989).

18 I am thinking here in particular of the state of criminological science nowadays in Italy. Some scholars, the majority, were initiated into their craft at the dissecting tables of the mortuary. Others learned their criminology in Faculties of Law, which, in Italy, as a legacy of the philosophical idealism taught by Gentile, are dominated by a visceral dismissal of the empirical sciences. I am more or less convinced that, in Italy, criminologists are the perfect example of those who have to teach themselves the nature of their subject. But this is probably not something limited to Italy; it applies also to Spanish speaking countries, is true at least in part also of criminology in France, and even perhaps of Germany.

19 Among recent writers in Italy De Leo and Patrizi (1992) seem to have taken the very opposite line to that argued here. Drawing on Luhmann's systems theory approach to modern society they purport to recognise in the very social complexity of criminality the factor that can serve to make it a unified object of analysis.

20 I use this term in the precise sense adopted and conceptually elaborated by Philippe Robert (1991) at the International Conference on Urban Safety, Drugs, and Crime Prevention (Paris, 18–20 November 1991).

21 Social control systems of this type take their form from artificially created processes of primary criminalisation. That which is prohibited is unconnected to any sentiments of disapprobation which exist a priori, and has no social or cultural referent; at most this may follow a posteriori. It is for this reason that we may consider it artificial. The social control of 'criminality' through technical prescriptions thus becomes a kind of technology of 'public order'.

22 Treating social control as a political question implies, as argued by Pitch (1989: 18 ff.),

that the situation described is one in which there are those who dominate and others who are dominated, and that these groups are in conflict. Those dominated are obliged to accept the logic of those in control, without sharing it, often actively resisting it because it represents interests in conflict with theirs. It is for this reason that social control has to become 'repression of resistance' and dissent against the ruling order.

23   Indeed, often the contrary is true. Those subject to social control may be seen as asking to be more closely integrated into society, in the sense that they may have legitimate expectations, even rights, to be integrated. For example, in the welfare state we demand the right to health, to education, and to social security. It is difficult to resist social control when it presents itself in this form.

24   I will offer only one illustration. Let us take the case of violence at football stadiums (this phenomenon in Italy has recently been examined in a penetrating study by Roversi, 1992), and seek to take into account the plurality of 'points of view' which are relevant.

The first set of views is that of the hooligans themselves. They certainly are representative of the youth culture of some subaltern sections of the population of large towns (in the British context this culture essentially belongs to the working class). Their collective actions of violence also express a culture of opposition in a political situation in which there are progressively fewer institutional forums in which certain conflicts can be aired.

Then there are the views of the victims. Often the authors and victims of this form of violence are the same people. What is sought out is physical conflict with followers of the adversary football club. All this reproduces and amplifies the antagonism on which their social identities are based. Other victims, however, include the outsiders involuntarily caught up by chance in these battles. On other occasions the goal is to engineer clashes with the police. This, certainly, serves even more to exalt the sense of an identity oppositional to that of the rest of society. But, at the same time, it also leads to the militarisation of controls at football stadiums, to massive police presence at railway stations and in controlling the trains used by fans. On the days of football matches entire zones of a city may be placed in a state of siege often, indeed, entire cities.   The point is clear. Any attempt to manage this social problem ends up by having large and complex repercussions for everyone's liberties.

References

American Friends Service Committee (1971) *Struggle for Justice: A Report on Crime and Punishment in America*. New York: Hill and Wang.

Aniyar De Castro, L. (1987) *Criminologia de la Liberacion*. Maracaibo: Universidad del Zulia.

Arlacchi, P. (1983) *La mafia imprenditrice*. Bologna: il Mulino.

Baratta, A. (1982) *Criminologia critica e critica del diritto penale*. Bologna: il Mulino.

Baratta, A. (1983) 'Problemi sociali e percezione della criminalità', *Dei Delitti e delle pene*, 1: 1–15.

Becker, H. (1963) *Outsiders: Studies in the Sociology of Deviance*. New York: Free Press.

Betti, M. and Pavarini, M. (1984) 'La tutela sociale della follia. Note teoriche sulla scienza e pratica psichiatriche di fronte alle nuove strategie di controllo sociale', *Dei delitti e delle pene*, 1: 161–83.

Calvino, I. (1988) *Lezioni americane: Sei proposte per il prossimo millennio*. Milan: Rizzoli.

Catanzaro, R. (1988) *Il delitto come impresa*. Padua: CEDAM.

Ceretti, A. (1992) *L'orizzonte artificiale: Problemi epistemologici della criminologia*. Padua: CEDAM.

Chambliss, W. J. (1978) *On the Take: From Petty Crooks to the Presidents*. Bloomington: Indiana University Press.

Chambliss, W. J. (1988) *Exploring Criminology*. New York: Macmillan.

Christie, N. (1981) *Limits to Pain*. Oslo: Universitetsforlaget.

Cohen, S. (1985) *Vision of Social Control*. Cambridge: Polity Press.

Cohen, S. (1988) *Against Criminology*. New Brunswick, NJ: Transaction Books.

Costa, P. (1974) *Il progetto giuridico: Ricerche sulla giurisprudenza del liberalismo classico*. Milan: Giuffré.

Creazzo, G. (1992) 'La differenza, le differenze', *Sicurezza e territorio*, 3: 12–14.

Cressey, D. R. (1969) *Theft of the Nation: The Structure of Operations of Organized Crime in America*. New York: Harper and Row.

Della Porta, D. (1992) *Lo scambio occulto: Casi di corruzione politica in Italia*. Bologna: il Mulino.

De Leo, G. (1986) 'Il crimine come problema e la sua spiegazione: nuovo realismo ed oltre', *Dei delitti e delle pene*, 3: 453–68.

De Leo, G. and Patrizi, P. (1992) *La spiegazione del crimine: Bilancio critico e nuove prospettive teoriche*. Bologna: il Mulino.

Del Olmo, R. (1981) *America Latina y su Criminologia*. Mexico DF: Siglo Veintiuno Editores.

Faccioli, F. (1983) 'Donne, devianza e controllo sociale', *Dei delitti e delle pene*, 1: 239–44.

Falcone, G. (1991) *Cose di Cosa Nostra*. Milan: Rizzoli.

Falcone, G. (1992) 'Lezioni sulla criminalitá organizzata, numero speciale di' *Sicurezza e territorio*.

Ferrajoli, L. (1989) *Diritto e ragione: Teoria del garantismo penale*. Napoli: Laterza.

Ferri, E. (1900) *Sociologia criminale*, (5th edn). Turin: UTET.

Fogel, D. (1975), *'We Are the Living Proof': The Justice Model for Corrections*. Cincinnati: Anderson.

Gadamer, H. G. (trad. ital. 1983) *Veritá e metodo*. Milan: Bompiani.

Garcia Mendez, E. (1985) 'Il Movimento e la Teoria per la abolizione del sistema penale e la discussione recente', *Del delitti e delle pene*, 3: 591–6.

Hamuer, J. and Maynard, M. (eds) (1987) *Women, Violence and Social Control*. London: Macmillan.

Hess, H. (1986) 'Criminalitá come mito quotidiano. Una difesa della criminologia come critica della ideologia', *Dei delitti e delle pene*, 1: 186–213.

Hobbs, D. (1988) *Doing the Business*. Oxford: Claredon.

Hulsman, L. (1983) 'Abolire il sistema penale?', *Dei delitti e delle pene*, 1: 71–90.

Kaplan, M. (1989) *Aspectos sociopoliticos del narcotrafico*. Mexico, DF: Istituto Nacional de Ciencias Penales.

Kinsey, R., Lea, J. and Young, J. (eds) (1986), *Losing the Fight Against Crime*. Oxford: Blackwell.

Lamberti, A. (1989) in Massimo Teodori (a cura di), *No alla legge governativa sulla droga, repressiva, illiberale, ingiusta*, Atti dell'incontro promosso da Gruppo Federalista Europeo della Camera, dal Gruppo Federalista Europeo Ecologista del Senato e del CORA, Roma, 14 febbraio 1989.

Lea, J. and Young, J. (1984) *What is to Be Done about Law and Order*. Harmondsworth: Penguin.

Lipton, D., Martinson, R. and Wilks, J. (1975) *The Effectiveness of Correction Treatment Studies*. New York: Praeger.

Matza, D. (1964) *Delinquency and Drift*. New York: Wiley.

Matza, D. (1969) *Becoming Deviant*. Englewood Cliffs, NJ: Prentice Hall.

Melossi, D. (1980) 'Oltre il "Panopticon". Per uno studio delle strategie di controllo sociale nel capitalismo del ventesimo secolo', *La questione criminale*, 2–3: 277–362.

Melossi, D. (1983) 'E' in crisi la "criminologia critica"? Saggio sul suo sviluppo, la situazione presente e una nuova prospettiva teorica', in *Dei delitti e delle pene*, 3: 447–70.

Michael, J. and Adler, M. J. (1933) *Crime, Law and Social Sciences*. New York: Harcourt, Brace and Company.

Pavarini, M. (1982) 'Introduzione' to *La Criminologia*. Florence: Le Monier.

Pavarini, M. (1985) 'Il sistema della giustizia penale trariduzionismo e abolizionismo', *Dei delitti e delle pene*, 3: 525–54.

Pavarini, M. (1992) 'Sistema dei partiti e corruzione politica', *Sicurezza e territorio*, 3: 9–11.

Pearce, F. (1976) *Crimes of the Powerful: Marxism, Crime and Deviance*. London: Pluto Press.

Pisapia, G. (1992) *La dimensione normativa della criminologia*. Padua: CEDAM.

Pitch, T. (1986) 'Viaggio intorno alla criminologia: discutendo con i realisti', *Dei delitti e delle pene*, 3: 469–89.

Pitch, T. (ed.) (1987) *Diritto e rovescio: Studi sulle donne e il controllo sociale*. Naples: ESI.

Pitch, T. (1989) *Responsabilitá limitate: Attori, conflitti, giustizia penale*. Milan: Feltrinelli.

Platt, T. and Takagi, P. (1977) 'Intellectuals for Law and Order: A Critique of the New "Realists"', *Crime and Social Justice*, 8: 1–16.

Robert, P. (ed.) (1991) *Le politiques de prévention de la délinquance a li'aune de la recherche: Un bilan international*. Paris: Editions l'Harmattan.

Roshier, B. (1989) *Controlling Crime: The Classical Perspective in Criminology*. Philadelphia: Open University Press.

Roversi, A. (1992) *Calcio, tifo e violenza: Il teppismo calcistico in Italia*. Bologna: il Mulino.

Ruggiero, V. (1992) 'Quando la criminologia evade il reale: Una critica del realismo criminologico', *Dei delitti e delle pene*, 1: 95–113.

Sgubbi, F. (1990) *Il reato come rischio sociale: Ricerche sulle scelte di allocazione dell'illecito penale*. Bologna: il Mulino.

Sica, D. (1992) 'La Corte dei Miracoli', *Sicurezza e territorio*, 2: 34–40.

Smith, Dwight C., Jr (1991) 'Wickersham to Sutherland to Katzenbach: Evolving an "official" definition for organized crime', *Crime, Law and Social Change*, 4: 135–54.

Sutherland, E. H. (1949) *White Collar Crime*. New York: Dryden Press.

Taylor, I., Walton, P. and Young, J. (eds) (1973) *The New Criminology*. London: Routledge and Kegan Paul.

Tenorio Tagle, F. (1991) *El Control Social de las Drogas en Mexico*. Mexico DF: Istituto Nacional de Ciencias Penales.

Vattimo, G. and Rovatti, P. A. (eds) (1983) *Il Pensiero debole*. Milan: Feltrinelli.

Ventimiglia, C. (1991) *Donne delle mie brame*. Milan: Franco Angeli.

Ventimiglia, C. (1992) *Nelle segrete stanze: Ricerca sul maltrattamento fisico e sulla violenza sessuale contro le donne*. Modena: Centro per le Pari Opportunitá.

Young, J. (1989) *Criminology: A Realistic Critique*. London: Sage.

Zincani, V. (1989) *La criminalitá organizzata: Strutture criminali e controllo sociale*. Bologna: CLUEB.

3

Social Control and the Politics of Reconstruction

Stanley Cohen

This chapter reflects on some implications from the distinctive discourse about social control that has emerged in Anglo-American and (to a lesser extent) European criminology, sociology and 'law and society' over the last 25 years. Although it contains other streams, this discourse has taken a clearly radical, revisionist or critical direction. Although it originated in the narrow confines of criminology and the sociology of deviance, it has spread to virtually every area of modern social life – not just crime and madness, but also family life, education, welfare, the body, the market, gender, sexuality and mass culture.

I have previously looked at overall trends in this literature, tried to classify the different ways of looking at 'social control' and identified subjects for further study (Cohen, 1989). This chapter moves into the more explicitly political terrain of 'social reconstruction'. This direction is, of course, relevant to the political choices facing democratic socialists in stable North American and West European societies today. My more immediate question, however, deals with the transfer of the critical discourse to societies outside the Western orbit that are undergoing the rapid and massive social reconstruction usually described as 'democratisation'. This notion has been applied to Third World and post-colonial countries in general, but my interest here lies more particularly in the two fascinating and fateful cases that occupy so much of our imagination today: the transition to democracy in Eastern Europe (and the ex-Soviet Union) and – in a very different context – in South Africa.

My exercise is deliberately disingenuous. In the first part of the chapter, I give a condensed, schematic and simplified reading of the discourse. In the second part, I try to imagine what this reading might look like to anyone currently engaged in the politics of reconstruction in those societies. This exercise is disingenuous because such intellectuals are by no means ignorant strangers to the literature.

Neither of these two parts pretends to be comprehensive: I emphasise themes in the social control discourse which have some political resonance and I choose only themes in the political discourse which may connect to issues of social control. I am not building theories or advocating policies – but trying to find some vantage points from which to observe theories and policies.

The discourse on social control

I will divide my review into three sections: first, some idea of the different ways of thinking about social control (grids); second, the main styles or forms of social control that have been studied and advocated; and third, the major empirical trends identified in Western structures and ideologies of social control.

Grids

There are three different traditions of thought about social control, each with its own literature, style and set of problems. We could call each of these three 'discourses'. Less grandly, these are different cognitive grids that the human sciences have used to talk about whatever looks like social control to them. I will call these simply: political; anthropological; deviance and crime.

Political The political grid is the oldest and goes back to the classic concerns of political philosophy, social and political theory. It deals with order, legitimacy and authority. It confronts the central problem in the liberal democratic tradition: how to achieve a degree of order, regulation and stability not inconsistent with the suppression of individual liberty. This, ever since the birth of the modern state, is the discourse of Leviathan. The history of this grid would be no less than an understanding of changes in the overall organisation, deployment, strategy and rationale of state power.

There is no need to elaborate on the continued relevance and persistence of this way of talking about social control. Political thinking has not been made redundant by the current round of the 'end of ideology' thesis – now called 'end of history' – nor by the proclaimed death of the master narratives of progress, either through benign liberal reform or Marxist-Leninist revolution. Where postmodernist theory has to be taken very seriously – and this is already being reflected in the social control literature – is in constructing a looser, less state-centred view of political power.

Anthropological The organic association between social control and the problems of a just political order (democracy, limiting state power, civil liberties, rights) became lost in American social science. In the Chicago School and then functionalism, the lines of the grid became those of socialisation, conformity, internalisation of norms, value consensus, etc. I call this 'anthropological' in the sense that the meta-project was to find processes (a key term) that were universal in all societies, but only varied in content. This attempt was initially grafted onto the Freudian and then the Parsonian narratives – and these legacies remain.

The anthropological grid, though, has taken many other forms – not all bound to psychological thinking. There are obvious historical referents in the vast literature comparing social control in traditional and modern societies. There are important (and now neglected) typologies such as

Riesman's distinction between social control which is 'tradition directed', 'inner directed', and 'other directed'. Other grand models abound, for example Lasch on the 'culture of narcissism', Elias on the 'civilising process' and postmodernists on the 'spectacle'. But although these grids are just as encompassing as the political, they do not touch the same issues of justice, rights or legality.

Deviance and crime   The third (and ostensibly most restricted) discourse deals with the organised, patterned responses to those normative violations which become categorised as deviance or crime. The intellectual origins of this grid have been recounted often enough. The revisionist chronology starts from the impact on criminological and legal thinking of the 'new deviancy theories' in the mid-1960s (labelling, interactionism); moves onto the next phase of the 'new criminology' (various conflict, neo-Marxist and state-centred theories of law and crime control); then records the unique discourse about social control developed under the spell of Foucault (surveillance, discipline, capillary power, etc.). In each phase – labelling, state-centred, Foucauldian – the grid becomes more imperialist, covering ever widening areas of social life. Thus, welfare *as* social control, education *as* social control, psychiatry *as* social control.

The historical object of this revisionist literature corresponds to the three master changes associated with the emergence of the modern state: first, the emerging state monopoly over social control through criminal law, policing and criminal justice; second, the development of grand systems of categorisation, expertise and professional power/knowledge; third, the segregation and incarceration of deviants into special institutions. Each revisionist phase developed its characteristic ways of talking – first about those master changes and then about the post-1960s movements aimed at unravelling, abolishing or bypassing the taken-for-granted structures of social control and finding alternatives.[1]

We are now, I believe, at the fascinating stage where these above three different grids of 'social control' are becoming less separate. In today's revision of revisionism – the endless self-referentiality of postmodernism – the lines are changing, the interfaces becoming more apparent.

For example: first, the state-centred model of deviance and control has given way to a looser image of bureaucratic and professional 'projects' not linked by any master plan. Intentions are unclear or unidentifiable; ideologies (such as the rule of law) not seen as fixed mystifications to be demystified, but as looser 'discourses' with (almost) infinitely variable meanings; alliances are pragmatic; techniques of control are 'relayed' without strategic foresight.[2] Above all, social control is not seen as an essentialist, universal thing.

Second, there are even more explicit boundary disputes about whether a particular form of control 'really' belongs to one category rather than another. Much of today's most interesting work consists of finding interfaces

– either empirical (between one form of social control and another) or theoretical (between those grids of thinking). One example is the continuing feminist expropriation of political concepts (repression, dominance, hegemony) to interpret areas of private life hitherto seen in the more universal language of socialisation. Then there is Garland's outstanding work on the sociology of punishment – which finally delivers the long promise of dissolving criminology and penology into the wider concerns of classical social theory.[3] Then again, there is the recent work by Rose (1990) on the 'governing of subjectivity' – which explicitly links projects of psychological power/knowledge with political notions about 'national well being', citizenship and 'governance'.

Third, there is an increasing receptivity to the anthropological grid. This was avoided in the past because we feared the ghost of Parsons and were reluctant to dissolve the study of social control into everything that is 'social'. It is clear enough now, that any use of concepts such as discipline, regulation or indeed social control, must lead into areas of social life not easily seen either as 'deviance' (as sociologists usually do) or as 'conflict' (as lawyers usually do). Note, for example, recent studies of surveillance, memory, privatisation, commodification, the policing of families or the regulation of desire. Note also virtually all feminist literature – where both the political and crime grids are seen as reproducing a male-centred view of social life in which only the formal, public, state sphere received attention. 'New' areas of social life (sexuality, body, gender, emotions, 'the heart') are seen as 'controlled', 'regulated', 'managed' or 'governed' in ways not easily understood by state-centred political theory (such as Marxism) and even less by law and criminology.

This work is stimulating and creative. But a difference remains between dissolving 'social control' into everything that is social (that is, all normative regulation of private and social life) and restricting the term to those forms of regulation embedded in organised programmes, projects and agencies operated by designated bureaucrats, experts and professionals and producing identifiable discourses of knowledge. Anyone approaching the social control literature from the outside, will have to note this important difference. Two other features should also not be missed.

First, there is the presence within each discourse – at the levels both of knowledge and power – of its counter forms. That is: movements of opposition, reform and resistance which might be expressed in conventional politics (pressure groups, social movements), aesthetics, theory, grand projects of liberation and utopia, visions of an alternative world of social control. This is obvious in the political grid, but also appears strongly in the crime/deviance grid (decarceration, community control, informal or popular justice, deprofessionalization, etc.). The anthropological grid has generated alternative ('new age') psychologies and, most notably, feminism. The claims of radical criminology, critical legal studies, anti-psychiatry and abolitionism are built in to each discourse. One set of knowledge is supportive of existing order; the other is subversive. Any outsider who wants to retain the distinction between factual and normative statements, would be hard pressed to find it here.

Second – and particularly important for the politics of reconstruction – is the 'hidden' history of what might be seen as another, fourth grid of social control: the market. This had little place in state-centred models and no place in discussions about crime and deviance. It appeared only in the political anthropology of the Frankfurt School. There is now a revived interest in this direction – with important work on consumerism, advertising, the commercialisation of desire, etc. Much postmodernist work on the spectacle, representation, globalisation, etc. can read from the vantage point of social control theory. A more obvious manifestation of market control is (as we shall see) the phenomenon of privatisation: the actual switch from state to market ownership and management of 'core' forms of social control such as policing and corrections. The narrower legalistic thinking which dominates current politics of reconstruction – for example, debates about replacing 'socialist legality' by liberal legalism – invariably ignore the erosion in Western democracies of state-centred formalism by modes of control dominated by the 'free' market.

Modes of social control

There are numerous ways to classify those modes of control observed within each grid and the interface between them: formal versus informal; public versus private; coercive versus consensual, etc. I will adopt the classificatory systems developed by sociologists who do not come from a critical or radical interest, but who think that they have produced a Durkheimian scheme of the 'elementary forms' of social control or of conflict management.[4] In my view, their claims to generalisation are unconvincing and their attempts to predict the precise social conditions under which one form of social control occurs rather than another are futile – but their classifications are well suited for any purpose. Four styles of social control are usually distinguished: punitive, compensatory, conciliatory and therapeutic.

The punitive style of control – as embodied in the entire criminal and penal law model – needs no explanation to lawyers and criminologists.[5] It has so dominated our intellectual landscape (in jurisprudence, philosophy, law, political science, etc.) that it is quite mistakenly taken to be paradigmatic of social control itself – rather than an extremely special and rare style of control.

We might remind ourselves of some of these special and rare features of the punitive style: it entails the infliction of pain (loss, harm, suffering); it must always identify an individual held responsible for the breaking of abstract rules (notably legal rules); it is moralistic in essence; it is coercive rather than voluntary and (an important feature to which we will return) it involves the transfer of social control functions to a third party – that is, the deviance or conflict is removed from the parties concerned (for example, victim and offender) and handed over to a specialised agency (usually the state's criminal justice system).

The next two styles of control have usually been subsumed under terms such as 'informal', 'community' or (misleadingly, as I will note) 'alternatives'. In the critical discourse – on informal justice, abolitionism, 'criminology as peacemaking' (Pepinsky and Quinney, 1991) etc. – they are always opposed to the penal law model. The many techniques – redress, compensation, reconciliation, mediation, arbitration, etc. – are variations on two styles, compensation and conciliation.

The compensatory style (redress, restitution, etc.) entails the repayment of debt from the offender to the victim. The offender is obliged to compensate the victim for damage or harm; once this has been done, the matter is theoretically over and settled. This is different from the punitive style not because 'nothing bad happens' to the offender, nor because he or she 'gets away', nor because the transaction is always voluntary. Theoretically, the difference is that the elements of intention, capacity and responsibility – so central to the penal law model – are less important. The connection between act and harmful outcome (consequences) is more important than act and prior mental state (intentions). This stress on damage rather than guilt should make this style of control less moralistic, more restorative. Sanctions are grounded not on the violation of abstract moral rules, but on a network of mutual obligations. This mutuality is further emphasised in systems of restitution which are collective, rather than individual.

In systems of conciliation, the parties involved (without necessarily being defined as victim and offender) work together (sometimes facilitated by a third party) to negotiate a mutually acceptable outcome. The eventual solution is arrived at through mutual bargaining and is not coerced by imposing external sanctions. The point is to reconcile people to each other.

Again, there is less focus on intent (as in the penal law) or even on harm (as in compensation or tort). In fact, there is no need to produce an identified 'offender' – blame is shared or not even allocated. The locus of control (in abolitionist terms) is neither act nor actor, but on the problematic relationship or situation. There are similarities to compensation (though the outcome is not so one-sided) – but this is totally different from the punitive style.

The putative 'radical' or 'critical' property of these last two styles has many different nuances. In the political grid, terms such as community justice, popular justice or people's courts are used. In the crime/deviance grid, we talk about alternatives to criminal justice, informal social control, community control or abolitionism. With a little poetic licence, we might see that both these critical messages derive from and appeal to the anthropological grid. That is, they both assume that somewhere out there – in the 'community', out of the reach of the state – there are universal, 'natural', 'organic' forms of control to be found and encouraged. Much of the second wave in the post-1960s critical discourse has been devoted to showing the problems or even dangers of this vision: cooption, widening of the net, disguised coercion, dispersal of discipline, etc.

Less frequently noted in this literature – but extremely important for the politics of social reconstruction – is the lack of correspondence between style and organisation. Thus 'popular justice' can (and often does) use punishment just as easily as reconciliation. And alternatively, methods such as compensation and reconciliation can be found in many conventional state or bureaucratic institutions.

In the therapeutic style, the focus is neither on the act/actor of the penal law nor the situation nor the relationship. The aim is to 'help' change the person of the deviant – either, in the psychodynamic model, to change internal psychic states or, in the behaviourist model, to produce external behavioural conformity. The process is not seen in moralistic terms as the punishment of a guilty, evil person, nor the fulfilment of obligations, nor the repair of damaged relationships.

The nature of the 'rules' violated or the conflicts to be settled are more obscure and complex in the therapeutic style than the others. For this reason, those working within the model still resist the claim that therapy is a form of social control at all. The obvious growth of the therapeutic style, though, and its invasion into areas previously dealt with through other forms of power/knowledge (the 'medicalisation of deviance' thesis) are of major significance in the social control landscape. Even more important than therapeutic systems where coercion is involved (involuntary hospitalisation, compulsory treatment of addicts, thought control of political dissidents), is the construction of new therapeutic categories (diagnoses, syndromes, classifications) – in areas such as sexual deviance, family violence, hyperkinesis, learning disorders, eating disorders, etc. In advanced Western societies, this is perhaps the major site for emergence of new forms of deviance, 'normalization' – and hence, social control.

There is obviously much more to be said about these four styles of social control and the vast literature each has generated. Sociologists have also usefully classified the different 'forms' through which each style might proceed or be organised – or not be invoked at all. An abused wife might suffer silently, apparently tolerating or normalising the violence directed towards her; she might call on her kinship network to take revenge; she might seek the aid of a counsellor either as a mediator or a therapist; she might take refuge in a shelter for battered wives; she might call the police and demand punishment.

Adopting again a typology from Horwitz (1990) we might distinguish between forms of (1) *unilateral* social control – such as inaction (tolerance, doing nothing) or avoidance (cutting off sight or further action) or exit (leaving the situation or relationship) or self-help (resorting to extra-legal methods such as vengeance or vigilantism – here, crime may be a form of social control); (2) *bilateral* social control – where both parties negotiate with each other or look for conciliation (sometimes with mutually agreed third party help, like lawyers in divorce cases); and (3) *trilateral* social control – that is, the mobilisation (for example by calling the police) of an official, formal control agency such as the criminal justice system, who may impose a solution regardless of the party or parties' wishes.

'Trilateral' control is usually seen as the historically dominant form. The replacement of private grievance by formalised public issue is taken as the defining feature of the modern state. In our context, however, it must be remembered that this form of social control is statistically highly abnormal. If we visualise a pyramid of social control to represent the spatial distribution of all forms and styles, only the tiniest triangle at the top would fall under the reach of criminal justice, professional and other specialised 'trilateral' organisations. The vast bulk of deviance flows through the channel of unilateral, bilateral or informal control. In this sense, we should not call *these* 'alternatives' but rather refer to the criminal justice and professional systems *as* 'alternatives'.

The theoretical task – way beyond my scope here[6] but highly relevant to any comparison between social control in different societies – is then to understand how certain methods become dominant. What is the 'social space' occupied by different forms? What are the interfaces between them? How autonomous is any form? These speculations usually lead to the often-noted paradox that the very social conditions which give rise to organised, trilateral control, particularly through punishment (greater individualism, more mobility, weakening of social bonds, social fragmentation, increasing social distance and hierarchy) are those which render such controls most ineffective.[7] The most moralistic of control styles becomes dominant just when the moral sentiment on which it rests is weakest.

Trends

Confining ourselves to formal or 'trilateral' social control – those forms embodied in organised agencies and programmes – let us briefly review the major empirical trends that have been picked up in the Western critical discourse. The term 'picked up', begs the question of whether these trends refer to actual developments on the ground or whether they are merely repetitive discursive themes. While the evidence is difficult to evaluate and while terms such as 'net-widening' have no doubt been abused, these themes do, I believe, reflect genuine changes. Commentators on the revisionist discourse (Nelken, 1990), though, correctly point to the unsatisfactory way in which the 'logics' of each trend is explained: how exactly, for example, does one trend appear as an 'alternative' or a 'supplement' to another? When is a social control form genuinely 'distinct' rather than merely the 'equivalent' of another?

I will concentrate on five themes that have preoccupied our recent literature. Each is a caricature of far more complex and contradictory processes.

Expansion, dispersal and intensification   We need not be attached to dystopian imagery nor to the 'dispersal of discipline' thesis to see that over the last two decades, formal social control systems in advanced Western societies have expanded, dispersed beyond their original bases and intensified their hold over those they reach. That is, more areas of social life are being subjected to organised forms of control, prevention, surveillance or formal categorisation; more forms of conflict or deviance are finding their way into the 'net'; more of the population are under management of these agencies.

It is beyond my scope to give detailed empirical evidence for all these trends. We may take two paradigmatic cases. The first is the internal organisational growth within criminal justice systems. The United States case may be too extreme to be paradigmatic, but it certainly corresponds to the above patterns. Besides the massive growth of the prison population – now some 420 per 100,000 of the population – high risk groups now have an extraordinary risk of being caught in the wider correctional net: some one in four young black males in California are now under supervision of the correctional system. The tendency for alternatives (such as electronic monitoring, house arrest, work release programmes, etc.) to lead to net widening and intensification, is even clearer than many of us thought a decade ago.[8]

A second case study is the wider process of the criminalisation. It is not just that more of the same old members of the underclass are being processed for committing the same crimes (or that more things are being done to a constant number of these old offenders) but that more areas of social life are subject to control through the punitive criminal law model. There are five notable examples: male sexualized violence and harassment; various other forms of family violence; corporate and business crime; environmental crime; and crimes of the state or violations of human rights.

One common thread runs through each of these examples: as previously dependent, weak, disenfranchised, or marginal groups become stronger (women, ethnic minorities, children, clients or consumers, victims) or find patrons to act on their behalf (notably by defining them as 'victims'), they look for legal means to redress past grievances or deal with conflicts that were previously tolerated or resolved informally – invariably to the disadvantage of the dependent party.

As I will note, this thread is of particular importance in periods of rapid social transition or social reconstruction. This is precisely when the tendency to find new laws or to apply punishments to those immune under the old laws is most appealing.

Elaboration of professional knowledge/power   Here I believe we are dealing with a tendency even more relentless (though less visible) than the expansion of the criminal justice network. Largely outside the reach of the law and largely an application of (or appeal to) the therapeutic style, a massive range of professional power/knowledge systems are being created.

This is 'control by categorisation'. Over the last decade, the social constructivist paradigm has shown this process in fine detail: family violence, hyperkinesis, dyslexia and other learning disorders, anorexia nervosa and other eating disorders, new sexual pathologies, defective parenting, narcissism, borderline personality, the whole range of addictions, adolescent personality disorder, and so on. Like the new criminalisation, the driving ideological force is progressive and well meaning. The area known as 'lifestyle control' (cigarette smoking, overweight) uses both forms: increasing punitive stigmatisation as well as the establishment of therapeutic modes such as self-help groups. Social constructionist studies of these processes, illustrate Foucault's crucial insight that these fine systems of power are not just negative and exclusory, but create new bodies of knowledge. To avoid the negative connotation of the term 'control', these techniques are increasingly seen as new forms for the 'governance' or 'management' of subjectivity.

Managerialism   Management is important in another sense as well. The new round of 'the end of ideology' game has left its mark in social control systems and ideologies. In the crime control business, we see an ascendancy of managerial, administrative and technocratic styles. The old liberal ideologies (treatment, rehabilitation, social reform) are discredited. The goal is to keep the criminal justice system in reasonable shape. Prison directors are not the 'moral architects' of the early nineteenth century, nor the professionals of the heyday of the treatment ideology; they are just as likely to be accountants.

In academic criminology 'managerialism' is reflected in various neo-classical movements, opportunity theory, rational choice theory and the emergence of the 'new reasoning criminal'. If people cannot be changed and societies cannot be transformed, then theories become less ambitious and lose their critical edge or indeed any social context.

Behaviourism, risk management and population control   The most influential variant of managerialism, is the increasing trend to population control. A number of related elements have made up this trend – each one with far-reaching implications for how we think about social control.

First – and already apparent some time ago – is the replacement at the hard end of the criminal justice system of psychodynamic models of change (based on inner psychic states) by behaviourist models based on external behavioural compliance. Instead of insight, conscience and internal moral conflict, we have relearning, resocialisation and the correction of defective social skills.

Second, there is the complementary trend to replace the determined offender of positivism by the rational choice offender of neo-classicism. This offender resembles both the creature of classical free market economics and the abstract legal subject of jurisprudence. He or she is amoral. Biography and social origin lose their explanatory and policy salience. Instead there is the new reasoning criminal, who sees opportunities and weighs up risks.

Third – and in consequence – the aim of social control becomes the reduction of opportunities for potential offenders and the increase of the risks they have to take. Target hardening, situational crime prevention, spatial and temporal opportunity reduction, crime prevention through environmental design, risk management – these are the preferred technologies. Social control moves from its standard *reactive* mode – only being activated when rules are violated – into a *proactive* mode, that is, anticipating, predicting, calculating in advance.

Fourth – and of enormous significance for the future of social control – the object of this discourse is the population rather than the individual. The blueprint is an 'actuarial regime' or 'risk society' (Reichman, 1986; Simon, 1987, 1988). Using the actuarial logic of drawing up life insurance tables, risks are calculated by statistical probability rather than referring to an actual person. The resulting styles of control include an increasing stress on surveillance and monitoring and the growth of compliance systems. Standards of conformity are established – airport security systems, employees given urine checks for drug use, lifts checked for safety standards – whether or not a deviant action has taken place.

Instead of altering individual behaviour, actuarial, surveillance and compliance regimes alter the physical and social structure in which individuals behave. This policy, we are assured, is both easier to implement than the old 'disciplinary regimes' and ultimately, more effective. It does not require a strong moral underpinning nor do you have to resort to direct coercion (and thereby run the chance of resistance).

Much more can be said about these trends and – particularly in our context – about their location in the private sector (see p. 74) and their political significance. As O'Malley (1991) nicely argues, the overall change under the New Right from the socialised (welfare) version of actuarialism to the private 'prudentialism' of 'looking after yourself' is mirrored in the crime control system. Just as the new reasoning offender is a creature who, like rational 'economic man' has no biography or values, but only makes choices, so the 'public' (the potential victim) has to make a choice to take preventive measures. This choice becomes a duty – you are blamed for apathy and lack of care (like women who have to take training courses to avoid 'rape-producing situations'). The New Right depends on the strong state (punitive sentencing, warehousing and incapacitation for those sectors of the underclass devoured and recycled by the criminal justice machine) and the free market, which with some help from the state, offers 'situational crime prevention' or private security system to a public with enough money and prudence.

All these trends together – grafted onto new technologies and the increased surveillance capacity of modern organisations (Dandeker, 1990) – have led sociologists of social control to some grim characterisations: the age of surveillance, the classified society, the managed society, the engineered society, the suspicious society, the self-monitored society, the transparent society, the maximum security society, etc. Whether or not we 'see' these futures, we cannot miss the emergence of modalities of social control that do not and cannot easily fit the standard typologies I reviewed earlier.

Of course, we are talking not about the total replacement of one form by another, but the simultaneous deployment of a variety of methods. Take again the example of 'lifestyle control'. The individual cigarette smoker may be punished (fined, for example, for smoking in a public place), encouraged to seek psychological treatment or (together with the overweight) not be hired by corporations seeking to reduce their medical insurance risks. Different styles may be used in combination: a divorce court ('mediation') may require ('punish') the partners to attend a programme ('therapy') about the psychological effects of divorce on children. Or (a genuine 'actuarial' style) potential marriage partners might be screened in advance for mutual compatability.

Privatisation   Along with managerialism and population control (though not always influenced by the same ideological currents), formal social control systems in advanced Western societes are moving through a process of privatisation. This process – as the increasing literature on the subject is beginning to show – is very complex and is not a simple 'return' to a pre-modern state form of crime control such as private policing.[9] Three important forms of privatisation have been noted.

The first lies within the traditional realm of the criminal justice system itself. Here, the most notable example is the massive growth of the private security industry. The buying or contracting out of policing and security functions (by the state, by corporations, by private individuals, by institutions such as universities) to private business, is a massive growth industry. In the United States, the number of private security personnel already exceeded the numbers of the regular uniformed police 20 years ago. A less marked shift has occurred in the correctional system – with partial privatisation of prisons and prison industries.

The second area – where professional rather than state agencies have always dominated – is the 'soft end' or therapeutic side of the control spectrum. There has been an increasing shift to the private sector of institutions, agencies and programmes dealing with troublesome juveniles and all forms of substance abuse. This is also happening in the market for controls over all sorts of 'disorders' – personality, sexual, eating, learning. Here, as in the private security business, we may begin to talk about the 'commodification of social control'.[10]

The third area – the one with the most obvious political resonance – is the overall cutback of welfare state provisions (in personal social services, health, education). Sometimes, these provisions are picked up by the private market, sometimes they disappear altogether and sometimes they are replaced by non-profit 'privatisation', that is, various forms of voluntarism, community networks, self-help, etc.

Political issues

Our question now, is whether the discourse I have just summarised has any relevance to the kind of urgent political debates that are taking place in Eastern Europe, South Africa or some countries in Latin America today: the dismantling of dictatorships; the building of democracy; ending racial discrimination; ensuring civil rights and the rule of law; advancing human rights and social justice?

At first sight, the connections should be there. The revisionist discourse on social control has been explicitly political in tone. Radical criminology, for example, tried to convert the interactionist dialectic of deviance/control into a sociology of law and hence a sociology of the state. The political message was even clearer in the various countermovements and utopian visions from the late 1960s onwards: popular justice; the abolition of punishment; society without law; criminology as peacemaking.

At closer glance, however, the very political vision which holds this literature together – the critique of existing structures, an anarchist utopianism, idealised control outside the reach of Leviathan – makes it somewhat remote from the immediate concerns and strategies that constitute conventional 'politics'. This remoteness, this visionary element, is precisely the 'left idealism' that has been attacked by the current wave of 'left realist criminology' in the United Kingdom (and its equivalents in Canada and the United States). The original (uneasy) combination of theoretical deconstructionism and libertarian utopianism is now seen as a passed and flawed 'moment'. To make criminology relevant, we are told, we must engage with the problem of crime as it is publicly defined: crime on the streets, fear of crime, victimisation of the powerless (the poor, the old, female victims of male sexualised violence). We must also challenge right-wing hegemony on its own terrain. This means reconstructing social democracy: arresting the decay of inner-city communities; solving problems in service delivery by the welfare state; defending formal rights; increasing police accountability, etc.

There is no need to accept the Realist's whole package, to concede their point in detecting a certain remoteness in the social control discourse. One can understand their impatience with concepts such as net-widening and expansion of discipline or movements such as abolitionism and de-professionalism. These ideas are condemned (wrongly, in my opinion) for being 'only' critical and not providing criteria for the choice between forms of control or even for conceding that some forms are more benign and desirable than others.[11] One can understand, particularly, the impatience with Foucault-inspired visions. These are criticised for not offering any judgement about whether 'the revolution' is worthwhile, for advocating only the impotent gesture of defiance by the heroic 'specific intellectual' – who is always on the move, refusing to be pinned down, going from one site of resistance to another.[12]

My own sense is that Foucault will become dramatically more rather than less relevant in the post-Cold War era. But an initial reading of the critical discourse on social control no doubt looks a little remote as we travel from the seminar rooms of academic postmodernism in the West. There are three reasons for this.

First – especially in the 'anthropological' trend I identified – the values which informed the original critical moment (social justice, equality) have given way to 'second order' concerns about subjectivity, privacy and the integrity of the self. These, needless to say, look expensive luxuries when faced with starvation, epidemic disease, state terror and discrimination. In those parts of the world locked in deep ideological conflict, massive injustice, swept between revolutionary violence and military control, with large parts of the population subject to torture, arbitrary arrest, disappearance and death squads – it looks a little self-indulgent to be talking about 'governing of the self'. When hunger is the problem, you cannot expect too much attention to be given to a feminist deconstruction of anorexia nervosa.

Second, the postmodernist rhetoric about the 'end of history' and the death of meta-narratives, comes to discredit precisely those 'meta-narratives' from which the struggle for democracy and human rights derive their potency. The politics of reconstruction appeals not to the local and relative, but to the universal and absolute. Little help is at hand from a cultural avant-garde engaged in discrediting the very universal metaphors which lent such struggles their normative and emotional appeal.

A third (and allied) problem goes back to the standard critique against Foucault-type theory: that this does not offer recognisable political alternatives or – more seriously – does not even offer the criteria for knowing why one alternative is any better than another. This is really a question about the role of the intellectual – which, in the context of criminology and social control, I have addressed in terms of the tension between intellectual scepticism and political commitment (Cohen, 1990). But if this solution hardly appeals in general, it is even less appealing in the societies that interest us here. In Eastern Europe and South Africa today, those critics and intellectuals who performed only an oppositional role for decades are now being offered a part in social reconstruction. Unlike the Left Realists in Britain who aspire to this role (but are not within the dominant political current), here intellectuals are actually being invited into positions of power: drafting constitutions and new laws, being consulted on a Bill of Rights, sitting on government commissions, even deciding which political prisoners from old regimes should be released and which new criminals should be made accountable.

At first sight, then, the critical discourse does not look promising. It has already become folklore to tell stories of Western radicals arriving in Warsaw, East Berlin and Prague with their avant-garde critique of formal legality – only to be laughed at by progressives who see their struggle precisely as achieving formal rights. Just as ludicrous might be the sophisticated critique of 'alternatives' in societies where there is hardly any critique of the old system. Or the Left Realist exhortation to 'work within the system' in societies organised around state terrorism.

But let us examine a number of specific issues where, I believe, the literature is more useful than it looks. It has something to offer precisely because the lawyers, politicians and aspiring *apparatchiks* who are now thinking about 'democratisation' are, for the most part, locked into a formal, legalistic state-centred model which gives little cognisance to the wider terrain of social control.

Legalism and formal rights

For obvious reasons, it *is* the 'formal, legalistic state-centred model' which remains at the heart of the debates – both within more static social democracies and our more dramatic cases. The redress of past grievances, the provision of formal legal rights, due processes, equality, accountability, the protection of basic human rights – these are the central issues. As I have suggested, the social control literature as such – even from the criminology/ sociology of deviance grid – is not immediately helpful here. Either it is uninterested in politics in this sense (because of its negative, idealist, deconstructive, visionary tone) or it is explicitly hostile to formalism.

Only critical legal studies offer some obvious relevance. This type of critical legacy is, paradoxically, important not so much for its normative or policy stance, but for its meta-theoretical position on formal rights and legality. Rejecting both the idealistic view of liberal legalism as a noble democratic achievement (to be defended unreflectively) and the instrumental view of liberal legalism as an ideology constructed as part of the ruling class game plan (to be criticised and demystified), we find an image of law as a 'plastic medium of discourse'.[13] Its texts, precedents, language and practices are capable of almost infinite variation. Law in the Third Reich (see Muller, 1991) was not law that advanced social justice and human dignity – but it was still 'law'. Even in South Africa – one of the most blatant ever historical cases of scrupulously legalised injustice – law was 'plastic' enough to allow limited victories for the oppressed (Ellman, 1991). Law could be a shield if not a sword.

There can be no doubt to anyone working in the human rights movement (as I have over the last decade) that the language of formal universal standards has to be defended.[14] And while international human rights conventions and laws do offer potential controls through mediation, compensation and negotiation, these methods usually occur at the level of contracting 'state parties'. At some point, especially when dealing with 'crimes of obedience' (Kelman and Hamilton, 1989) – genocide, disappearances, state terror, torture – the issue of personal responsibility and legal culpability has to be confronted and hence the use of punishment. In these contexts (as observers in Chile, Argentina and similar countries have noted) the rhetoric of 'reconciliation' far from being progressive, is an elaborate attempt to rewrite history and avoid moral accountability.

The transfer of formal legalism to societies going through democratisation raises, of course, many more complex issues than I can even mention here. I list only a few examples of the paradoxes that are being lived through in the struggle for social justice:

- While the broader notion of 'human rights' (appeals to international standards, Helsinki Watch ideals, universal declarations) was central in the phase of resistance, it turns out that these norms are not easily translatable during social reconstruction – where the narrow notion of 'civil liberties' seems to work better.
- While formal rights and the penal code can indeed be used for state crime and the redress of political grievances, the deployment of standard criminal justice methods against 'ordinary' crime, very quickly exposes the same defects which have rendered the model so useless and counterproductive in the West.
- Democratic notions such as accountability are easily transferred by the old bureaucracies into self-protecting ideologies. In South Africa, for example, the police resist genuine democratisation by appealing to a technological 'non-political' role in which they are accountable only to themselves (Steytler, 1991). In order to improve their image and achieve some legitimacy during the transitional period, they present themselves as a neutral, crime fighting, professional force which has to be kept 'independent' of public accountability. In Poland, the Communist Party's power to appoint and remove judges at whim, is replaced by a democratic system in which permanent judicial appointments are not subject to political interference – thereby leaving intact the same corrupt judges who had not withdrawn from the old system.[15]

I am not arguing that some inevitable tragedy will repeat itself in which formal legalism will be constructed only to have to be deconstructed. But I am arguing against those who see critical theory and movements such as abolitionism as expensive luxuries which must be put aside for the moment. As Falandycz notes – reflecting on his reading of critical theory in Poland during the resistance years and today – the 'negative' tone of abolitionism is not at all remote: 'we are not creating or inventing anything new and good, but we only want to abolish what is old and bad' (Falandycz, 1991).

Informalism and popular justice

The mirror image of our discussion of formal legalism applies to any contemplation of the role of 'alternative' forms of justice and control. A very special debate deals with the role of popular justice (people's courts, etc.) during and after the transition. Let me give three examples of types of issues raised.

Prefigurative justice or vigilantism?   There has been a sustained attention in South Africa to the network of 'people's courts' that grew up in the townships as a popular alternative to the blatantly unjust and repressive formal system.[16] One record sees this experience as 'prefigurative justice' – that is, a creative resistance to the state which anticipates what real social justice will look like after the revolution. Another record finds signs of populist violence of the worst kind – 'self-help social control' which degenerates into vigilantism, banditry, kangaroo courts, settling of scores. Yet another record sees a continual tension between these forms or else oscillations between one historical period to another.

To my mind, this is a classic case where the notion of a 'plastic medium of discourse' applies to popular justice just as it does to formal legalism. The form can appear both in desirable and undesirable guises. And there is no fixed congruence between the legitimising ideology ('the people', 'the mass line', 'alternatives', 'resistance') and the style of social control. Popular justice can be conciliatory and mediatory, it can be beautifully nuanced, it can appeal to local tradition – but it can also be crudely punitive (corporal punishment, kangaroo courts, 'necklacing', collaborator killing, death squads). It can also be based on the political version of the disciplinary mode – in which the benign notion of the 'whole person' becomes the terror of thought control, resocialisation into 'correct thinking' and coercive models of how ideal comrades of the future should conduct themselves.

Interface with state system?   Given that popular justice is legitimised by the struggle – that is, is constructed as a critical, negative ideology – what happens when the regime begins to change? In one view, the popular forms will 'dissolve' as their demands are met by a more receptive state. A less benign view of this transition sees the state as coopting any forms of resistance which might contain a latent opposition to its new hegemony.

In any event, it is clear that when popular, alternative forms loose their oppositional status, questions of 'interface' with the new emerging state system become critical. One possible relationship (long noted by students of informalism in the West) is one of dependence: the alternative system always exists in the shadow of the state, which filters out cases, and then passes on the less important, 'junk cases'. Another possibility is that the informal system does the initial filtering and then refers to the state those cases which are beyond its jurisdiction. In both possibilities, a question of political priority arises: if you try to strengthen popular justice, this might leave the state unreformed; if you concentrate on reforming the state, the popular system might wither away.

Defence or reconstruction?   Another tension arises from the powerful appeal that I have already noted to the formal penal law as a form of redress. For people under oppression – whether the crude oppression of military rule, state terror, Stalinism or apartheid or more subtle forms of discrimination – injustice is experienced as a breach of expectations about rights. In the same way that these people resorted to the informal economy at the economic level or the underground press at the cultural level, so at the social control level, they resorted to popular justice (self-help) or avoidance (through lack of access to the formal system). Informalism was a defence against a state system seen as repressive – either because it denied people's lived experience of social injustice or offered them ineffective, unfair and biased forms of redress.

It was this perception of law as powerful, pervasive and unjust that inspired the search for alternatives in the West. But under reconstruction – certainly in South Africa and Eastern Europe – there are high hopes for the formal system. It is seen to offer not just a defensive shield but an attacking sword. The hope and expectation is that law will now decode people's lived injustice in a fair, responsive and active way (particularly by punishing those responsible for past crimes and by reallocating resources). Even in (or especially in) countries like South Africa where the bulk of the population see formal legality as totally unjust and illegitimate, the assumption is made that the new system will provide justice. The content is criticised rather than the form.

Under these circumstances – as I have already suggested – it is harder to find an intellectual space to talk about 'alternative' forms of social control. New regimes try to prove their democratic credentials by replacing old laws with new laws, proclaiming a bill of rights, carrying out constitutional reforms. Interstitial areas of social control will remain invisible unless voices from critical theory and feminism are applied to the spheres of justice, welfare and therapy.

Civil society and the realm of the political

Many of the familiar issues in the social control literature – formal state control versus informal community control, tolerance for 'semi-autonomous fields' – appear today in a slightly different form in the debate (especially in Eastern Europe) about 'civil society'.

It is way beyond my scope to review this concept's complicated genealogy (from Locke, Hegel, Marx, Gramsci, et al.) and its current usage – in arenas as different from each other as Eastern Europe and post-colonial Africa.[17] The non-idealistic usage of the concept is extremely vague – covering sometimes all institutions between the family and the state, sometimes only institutions that confront or withdraw from ('exit') the state; sometimes any form of associational and political life (such as voluntary associations) beyond state domination. The relationship between civil society and, on the one hand, 'society' in general and on the other, the state, is seldom clear; the metaphors here range from bridge, buffer, agent, symbol, regulator and intermediary.

The more idealistic usage of the concept – although open to different political judgements – is at least much clearer. In the original political philosophy of liberalism, 'civil society' referred to a free, natural realm of society outside the legitimate sphere of the state and 'politics'. Although the term itself disappeared from the political lexicon, this idealistic sense remains very much alive in the discourse of liberal democracy. In Gramsci's version, civil society acquired a different, but still positive, idealistic twist: the final achievement of socialism would come when the state would not so much wither away, but be absorbed by an extended civil society that replaced coercion with administration and participation. Some permutations of both these ideals appear in contemporary attempts – such as Keane's – to revive the concept and mould it onto a postmodernist theory about political power.

How does any of this connect to our interest in social control?[18] The link lies in the boundaries that liberalism imposed on coercive state control. In theory, the government's obligation was to foster the self-controlling aspects of civil society: people should want to conform, if not they should be subject to civil control and only as a last resort would formal state control be applied. Classic liberalism abandoned as dystopian the dream of totally administered society; instead it looked for a natural domain of freedom and self-regulation.

In practice, as Rose and Miller argue, the private realm so 'freed' and constituted by the state as 'non-political', became subject to new technologies of control (through experts and professionals) – sometimes genuinely autonomous from the state, sometimes forming 'strategic alliances' with the state. In these new 'sites' – the family, welfare, leisure, crime control, the body, sexuality – power becomes 'not so much a matter of imposing constraints upon citizens as of "making up" citizens capable of bearing a kind of regulated freedom' (Rose and Miller, 1992: 174). The ideals of privacy and civic society assumed the existence of a new type of citizen/subject: one that did not require too much external, coercive control. These ideals were not mere mystification, a disguise for the extension of state power:

> Liberal mentalities of government do not conceive of the regulation of conduct as dependent only upon political actions: the imposition of law; the activities of state functionaries or publicly controlled bureaucracies; surveillance and discipline by an all-seeing police. Liberal government identifies a domain outside 'politics' and seeks to manage it without destroying its existence and autonomy. (Rose and Miller, 1992: 181)

This is just the domain in which the major bureaucratic, professional (notably therapeutic or welfare) and managerial projects of social control operate.

Echoes of the ideal of 'civil society' (again, without the term itself being used) could also be found in the 1960s liberal rhetoric on social control. The popular appeals to freedom, tolerance and permissiveness carried the message of 'doing your own thing'. But their intellectual versions – notably in the debates about decriminalisation, crimes without victims, drugs, etc. – assumed that once certain forms of deviance were extracted from the reach of the state ('not the law's business' was a common slogan) then they would be dealt with by other, more benign, forms of control: tolerance, self-help, education, alternative therapies (growth, self-actualization, co-counselling), networks of mutual care, mediation, etc. The gay community was seen as providing a model for a new 'culture of civility'. All this would take place in civil society – a sphere of 'decentralised community control' organised by volunteers, victims, ex-deviants, people 'from the community'. Thus: self regulation, rather than regulation by the state (or, a possibility not considered then) by the market.

In practice, as we have noted, the interlocking network of social control projects – 'owned' by professional monopolies or by private corporations – hardly add up to 'self-regulation'. The pristine vision itself has also been transformed. There has been the general liberal retreat, the ascendancy of neo-conservatism and – from another direction – the feminist critique of liberal tolerance in areas such as pornography (no longer a 'crime without a victim') and its demand that the once 'private' realm of the family be subject to more formal control in order to protect women from male violence. Much of this debate can be reinterpreted in the terms of civil society. The phenomena of the new criminalisation, net-widening and – in a different way – privatisation, all carry profound implications for how we see the boundaries between state and society. There will be conditions under which the state cannot tolerate alternatives such as oppositional popular justice. On the contrary, there will be conditions when it encourages 'tolerance' (in the form of benign neglect – the plight of the homeless and the decarcerated mentally ill) or (as in Thatcherite Britain) cynically preaches the morality of voluntarism, altruism and self-sufficiency to avoid government responsibility for social welfare.

How do these debates look in our more dramatic examples of political reconstruction? In Eastern Europe, as I have noted, the concept of civil society is now quite explicitly invoked to refer to the social space that is open for 'reoccupation' when the strong state collapses. State socialism had controlled, extinguished or absorbed the institutions of civil society – that is, there was no viable institutional space between family and state. Intellectuals, progressives, trade unionists and church leaders now look to a revival of civil society in the most idealistic sense of the concept. There is a Manichean view of the state as bad, the enemy – and civil society as noble and benign.

In Poland, for example, there was much talk during the resistance about the long dormant institutions of civil society that would emerge from the ashes when the state withered away. What is now being realised, however, is that many of these institutions (the informal economy, the underground press) took their character from their opposition to the state. Once the state weakens as an 'opponent', then those institutions lose their alternative or critical status. Who needs an underground political press when political views are not subject to state censorship?[19] Further, not only may civil society turn out to be weaker than expected, but might exhibit some extremely unpleasant features – ethnic prejudice, discrimination, anti-Semitism, violence to strangers – previously suppressed by the state monopoly on coercive control.

In the debate about democratisation then, the civil society literature offers an interesting opening to our more familiar terrain of social control. Another way of looking at the problem is to query the relationship between those different grids of social control. When the relationship is tight, we have a classic totalitarian or 'state-saturated' society. The grids cannot be separated from each other: political indoctrination pervades socialisation (the anthropology of correct thinking); crime is always politicised; the model of the good citizen is the child who informs on his or her own parents. When the relationship between the grids is loose, then all sorts of 'semi-autonomous fields' of social control are tolerated or encouraged. (This vision, in turn, may be less appealing when the resultant forms of non-statist, control become manipulated by the market for private profit.)

The concept of civil society also resonates with another debate in the social control literature: how large is the realm of the political? And what is the relationship between crime and politics? A persistent trend in the Western critical tradition has been to politicise more areas of social life. There is the feminist inspired slogan that 'the personal is political'; there was the brief moment in radical criminology – still very relevant to societies like South Africa[20] – where criminals became proto-revolutionary heroes; there was the overall theoretical drift to define the content and enforcement of the criminal law in political terms. Matza's ironical comment that the 'success' of criminological positivism was to separate the study of crime from the study of the state, became a cliche. The message was clear – 'bring the state back in' – and was clearly reflected in the revisionist criminological and social control literature.

At the theoretical level, this literature has become less state-centred. More importantly, it has been realised that the actual experience of state-saturated societies shows the appalling dangers of politicising the whole realm of social control. Perhaps a separation of deviance from politics – in the sense envisaged by the liberal democratic ideal of civil society – is what we should be looking for. It is, though, very difficult to separate politics and deviance when past political crime and present political crime, political corruption and collusion with organised crime are key problems facing post-communist regimes.

Categorisation and professionalism

The debates about state, law, rights and civil society form the very essence of the politics of reconstruction. Everybody uses this language. Much less familiar, though, are questions of professionalism, therapy and the whole process as control through categorisation.

Here, it seems to me, that both the strengths and the weaknesses of the social control discourse are most visible. The strengths lie at the theoretical and meta-theoretical level: the rich and nuanced accounts – from feminism, the social constructivist paradigm, discourse analysis, historians – about how categories of deviance and control are created and managed. There is no reason why these models should not be applied elsewhere, especially in understanding such processes as the transference of therapeutic fashions or diagnostic categories from core to peripheral cultures (for example, through professional journals, academic patronage and international conferences).

The weaknesses lie at the political and social policy level. Like pristine anti-legalism, so pristine anti-professionalism looks remote to the weak, poor and marginalised who have never been able to afford professional services. The dangers of overprofessionalism, though – the disabling effect of radical monopolies, the fetish of certification, the creation of self-serving elites – still have to be pointed out. And the more desirable forms of self-help and community support are still very much alive.

The wider process of categorisation resists easy political judgements. Only by being sensitive to the individual case and by invoking clear value preferences, can we suggest whether any particular instance of construction will turn out to be benign or malignant.

Privatisation, surveillance and actuarial control

None of the trends I identified in Western social control systems and ideologies – managerialism, privatisation, surveillance, actuarial control – arose because of some inexorable drive to rationalisation. Nor can they be understood as some form of technological determinism. Nor are they inevitable by-products of progress. And they are by no means uniform and irreversible. Because these trends are taking place in California we cannot simply predict that they will soon happen in Czechoslovakia.

But something can be learned, if not prevented, by studying this literature. At one level, these modes and technologies of control will be transferred, whether we like it or not. The globalisation of information systems, the standardisation of the mass media and the loss of a 'sense of place' (Meyrowitz, 1985) – all of which happen despite the resurgence of separatism and nationalism – facilitate the export of control methods which offer a quick solution to growing problems of street crime. Private security systems, for example, have an obvious attraction. And now that Disneyland has been exported from California to France, the next stage might be Poland – reproducing not just the spectacle, but its distinctive system of proactive social control (Shearing and Stenning, 1985).

Conclusion

There is no way to conclude a chapter like this by 'recommending' certain forms of social control rather than others – either in general or for any single case of political reconstruction. The choices are never all available and they are always constrained by value and political preference, by available resources and by existing control structures and interests. It is always easier to start new projects than dismantle old ones. And consequences can never be predicted from intentions. All we can do is suggest some guidelines for two forms of success – instrumental and normative.

The criteria for instrumental success – 'what works' – are taken for granted in the conventional discourse. And Left Realist criminology is correct in pointing out that these conventional criteria of effectiveness (such as reducing victimisation or fear of crime) cannot be deconstructed away. If anything, these criteria need extension by seeing freedom from fear as a universal human right. But any such extension must lead us into the old political debate about how to achieve order, regulation, stability and protection without infringing on individual liberty. That is, we are not just talking about effectiveness but justice.

Those general typologies of social control I considered earlier, offer a much blunter criterion of instrumental success: social control is effective to the extent that the efforts of the controllers actually change the behaviour of potential deviants (Horwitz, 1990: Ch. 11). This criterion leads us to familiar but still interesting suggestions: that control systems must be able to communicate their ability to impose sanctions and give rewards; that official efforts must coincide with or be able to alter informal definitions; that the effectiveness of control increases if interactional costs (shame, honour, loss of attachment) increase, etc. Following these lines, some clear examples of 'what works' can be singled out – for example, the social control of AIDS within the gay community where official warning systems were reinforced by tight interactional bonds. But – claims to the contrary – these propositions hardly provide any hard rules or if so, these are only at the most obvious level – for example, that preventive social control systems are most effective within small, closely knit and homogeneous groups.[21]

By 'normative success' I mean the extent to which social control generates a symbolic arena in which value choices can be clarified. The criteria here are oriented to means rather than ends. Or the ends – social justice, democracy, human rights – are themselves subject to normative rather than empirical evaluation. Here, we might each make our own list. Mine would include a preference for methods that result in integration rather than exclusion; that (following Nils Chistie) abolish or reduce to the minimum the amount of deliberately inflicted pain; that allow for active citizen participation; that reduce the power of professional and bureaucratic monopolies; that provide for accountability and democracy within the organisation, and so on.

What I have tried to suggest in this chapter, is that any such list – difficult as it is to construct in the most stable of societies – becomes even more problematic during the dramatic politics of social reconstruction.

Notes

An earlier version of this chapter was presented at the Conference 'Strafrecht, soziale Kontrolle, soziale Disziplinierung', in Bielefeld, Germany, 6–8 December 1991 and has been published as (1993) 'Soziale Kontrolle und die Politik der Rekonstruktion', in D. Frehsee et al. (eds), *Strafrecht, soziale Kontrolle, soziale Disziplinierung*. Opladen: Westdeutscher Verlag. I am grateful to David Nelken and Clifford Shearing for comments.

1 My book *Visions of Social Control* (Cohen, 1985) synthesises the late 1970s–early 1980s work within the crime/deviance grid of social control. Subsequent texts in this tradition dealing with more recent (especially feminist) work include Edwards (1988) and Davis and Stasz (1990).

2 For an explicit example of this new thinking – in the case of psychiatry as social control – see Miller and Rose (1986) and Rose (1990).

3 Garland (1990). See also Dandeker (1990).

4 The best known example is the work of Donald Black; see most recently Black (1989). For a useful synthesis of this approach, Horwitz (1990).

5 But only Garland (1990) gives us the most sustained *sociological* examination of punishment.

6 On punishment, see again Garland (1990). Note also Nelken's (1990) distinction between 'correspondence', 'corrective' and 'constitutive' models of the connections between broader social trends and social control developments. The correspondence model looks for congruence between overall social trends and particular changes in social control; the corrective model sees changes in social control as the converse of other changes (for example, formal, trilateral methods increasing to compensate for weak informal control); the constitutive approach sees responses to deviance as shaping and constituting the phenomenon itself.

7 This paradox explains current interest in Durkheimian-derived 'control theories' and the interesting attempts (especially, Braithwaite, 1989) to ground formal social controls on foundations such as shame and reintegration. It is beyond my scope to deal with the theoretical debate here: the claim that punitive-moralistic controls dominate when their social base is weakest contradicts Durkheim's idea that the social solidarity of modern society rests on other forms of law and regulation.

8 For a fine case study of the net-widening and intensification within one system, see Tom Blomberg's current work on 'sanction pile up' within the Florida juvenile justice system. (Blomberg, forthcoming). For a rich empirical analysis of the overall American juvenile justice system – the 'get-tough' track of capture and confinement as well as the less visible track of observation – see Gordon (1991).

9 Feeley (1991) highlights one of the less obvious functions of privatisation: its potential to expand the state's capacity to punish.

10 Ewick (1993) uses one example – an advertisement for Remuda Ranch, a residential treatment centre for women suffering from anorexia and bulimia – to show how social control (particularly therapeutic technologies for the control and care of the self) is transformed into a commodity and made available by corporations to those who can (and are persuaded by advertising that they want to) purchase it.

11 My concern in this chapter is more with the substantive themes in the social control discourse than its theoretical stance. I deal elsewhere with the connections between deconstructionist-type theory and policy choices (Cohen, 1990).

12 The Foucault industry has generated a massive debate on this point; for a review, see Keenan (1987).

13 This phrase is used by Gordon (1988) in a useful popular summary of critical legal studies.

14 Not just against the right and anti-democratic forces, but also – as I have suggested in the case of torture – against the vanities of postmodernism (Cohen, 1991). For a fine polemic against the excesses of Baudrillardian postmodernism – this time, in its attempted denial of the reality of the Gulf War – see Norris (1992).

15 I am grateful to Lech Falandycz for this example.

16 On non-state judicial systems in South Africa and their possible future in a post-apartheid era, see Burman and Scharf (1990).

17 For a current revival of the principles of civil society, see Keane (1988a, 1988b); for a more sceptical view see Wood (1990). On the use of the concept by Africanists, see papers from 'International Conference on Civil Society in Africa', (Truman Research Institute, Hebrew University, Jerusalem, January 1992). Papers from an earlier conference on the same subject appear in Rothchild and Chazan (1988).

18 The only explicit connection I have seen between the social control and civil society literatures is Rose and Miller (1992).

19 The ironies of what might happen to the creative, critical spirit when playwrights become presidents have, of course, been noted – especially by Havel himself (Havel, 1991).

20 On political violence in South Africa, see Manganyi and du Toit (1990).

21 Braithwaite's theory and advocacy of crime control through communitarian, reintegrative shaming is one of the few convincing attempts that go beyond the obvious. He is also sensitive to 'success' in both the instrumental and normative senses.

References

Black, Donald (1989) 'The elementary forms of conflict management', in *New Directions for the Study of Justice, Law and Social Control*. New York: Plenum Press.

Blomberg, Tom and Lucken, Karol (1994) 'Stacking the deck by piling up sanctions', *The Howard Journal*, 33(1) 62–80.

Braithwaite, John (1989) *Crime, Shame and Integration*. Cambridge: Cambridge University Press.

Burman, Sandra and Scharf, Wilfried (1990) 'Creating people's justice: street committees and people's courts in a South African city', *Law and Society Review*, 24(3): 693–744.

Cohen, Stanley (1985) *Visions of Social Control: Crime, Punishment and Classification*. Cambridge: Polity Press.

Cohen, Stanley (1989) 'The critical discourse on social control: notes on the concept as hammer', *International Journal of the Sociology of Law*, 17: 347–57.

Cohen, Stanley (1990) 'Intellectual scepticism and political commitment: the case of radical criminology', Bonger Memorial Lecture, University of Amsterdam.

Cohen, Stanley (1991) 'Talking about torture in Israel', *Tikkun* 6(6): 23.

Dandeker, Christopher (1990) *Surveillance, Power and Modernity*. New York: St. Martins Press.

Davis, Nannette and Stasz, Clarice (1990) *Social Control and Deviance: A Critical Perspective*. New York: McGraw Hill.

Ellman, Stephen (1991) *In a Time of Trouble: Law and Liberty in a State of Emergency*. New York: Oxford University Press.

Edwards, Anne (1988) *Regulation and Repression: The Study of Social Control*. London: Allen and Unwin.

Ewick, Patricia (1993) 'Corporate Cures: The Commodification of Social Control', in A. Sarat and S. Silbey (eds), *Studies in Law, Politics and Society*, vol. 13. Greenwich: JAI Press.

Falandycz, Lech (1991) 'Abolitionism: between necessity and utopia', in Z. Lasocik (ed.), *Abolitionism in History: On Another Way of Thinking*. Papers from International Conference on Penal Abolition, Warsaw University.

Feeley, Malcolm M. (1991) 'The privatization of punishment in historical perspective', in W. T. Gormley (ed.), *Privatization and its Alternatives*. Madison: University of Wisconsin Press.

Garland, David (1990) *Punishment and Modern Society*. Oxford: Oxford University Press.

Gordon, Diana R. (1991) *The Justice Juggernaut: Fighting Street Crime, Controlling Citizens*. New Brunswick, NJ: Rutgers University Press.

Gordon, Robert (1988). 'Law and ideology', *Tikkun*, 3(1).

Havel, Vaclav (1991) 'Uncertain strengths: an interview', *New York Review of Books*, 15 August.

Horwitz, Alan V. (1990) *The Logic of Social Control*. New York: Plenum Press.

Keane, John (ed.) (1988a) *Civil Society and the State*. New York: Verso.

Keane, John (1988b) *Democracy and Civil Society*. London: Verso.

Keenan, Tom (1987) 'The paradox of knowledge and power: reading Foucault on bias', *Political Theory*, 15(1): 5–37.

Kelman, Herbert C. and Hamilton, V. Lee (1989) *Crimes of Obedience*. New Haven, CT: Yale University Press.

Manganyi, N. Chabani and Du Toit, Andre (eds) (1990) *Political Violence and the Struggle in South Africa*. London: Macmillan.

Meyrowitz, Joshua (1985) *No Sense of Place: The Impact of Electronic Media on Social Behaviour*. New York: Oxford University Press.

Miller, Peter and Rose, Nikolas (eds) (1986) *The Power of Psychiatry*. Cambridge: Polity Press.

Muller, Ingo (1991) *Hitler's Justice: The Courts of the Third Reich*. Cambridge, MA: Harvard University Press.

Nelken, David (1990) 'Alternative logics in criminal justice', in R. Light (ed.), *Public and Private Provisions in Criminal Justice*. Bristol Centre for Criminal Justice.

Norris, Christopher (1992) *Uncritical Theory: Postmodernism, Intellectuals and the Gulf War*. London: Lawrence and Wishart.

O'Malley, Pat (1991) 'After discipline? Crime prevention, the strong state and the free market', paper presented at the Law and Society Association Annual Conference, Amsterdam.

Pepinsky, Harold and Quinney, Richard (eds) (1991) *Criminology as Peace Making*. Bloomington: Indiana University press.

Reichman, Nancy (1986) 'Managing crime risks: towards an insurance based model of social control', *Research in Law and Social Control*, 8: 152–72.

Rose, Nikolas (1990) *Governing the Soul: The Shaping of the Private Self*. London: Routledge.

Rose, Nikolas and Miller, Peter (1992) 'Political power beyond the state: problematics of government', *British Journal of Sociology*, 43(2): 173–205.

Rothchild, Donald and Chazan, Naomi (eds) (1988) *The Precarious Balance: State and Society in Africa*. Boulder, CO: Westview Press.

Shearing, Clifford and Stenning, Peter (1985) 'From the panopticon to Disneyworld: the development of discipline', in A. N. Doob and E. L. Greenspan (eds), *Perspectives in Criminal Law*. Aurora: Canada Law Book Co.

Simon, Jonathan (1987) 'The emergence of a risk society: insurance, law and the state', *Socialist Review*, 95: 61–89.

Simon, Jonathan (1988) 'The ideological effects of actuarial practices', *Law and Society Review*, 22: 772–800.

Steytler, Nico (1991) 'The South African Police and law enforcement in a new South Africa: The quest for legitimacy', paper presented at Law and Society Association annual conference, Amsterdam.

Wood, Ellen M. (1990) 'The Uses and Abuses of "Civil Society"', in R. Miliband (ed.), *The Socialist Register*. London: Merlin Press.

4

The Fragmentation of Criminology

Richard Ericson and Kevin Carriere

Criminology is a fragmented field of enquiry. As such, it is subject to criticism and marginalisation among academics. This situation worries criminologists and is a matter of a great deal of debate among them. For example, the lead article in a recent edition of *The Criminologist* states that 'within the last few years there has been considerable discussion surrounding the notion that criminology is fragmented and has stagnated' (Stitt and Giacopossi, 1992: 1).

In this chapter we ask why criminology is so fragmented. Our answer is that the fragmentation of criminology is part of wider processes of fragmentation in the academy, in other social institutions, and in the 'risk society'. First, we consider criminology in the context of an academic world that is fragmented. Criminology participates in the blurring of disciplinary boundaries that is occurring in all areas of modern science. It is a depository of multiple academic discourses, and a generator of blurring among disciplines, because it is an interdisciplinary field. Second, we explain the fragmentation of criminology in the context of institutional responses to crime that are also increasingly fragmented. Crime and its regulation are part of the practices and discourses of all major social institutions, for example economy, law, science, politics, medicine, education, insurance, military, business enterprise and mass media. In producing discourses about how myriad institutions define and respond to crime, criminology inevitably articulates fragmentation within and among those institutions. Third, we examine both multi-institutional responses to crime and criminological efforts to understand those responses in the context of societies increasingly driven by the monitoring of risks and provision of security. The fragmentation of risk definition, assessment, management and distribution in contemporary societies is contributing both to the fragmentation of institutional responses to crime and to criminological efforts to understand those responses.

Fragmentation within the academy

The fragmentation of academic literatures and the blurring of disciplinary boundaries is occurring across modern science (Capra, 1976; Lyotard, 1984; Giddens, 1987). Marcus (1986: 166) has declared: 'In anthropology and all other human sciences at the moment, "high" theoretical discourse – the body of ideas that authoritatively unify a field – is in disarray.' As the boundaries of modern science dissipate, and as interdisciplinary fields become ascendant, many academics experience vertigo.

> A conceptual revolution in the humanities and social sciences has given new vigor to inquiries about cultural studies in a variety of fields over the past twenty years, but that ongoing revolution leaves investigators with no stable ground on which to stand. A dizzying succession of new methods and theories has shattered disciplinary paradigms, forced scholars to engage in bold departures from their own training, to become 'specialists' in fields with few acknowledged experts and few firm standards of evidence and argument. My own inquiries have often left me between fields – too historical for the sociologists, too sociological for the linguists, and too linguistic and too sociological for the historians. (Lipsitz, 1990: vii–ix)

Within the academy, responses to the fragmentation of criminology vary. Some scholars who are cited by criminologists, but who do not see criminology as their field, simply ignore the issue. Criminologists who are disillusioned by the very thing that constitutes the field, namely its multidisciplinary and fragmented character, offer essentialist solutions. The essentialist solutions include treating criminology as an effective politics of crime control, or as a branch of a particular master discipline, or as a unified critical practice. Each of these essentialist solutions ignore the fact that the

> search for final solutions to questions about truth, rationality and knowledge could lead to the 'freezing over of culture' and the 'dehumanization of human beings' . . . the Platonic quest for a final, rational justified consensus based on access to an eternal Truth is actually a manifestation of what Nietzsche called a 'craving for metaphysical comfort': the desire to close off inquiry, to calcify a privileged set of descriptions, and to 'escape our humanity' by becoming properly programmed machines. (Guignon and Hylery, 1990: 339)

Most criminologists respond to fragmentation by identifying their discipline and their selves with the template of the criminal law institution. They join with those working within that institution to produce a discourse about crime and its regulation. This response entails patrolling the boundaries of their institution to police what other knowledges or forms of expertise will be allowed as they fit their discourse. Driven by practical questions, practices and power relations of those working within the criminal law institution, this criminology begins with questions of reform and improvement – What is faulty? How can it be corrected? How can it be made more efficient? – rather than questions arising from problems and academic puzzles derived from scholarly literature. This criminology of applied knowledge and social necessity (Rock, 1988) has always been dominant, but it has become predominant in the past decade through versions of what constitutes an effective politics of crime control.

In the form of Right Realism, academic criminology becomes synonymous with the institution of criminal law and the effective politics of crime control favoured by those who control that institution at a given time and place (Wilson and Herrnstein, 1985). Such efforts to make criminology the institutional voice of criminal law create all sorts of analytical problems. For example, agencies that participate in the criminal law institution, such as the police, tend to be essentialised as criminal law enforcers, which leads analysts to neglect other aspects of police work including their participation in many other institutions (for example, Sherman et al., 1989; Sherman, 1992). Moreover, the ways in which crime and its regulation are constituted by, and constitute, other institutions and their subject populations are ignored by those whose criminology does not go beyond the discourse of the criminal law institution.

Right Realism arose in the United States as a political strategy for addressing the urban decay and underclass produced by the very conservative forces with which it identifies. Grounded in assumptions of consensus and unified interest, Right Realism is oriented to all right-thinking people who believe that the criminal law institution is there to protect their persons and property through strong measures of general deterrence, specific deterrence and incapacitation. It sympathises with the propertied, in particular with trying to prevent their reserves of peace and prosperity from becoming preserves fortified to the hilt against the desperate urban poor (see the descriptions by Davis, 1990: Ch. 4; Reich, 1991). Their criminology is the ideological and technological arm of a criminal law institution left with too much of the burden for shoring up the spatial, material and social 'disorder and decline' (Skogan, 1990). Their preferred technologies include, for example, longitudinal studies that identify the criminal other and justify his or her differential treatment (for example, Farrington et al., 1986); and, they also include research that is meant to assist in the calibration of the 'scale of punishment' (Zimring and Hawkins, 1990), where prison is taken for granted as *the* response to crime and the refinement of penal technique is the only puzzle left.

While Right Realism defines itself with a conservative world view, Left Realism arose in the United Kingdom as a political strategy for challenging the law and order politics of the Conservative government (Lea and Young, 1984; Young, 1986, 1988a). As Michalowski (1991: 30) has pointed out, Left Realism was also born through a critique of two academic traditions in criminology: the cultural school, concerned with moral panics and other symbolic aspects of crime (Cohen, 1972; Hall et al., 1978); and, Marxist approaches, concerned with the plight of criminals (Taylor et al., 1973). Identifying with the consumers of criminal justice, especially crime victims who are poor and otherwise disadvantaged, Left Realism asks how the criminal justice system can meet their needs more adequately. In contrast to Right Realists who believe that the police are already in touch with essential community interests, Left Realists challenge state definitions by documenting community interests through victimisation and fear of crime surveys. Survey data are treated as indicative of essential community interests. They are used as a template for rationalising formal policing practices, and for making the police more accountable to the urban poor and other minorities.

Left Realists focus almost exclusively on those who suffer most in criminal victimisation and yet have the fewest resources to defend themselves or to seek compensation (for example, Jones et al., 1986; Young, 1988b). Part of a wider politics of 'community', the central concern is state responsibility for the just distribution of risks through security measures such as social insurance and protective services (Young, 1988a; see generally Burchell et al., 1991). Led by criminologists who appeared more radical in the 1970s, Left Realists have adjusted to a 1980s and 1990s 'realism' that really entails joining the ranks of those who take a pragmatic, piecemeal, administrative approach to the field on behalf of particular interests.

Between these extremes of what constitutes an effective politics of crime control is a liberal approach that both Right and Left Realists see as unrealistic. This approach is embodied in the academy in some departments of criminal justice (for example, Ashworth, 1988; Griffiths and Verdun-Jones, 1989). This form of criminology is essentially concerned with the just administration of criminal law conceived in terms of due process of law, and efficiency and humaneness in its administration. Various knowledges are assessed, and the technologies associated with those knowledges are selected, in terms of whether they meet the due process, efficiency and humaneness parameters of the criminal justice institution.

Criminologists who commit themselves to one of these three positions on the politics of crime control typically defend their position vehemently, which includes heaping scorn on opposing positions that are not politically correct. The result, at least among those committed to criminology as an effective politics of crime control, is a field that is not only fragmented but fractured. Meanwhile, criminologists driven by an effective politics of crime control are scorned in turn by those who feel such work is not significant academically because it does not take its lead from core theoretical puzzles of a master discipline. Academic purists argue that there is no scholarly benefit from research that begins with questions of pragmatic penal technique and reform. To accept pragmatic control questions as the first principle of enquiry is to concede that criminology is as Foucault (1977) depicted it in his harshest criticisms: a technology for the suppression and management of crime, conservative in character and devoid of serious intellectual content. In support of their stance, academic purists point to cases where the most significant intellectual breakthroughs derive from master disciplines 'outside' of criminology.

Academics who speak from a master discipline 'outside' of criminology essentialise the field as being synonymous with the theoretical puzzles and preferred methodologies of their discipline. While such a stance is taken, for example, by historians, psychologists, political scientists, semioticians and philosophers, it is exemplified in recent statements of sociologists.

John Hagan (1989) proselytises 'structural criminology'. He ends a recent collection of his research papers on his approach with a piece entitled 'The future of structural criminology'. This piece includes a vehement defence of his version of sociological criminology through an attack on those he terms 'sociological discontents'. Criminology is neither other academic disciplines nor an effective politics of crime control. Criminology is his brand of positivistic sociology.

> If sociology is the scientific study of social relations, then the approach outlined in this volume is not only a structural criminology, but a sociological criminology as well. The sociological tradition has long been ascendant in criminology [see Gibbons, 1979], but today is under attack. The attack comes on the one hand from those who see criminology as its own 'fully autonomous discipline' [for example Thomas, 1984], and on the other hand from those in other disciplines [for example Wilson, 1975] who believe their own or some grander combination of disciplines provides a better approach to the study of crime and delinquency. The structural approach outlined in this volume is inherently opposed to the separation of criminology from sociology, arguing instead that the structural foundations of sociology make its explanatory role necessary for an understanding of crime and delinquency. The policy analysis of crime leaves off where the sociological study of crime and delinquency began. Sociologists, it seems, may still be uniquely suited to pursue the causes of these behaviours regarded by others as disreputable. (Hagan, 1989: 257–8)

Hagan attempts to disqualify or render subservient alternative methods and disciplines. He does so through the use of metaphors of war such as 'attack' (cf. McGaw, 1991), which are aimed at securing his ontological terrain. The activities of 'discontents' are characterised as subsidiary, unreasonable or ex-centric. In the face of such academic essentialism and imperialism, Foucault (1980b: 565) asked rhetorically: 'Should the actual question not be what forms of knowledge do you want to disqualify, if you ask me "is it science"?'. Positivists such as Hagan 'find themselves treating as their object what is in fact their condition of possibility' (Foucault, 1972: 364).

Clifford Shearing (1989) argues that criminology is essentially concerned with the sociological problem of order. Any criminology that focuses on crime is political because crime itself is a political rather than technical construct. Therefore, not only are those who take one of the three positions on an effective politics of crime control dismissed as politically rather than academically motivated, so too are sociologists such as Hagan who focus their analysis on the causes of and social reaction to crime. Against 'crime-ology', Shearing is for 'internally driven agendas and boundaries' (1989: 172) of his discipline. With the sociological problem of order as his agenda, Shearing draws boundaries which reduce and essentialise criminology to sociology, and a rather traditional sociology at that.

> It is our failure to translate our theoretical insights and the practices they promote into a disciplinary definition that has produced the straight-jacket of crime-ology. It is because we have allowed ourselves, in our definition of our discipline, to remain so closely tied to the 'natural attitude' that pervades practical political and policy discourse, that we have created barriers, perhaps the appropriate metaphor would be a prison, that has stifled the development of our discipline . . . The struggle over order, the activity that seeks to guarantee it, and the activity that resists the realization of this guarantee, either in part or in whole, is the phenomenon that gives unity to criminological research and teaching. Ordering both includes crime-ology and goes beyond it in precisely the way that work in our discipline in fact does . . . [I]t is not crime that is our central topic but the struggle around order and the products it produces, among which are crime and criminal

justice. Only then will criminology truly reflect its beginnings and the vision that inspired it. (Shearing, 1989: 173, 176, 178)

Shearing and Hagan are typical of criminologists who yearn for order in the field. It comes as no surprise that what 'truly reflects' the tradition of criminology turns out to be a truth derived from their own master discipline.

Fragmentation within the field also results in a sense of dis-ease for some academics who operate under the broad rubric of 'critical' or 'radical' criminology. Despite the fact that the hegemony of Marxism has faded, and it no longer enjoys a monopoly as *the* voice of *the* left (Laclau and Mouffe,1985), some criminologists are still trying to forge unification among critical forces. For example, in a recent book entitled *New Directions in Critical Criminology*, the editors argue that perspectives as diverse as Left Realism, feminism, postmodernism and peacemaking should be viewed as complementary (MacLean and Milovanovic, 1991: 1). This statement is made despite the fact that some of the contributors to this collection recognise the difficulties associated with such a position. The final article in this collection, entitled 'The future of critical criminology', asserts that the term '"critical criminology" is a metaphor for those of us who work in a common tradition with common goals' (Schwartz, 1991: 119). Such attempts to unify the field betray a nostalgia for the enlightenment fantasy of the pursuit of freedom through the collection and synthesis of truth, as well as the Marxist fantasy of a united revolutionary class. From any Realist perspective, there is no consideration of the possibility that scientific and technical knowledge may not be cumulative: 'At most, what is debated is the form that accumulation takes – some picture it as regular, continuous, others as periodic, discontinuous and conflictual' (Lyotard, 1984: 7).

In their attempts to impose an artificial order and unity upon the field, academic essentialists proceed by criticising the truths of their opponents as being reductionist and essentialist. Ironically, they then advance an alternative that is itself reductionist and essentialist. This paradox can be avoided, however, if criminologists stop worrying about discipline and order in the field and start celebrating its fragmented character. The only problem with the fragmentation of criminology is criminologists who fret about it. Problems arise when criminologists essentialise the field within their preferred template of political and/or academic correctness.

The drive to essentialise is itself a worthy topic for research. For example, Rabinow (1986: 253) suggests research on the 'micropolitics of knowledge in the academy'. A reflexive criminology must be sensitive to the immediate political conditions and institutional contexts that encourage essentialism.

Asking whether longer, dispersive, multi-authored texts would yield tenure might seem petty. But those are the dimensions of power relations to which Nietzsche exhorted us to be scrupulously attentive. The taboo against specifying them is much greater than the strictures against denouncing colonialism . . . Just as there was formerly a discursive knot preventing discussion of exactly those field practices that defined the authority of the anthropologist, which has now been untied (Rabinow, 1977), so, too, the micropractices of the academy might well do with some scrutiny. (Rabinow, 1986: 253)

Fragmentation is endemic to the human sciences because of their particular place in the modern *episteme* (Foucault, 1972: esp. 344–87). Foucault situates the development of the human sciences within the context of other scientific discourses on life, labour and language. Arguing that the title of human 'sciences' is a misnomer, he says:

> what renders them possible, in fact, is a certain situation of vicinity with regard to biology, economics and philology (or linguistics); they exist only in so far as they dwell side by side with those sciences – or rather beneath them, in the space of their projections . . . the configuration that defines their positivity and gives them roots in the modern *episteme* at the same time makes it impossible for them to be sciences. (Foucault, 1972: 366)

For Foucault, the precarious status of the human sciences on the landscape of the modern *episteme* makes the blurring of disciplinary boundaries and interdisciplinary dialogue inevitable.

> [H]ence the frequent difficulty in fixing limits, not merely between the objects, but also between the methods proper to psychology, sociology, and the analysis of literature and myth . . . In this way all of the human sciences interlock and can always be used to interpret one another: their frontiers become blurred, intermediary and composite disciplines multiply endlessly, and in the end their proper object may even disappear altogether. (Foucault, 1972: 357–8)

Criminology has the same theoretical ambitions as the disciplines that constitute it and are constituted by it. It is therefore no surprise that important theoretical breakthroughs occur in conjunction with other disciplines. A few recent developments are illustrative.

Foucault's interest in the institutional basis of historical memory has an affinity with Nietzsche's passionate plea for us to 'remember' the role of institutions in mediating history through 'the will to tradition, to authority, to centuries long responsibility, to solidarity between succeeding generations backwards and forwards in infinitum' (Nietzsche, 1968 [1889]: 93). In turn, Foucault's work has, of course, penetrated and transformed the boundaries between a wide range of academic disciplines and fields, including criminology.

Literary studies are influencing criminology. For example, following Burke (1989), Gusfield (1981) and Wagner-Pacifici (1986) have used literary theory to analyse public culture discourse about crime and criminals. The law-as-literature field has shown similar cross-fertilisation among disciplines (Posner, 1990), as has the study of how law criminalises and regulates writing and other forms of representation (Stewart, 1991).

Historians, political scientists and sociologists have converged on questions about how institutions and their authorities imprint social reality, and thereby constitute their identities, ideologies and authority, through discourses and practices of crime and punishment (Gladstone et al., 1991). This has led to changes in each discipline. Historians have become more sensitive to wider questions in social and political theory, while sociologists and political scientists have better anchorage for understanding the institutions and reform processes that are the objects of their enquiries.

At the same time criminology helps to make clear that there are distinct differences among and within academic disciplines. Academic disciplines cannot be entirely folded into one another and made a single entity. This consideration is related to the point that there are limits to any given body of knowledge and its ways of knowing. Criminology tells us a great deal about the limited character and methodologies of particular disciplines.

In the light of the above considerations, the fragmentation of criminological literature and the blurring of disciplinary boundaries cannot be thought of as representing an acute phase that must be endured until the field can be properly diagnosed and corrected. Rather, the fragmentation of criminology is a chronic condition. While the growth in the academy and in its myriad discourses and communications media mean that criminology has become more fragmented, this merely represents an accentuation of what has always been the case.

If a criminologist takes this view, he or she also lets go of the belief that academic consensus is possible or desirable, since all narratives of crime can never be united. An ultimate vision of truth and synthesis of knowledge is fantasy. The truths that constitute scientific knowledge can no longer be thought of as individual pieces of a puzzle to be put together to form a whole. While a celebration of fragmentation is not limited to those who write from a postmodernist position, Lyotard's conclusion to *The Postmodern Condition* is exemplary. In the face of unifying meta-narratives such as science and Marxism, he says:

> We have paid a high enough price for the nostalgia of the whole and the one, for the reconciliation of the concept and the sensible, of the transparent and the communicable experience. Under the general demand for slackening and for appeasement, we can hear the mutterings of the desire for a return of terror, for the realization of the fantasy to seize reality. The answer is: Let us wage war on totality; let us be witness to the unpresentable; let us activate the differences and save the honour of the name. (Lyotard, 1984: 81–2)

When fragmentation is viewed as the norm, a situation of reverse onus is created. Concern shifts from the problem of fragmentation in criminology to those who view the fragmentation of criminology to be a problem. Pluralism is no longer viewed as indicative of a crisis of knowledge. The analytical eye becomes focused instead on those wishing to unify and essentialise the field, and to silence antagonistic voices (Cheal, 1990). There must be an interrogation of any authoritative claims over what is reputable.

A fragmented criminology does not lack direction. To portray criminology as lacking in direction is disrespectful of the interested parties – often ex-centrics such as the poor, women, blacks and gays – who have resisted and forced a wider range of political issues and methodologies onto academic agendas (Hutcheon, 1989: esp. 57–73). The fragmentation of criminology can be viewed as indicative of the collapse of conservative orthodoxies which were previously more successful at imposing a relatively monolithic order upon the field. Scholars can enjoy using the fragments to create mosaics. For example, Butler (1990) says that her analytical strategy in the area of gender deviance is based on a desire

> to affirm those positions on the critical boundaries of disciplinary life. The point is not to stay marginal, but to participate in whatever network of marginal zones is spawned from other disciplinary centers and which, together, constitute a multiple displacement of those authorities. The complexity of gender requires an interdisciplinary and postdisciplinary set of discourses in order to resist the domestication of gender studies or women studies within the academy and to radicalize the notion of feminist critique. (Butler, 1990: xiii)

It is peculiar indeed to still find criminologists who essentialise the field in the ways discussed above. To be other than highly reflexive can only lead to frustration and a narrowness of focus. Perhaps it is their tendency to be insufficiently reflexive in a highly reflexive world that leads some criminologists to question the relevance of a lot of criminology, and to retreat into either a narrow political concern or a single discipline that they believe will finally allow mastery.

Ethnocentric in terms of discipline and political position, many criminologists persist in believing that what they do is most central and worthwhile, while other approaches are worn, unproductive, or simply wrongheaded. As is characteristic of all forms of ethnocentrism, they experience dis-ease about disciplinary boundaries that are blurred or disintegrating. This heightens their anxiety about the value of their own projects and the distinctiveness of their own academic identity. They react by trying to essentialise criminology into a more unified, even singular project, and to proselytise in terms of that project. Of course their efforts intensify and proliferate the very thing they are trying to avoid, that is an acute sense that the field is coming apart. The only viable *academic* sensibility is to encourage people to let their minds wander, to travel intellectually across the boundaries and frontiers and perhaps never return to them. It is connections with myriad cultures of knowledge that are crucial for the vitality of criminology.

> It is the field of academic study sufficient unto itself, ignoring and contemptuous of cognate disciplines, that is in terminal crisis. The fact that criminology is unsure of its precise location and its relation to the wider project of social science is what keeps it relevant and engaged. (Hunt, 1990: 658)

Fragmentation in institutional responses to crime

In the process of analysing myriad institutional responses to crime, criminology confronts fragmentation within and among social institutions. Criminology inevitably articulates the local, differentiated discourses in other social institutions and mediates clashes among these discourses, which in turn contributes to the fragmentation of criminology.

An institution is an established community with particular interests. The activity of institutional communities is not limited by the boundaries of any geographical territory or nation state. Institutions know no such boundaries. The main activity of institutions is the communication of knowledge to enact an environment that facilitates particular constellations of interests (Weick, 1979; Douglas, 1986). In this way, the concepts of institution, community and communication are inextricably bound up (Ericson et al., 1993). Knowledge is communicated with respect to material components (buildings, mechanical technologies, objects), cultural aspects (traditions, rituals, scientific technologies, legal technologies) political processes (it must be legitimised), and social dimensions (all of the above are reproduced through social communicative acts).

Discourse is the institutional communication of meaning through these material, cultural, political and social elements (Macdonnel, 1986; Valverde, 1990, 1991). Discourse does not represent a pre-linguistic or objective reality, it is constitutive of realities. It is entwined with the material, cultural, political and social relations that provide the context for how people think, feel, speak, write, dress, design their buildings and so on. Human activities and technologies are therefore simultaneously 'real' and linguistic, 'elements of a discourse that . . . transcends and makes redundant the usual distinctions between language and reality' (Valverde, 1990: 71). When language and reality are seen in these terms, distinctions between, for example, knowledge and ideology (Foucault, 1980a), sign and referent (Baudrillard, 1983), narrative and non-narrative knowledge (Lyotard, 1984), and art and science (Nisbet, 1976), become less distinctive.

Criminologists study, and participate in, how the discourse of the criminal law institution relates to other institutional discourses in the allocation of resources (for example, by guaranteeing and protecting relationships; by intervening to enforce policies and programmes); the regulation and resolution of conflict (for example, by providing principles and procedures for doing so); and, keeping the peace (for example, by establishing rules of behaviour and enforcing violations with sanctions). The focus is how mechanisms of criminal law coordinate institutional activities and help to constitute society's authority system. That is, these mechanisms are not only a set of rules and bureaucratic roles and practices, but also a distinctive way of communicating culture and identity, telling people both what to do and who to be. As such, the mechanisms of criminal law involve a dialectic between agency and structure (Sewell, 1992). Going beyond the simple binary oppositions characteristic of other discourses – for example, between repression and liberation, enabling and constraining features, due process and crime control – criminologists construe criminal law in broader institutional contexts: as, for example, a site of political conflict and struggle; a vehicle for political, economic, cultural and social dominance; and, a means of constructing culture and expressing dominant cultural values.

In contemporary societies possessed by bureaucracies and therefore obsessed with procedure (Habermas, 1975; Dandeker, 1990), procedural discourses become especially important to criminology. There is reciprocal influence between criminal procedure and the procedures used in other forms of law, social institutions, organisations and groups. Procedures combine with moral considerations to provide a discourse of procedural propriety that sustains the legitimacy of institutions. For example, criminologists examine how the public pronouncements, specific provisions and case decisions of constitutional law – such as the Canadian Charter of Rights and Freedoms – influence the procedural conceptions of various institutions (Ericson, 1985; Mandel, 1989; Roach, 1991). Criminology addresses the extent to which the procedural conceptions of criminal law permeate other institutions and thereby affect their autonomy, result in a merging of practices, and influence the interchangeability of both their professional staffs and their clienteles (Lowman et al., 1987; Menzies, 1989; Chunn, 1992). There is also increased concern with how the conceptions of procedure fostered by criminal law relate to accountability and legitimacy in various institutions, and thus to the constitution of institutional positions and authority (Stenning, forthcoming).

The discourses of criminology, criminal law and other institutions sometimes meet and cohere, and at other times they meet and conflict. In what follows we use as examples the relation between criminology and criminal law, medicine, the mass media, the military, and political institutions, although many additional institutions could be used as examples.

There is a long history of medical discourse being brought in to fit particular needs of criminal law, especially with respect to the disposition of offenders (Garland, 1985, 1988). Early criminology was dominated by medical discourse because it fitted so well with the practical needs and pragmatic justifications of criminal sentencing. The dominance of medical discourse in criminology only began to recede in the 1960s (Rock, 1988). Criminality, along with other forms of deviance, continues to be heavily medicalised through the combined discourses of criminal law and psychiatry (Menzies, 1989).

The discourses of the mass media institution also fit well with criminal law in constituting crime, law and justice (Ericson et al., 1989, 1991; Ericson, 1991; Schlesinger et al., 1991; Sparks, 1992). Criminal law agencies, especially the police, are members of the deviance-defining elite with preferred access to the mass media. This access allows them to engage the mass media directly in law enforcement, for example, in mobilising informants (Carriere and Ericson, 1989; Ericson, 1989). It also allows criminal law agencies to frame how particular events, issues, responsibilities and solutions are understood and deemed viable. More generally, preferred access allows them to create the contemporary myths of crime, law and justice, to turn stories of what is into stories of what ought to be with important implications for popular understandings of morality, procedural propriety, and hierarchy.

The military institution has had a dominant influence on bureaucratisation in general, and on criminal law bureaucracies in particular

(Dandeker, 1990). For example, the police and prisons continue to organise in military terms. Their versions of organisational order, of morality, procedure and hierarchy, are distinctly militaristic, in spite of various 'community policing' and 'community corrections' innovations. At the same time, especially in the United States, the military model is as pervasive as the medical model in efforts to colonise the control of crime and other forms of deviance. 'War on . . . ' military metaphors abound, for example the 'war on crime' and the 'war on drugs'. So pervasive is the military model that even seemingly benevolent efforts to alleviate the causes of crime are based in militaristic sensibilities, for example the 'war on poverty'. Beginning with the American Declaration of Independence (White, 1984), the belief has been created that metaphors of war are the best way to justify policies and to move people both emotionally and practically to fight 'suitable enemies' (Christie, 1986).

As illustrated in research addressing the war on drugs (for example, Scheingold, 1990; McGaw, 1991), military discourse does not simply function as rhetoric in public culture to rouse the masses. It also relates to the practices of criminal law bureaucracies, especially the police. Coincident with the 'war on . . . ' sensibility and the militarism mentality, criminologists studying police have adopted what is best termed General Schwartzkopf Criminology (Ericson, 1994). This criminology analyses how the police, like the military, deploy personnel and use strategies and tactics to secure a territory against those who threaten its people and things. The emphasis is on how military-type bureaucracy, discipline, technology, deployment and coercion fight criminal sources of insecurity (Kelling et al., 1974; Sherman et al., 1989; Skogan, 1990; Sherman, 1992).

Myriad groups and organisations that make up the political institution use crime and the reform of the criminal law as vehicles for communicating their own concerns and interests. The study of criminal law reform is especially fruitful in illustrating both that crime, and reaction to crime, are defined politically, and that crime in turn connects to political concerns and interests well beyond the regulation of undesirable conduct. Perhaps the best illustration of this point is research on victims' movements (Rock, 1986, 1990; Fattah, 1992). However, there are many other studies, especially the work of Gusfield (1981, 1989), which teach that various political and professional groups use crime and its regulation as a vehicle for creating their role on the political stage, a role that in turn allows them some purchase on how crime *and* other aspects of institutional life are understood and managed. This research also provides instruction on how such communications about crime and its regulation articulate with efforts by the groups concerned to imprint a particular template of moral order and regulation. Research has shown that there are areas such as child abuse in which criminal law reform is accomplished routinely because it is already rooted in moral consensus (Nelson, 1984; Best, 1990); areas such as impaired driving and narcotics use in which the moral consensus has to be constructed through legal change (Gusfield, 1981; Giffen et al., 1991); areas such as abortion in which any effort at law reform perpetuates moral conflict (Kellough, forthcoming); and areas such as private policing under administrative law which are not even on the reform agenda because there is moral ambiguity or moral concerns are silenced (Shearing and Stenning, 1983; Friedland, 1990).

Several academic disciplines – in particular history, political science and sociology – have converged on these questions of how various institutions participate in communications about criminal law to enhance their respective discourses and practices. These disciplines have a common concern with how institutions and their authorities imprint social realities through a focus on crime and its regulation, and with how this imprint helps to legitimise some and marginalise others. There is an attendant focus on the lack of fit and clashes between discourses. This focus provides instruction about the relative power of discourses and institutions, where power is seen in relational terms following Foucault.

A basic question concerns the mechanisms through which the criminal law institution regulates knowledge possession and use, resulting in the accretion of knowledge/power advantages to some over others. For example, criminal law polices its own institutional boundaries with respect to the types of expertise it allows as evidence in dispute settlement (Freidson, 1986; Nelken, 1990). On a general level, some institutions and their discourses are given more licence than others. For example, medical discourse tends to be mitigating while sociological discourse is often aggravating in the criminal courts. At the same time, even with respect to more permissible discourses, rules of evidence, judgments and discretion are used to protect the authority of legal reasoning and discourse over the claims of experts and their peculiar reasoning and discourse. The institutional hegemony of criminal law is maintained by protecting its own ways of producing meaning, its own knowledge systems in the wider environment of other institutional discourses with claims to authority (Ericson and Baranek, 1982).

The more general question here is the division of expert knowledge and labour among institutions and associated professions, as this affects criminal law jurisdiction (Abbott, 1988; Gusfield, 1989; Ericson, 1994). How is criminal law jurisdiction won and lost in terms of expertise embodied in people (professionals) and embedded in institutions and their technologies? As the courts recognise in granting professional privilege and standing to expert witnesses, it is not professional formal education, credentials and institutionalisation that are most important but rather abstract knowledge combined with skill and practical experience (Freidson, 1986: Ch. 5; Smith and Wynne, 1989; Mayo and Hollander, 1991). Professions define themselves and their jurisdiction in terms of control of abstract knowledge, and of the practical technologies and techniques abstract knowledge generates. Abstraction allows ongoing redefinition and defence of problems and tasks, and the seizure of new tasks (Abbott, 1988: 8–9).

Beyond these inter-institutional mechanisms of contesting permissible discourse about crime and criminal law enforcement, there are some respects in which the communication of crime and its regulation in other institutions is of greater significance than how it is communicated within the criminal law institution. For example, the mass media is the most pervasive and persuasive institution through which people experience crime, law and justice in everyday life (Ericson et al., 1989, 1991; Sparks, 1992). In contrast to the high visibility of crime and criminal law in the mass media, business enterprise maintains low visibility by refusing to communicate more widely crimes within its jurisdiction. Business enterprise does not report most crime to the police, thereby shutting out any prospect for the involvement of criminal law (Shearing and Stenning, 1983). It participates in the construal of its nefarious activities as matters for compliance law enforcement under administrative law rather than as criminal (Pearce and Tombs, 1990). Business enterprise defines what is deemed criminal in other institutional spheres in relation to its own framework for regulation, for example seeing property violations in terms of loss prevention and mechanisms of cost accounting (Shearing and Stenning, 1982). At the same time business enterprise defines as crime activities that are seen in other institutional spheres as legitimate conduct or rights, for example using the term 'crime' in relation to strikes and picketing (South, 1988).

The fragmentation of risk

The fragmentation of institutional responses to crime, and the participation of criminology in that fragmentation, are in turn related to more general social trends. In particular discourses of risk – emanating from several quarters, but especially the institution of insurance and efforts to regulate the environment – are imposing alternative templates on the control of crime and other social deviance. It is now possible to contend that we live in a 'risk society' (Giddens, 1990, 1991; Beck, 1992a, 1992b) in which the demand for knowledge useful in risk definition, assessment, management and distribution is refiguring social organisation. Part of this refiguration is a fundamental shift in the position of the criminal law institution in regulatory space, a space that is now being constructed through concerns of vulnerability, risk, efficiency and accountability (Ericson, 1994). Discourses of risk penetrate a range of institutions and have bearing upon how the criminal law institution and its operatives think and act (Reichman, 1986; Simon, 1987, 1988; O'Malley, 1991, 1992). Criminologists are very much a part of the assessment and management of risk for various legal, economic, military, mass media, insurance, medical, educational, welfare, and business enterprise institutions. Such participation is the basis of criminological expertise and its marketability.

The risk society is constituted by three logics of risk that influence the discourse and practice of the criminal law institution. First, there is a negative logic. Threats and dangers, and fears about them, are dealt with by the construction of 'suitable enemies' (Christie, 1986) and attendant negative labelling, denial, avoidance and exclusion. Solidarity is based in a communality of fear. In some cases, such as the 'war on drugs', insecurities are cultivated and focused on unfortunate people to gain political purchase and to offset the endemic insecurity experienced more generally in everyday life (Christie, 1986; Ehrenich, 1989; Scheingold, 1990; McGaw, 1991).

Second, there is a logic of controlling the irrational by rational means. Fear becomes a basis for rational action. People turn to experts, such as criminologists, to rationalise fears and make probability choices. Science, including criminology, replaces traditional controls of fear and insecurity, such as those provided by religion. There is a secularisation of risk and danger and an attendant awareness that risks cannot be counteracted through knowledge that is not scientific: 'No amount of collective coughing, scratching or sighing helps. Only science does' (Beck, 1992a: 212). Specialists in the rational are drawn into the realm of the irrational, or at least into different rationalities. Science is forced to address the less rational aspects of risk perception in political culture and becomes a rhetorical force in the politics of risk. The more rigorous the scientific standard of risk, the greater the perceived risk and fear, and the greater the likelihood that other risks will be overlooked. There is no escape from the rationalisation of risks.

Third, there is a logic of insurance. The concept of risk is a neologism of insurance. In modernity the institution of insurance is central to the rationalisation of risk (Evers and Nowatny, 1987; Reiss, 1989; Ewald, 1991a, 1991b; Lau, 1992). Insurance makes risks objectified, as an accident; calculable, as a matter of probability; collective, as a distribution among groups; capital, as a means of capital accumulation and as a guarantee against loss of capital; and legal, as subject to contract and adjudication. Insurance has become a dominant cultural template. It is so pervasive that the risk society is envisaged as a vast system of insurance (Ewald, 1991a: 210), a 'generalizable technology for rationalizing societies' (Defert, 1991: 215) and selves in everyday life. As such insurance technology constitutes society and its various security institutions, including the criminal law institution (Reichman, 1986; Simon, 1987, 1988; O'Malley, 1991, 1992). It produces social configurations based on particular interests and memberships in risk categories, which in turn affect inclusion and exclusion, hierarchy, solidarity and justice.

The three logics of the risk society refigure institutional logics of social hierarchy, integration and justice. Social integration is enhanced through a communality of fear which joins the communality of need as a socially binding force and basis of solidarity (Beck, 1992a, 1992b). There is a drift in the public agenda away from economic inequality to the distribution and control of risks. The values of the unsafe society displace those of the unequal society (Beck, 1992a, 1992b; Lau, 1992). This sensibility is enhanced by the logic of insurance in particular, which offers solidarity and justice through common interests in the distribution of risk. Risks cut across traditional categories and boundaries based on class, labour and property, blurring and even refiguring those bases of hierarchy and boundary maintenance.

The risk society shifts the focus on deviance–control–order to a focus on knowledge–risk–security. The concern is less with the labelling of deviants as outsiders, and more on developing a knowledge of everyone to ascertain and manage their place in society. The concern is not so much a control of deviants in a repressive sense, but the constitution of populations in their respective risk categories. The concern is not only with security as a predictable spatial environment, but also with a plethora of insurance mechanisms that guarantee healthy, productive 'human resources'. Through insurance schemes government capitalises human resources as risks, and services its investment through 'an intimate regular presence in the existence of citizens' (Defert, 1991: 232). Of course this 'intimate regular presence' is not personal or face-to-face, nor does it control directly. Rather, it is constituted by the surveillance capacities of expert systems of risk management and their communications media: 'The rationalization of security . . . is inherently open-ended . . . it deals not just in closed circuits of control, but in calculations of the possible and the probable' (Gordon, 1991: 35–6).

These developments influence the criminal law institution substantially. For example, the police increasingly respond, think and act in terms of the knowledge demands for risk management of various security institutions (Ericson, 1994). That is, whether they are handling criminal activity or other social deviance, the police treat something as actionable only if it fits with the knowledge demands of other institutions: insurance companies, regulatory agencies, criminal courts, health agencies, government statistics bureaux, etc. The police are reactive not only at the individual level of responding to calls for service, but also at the institutional level of satisfying the knowledge demands of other security institutions. Police work itself is transformed. The police become knowledge brokers and expert advisers on risk to other institutions. They no longer police a community based on sharing, reciprocity, tradition, special face-to-face relationships, and local space with a sense of immediacy. Rather they police communities constituted by major institutions and their respective interests. In this community of institutional interests tradition diminishes the more it is penetrated by the risk technologies of major institutions. Communications are extra-situational more than face-to-face, mediated by electronic technologies that offer surveillance of populations. In this environment of surveillance – of the production of knowledge for the management of populations (Dandeker, 1990) – community policing turns out to be communications policing (Ericson et al., 1993).

These shifts are not a sign that criminal law and other components of the legal institution are becoming less powerful. At least in Anglo-American jurisdictions, there has been an enormous growth in legislation, in policing capacity (the size and characteristics of bureaucracies involved in legal regulation), in levels of enforcement (the populations subject to control, potentially and actually), and in law talk in political culture and popular culture (influencing how we think and imagine the real). Law grows as it coheres with other institutional discourses of risk in accomplishing social organisation. The growth in law is associated with the increasingly complex division of knowledge and labour among risk institutions, and the attendant features of social distance and inequality. The growth in law also relates to the growth in and complexity of knowledge, especially scientific knowledge, and of technology.

Criminology has also expanded enormously in the past decade. It too has grown because it articulates with the three logics of risk, and their translation into risk assessment and management practices. Criminologists help myriad institutions construct suitable enemies, control the irrational by rational means, and apply insurance-formatted technologies. As such criminologists contribute to an increasingly destructured, fragmented, and reflexive existence in risk society.

The fragmentation of criminology is part of wider processes of fragmentation in the academy, in other social institutions, and in the risk society. These wider processes explain why criminologists who try to essentialise the field as an effective politics of crime control or as a single academic discipline experience increasing frustration and 'stagnation' (Stitt and Giacopossi, 1992). It is preferable to engage the fragmentation of criminology for what it is, the inevitable result of academic and institutional change in risk society.

References

Abbott, A. (1988) *The System of Professions: An Essay on the Division of Expert Labor*. Chicago, IL: University of Chicago Press.

Ashworth, A. (1988) 'Criminal justice and the criminal process', in P. Rock (ed.), *A History of British Criminology*. Oxford: Oxford University Press.

Baudrillard, J. (1983) *Simulations*. New York: Semiotext(e).

Beck, U. (1992a) 'Modern society as a risk society', in N. Stehr and R. Ericson (eds), *The Culture and Power of Knowledge*. Berlin and New York: de Gruyter.

Beck, U. (1992b) *The Risk Society*. London: Sage.

Best, J. (1990) *Threatened Children*. Chicago, IL: University of Chicago Press.

Burchell, G., Gordon, C. and Miller, P. (eds) (1991) *The Foucault Effect : Studies in Governmentality*. Chicago, IL: University of Chicago Press.

Burke, K. (1989) *On Symbols and Society*. Chicago, IL: University of Chicago Press.

Butler, J. (1990) *Gender Trouble: Feminism and the Subversion of Identity*. New York: Routledge.

Capra, F. (1976) *The Turning Point: Science, Society and the Rising Culture*. New York: Simon and Schuster.

Carriere, K. and Ericson, R. (1989) *Crime Stoppers: A Study in the Organization of Community Policing*. Toronto: Centre of Criminology, University of Toronto.

Cheal, D. (1990) 'Authority and incredulity: sociology between modernism and postmodernism', *Canadian Journal of Sociology*, 15(2): 129–48.

Christie, N. (1986) 'Suitable enemies', in H. Bianchi and R. Van Swaaningen (eds), *Abolititionism – Towards a Non-Repressive Approach to Crime*. Amsterdam: Free University Press.

Chunn, D. (1992) *From Punishment to Doing Good*. Toronto: University of Toronto Press.

Cohen, S. (1972) *Folk Devils and Moral Panics*. London: Paladin.
Dandeker, C. (1990) *Surveillance, Power and Modernity: Bureaucracy and Discipline from 1700 to the Present Day*. New York: St Martin's Press.
Davis, M. (1990) *City of Quartz*. London: Verso.
Defert, D. (1991) ' "Popular Life" and insurance technology', in G. Burchell, C. Gordon and P. Miller (eds), *The Foucault Effect: Studies in Governmentality*. Chicago, IL: University of Chicago Press.
Douglas, M. (1986) *How Institutions Think*. Syracuse: University of Syracuse Press.
Ehrenich, B. (1989) *Fear of Falling: The Inner Life of the Middle Class*. New York: Pantheon.
Ericson, R. (1985) 'Legal inequality', in S. Spitzer and A. Scull (eds), *Research in Law, Deviance and Social Control (Volume 7)*. Greenwich, CT: JAI Press.
Ericson, R. (1989) 'Patrolling the facts: secrecy and publicity in police work', *British Journal of Sociology*, 40: 205–26
Ericson, R. (1991) 'Mass media, crime, law, and justice: an institutional approach', *British Journal of Criminology*, 31: 219–49.
Ericson, R. (1994) 'The division of expert knowledge in policing and security', *British Journal of Sociology*, 45: 149–70.
Ericson, R. and Baranek, P. (1982) *The Ordering of Justice: A Study of Accused Persons as Dependants in the Criminal Process*. Toronto: University of Toronto Press.
Ericson, R., Baranek, P. and Chan, J. (1989) *Negotiating Control: A Study of News Sources*. Milton Keynes: Open University Press; Toronto: University of Toronto Press.
Ericson, R., Baranek, P. and Chan, J. (1991) *Representing Order: Crime, Law and Justice in the News Media*. Milton Keynes: Open University Press; Toronto: University of Toronto Press.
Ericson, R., Haggerty, K. and Carriere, K. (1993) 'Community policing as communications policing', in D. Dölling and T. Feltes (eds), *Community Policing*. Holzkirchen: Felix-Verlag.
Evers, A. and Nowatny, H. (1987) *Über den Ungang mit Unsicherheit*. Frankfurt: Suhrkamp.
Ewald, F. (1991a) 'Insurance and risk', in G. Burchell, C. Gordon and P. Miller (eds), *The Foucault Effect: Studies in Governmentality*. Chicago, IL: University of Chicago Press.
Ewald, F. (1991b) 'Norms, discipline and the law', in Robert Post (ed.), *Law and the Order of Culture*. Berkeley: University of California Press.
Farrington, D., Ohlin, L. and Wilson, J. (1986) *Understanding and Controlling Crime*. Berlin: Springer-Verlag.
Fattah, E. (1992) *Toward a Critical Victimology*. London: Macmillan.
Foucault, M. (1972) *The Order of Things: An Archaeology of the Human Sciences*. New York: Random House.
Foucault, M. (1977) *Discipline and Punish: The Birth of the Prison*. New York: Pantheon.
Foucault, M. (1980a) 'Truth and power', in C. Gordon (ed.), *Power–Knowledge: Selected Interviews and Other Writings*. New York: Pantheon.
Foucault, M. (1980b) 'Debat avec Michel Foucault', in M. Perrot (ed.), *L'impossible Prison: Recherche sur le systeme penitentiaire au XIX siecle*. Paris: Sevil.
Freidson, E. (1986) *Professional Powers: A Study of the Institutionalization of Formal Knowledge*. Chicago, IL: University of Chicago Press.
Friedland, M. (ed.) (1990) *Securing Compliance*. Toronto: University of Toronto Press.
Garland, D. (1985) *Punishment and Welfare*. Aldershot: Gower.
Garland, D. (1988) 'British criminology before 1935', in P. Rock (ed.), *A History of British Criminology*. Oxford: Oxford University Press.
Gibbons, D. (1979) *The Criminological Enterprise*. Englewood Cliffs, NJ: Prentice-Hall.
Giddens, A. (1987) *Social Theory and Modern Sociology*. Cambridge: Polity Press.
Giddens, A. (1990) *The Consequences of Modernity*. Cambridge: Polity Press.
Giddens, A. (1991) *Modernity and Self-Identity: Self and Society in the Late Modern Age*. Stanford, CA: Stanford University Press.
Giffen, J., Endicott, S. and Lambert, S. (1991) *Panic and Indifference: The Politics of Canada's Drug Laws*. Ottawa: Canadian Centre on Substance Abuse.
Gladstone, J., Ericson, R. and Shearing, C. (eds) (1991) *Criminology: A Reader's Guide*. Toronto: Centre of Criminology, University of Toronto.

Gordon, C. (1991) 'Governmental rationality', in G. Burchell, C. Gordon and P. Miller (eds), *The Foucault Effect: Studies in Governmentality*. Chicago, IL: University of Chicago Press.

Griffiths, C. and Verdun-Jones, S. (1989) *Canadian Criminal Justice*. Toronto: Butterworths.

Guignon, C. and Hylery, D. (1990) 'Biting the bullet: Rorty on private and public morality', in A. Malachowski (ed.), *Reading Rorty*. Cambridge, MA: Blackwell.

Gusfield, J. (1981) *The Culture of Public Problems*. Chicago,IL: University of Chicago Press.

Gusfield, J. (1989) 'Constructing the ownership of social problems: fun and profit in the welfare state', *Social Problems*, 36: 431–41.

Habermas, J. (1975) *Legitimation Crisis*. Boston, MA: Beacon.

Hagan, J. (1989) *Structural Criminology*. Cambridge: Polity Press.

Hall, S., Critcher, C., Jefferson, T., Clarke, J. and Roberts, B. (1978) *Policing the Crisis*. London: Macmillan.

Hunt, A. (1990) 'Criminology: what's in a name? a response to Clifford Shearing', *Canadian Journal of Criminology*, 32: 657–8.

Hutcheon, L. (1989) *A Poetics of Postmodernism: History, Theory, Fiction*. New York: Routledge.

Jones, T., MacLean, B. and Young, J. (1986) *The Islington Crime Survey*. Aldershot: Gower.

Kelling, G., Pate, A., Dieckman, D. and Brown, C. (1974) *The Kansas City Crime Preventive Patrol Experiment*. Washington, DC: The Police Foundation.

Kellough, G. (forthcoming) *The Abortion Controversy*. Toronto: University of Toronto Press.

Laclau, E. and Mouffe, C. (1985) *Hegemony and Socialist Strategy: Towards a Radical Democratic Politics*. Thetford: Thetford Press.

Lau, C. (1992) 'Social conflicts about the definition of risks: the role of science', in N. Stehr and R. Ericson (eds), *The Culture and Power of Knowledge*. Berlin and New York: de Gruyter.

Lea, J. and Young, J. (1984) *What is to be done about Law and Order*. London: Penguin.

Lipsitz, G. (1990) *Time Passages: Collective Memory and American Popular Culture*. Minneapolis: University of Minnesota Press.

Lowman, J., Menzies, R. and Palys, T. (eds) (1987) *Transcarceration: Essays in the Sociology of Social Control*. Aldershot: Gower.

Lyotard, J.-F. (1984) *The Postmodern Condition: A Report on Knowledge*. Minneapolis: University of Minnesota Press.

Lyotard, J.-F. (1989) 'Lessons in paganism', in A. Benjamin (ed.), *The Lyotard Reader*. Oxford: Blackwell.

Macdonnel, D. (1986) *Theories of Discourse*. Oxford: Blackwell.

McGaw, D. (1991) 'Governing metaphors: the war on drugs', *The American Journal of Semiotics*, 8: 53–74.

MacLean, B. and Milovanovic, D. (1991) 'On critical criminology', in B. MacLean and D. Milovanovic (eds), *New Directions in Critical Criminology*. Vancouver: The Collective Press.

Mandel, M. (1989) *The Charter of Rights and the Legalization of Politics in Canada*. Toronto: Wall and Thompson.

Marcus, G. (1986) 'Contemporary problems of ethnography in the modern world system', in J. Clifford and G. Marcus (eds), *Writing Culture: The Poetics and Politics of Ethnography*. Berkeley: University of California Press.

Mayo, D. and Hollander, R. (eds) (1991) *Acceptable Evidence: Science and Values in Risk Management*. New York: Oxford University Press.

Menzies, R. (1989) *Survival of the Sanest*. Toronto: University of Toronto Press.

Michalowski, R. (1991) 'Niggers, welfare scum, and homeless assholes: the problems of idealism, consciousness and context in Left Realism', in B. Maclean and D. Milovanovic (eds), *New Directions in Critical Criminology*. Vancouver: The Collective Press.

Nelson, B. (1984) *Making an Issue of Child Abuse*. Chicago, IL: University of Chicago Press.

Nelken, D. (1990) 'The truth about law's truth', European University Institute Working Paper. Florence, Italy: Law Department.

Nietzsche, F. (1968 [1889]) *Twilight of the Idols*. London: Penguin.

Nisbet, R. (1976) *Sociology as an Art Form*. Oxford: Oxford University Press.

O'Malley, P. (1991) 'Legal networks and domestic security', *Studies in Law, Politics and Society*, 11: 171–90.

O'Malley, P. (1992) 'Risk, power and crime prevention', *Economy and Society*, 21: 252–75.

Pearce, F. and Tombs, S. (1990) 'Ideology, hegemony and empiricism: compliance theories of regulation', *British Journal of Criminology*, 30(4): 423–43.

Posner, R. (1990) *Law as Literature*. Cambridge, MA: Harvard University Press.

Rabinow, P. (1977) *Reflections on Fieldwork in Morocco*. Berkeley: University of California Press.

Rabinow, P. (1986) 'Representations are social facts: modernity and postmodernity in anthropology', in J. Clifford and G. Marcus (eds), *Writing Culture: The Poetics and Politics of Ethnography*. Berkeley: University of California Press.

Reich, R. (1991) 'Secession of the successful', *New York Times Magazine*, 20 January.

Reichman, N. (1986) 'Managing crime risks: toward an insurance based model of social control', *Research in Law and Social Control*, 8: 151–72.

Reiss, A. (1989) 'The institutionalization of risk', *Law and Policy*, 11: 392–402.

Roach, K. (1991) 'The charter and the criminal process', in J. Gladstone, R. Ericson and C. Shearing (eds), *Criminology: A Reader's Guide*. Toronto: Centre of Criminology, University of Toronto.

Rock, P. (1986) *A View from the Shadows*. Oxford: Oxford University Press.

Rock, P. (1988) 'The present state of criminology in Britain', in P. Rock (ed.), *A History of British Criminology*. Oxford: Oxford University Press.

Rock, P. (1990) *Helping Victims of Crime*. Oxford: Oxford University Press.

Scheingold, S. (1990) 'The war on drugs in context: crisis politics and social control', paper to the Law and Society Association Meeting, Berkeley, CA, June.

Schlesinger, P., Tumber, H. and Murdock, G. (1991) 'The media politics of crime and criminal justice', *British Journal of Sociology*, 42: 397–420.

Schwartz, M. (1991) 'The future of critical criminology', in B. MacLean and D. Milovanovic (eds), *New Directions in Critical Criminology*. Vancouver: The Collective Press.

Sewell, W. (1992) 'A theory of structure: duality, agency and transformation', *American Journal of Sociology*. 98: 1–29.

Shearing, C. (1989) 'Decriminalizing criminology: reflections on the literal and tropological meaning of the term', *Canadian Journal of Criminology*, 31: 169–78.

Shearing, C. and Stenning, P. (1982) 'Snowflakes or good pinches – private security's contribution to modern policing', in R. Donelan (ed.), *The Maintenance of Order in Society*. Ottawa: Ministry of Supply and Services.

Shearing, C. and Stenning, P. (1983) 'Private security: implications for social control', *Social Problems*, 30: 493–506.

Sherman, L. (1992) 'Attacking crime: policing and crime control', in M. Tonry and N. Morris (eds), *Modern Policing*. Chicago, IL: University of Chicago Press.

Sherman, L., Gartin, P. and Buerger, M. (1989) 'Hot spots of predatory crime: routine activities and the criminology of place', *Criminology*, 27: 27–55.

Simon, J. (1987) 'The emergence of a risk society: insurance, law and the state', *Socialist Review*, 95: 61–89.

Simon, J. (1988) 'The ideological effects of actuarial practice', *Law and Society Review*, 22: 772–800.

Skogan, W. (1990) *Disorder and Decline*. New York: Free Press.

Smith, R. and Wynne, B. (eds) (1989) *Expert Evidence: Interpreting Science in Law*. London: Routledge.

South, N. (1988) *Policing for Profit: The Private Security Sector*. London: Sage.

Sparks, R. (1992) *Television and the Drama of Crime: Moral Tales and the Place of Crime in Public Life*. Buckingham: Open University Press.

Stenning, P. (ed.) (forthcoming) *Accountability in Criminal Justice*. Toronto: University of Toronto Press.

Stewart, S. (1991) *Crimes of Writing*. New York: Oxford University Press.

Stitt, B. and Giacopossi, D. (1992) 'Trends in the connectivity of theory and research in criminology', *The Criminologist*, 17(4): 1–5.

Taylor, I., Walton, P. and Young, J. (1973) *The New Criminology*. New York: Harper and Row.

Thomas, C. (1984) 'From the editor's desk', *Criminology*, 22: 467–71.

Valverde, M. (1990) 'The rhetoric of reform: tropes and the moral subject', *International Journal of the Sociology of Law*, 18: 61–73.

Valverde, M. (1991) *The Age of Light, Soap and Water: Moral Reform in English Canada*. Toronto: McClelland and Stewart.

Wagner-Pacifici, R. (1986) *The Moro Morality Play: Terrorism as Social Drama*. Chicago, IL: University of Chicago Press.

Weick, K. (1979) *The Social Psychology of Organizing*, 2nd edn. Reading, MA: Addison-Wesley.

White, H. (1984) *When Words Lose their Meaning*. Chicago, IL: University of Chicago Press.

Wilson, J. (1975) *Thinking About Crime*. New York: Basic Books.

Wilson, J. and Herrnstein, R. (1985) *Crime and Human Nature*. New York: Simon and Schuster.

Young, J. (1986) 'The failure of criminology: the need for radical realism', in R. Matthews and J. Young (eds), *Confronting Crime*. London: Sage.

Young, J. (1988a) *Realist Criminology*. London: Sage.

Young, J. (1988b) 'Risk of crime and fear of crime: a realist critique of survey based assumptions', in M. Maguire and J. Ponting (eds), *Victims of Crime: A New Deal*. Milton Keynes: Open University Press.

Zimring, F. and Hawkins, G. (1990) *The Scale of Imprisonment*. Chicago, IL: University of Chicago Press.

5

The Constitution of Constitutive Criminology: a Postmodern Approach to Criminological Theory

Stuart Henry and Dragan Milovanovic

Constitutive criminology is concerned with identifying the ways in which the interrelationships between human agents and their social world constitute crime, victims and control as realities. It is oriented to how we may deconstruct these realities and to how we may reconstruct less harmful alternatives. Simultaneously, it is concerned with how emergent socially constructed realities themselves constitute human agents with the implication that, if crime is to be replaced, this necessarily must involve a deconstruction and reconstruction of the human subject. It is towards a statement of the assumptions underlying the constitutive position that this chapter is directed.

In a recent review of the postmodernist contribution to legal theory Hunt (1990: 539) accurately describes the aspiration of the 'constitutive' version of postmodernism as being 'to grasp both discourse and practice . . . to hang on to the coexistence and mutual determination of practices and discourses, structure and agency'. Referring to some founding theoretical traces of 'constitutive theory' (Fitzpatrick, 1984; Giddens, 1984; Henry, 1987; Hunt, 1987; Harrington, 1988). Hunt says:

> Perhaps this project has not been sufficiently developed to merit the slightly grand description 'theory'. . . . This sense of 'theory' is not one of a complete or formal model as a condensation or concentration of reality; rather it is a sense of theory as a provisional metaphor, as a potentially useful way of thinking and saying something new. Such a view of theory makes no claims to Truth or truths . . . it involves a conception of theory without guarantees. (1990: 539)

He further argues that while there is much of value to the approach, 'the deeper problem remains of the negative face and . . . most visible face, of postmodernism' which stems from its basic nihilistic and relativistic tendencies concealed in the radical guise of deconstructionism (see for example Derrida's [1981] and Fish's [1982] 'antifoundationalist' positions).

In this chapter we shall move the constitutive project in criminology from its tentative and uncertain beginnings towards a clear and concise statement. Based on our theoretical explorations to date (Henry and Milovanovic, 1991; Milovanovic and Henry, 1991), we shall define the underlying assumptions in the context of the paradigmatic analytical framework developed by Young (1981) for 'thinking seriously about crime'. In laying out the framework we will consider five interrelated dimensions which together make up the theory. First we will discuss the view of human nature. The key issue here will be to describe our fundamental assumptions about the interconnectedness of human agency. Second, we will explain our view of social order; the vision we hold of society and the global context. Third, will be a discussion of constitutive assumptions about law and our definition of crime. Fourth, we will identify the dialectical causal model that this theory so far has implied. Fifth, will be a description of the criminal justice policy implications that follow from our approach, and within this context an outline of the system of administering justice that is logically consistent with these assumptions, together with our philosophy of intervention. This moves beyond the either/or dichotomy of individual punishment or rehabilitation/treatment towards the deconstruction of crime.

By employing this method we strive to demonstrate not only the specificity of the main assumptions of constitutive criminology but also suggest that postmodernist theory, at least in its constitutive form, is anything but pessimistic. Indeed, in contrast to Hunt and other recent critics (for example, Teubner, 1992), we believe constitutive theory offers an optimistic realism that resolves the dilemma of deconstruction through the promise of reconstruction.

Of vital importance to any vision of criminological theory is a consideration of the way human agents are perceived and the nature of the social structure in which they are seen as acting. We will thus begin by looking at the constitutive view of human nature and social order which, consistent with our position, cannot be treated separately.

Human nature and social order

We view humans as active agents producing their social world. This production is both continuous and continual, although not necessarily self-reflective. It is continuous with regard to the ongoing production and reproduction of existing social order. It is continual in that the world produced by human agency is only episodically perceived as the outcome of its own authorship. For the most part humans are what Matza (1969) referred to as 'pacified'. Because of what are encountered as overbearing conditions, these 'subjects' submit to the dictates of their circumstances. This amounts to a connivance in their own subordination to the agency of others.

Most humans are partially blind builders; intermittently aware that what they build is constructed by them, yet experientially subjected to the constructions they see in others. Typically, humans export their own agency to its product and to others with whom they interact. They see themselves more acted on than acting. So much is reification.

Some support for this position is evident in various classical commentaries that recognise both the freedom and constraint governing human lives. The issue is not one or the other, nor the time–space dualism of now one, then the other. Rather it is a duality of *both* freedom and constraint. Humans are intrinsically social beings who create the world in which they live, but not under conditions they have chosen for themselves: 'Rather on terms immediately existing, given and handed down to them' (Marx, 1852: 115). They are social agents, potentially open to development and change but only under the right structural conditions (Geras, 1983).

As a result, only rarely is the world perceived as open to transformation and change by those who experience it. Even then it is as subjects confronting the 'invitational edge', a bifurcation point where identities seem to change fundamentally. From this viewpoint, people's qualities are not envisioned as fixed but open to change through their relations with others. Such change is possible because of the potentials inhering in human qualities of reflexivity about oneself and sensitivity to others to whom we relate and with whom we can empathise.

Humans are also *both* individually self-interested and socially coopera-tive. Denial of either one of these apparently opposed dimensions is itself an actively sustained ideological construction with real and often negative consequences for self and others. Humans are interconnected agents rather than entirely free 'individuals'. Constructing the delusion of personal freedom can spur the action that sustains and symbolises that claim through physical and momentary displays of difference, individuality, uniqueness, art, and style. Changing jobs and neighbourhoods, leaving lovers and old lives to make new ones, taking a step beyond the invitational edge, often provides a sense of personal control, a security from the precariousness of human existence that comforts restless souls. Regardless of its rationality and emotion, it is nothing if not display.

The substance of being human must entail what preceded us as biography, what looms ahead as prospect, caught in the contingent moment of the here and now. People are process. Humans are social projects in their own making. No amount of delusionary display can sever the fundamental intersubjectivity of the human being. Without the discursive medium constructed with others through which people converse with themselves, without their unique turn of our cultural conglomerate of meaning, they would cease to exist. Connectivity to others is a partial life blood that constitutes the self; but it is as separate entities, that the intersubjective discursive medium is invoked, through *it* that meaning is created and interpreted, and in terms of it that structures are reproduced. Without the individual human agent there would be no intersubjectivity, no society. In short, freedom and constraint, agency and subject are mutually implying, co-present themes in the constitution of human beings. Human agency is connected to the structures that it makes, as are human agents to each other.

Human agents can be envisioned as unique, with a multiplicity of needs, drives, desires, and abilities, *and* as intersubjectively constituted. Any subsuming of these qualities to some 'equal' measure must be read as an imposition, a reification by submission to macro-constituted forms of capital logic, an idealisation of relations constitutive of the capitalistic mode of production which exaggerates the importance of vertical power hierarchy.

Just as agents make structure so the structure makes agents through discourse. A central issue in constitutive criminology's vision of human nature is the role of human agents' discursive practices. This is not to reify human subjects by giving priority to their discourse, as though this somehow operated independently of those using it. Rather it is to stress again the interwovenness of agency-discourse-structure.

The use of particular ways of talking, as in Cohen's (1985) 'control talk', Manning's (1988) 'organisational talk', or Milovanovic's (1986; 1988; 1992a) and Thomas' (1988) 'law talk', both reflects, continuously constitutes and reconstitutes narratives that provide the continuity to reproduce social structures of crime and its control, in time and space. As Knorr-Cetina and Cicourel (1981) have argued, human agents transform events that they see or experience as micro-events into summary representations, or mind patterns, by relying on routine practices through which they convince themselves of having achieved the appropriate representation of those events; these are then objectified in coherent narrative constructions. Narrative constructions are essentially composed of signifiers (the most manifest form being words that are routinely invested with value) coordinated by the semiotic axes of paradigm (that is, the repository of available signifiers with delineated meanings) and syntagm (that is, the codes governing the correct placement of signifiers in utterances or sentences in order to make sense).

In the constitutive criminological vision, social structures are the categories of classification of the events that they allegedly represent. As such they are strengthened by routine construction in everyday life and by activity organised in relation to them, as though they were concrete entities. The principal means through which social structures are constituted is language use and the discursive practice of making conceptual distinctions through the play of differences (Derrida, 1973, 1981; Lacan, 1977). At the macro, societal level, in Western industrial society, capital logic and the integrally related processes of rationalisation provide the medium through which people constitute categories that capture essential relations. Not the least are rhetorical structures, figurative expressions, metaphors, cliches, and verbal mannerisms that are used as primary signifiers of meaning.

At the levels of intersubjective communication, organisational processing, and capital logic, discursive practices are given anchorings, a 'pinning down' (Lacan, 1977; Manning, 1988; Milovanovic, 1992a; 1992b). In other words, humans use discursive practices to produce texts (narrative constructions), imaginary constructions, that anchor signifiers to particular signifieds, producing a particular image claiming to be the reality. These texts become the semiotic coordinates of action, which agents recursively use, and in so doing, provide a reconstruction of the original form. Consider, for example, Freire's (1985) literacy campaigns where what must be first confronted is the alien texts (constituted by value-laden signifiers and particular paradigmatic and syntagmatic codes) imposed upon indigenous peoples by colonisers.

Once social structures are constituted as summary representations, their ongoing existence depends upon their continued and often unwitting reconstruction in everyday discourse, a discourse replete with tacit understandings whose basis lies outside the realm of intrinsic intersubjective communication and intersubjectively established meaning. Core meaning constructs are typically pre-constructed elsewhere as part of our common 'stock of knowledge' (Schutz, 1967; Manning, 1988). Agents in organisational settings, for example, tend to reduce feedback which represents contaminating and disruptive 'noise' and in the process infuse existent explanatory discursive categories and texts with energy and sustenance.

In order to sustain abstractly constructed distinctions, these are made applicable to events, in spite of the contradictory evidence that comes from renewed micro-interaction. Contradictory evidence and potential disruptions are engendered by the internal transfer of messages, a basis of instability that is best negotiated by framing it into already understood narrative constructs that 'beg' us to make old reaffirming sense of the new nonsense (Goffman, 1974, 1981; Manning, 1988; Thomas, 1988).

Organising action to defend representations – framed and objectified in narrative texts – is one of the principal means of both defending and conferring object-like reality upon them, providing life, form, energy, sustenance and a high degree of permanence. As we shall see below this is how we see what criminal justice presently does (though not what we think it should do) through prevailing current constructions.

Capital logic is a ubiquitous rationalising form; the more investment that is made in it, the more difficult it is to sustain that which it is not. This is not to imply conspiracy but to specify formal function, for while defending the wider totality, agents and agencies also compete to defend their own integrity within the framework of capital logic (Jessop, 1982). Criminal justice practitioners, then, are defenders of prevalent constructions as well as of their own current identities tied to and fed by the agencies that they staff.

Law and normative orders

Most traditional sociological theories of law are narrowly defined. They regard law as an object, separate from, produced by, and subject to, the actions of external social forces, whether these be society, classes, groups, agencies etc. (Griffiths, 1979). In contrast, the perspective we take on law is closer to that of legal pluralism (Gierke, 1900; Ross, 1901; Ehrlich, 1913; Gurvitch, 1947) than to any other position. However, it is a postmodern constitutive version of recent critical pluralist theory (Fitzpatrick, 1984; Santos 1985, 1987; Henry, 1987; Hunt, 1987; Merry, 1988; O'Malley, 1988).

Constitutive theory is based on the idea that law is, in part, social relations and social relations are, in part, law (Fitzpatrick, 1983a, 1983b, 1984). It is the movement and tension whereby these are socially constituted, 'the way "society" is produced *within* "law"' (Nelken, 1986: 325), rather than how they interact, that is crucial to understanding the law–society interface. Thus, instead of assuming that state law is the hub of social control whose spokes radiate as unidirectional pathways of influence to other social and normative orders, constitutive theory also directs our attention to the reverse process: forms and mechanisms whereby legal-relations are penetrated by extra-legal social relations. A constitutive approach examines both the presence and the source of other social forms, 'which are not simply variant forms of legal reasoning but derive their significance and their legitimating capacity from the forms of social relations from which they originate' (Hunt, 1987: 18).

It is not, then, just that law is created by classes or interest groups to maintain or increase their power. Rather, some of the relations of these groups, particularly their rules and procedures are, and indeed become, the relations of law. This suggests that 'any site of social relations is likely to be traversed by a variety of state and non-state legal networks' and that 'what constitutes "the law" in any specific context will depend upon which legal networks (or more precisely which parts of which networks) intersect in that context, how these orders are mobilized, and how they interact' (O'Malley, 1988: 4–5).

Thus, instead of treating law as an autonomous field of enquiry linked only by external relations to the rest of society, or assuming 'law' and 'society' are concrete entities that 'influence' or 'affect' each other, the constitutive approach takes law as its subject of enquiry but pursues it by exploring the interrelations 'between legal relations and other forms of social relations' (Hunt, 1987: 16; Nelken, 1986: 324). More accurately, then, we may speak of interpenetration rather than interaction or cause and effect.

One of the first to recognise the mutuality between state law and non-state forms was Moore (1973). She argued that law is not a fixed autonomous entity but a 'semi-autonomous field' which, while having rule-making and enforcement capacity, is also 'vulnerable to rules and decisions and other forces emanating from the larger world by which it is surrounded'. She argues that law is 'set in a larger social matrix which can and does affect and invade it' (Moore, 1973: 720).

Considering this interrelationship some draw on Foucault's (1977) demonstration that the modern era has seen state control dispersed into the social fabric to become part of a hidden totality of surveillance. Important too, is Foucault's (1979) 'rule of double conditioning' in which power is exercised, not only from the top, but through distinct, localised machinery, which itself is only effective as part of a general overarching strategy of power. At the same time as the general strategy is distinct it is also, in turn, dependent for its effectiveness on local strategies. Deleuze and Guattari (1987) have also indicated that we can conceptualise power relations as beginning with political economy, following a path by which recipients make use of the essential relational terms, and ending by subjects interjecting the essential hierarchical forms as constitutive of psychic economy. We add, however, that identifying any particular moment along this path would indicate not simply a passive receiving subject, but an agent who actively incorporates elements from 'above' within existing narrative constructions in producing coherent texts.

Fitzpatrick (1984), much influenced by Foucault, has developed the idea of 'integral plurality'. He says that the reason state law is, in part, shaped by the plurality of other social forms, while these forms are simultaneously being shaped by it, is because 'elements of law *are* elements of other forms and *vice versa*' (Fitzpatrick, 1984: 122). While law incorporates other forms, transforming them into its own image and likeness, the process is not unilateral but mutual, such that 'law in turn supports the other forms but becomes in the process, part of the other forms' (Fitzpatrick, 1984: 122). As such, 'state law is integrally constituted in relation to a plurality of other social forms' and 'depends on social forms that tend to undermine it' (Fitzpatrick, 1984: 118). His theory of integral plurality is a considerable advance, both over earlier legal pluralism, and over critical legal theory, for it demonstrates that there is not so much a unilinear relationship with other social forms but rather that 'law is the unsettled product of relations with a plurality of other social forms. As such, law's identity is constantly and inherently subject to challenge and change' (Fitzpatrick, 1984: 138). Fitzpatrick's fundamental insight is to recognise that state law obtains some of its identity from its interrelationship with non-state forms and vice versa; that without this connection each would be constitutively different. He argues elsewhere (Fitzpatrick, 1988) that the interrelations between state law and non-state normative orders forms new entities, as a common discourse and set of practices is worked out between participating arenas of power. This is particularly evident in the context where law is being synthesised from other existing sets of rules and norms. Fitzpatrick says that in the process of synopsis of existing rules and practices the participating networks retain their own relative autonomy, but 'integrating homologies' (corresponding structures) are formed which merge selected elements of the component networks into an emergent whole that becomes new law. What we can draw from the theorising of Fitzpatrick, Foucault (1977, 1979) and others such as Deleuze and Guattari (1987), is that unilateral top-down discursive constructions in law, as stipulated by some instrumental Marxists, distracts us from addressing the complexities involved.

O'Malley, similarly, describes such attempts at legal synthesis as 'synoptic projects' which

> disaggregate the elements of the participating powers, ignoring, suppressing or denying incompatible and irreverent elements, combining and translating useful elements into the new formation. Although the component powers are changed by this process, they do not cease to have their own distinct and quite possibly hostile existence. (1988: 6)

O'Malley claims that these 'synoptic projects' are most likely to occur where changing conditions, such as the emergence of obstacles to the continued effectiveness of existing arrangements, make their continued operation problematic. In other words, agents more often imperceptively confront bifurcation points, where the problematic nature is of such magnitude that existent and otherwise explanatory narrative constructions fail to provide convincing resolutions. This does not mean, however, that the newly created narratives will necessarily become objectively more correct; only that they will now become discursive coordinates for further social action. For Teubner (1992) law is the outcome of a process of 'interdiscursivity' where intra-organisational legal discourse 'productively misunderstands', and misreads (through their rereading, reinterpreting, reconstructing and reobservation) 'organizational self-production as norm production and thus invents a new and rich "source" of law' (Teubner, 1992: 1453–4). A similar misreading occurs, says Teubner, when the organisation reincorporates legal rules developed and refined in disciplinary proceedings and makes use of them to restructure its organisational decision making.

In summary, recent developments in constitutive legal pluralism take a postmodernist stance and argue that law is mutually constituted through social relations and discursive misreading. The discursive processes of non-state normative orders with which state law is interrelated and interwoven provides a significant context of synoptic projects wherein old power is moulded into new forms. Although constructively critical of this new legal pluralism from the perspective of legal autopoiesis, Teubner (1992: 1443) accurately observes that the position assumes that the relations between the legal and the social are characterised by 'discursive inter-wovenness', 'are highly ambiguous, almost paradoxical: separate but intertwined, closed but open'. He argues that this new legal pluralism is 'no longer defined as a set of conflicting social norms in a given social field, but as a multiplicity of diverse communicative processes that observe social action under the binary code of legal/illegal' (Teubner, 1992: 1451). However, nowhere does Teubner indicate the potentials for a possible replacement discourse out of which alternative narrative construction could take place. Thus, at best, a praxis not a transpraxis is partially explained.

A constitutive concept of law differs from the liberal–legal conception in that law is understood as having the power to frame politics and legal processes – doctrine and institutions shape political possibilities (Gordon, 1984; Brigham and Harrington, 1989). The Western notion of the 'juridic subject', for example, can only be understood in its inherent dualistic relation of being both a constitutive element and a recursive outcome of the practice of capital logic. As Henry (1983) argues, with such an approach we begin to see the possibility of transcending the view that law is either a product of structure or the outcome of interaction. We begin to see how informal social control is not so much an alternative form of law but a necessary part of the ideological process whereby the crystallised, formal-ised, object-like qualities of law are created and sustained in an ongoing manner, albeit within a different arena. Thus constitutive criminology directs our attention to the way law, crime and criminal justice are conceptualised and implied as though they are objective realities having real consequences, consequences we attribute to their claim, but that they do not possess in any intrinsic sense.

Institutions of law seen in this way, then, are the organised acting out of discursively produced 'control thoughts', whose very action reflects on the reality of that which they are organised to defend. Brigham's (1987) research on social movements demonstrates how these are 'constituted in legal terms when they see the world in those terms and organize themselves accordingly. . . . Legal forms are evident in the language, purposes, and strategies of movement activity as practice' (Brigham, 1987: 306).

The definition of crime

If law is constituted through its mutual relations with other social orders, what does this imply where it is used to define what counts as 'crime'? In the traditionally simple positive definition, crime is what the state defines as punishable behaviour. But such a statement misses much of what it means to define an act as a crime. Crime is not just what is defined in the written laws or rules, nor is it merely judicial declarations accumulated as precedent. This is mere tautology. To say this is to say nothing of how particular instances of behaviour are interpreted. It is to say nothing of how instances of meaningful action are transformed from the meaning they have for the participants to the meaning they are given by the legal functionaries who make the behaviour stand for, exemplify, or be another case of this or that type of offence. It is to say nothing of what actors and agencies are involved in the definition of whatever took place to make it into crime. It is to say nothing of what dimensions had to be exaggerated and what had to be omitted or discounted for the instance to be made to fit the general case. Finally, it says nothing of the work done by alleged perpetrators and apparent victims (themselves categories in the making of crime) for these people to declare a 'crime' had occurred. The legalistic definition of crime merely provides closure where robust debate must begin. Legal syllogistic reasoning, a linear logic, for example, can only be effective where a body of assumed major premises remain non-problematic. So what is a constitutive definition of crime?

Crime is a socially constructed category. It is a categorisation of the diversity of human conflicts and transgressions into a single category 'crime', as though these were somehow all the same. It is a melting of differences reflecting the multitude of variously motivated acts of personal injury into a single entity 'violent crime' or 'sub-type of violent crime'. It is the celebration of the homogeneous.

But does this mean the behaviour and the experience in the interaction that subsequently resulted in this classificatory and translation work is unreal, fictional, imagined? Of course not. Only some radical realists seem to imagine that postmodernist criminology adheres to this view. Let us be very clear. What is taken to be crime involves pain and conflict and an instance of harm. People involved in the relations that are taken to be 'crimes' are for the moment in relations of inequality. Thus crime, as we define it here, is the expression of some people's energy to make a difference over others and is the exclusion of those others who in the instant are rendered powerless. Crimes are nothing less than moments in the expression of power such that those who are subjected to these expressions are denied their own contribution to the encounter and often to future encounters. Crime then is the power to deny others. It is the ultimate form of reification in which those subject to the power of another suffer the pain of being denied their own humanity, the power to make a difference. The victim of crime is thus rendered a non-person, a non-human. The victim is nothing. That is the harm of crime. That is its pain. Crime is the expression of power, the master of power and the handmaiden of pain.

So what of law and crime? Law does not include most of the behaviours that fit our definition of crime. Law is a very partial list of harms. An adequate listing of law to capture the behaviour that we define as crime would have to start from the contexts of pain resulting from such denials of others. It would thus have to include much of what currently stands for business practices, governmental policies, hierarchical social relations, and a lot of what occurs in family life, since these arenas of power are premised upon the inequality that liberates the expression of the power to create pain.

The significance of the interconnectedness of law with other social forms is that law will inevitably contain the self-same expressions of power that create the crime that is subsequently omitted from its definition. Celebrating, uncritically, the existing definition of crime and the rule-of-law ethic, then, can further constitute and reconstitute existing power relations, suffering and pain in more insidious forms such as when the more powerful benefit from otherwise perceived 'free' contractual relations. This is not the same, for example, as saying corporate interests shape the law so that they are immune from prosecution and thereby free to create harm. Rather it is saying that corporations, as expressors of power, like the state or the family, will inevitably constitute law to reflect the legitimacy of their power and the illegitimacy of the power of others. This is why, from our perspective, much of what counts as business, governmental policy, hierarchical social relations, family and the state is crime. It is why homelessness can be a crime (Barak, 1991b) and why neglect of health and safety regulations are crimes, why sexual harassment and domestic violence (whether in emotional torment or physical beating from either spouse to the other) are crimes. It is especially why child abuse is a crime and it is why suicide may sometimes be, yet also why doctor-assisted suicide is most always not a crime. Indeed, it is why emotional terror by employers over employees through at-will employment should be a crime. Finally, it is why the actions of agencies of government are also crime. This is not in the sense of specific incidents such as police brutality (as in the case of Rodney King and several similar beatings of those held in custody by government agencies on a global scale) but rather in the sense of the pervasive crimes of domination that Bourdieu (1977: 192) describes as 'symbolic violence'. This is a form of domination which is exerted through the very medium in which it is disguised wherein it is the 'gentle, invisible form of violence, which is never recognized as such, and is not so much undergone as chosen, the violence of credit, confidence, obligation, personal loyalty, hospitality, gifts, gratitude, piety' (Bourdieu, 1977: 192). But we have forgotten this dimension of domination and neglected to see how this power play can itself be crime.

Again, let us be very clear. The activity of many of those in the institutions in Western industrial society is premised on the exercise of power over others and the witting or unwitting denial of others' right to make a difference. The activity of those who deliver such power is crime. It is crime because it harms.

Crime then must be redefined in terms of the power to create harm (pain) in any context, and law can only be reconstituted (because of its inter-relations with other social orders) by reconstituting the relations of other social forms with which it is interrelated. Thus our position on law and the nature and definition of crime suggests that it is not only through changing laws that social forms can change to reduce harm but that changing social forms is necessary so that harm is not carried under the guise of law, in the expression of power over others. (Herein lies our opposition to the state use of capital punishment and the existing forms of criminal justice.)

In short, premised upon our view of law and crime, law is not just a definer of crime, it is also the maker of crime. This is because it conceals some people's harms by reflecting power relations, and it manifests crime through its own exercise of power over others, especially those whose own activities have not been to deny others their own expression, such as in the case of consensual 'crimes', or 'crimes without victims' (Schur, 1965).

The causes of crime

Constitutive criminology rejects traditional approaches to criminological theory that reduce crime to an outcome of micro causes or macro contexts. Our position calls for an abandoning of the futile search for causes of crime since this activity simply elaborates the distinctions that maintain crime as a separate reality, while failing to address how it is that crime is a part of society. Without acknowledging its integral nature no analysis of cause can lay an adequate foundation for effective criminal justice policy. From our perspective crime is not so much caused as it is constructed through human processes of which it is one. Crime is the ongoing, recursively produced outcome of numerous different contexts of meaningful interaction, only some of which fit our definition of crime as the exercise of the power to deny others. The model of causality that best captures our notion of how crime is constituted is that of dialectics. We take this to mean co-determination and mutual interrelation.

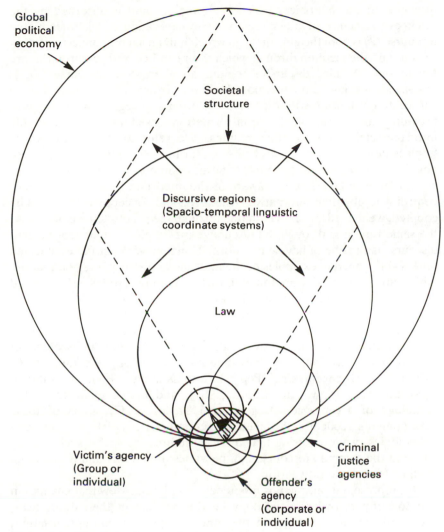

Figure 5.1   *The discursive constitution of crime*

Co-determination can be represented as several overlapping spheres (as in a Venn diagram) that illustrate how the constitutive social fields or forms are related to each other (see Figure 5.1). Each of the principal component agencies (offenders, victims, criminal justice, law, society and discursive regions) exist partly as separate and partly as common social constructions. We refer to discursive regions in the plural since a number of relatively autonomous and stable regions exist, within which acceptable narrative constructions may take place. Also it may be important here to reflect on the differences between discourse.

It is apparent to us that regions of social structure whose agents generate self-referential discourse (1), might be distinguished from the generation of discourse at the interstices which itself merges and is absorbed by the discursive structure of other regions. The generation of such negotiated discourse (2) is both the glue through which human agents connect different regions and the medium through which their conflicts and compromises are fought out. A third discursive region, an alternative discourse (3), is envisaged, having a quality not dissimilar from (1) except that it is constituted in tension with the prevalent discursive regions with a view to providing an alternative for transformation based upon its inevitable interconnectedness with other regions. We refer to this alternative as 'replacement discourse' as we shall see later in the chapter. While it is not possible for replacement discourse to be autonomous, it is possible for those generating it to be reflexively aware of the importance of the dialectics of control whereby their alternative structuring and conceptualisation can be coopted, weakened and contaminated through the negotiated region (2). At the same time it is through the discursive interstices (2) that replacement discourse is capable of having transformational power over the established orders (1). Concrete examples of the alternative discursive region that are critical and self-reflexive are found in various feminist groups, self-help and mutual aid groups and in cooperative and certain other collectively oriented gatherings and range to the less consciously aware alternatives as found, for example, in hidden economies. Critically aware replacement discourse is also reflected in the more overt attempts to develop a discourse of transformation as found in 'newsmaking criminology' (Barak, 1988), 'criminology as peacemaking' (Pepinsky and Quinney, 1991), 'oppositional legal discourse' (Selva and Bohm, 1987), and in the emergence of a 'sociology of acceptance' (Bogdan and Taylor, 1987). Each of these developments recognise the need to generate alternative concepts and cosmologies, while realising that there is minimal room for such activity owing to the common discourse that pervades the totality and is the initial medium for any alterative form.

This representation, then, is intended to depict our view that changes in one constitutive order, which may be the product of their differences, necessarily produce changes in the other. Given this conceptualisation, changes occur, not because these various components direct the other, nor because they interact with the other but because some of what constitutes each *is* the other, just as some of the other is constituted by each. Nor is the extent of co-determination fixed, but is an ever-changing socially constructed dynamic wherein each integral element is sometimes constructed as more corresponding with (represented in our diagram as more overlapping) and sometimes as more divergent from other constitutive elements.

Crime, as we define it, is the ongoing and emerging outcome of such a dialectical process. It is a process that enables some people to sometimes believe it is possible, and often even acceptable, to act on the differences that they create, in such a way as to deny others the freedom to make their own differences. It includes symbolic violence, the violence of language, that maintains a culture of silence among those denied a stable discourse out of which their pain and suffering can be articulated (see also Freire, 1985). In short, an analysis of the cause of crime is not a matter of factors but a matter of the dialectics of power and control.

Power implies creation and denial; the ability and the will to force others to comply. The exercise of power over others in such a way that causes them pain, loss and deprivation is not only an individual choice or a biological trait, it is also a socially and culturally sanctioned and celebrated feature of institutions, economy and polity in Western industrial society (as well as in many other societies) and as these are interrelated in the global political economy. In order to understand how some individuals conceive of and accumulate the skills necessary to exercise power over others it is necessary to examine how both the global order and within that, particular societies, are constituted in such a way as to celebrate inequalities (that is, differences of power). It is necessary to examine how institutions and governments support ideological practices that result in the delusion that anyone is somehow separate from, different from and unconnected to, others in the national and global context. It is necessary to explore the state and institutional processes that bolster some individuals and groups to accumulate the power to cause pain, whether through cultural hegemony, organisational strategy or personal will. We need to understand how, while exercising their own power that denies others, these institutional processes reward the power to cause pain and how conceptual and discursive practices enable this process to become pervasive, all corrupting and undermining of any that seek to counter it. Crime, then, is 'caused' when people lose sight, through institutional and other processes, of the humanity and integrity of those with whom they relate and who their actions and interactions affect.

Crime, then, is not caused by things but by processes. These are dialectical processes that episodically allow people to believe that they are somehow free from their relations with others. These are processes that allow people to believe that they can be independent, individuals in so far as that means insulated from others. They are processes in which others are allowed to be known only through the ultimate denial of person, the stereotypical categories of classification and summary.

Perhaps an illustration of our approach to the 'causes of crime' is in order. Let us take the example of middle managers and corporate crime (Clinard, 1983) to illustrate the case for dialectics of human process wherein crime is the power to deny others. Middle managers blame top management for corporate crime. They accuse top managers of setting 'the ethical tone', 'the pattern', 'the standards', 'an example', for it was they who 'gave the orders' to the 'troops below'. Managers accuse their superiors of knowing about corporate crime and of putting undue pressure on them to cut costs and corners in order to maximise profits. As one of Clinard's (1983) managers laments, 'You start out of college with high ideals and due to pressures these ideals deteriorate during one's corporate experience. Middle management violates their ethics mainly to get the job done' (see also Vandivier, 1972). This discursive practice of 'pointing the finger' of corporate responsibility at those above is revealed in its most dangerous form when structured by state, institutional and personal interests. For example, while middle managers are generally in favour of reporting serious worker safety violations to control agencies, they reject the idea of reporting price fixing, serious illegal rebates and kickbacks and illegal payments to foreign officials (Clinard, 1983). The reason given for this is a mixture of corporate loyalty and self-preservation within a power hierarchy. Many, for example, take the view that such matters were 'not their business': 'price fixing is none of middle management's damn business. If there is a general in charge you do not blow the whistle on him.' Thus, as another of Clinard's respondents declared: 'I'm not running the corporation. I am not the CEO. I am in middle management and price fixing is not my business.' The question of another was 'Am I God that I should go to the government on a top management price-fixing agreement and sacrifice myself?' 'None of my business', 'Not my responsibility' and for the sole manager who believed that he owed a greater loyalty to his fellow human species than to the corporation the response was: 'He should find another corporation more compatible with his own values.' The point should be clear. Crime is contrived by the discursive construction of differences that allow people, here middle managers, the delusion that they are unconnected to those with whom they interrelate, and are divorced from their own species.

We concur with Box (1983) when he argues that 'Any discussion of crime must be cognizant of the fact that serious adverse consequences can and often do follow from being indifferent to the outcome of one's actions or inactions' and that 'corporate crime should be conceptualized so as to include omission as well as the more obvious acts of commission' (Box, 1983: 20–1). From this we can infer that it is not only individuals that are 'guilty' but the process through which it is possible to isolate oneself, and the institutional support for such processes that reflects the wider societal power hierarchy.

By this measure the cause of corporate crime is little different from the cause of state crime (see Barak, 1991a; Henry, 1991). The process resulting in the harms of corporations can be compared with that of Lieutenant William L. Calley whose 'middle management' role in the 1968 massacre in the Vietnamese village of My Lai of old men, women and babies, reflects much the same contextual process of pressure, obedience to authority and self-preservation in the structural context of a rigid power hierarchy and the use of discursive practices to deny the human agency of the other. Calley explains:

> I wasn't taught at OCS to use common sense. I was taught, 'Do this! Do this like this!' . . . I went to school in the 1950's remember and it was drilled into us from grammar school on, '*Ain't is bad, aren't is good, communism's bad, democracy's good. One and one's two,* etcetera,' until . . . we just didn't think about it . . . I was a run-of-the-mill average guy . . . I always said *the people in Washington are smarter than me.* If intelligent people told me, 'Communism's bad. It's going to engulf us, to take us in,' I believed them . . . Personally I didn't kill any Vietnamese that day. I mean, personally. I represented the United States of America. My country . . . (Captain) Medina was right behind me and pulling my string. And the colonel his? I passed by PFC Meadlo. He still had the Vietnamese there. I didn't even stop. I said,

'Damn it! You said *I know what to do with these goddam people*. Get rid of 'em.' I meant – hell, I didn't know. I didn't think this out. I meant, 'Get rid of 'em.' I meant, 'Go wave a magic wand. And say "Disappear"'. I meant 'Waste them', but I didn't think of what *that* meant. If it meant to Meadlo, 'Kill them' I must admit it. I had that meaning. I had those orders: 'Get in the damn position'. A hundred meters ahead, and the Vietnamese were all in the goddamn way. I wasn't playing games here! I said to Meadlo, 'Get them on the other side of the ditch. Or get rid of 'em!' (Calley, 1974: 341–7, original emphasis)

Similarly, Clinard's managers represent their corporations taking orders from top management, under pressure to reach goals, to cut corners while preserving their own threatened existence. What 'causes' the crime in any of these cases is the structure, ideology and invocation of discursive practices that divides human relations into categories, that divides responsibility for others and to others into hierarchy and authority relations. Such a process is the most lethal devised by man. At once it both commands action towards goals, themselves seemingly harmless and limits a person's responsibility to others, now classified as one or other lesser, disposable category, summarised as 'not my business'. The German atrocities against the Jews, the CIA's activities in attempting and succeeding in murdering 'undesirable' members of foreign governments, the McCarthy attacks on free speech, the governmental attacks against the unionisation movement in the early part of this century, the American My Lai massacre, from Watergate, to Iran-Contra, from car hijacking to serial murder, to the emerging open forms of 'ethnic intimidation crimes', and from drug dealing to domestic violence, all are 'caused' through the dialectical discursive process that allows individuals to fuse observations of difference with evaluations of worth, structured by a power hierarchy that manifests in the denial of others as human beings. Were this not so, were people imbued with a sense of connectedness to others and to life, were the silence on 'individual freedom' rather than intersubjectivity, there would be considerably less likelihood of the power play that is crime. This leads us then to the appropriate criminal justice policy for such a constitutive view of crime.

Criminal justice policy and practice

It might be appropriate to first clarify what we mean by criminal justice policy since this idea is prone to numerous and varied interpretations. Policy refers to a course of action deliberately adopted or intended but there is some ambiguity (Harrison, 1964: 509). With *criminal justice* 'policy' the term may indicate the existence of a considered intention, plan or programme but it is often used to refer to a course of action where a planned programme does not exist, but rather describes what practitioners of criminal justice do or did. Further it is used to refer to a series of policies rather than one policy. We shall first describe what we believe existing criminal justice policy does in contributing to the constitution of crime and go on to state what we believe it should do consistent with our constitutive theoretical approach.

Criminal justice policy as it is currently constructed involves the generation of an ideology supported by a series of sometimes implemented
strategies that ostensibly are designed to 'remove' the behaviour allegedly
represented by the category 'crime' (failing to recognise the dialectic of
control wherein attempts to oppose add energy and vitality to that which is
opposed, and thereby constitute it; see Henry and Milovanovic, 1991).
These strategies are episodically implemented by members of a hierarchi-
cally divided power structure (government), through its varied semi-
autonomous agencies that we may refer to as control forms or control
institutions. From the perspective of constitutive criminology, control
institutions are the relations among human agents, acting to police the
conceptual distinctions among discursively constructed social structures.
Such policing of distinctions is a process mediated by the availability
(through intersubjective relations) of a sedimented, differentiated symbolic
system, a repository of value-laden, politically anchored signs. Once
constituted these relations, expressed in symbolic form, themselves become
structures and, as agencies and institutions, have relative autonomy. In turn,
they too are policed by further 'private' or internal relations of control.
Thus, signifying chains, narrative constructions, objectified bits and pieces
of everyday activity float within specific discourses. Within these discourses
distinctive, discursive subject-positions exist that structure what can be
framed, thought and said. Assuming these positions and appropriating
semiotic forms within particular discursive regions allows coherent narrative
constructions. Tacit understanding (Manning, 1988) is rooted in these
subterranean semiotic systems that continuously receive support through
their use.

Seen in this way, then, criminal justice policy is the ideology and the plan
for the organised acting out of discursively produced 'control thoughts',
whose very action reflects on the reality of that which they are organised to
defend. Control institutions are rooted in control discourse and in their own
parent social structures (see Figure 5.1) and cannot be divorced from them,
but nor can the structures exist without their control forms since each implies
the other as we saw earlier.

But as we also describe above, criminal justice policy and practice is not
only crime over others (through its expression of the power to deny others),
it also partially constitutes the very crime with which it is interrelated. The
ideology and practice of criminal justice is some of what crime is, as when
offenders use the criminal justice system as a status conferring institution,
through which they can 'rise' with increasing prestige among peers, or in
providing a justification for any personally felt or attributed inadequacies, or
as psychic mechanisms of release, a form of pacification where the agent
surrenders him or herself to the dictates of circumstance. The criminal
justice system is also coopted as a resource and utilised principally as an
educational and training ground for the relations of power by those who
subsequently refine and reproduce offending behaviour.

The duality of criminal justice policy and practice as constitutive of crime can further be illustrated through critical discussions on the notion of 'fighting crime' and most recently 'fighting the war on drugs' (Johns, 1992). In a microcosmic form, undercover work of policing in the 1980s, as those like Gary Marx (1988) and Bob Weiss (1987) have so poignantly documented, has produced the new 'maximum-security society'. Here, there is an increasing emphasis by control agents on developing dossiers in computerised form; an increasing use of predictive and actuarial instruments that focus on producing predictive statements about persons in particular created categories; and an obsession to find the 'predisposed' criminal which has led to an extreme manipulation of the environment to induce the very criminality which is the controller's own creation. It is concluded that the resultant new transparent society has seen the erosion of traditional notions of privacy such that even the citizenry has been recruited to monitor others as well as themselves for deviance or deviance proclivities (Marx, 1988; Einstadter and Henry, 1991). At the same time, however, the constitutive nature of the dialectic of control is as apparent in its oppositional form. Indeed, it is ironic that in seeking to defend people against control agent invasion of their lives, critical criminologists have acceded to support the ideological protection of privacy while being silent on the theft of that which was traditionally held in common. Protecting privacy is nothing less than ideological legitimisation for the theft of the common (Einstadter and Henry, 1991; Einstadter, 1992).

These criminal justice practices lead to a high premium on collecting, filtering, categorising and disseminating increasingly complex information framed in coherent narrative constructions (Jackson, 1988; Manning, 1988; Thomas, 1988). The process of constructing meaning intersubjectively is abdicated or usurped by agents of organisations who use these constructions as the criteria by which to further survey, control and act on subjects, particularly those in predicted high risk categories in the existing social arrangements. Simultaneously, they are given inadvertent ideological support through oppositional attacks on the automation of social control instruments. These are attacks by critical theorists and reformers alike, who take as given, many of the concepts, presuppositions, or working hypotheses of these same agents of control, in the end, reproducing the recursive machine.

The observation that power begets crime and is manifest (among other arenas of 'civil' society) as criminal justice policy, occurs because institutions of social control are framed within the context of recursively constructed symbolic systems. Organisational agents, including control agents, must produce the appearance of stable meaning in the very process of controlling deviance. Hence, human agents' semiotic work stabilises drifting meanings, giving a particular meaning that is formalistic, rationalistic and logical, producing the appearance of a stable and static semiotic grid which henceforth anchors the multiplicity of forces in movement (Milovanovic, 1992b).

In Western industrial political economies meaning construction based on

'purposive rational action' (as opposed to shared intersubjectively constituted meaning) (Habermas, 1984, 1987) increasingly underlies the constitutive process within the semiotic grid producing narrative coherence. This
becomes the narrative structure (text) that conveys images of deviant
behaviour and simultaneously as it is invoked by agents produces those
agents that are its supports. Such is the making of the subject as control
agent. Those who, in their non-reflexive practices, oppose images of
deviance, as we have said, more often inadvertently affirm the reality of
their existence. Such is the dialectic of control (see above, and Henry and
Milovanovic, 1991). Organisational imperatives, reflecting human agency
deference to concepts of rationalisation and capital logic, rely on signifying
practices by those agents. The agents in turn rely on a tacit understanding in
constructing meaning (Manning, 1988). The outcome of this constitutive
work is the organisational supports, deviant cases, correctors and rebels who
unwittingly purify these structural distinctions in their critical attack on its
assumed operating principles. Oppositional narratives (texts), for example,
are most often replete with the very core imageries, metaphors and signifiers
that are the supports of a hierarchical and dominating apparatus. By
activating system-supportive imageries and then attempting to react and
negate does not in itself produce alternative imageries of what could be. The
'at best' – react and negate – turns often to be 'at worst', for the cancelling of
a negation by a negation in the Hegelian sense does not produce
transcendence, only at best destruction at one level, but a reconfirmation of
system generated elements at another (Milovanovic, 1988; Thomas, 1988;
Bannister and Milovanovic, 1990).

Social control agents in their practice of criminal justice policy both
produce and sustain deviant categories, and they tacitly frame coherent
narratives on 'what happened', hence objectifying interactive experience.
These objectifications become increasingly the anchoring points for micro-
constructions which in turn sustain the organisationally framed narrative.
This constitutive process is recursive and self-referential, cyclically generating a more refined and purified version of the substance of their actions, as
object.

To refer to control institutions as relatively autonomous, then, is not to
say they are separate from the wider social structure since they are part of its
constitution. It is to say, rather, that recursivity reinforces conventional
notions, giving permanence and stability to them. Nor do control institutions support the wider structure simply because that is their assigned
social function. Such a vision is rabidly reifying. Rather, as Fitzpatrick
(1984) again reminds us, control institutions support the relations of
reproduction within the totality of society because they *are* some of those
relations of reproduction (see again Figure 5.1). Likewise the 'internal'
relations that monitor control institutions *are* some of the relations of the
control institutions that they police. A police agency would not be what it
was without the relations that police it, informal or otherwise, and that
would not be what it was without human agents' action. As a result, any

examination of control institutions that analyses them outside of the structural context that they police or which ignores the internal relations that police them, or that ignores human agents' recursive action, is producing a partial account that itself becomes part of the constitutive discourse that sustains their reproduction. Concomitantly, any challenging practices whose agents are not sensitive to the reconstituting effects of their very practices, further reproduce, elaborate and stabilise the existing structural arrangements. Thus, although relations of control are most visible in their institutional form as criminal justice policy and practice, this should not lead us to neglect their pervasive presence in informal and alternative modes of control or even in Foucault's (1977) sense of a dispersed disciplinary technology pervasive throughout our society. Neither should it lead us to gloss the human agent's renditions and intersubjective creative work which daily makes these relations into organisations and structures. Rather such insight leads us to the challenge of constitutive criminology and the central problematic of postmodernist thought: how do we deconstruct crime and reconstruct that which is not crime? In other words, how do we reconstruct the kinds of relations that affirm others' right to make a difference while preventing their right to make a difference denying that of others. What would a criminal justice policy that adopted such an approach look like? What implications would such an approach have for the practices of controlling or (more accurately, according to our analysis) minimising harm? We can only hint at these issues in this chapter since essentially we are here outlining the assumptions of theory. Indeed, we have given some consideration to these matters in our previous work (Milovanovic and Henry, 1991) and will do so more fully in a work in progress (Henry and Milovanovic, forthcoming). However, we would be remiss not to at least repeat our basic position here.

First, we believe that the logic of our analysis suggests that criminal justice policy be directed at all the constitutive process components that constitute crime. Thus any tinkering with one element, such as offenders, or victims, or law or criminal justice agencies, or the wider political economy, without recognising that these are set in a global political economy, must be a partial response. We believe such a policy is destined to do little more than change the face of the criminal form. Criminology and its implied criminal justice policy must begin with global economy since it is with global economy that power, however directed by particular nation states, is most widely constituted. Within this context, particular societal structures must be reconstituted through sociopolitical policies that deconstruct the power of their politics and that emphasise the interdependence and intersubjective nature of human relations. Thus social and economic 'policies' must become occasions of transpraxis. If praxis is taken to be purposive social activity born of human agents' consciousness of their world, mediated through the social groups to which they belong, then this must be supplanted by the richer notion of transpraxis. Transpraxis assumes that critical opposition must be aware of the reconstitutive effects – the reproductions of exploitative

relations of power – in both supportive and oppositional activity. Transpraxis must be facilitated by 'replacement discourse'. Replacement discourse, as we conceive it, is not merely another package of ways to talk and
make sense of the world, but a language of 'transpraxis'. It is a non-
reificatory connecting of the way we speak with our social relations and
institutions, such that through its use we are continuously aware of the
interrelatedness of our agency and the structures it reproduces through the
constitutively productive work of our talking, perceiving, conceptualising
and theorising. An alternative discourse, a replacement discourse, may only
arise as alternative accounts are given hearing at every level of crime control
proceedings (Gilsinan, 1982: 236; De Haan, 1990). A replacement discourse
would capture 'the fluid nature of criminal violations and the legal
processing of such infractions' (Gilsinan, 1982: 243). It would envelope not
just the declarations of policy but the ways its practitioners and policy
makers distinguish their reality from the totality. It would require a 'bringing
back in' of the underemphasised, informal, unofficial and marginalised
practices (the unspoken) that are part of the totality of power that passes for
crime control. It would provide alternative signifiers, diverse discursive
subject-positions and a semiotic grid (paradigm/syntagm) from which
alternative narrative constructions can occur which de-privilege categoris-
ations, abstractions and formalisations that sustain forms of inflicting pain
and suffering. This notion, in principle

> (a) . . . includes almost every conceivable reaction to an event – individual,
> collective, structural, material, or immaterial. (b) It implies that response is
> mandatory, without pre-defining the event as a crime, an illness, or anything else.
> (c) It invites analysis of the event before deciding or choosing a proper response.
> [And] (d) . . . it invokes the consideration of historical and anthropological forms
> of dispute settlement and conflict resolution for possible cues to rational forms of
> response. (De Haan, 1990: 158)

De Haan's suggestion is for providing various (repressed, marginalised)
discursive practices a forum for genuine consideration. Only with such a
comprehension of the totality and the contribution of these excluded parts to
the reality-making process, is it possible to provide an alternative understanding of the phenomena of crime and crime control in our society. Only
from such an understanding of the total constitutive process is it possible to
generate a replacement discourse that begins the deconstruction of crime
and crime control, the correction of corrections and the ultimate criminal
justice policy that denies itself.

References

Bannister, Shelley and Milovanovic, Dragan (1990) 'The necessity defense, substantive justice
    and oppositional linguistic praxis', *International Journal of the Sociology of Law*, 18: 179–98.
Barak, Gregg (1988) 'Newsmaking criminology: reflections on the media, intellectuals, and
    crime', *Justice Quarterly*, 5: 565–87.
Barak, Gregg (ed.) (1991a) *Crimes by the Capitalist State: An Introduction to State Criminality*.
    Albany: SUNY Press.

Barak, Gregg (1991b) *Gimme Shelter: A Social History of Homelessness in Contemporary America*. Westport, CT: Praeger.

Bogdan, Robert and Taylor, Steven (1987) 'Towards a sociology of acceptance: the other side of the study of deviance', *Social Policy*, 18: 34–9.

Bourdieu, Pierre (1977) *Outline of a Theory of Practice*. Cambridge: Cambridge University Press.

Box, Steven (1983) *Crime, Power and Mystification*. London: Tavistock.

Brigham, John (1987) 'Right, rage and remedy: forms of law in political discourse', *Studies in American Political Development*, 2: 303–16.

Brigham, John and Harrington, Christine (1989) 'Realism and its consequences: an inquiry into contemporary sociolegal research', *International Journal of the Sociology of Law*, 17: 41–62.

Calley, William L. (1974) 'So this is what war is' in C. H. McCaghy, J. K. Skipper Jr, and M. Lefton (eds), *In Their Own Behalf: Voices from the Margin*. Englewood Cliffs, NJ: Prentice-Hall.

Clinard, Marshall B. (1983) *Corporate Ethics and Crime: The Role of Middle Management*. Beverly Hills, CA: Sage.

Cohen, Stanley (1985) *Visions of Social Control*. Oxford: Polity Press.

De Haan, Willem (1990) *The Politics of Redress: Crime, Punishment and Penal Abolition*. Boston, MA: Unwin Hyman.

Deleuze, Gilles and Guattari, Felix (1987) *A Thousand Plateaus*. Minneapolis: The University of Minnesota Press.

Derrida, Jacques (1973) *Speech and Phenomena*. Evanston, IL: Northwestern University Press.

Derrida, Jacques (1981) *Positions*. Chicago, IL: The University of Chicago Press.

Ehrlich, Eugene (1913) *Fundamental Principles of the Sociology of Law*, Cambridge, MA: Harvard University Press.

Einstadter, Werner J. (1992) 'Asymmetries of control: surveillance, intrusion, and corporate theft of privacy', *Justice Quarterly*, 9(2): 285–98.

Einstadter, Werner J. and Stuart Henry (1991) 'The inversion of the invasion of privacy?', *The Critical Criminologist*, 3 (Winter): 5, 7.

Fish, Stanley (1982) 'With compliments of the author: reflections on Austin and Derrida', *Critical Inquiry*, 8: 693–821.

Fitzpatrick, Peter (1983a) 'Law, plurality and underdevelopment', in D. Sugarman (ed.), *Legality, Ideology and the State*. London: Academic Press.

Fitzpatrick, Peter (1983b) 'Marxism and legal pluralism', *Australian Journal of Law and Society*, 1: 45–59.

Fitzpatrick, Peter (1984) 'Law and societies', *Osgoode Hall Law Journal*, 22: 115–38.

Fitzpatrick, Peter (1988) 'The rise and rise of informalism', in R. Matthews (ed.), *Informal Justice?* London: Sage.

Foucault, Michel (1977) *Discipline and Punish*, Harmondsworth: Penguin.

Foucault, Michel (1979) *The History of Sexuality Volume I: An Introduction*. London: Allen Lane.

Freire, Paulo (1985) *The Politics of Education*. South Hadley: Bergin and Garvey Publishers.

Geras, Norman (1983) *Marx and Human Nature Refutation of a Legend*. London: New Left Books.

Giddens, Anthony (1984) *The Constitution of Society*. Oxford: Polity Press.

Gierke, Otto (1900) *Political Theories of the Middle Age*. Cambridge: Cambridge University Press, 1958.

Gilsinan, James (1982) *Doing Justice: How the System Works – As Seen by the Participants*. Englewood Cliffs, NJ: Prentice-Hall.

Goffman, Erving (1974) *Frame Analysis*. New York: Harper and Row.

Goffman, Erving (1981) *Forms of Talk*. Oxford: Blackwell.

Gordon, Robert W. (1984) 'Critical legal histories', *Stanford Law Review*, 36: 57–125.

Griffiths, John (1979) 'Is law important?', *New York University Law Review*, 54: 339–74.

Gurvitch, Georges (1947) *The Sociology of Law*. London: Routledge and Kegan Paul.

Habermas, Jürgen (1984) *The Theory of Communicative Action. Vol. 1. Reason and the Rationalization of Society*. Boston, MA: Beacon Press.

Habermas, Jürgen (1987) *The Theory of Communicative Action. Vol. 2. Lifeworld and Sytem: A Critique of Functionalist Reason*. Boston, MA: Beacon Press.

Harrington, Christine (1988) 'Moving from integrative to constitutive theories of law: comment on Itzkowitz', *Law and Society Review*, 22: 963–7.

Harrison, Wilfrid (1964) 'Policy', in J. Gould and W. L. Kolb (eds), *A Dictionary of the Social Sciences*. London: Tavistock.

Henry, Stuart (1983) *Private Justice: Towards Integrated Theorizing in the Sociology of Law*. London: Routledge and Kegan Paul.

Henry, Stuart (1987) 'The construction and deconstruction of social control: thoughts on the discursive production of state law and private justice', in J. Lowman, R. Menzies and T. Palys (eds), *Transcarceration: Essays in the Sociology of Social Control*. Aldershot: Gower Press.

Henry, Stuart (1991) 'The informal economy: a crime of omission', in G. Barak (ed.), *Crimes by the Capitalist State: An Introduction to State Criminality*. Albany, NY: SUNY Press.

Henry, Stuart and Milovanovic, Dragan (1991) 'Constitutive criminology: the maturation of critical criminology', *Criminology*, 29: 293–315.

Henry, Stuart and Milovanovic, Dragan (forthcoming) *The Constitutive Theory of Criminology and Criminal Justice*.

Hunt, Alan (1987) 'The critique of law: what is 'critical' about critical legal theory?', *Journal of Law and Society*, 14: 5–19.

Hunt, Alan (1990) 'The big fear: law confronts postmodernism', *McGill Law Journal*, 35: 507–40.

Jackson, Bernard (1988) *Law, Fact and Narrative Coherence*. Liverpool: Deborah Charles Publications.

Jessop, Bob (1982) *The Capitalist State*. New York: New York University Press.

Johns, Christina (1992) *The War on Drugs*. Westport, CT: Praeger.

Knorr-Cetina, Karen and Cicourel, Aaron (1981) *Advances in Social Theory and Methodology: Toward and Integration of Macro- and Micro-Sociologies*. London: Routledge and Kegan Paul.

Lacan, Jacques (1977) *Ecrits*, trans. A. Sheridan. New York: Norton.

Manning, Peter (1988) *Symbolic Communication: Signifying Calls and the Police Response*. Cambridge, MA: The MIT Press.

Marx, Gary (1988) *Undercover: Police Surveillance in America*. Berkeley: University of California Press.

Marx, Karl (1852) 'The eighteenth Brumaire of Louis Bonaparte', in K. Marx and F. Engels, *Werke* in E. Kamenka (ed.), *The Portable Marx*. Harmondsworth: Penguin, 1984.

Matza, David (1969) *Becoming Deviant*. Englewood Cliffs, NJ: Prentice-Hall.

Merry, Sally (1988) 'Legal pluralism', *Law and Society Review*, 22: 869–96.

Milovanovic, Dragan (1986) 'Juridico-linguistic communicative markets: towards a semiotic analysis', *Contemporary Crises*, 10: 281–304.

Milovanovic, Dragan (1988) 'Jailhouse lawyers and jailhouse lawyering', *International Journal of the Sociology of Law*, 16: 455–75.

Milovanovic, Dragan (1992a) *Postmodern Law and Disorder: Psychoanalytic Semiotics, Chaos and Juridic Exegeses*, Liverpool: Deborah Charles Publications.

Milovanovic, Dragan (1992b) 'Rethinking subjectivity in law and ideology: a semiotic perspective', *Human Justice*, 4(1): 31–53.

Milovanovic, Dragan and Henry, Stuart (1991) 'Constitutive penology', *Social Justice*, 18: 204–24.

Moore, Sally Falk (1973) 'Law and social change: the semi-autonomous field as an appropriate subject of study', in S. F. Moore (ed.), *Law as Process*. London: Routledge and Kegan Paul.

Nelken, David (1986) 'Beyond the study of "law and society"?: Henry's private justice and O'Hagan's the end of law', *American Bar Association Research Journal*, 2: 323–38.

O'Malley, Pat (1988) 'Policing domestic security', *mimeo*. Bundoora, VIC: Department of Legal Studies, La Trobe University.

Pepinsky, Harold and Quinney, Richard (1991) *Criminology as Peacemaking*. Bloomington: Indiana University Press.

Ross, Edward (1901) *Social Control: A Study of the Foundations of Social Order*. New York: Macmillan.

Santos, B. (1985) 'On modes of production of law and social power', *International Journal of the Sociology of Law*, 13: 299–336.

Santos, B. S. (1987) 'Law: a map of misreading. Toward a postmodern conception of law', *Journal of Law and Society*, 14: 279–302.

Schur, Edwin M. (1965) *Crimes Without Victims*, Englewood Cliffs, NJ: Prentice-Hall.

Schutz, Alfred (1967) *The Phenomenology of the Social World*. Evanston, IL: Northwestern University Press.

Selva, Lance and Bohm, Bob (1987) 'Law and liberation: toward an oppositional legal discourse', *Legal Studies Forum*, 113: 255–76.

Teubner, Guenther (1992) 'The two faces of Janus: rethinking legal pluralism', *Cardozo Law Review*, 13: 1443–62.

Thomas, Jim (1988) *Prisoner Litigation: The Paradox of the Jailhouse Lawyer*. Totowa, NJ: Rowman and Littlefield.

Vandivier, Kermit (1972) 'Why should my conscience bother me?', in R. L. Heilbroner (ed.), *In the Name of Profit*. New York: Doubleday.

Weiss, Robert P. (1987) 'From "slugging detectives" to "labor relations"', in C. D. Shearing and P. C. Stenning (eds), *Private Policing*. Beverly Hills, CA: Sage.

Young, Jock, (1981) 'Thinking seriously about crime: some models of criminology', in M. Fitzgerald, G. McLennan and J. Pawson (eds), in *Crime and Society: Readings in History and Theory*. London: Routledge and Kegan Paul and the Open University Press.

6

Criminology, Modernity and the 'Truth' of the Human Condition: Reflections on the Melancholy of Postmodernism

Wayne Morrison

Introduction: melancholic times?

> [Contemporary] Criminologists are pessimists and cynics. There seem good reasons for this. Our science has largely failed to deliver criminal justice policies that will prevent crime. The grand 19th century utilitarian doctrines – deterrence, incapacitation, rehabilitation – are manifest failures. The return to classicism in criminology – the just deserts movement – has been worse than a failure. It has been a disastrous step backwards. (Braithwaite, 1992: 1)

> A general theory of crime must be a general theory of the social order. (Gottfredson and Hirschi, 1990: 274)

These quotes express two central issues for the future of criminology. First, the current 'mood' of Western societies, a feeling that some writers have referred to as the 'collapse of the confidence of modernity'; second, the relationship between the 'doing' of criminological theorising and its place in general or 'meta'-theoretical conceptions of the social body, images and discourses which situate and legitimise (either explicitly or implicitly) criminology.

Both issues are problematic, indeed it is symptomatic that Gottfredson and Hirschi (1990), while making the second statement at the end of a large and controversial book, actually did not make any attempt to place their 'general theory of crime' within an articulated vision of the social order.

The contemporary sociocultural mood impacts both upon individual projects of writers and in structuring the context in which criminology will have to work. For example, in my attempt to avoid the pessimism, as Braithwaite characterised criminology experiencing, the original beginning to this chapter became a recipe for depression:

> In considering a future for criminology, take a few basic points of the sociocultural context: modernity is exhausted, the working class movements are exhausted, the dreams of social justice are dead, the only discourse which is listened to by those in power is economics (and most economics professors say that their discipline is discredited, it has failed to come up with bodies of predictable generalisations or laws, hence governments run on guesses which the public cannot understand), most people in the society held out as the bastion of democracy (namely, the USA) do not even bother to vote; the result of prohibiting drugs is that they are tearing

apart the youth of Western countries, social divisions are increasing. With rehabilitative and preventive measures having failed, the future of criminology will be to come up with strategies of penal control in increasingly divided societies.

What ties these two issues together is the ascription of our contemporary situation throughout the Western world as 'postmodern'. Postmodernity is defined as a time of great ambivalence and doubtful self-questioning where the intellectual traditions which have driven modernity stand exhausted. Postmodernity is an age of mass communication where no intellectual or ideological position can stand alone but is constantly surrounded with other perspectives, other ideas; where no experience appears entirely personal and where the 'social' becomes a mass of impressions and imagery, or to use the jargon – an interactional site of various significants and signifiers, fragmenting, dislocating, representations impacting without referents, locations without fixed walls of interiority or exteriority.

In terms of doing social theory what was common to my various, now discarded, beginnings was the feeling that as we move to the end of the twentieth century it has become hard, very hard, to make coherent sense of the experiences of social life. Moreover, and as importantly, it is also hard to articulate and develop any shared understanding of the kinds of societies we currently inhabit. The big concepts borrowed from the traditions of Marx, Weber and Durkheim appear to fail in conveying a sense of having touched the essence of the currently developing social body.

Baudrillard described the postmodern condition in terms of an endgame:

> Post-modernity is neither optimistic nor pessimistic. It is a game with the vestiges of what has been destroyed. This is why we are 'post' – history has stopped, one is in a kind of post-history which is without meaning. One would not be able to find any meaning in it. So, we must move in it, as though it were a kind of circular gravity. We can no longer be said to progress. . . . Right now one can tumble into total hopelessness – all the definitions, everything, it's all been done. What can one do? What can one become? And post-modernity is the attempt – perhaps it's desperate, I don't know – to reach a point where one can live with what is left. It is more a survival among the remnants than anything else. (Baudrillard, 1984: 25)

The emotional state of melancholy impacts:

> Melancholy is the fundamental tonality of functional systems, of the present systems of simulation, programming and information. Melancholy is the quality inherent in the mode of disappearance of meaning, in the mode of volatilization of meaning in operational systems. (Baudrillard, 1984: 39)

Melancholy is the emotive flipside of nihilism. It is a feeling of engagement without joy, without energy, or boredom with the prospect of the future. It is postmodern in that the despair and alienation of modernity, the depressed rasp of Billie Holiday for instance, were cast against the understanding that there was always something other, some structure to be built that would overcome and that these structures, call them just societies for want of a better name, were achievable in this world. Aesthetically, the modern sensibilities suggested that there was a realm of purity achievable and knowable to humans, that love and effort were important, that even in suffering redemption could be found and that this would occur within the time and space constraints of modernity – indeed that this understanding would define the purpose of modernity itself. Thus the experiential form of modernity can be seen in terms of journeying – a combination wherein the happiness of the individual was to be found in the construction of just, secure and happy societies as the end of modernity; societies which would allow human autonomy to flourish inside a true solidarity. These understandings contained a central thesis of the human condition, an argument that humanity was social and its telos, its happiness and all the totality of its being, what we might call the truth of the human condition, was to be found within social processes and indeed, within the creative powers of mankind working on the basis of secure knowledge about these processes. Modernity passes into postmodernity with the realisation that the journey is without end, that in important ways 'this' is the endgame and instead of dreaming of utopia, of travelling in hope for the future, we turn to the present.

But where and what are we? It is all too apparent that what passes for much of individual autonomy is loneliness, indifference, brutality. It has become commonplace to assert that the projects of modernity are dead. The big stories, the meta-narratives and the grand social projects no longer have their appeal, their promises lost in disillusionment, their truths subject to scepticism and doubts, acceptable only to those who share a specific range of assumptions, untrue to those who do not – hence 'meaning' relativises and vanishes. In this 'decentring of experience' the quest for a truly human social solidarity appears compromised. Human needs become relative, values subjective, concern for the welfare of others either a patronising instrument in their oppression or a misguided allocation of resources which will intensify the problem, and the impetus of doing criminology, energetic when criminologists were assured that virtue was on their side, becomes dissipated in a world after virtue. But what, reflexively, does this end of meaning mean? And what sort of answer is it to say we are in postmodernity? And if the future of criminology is to operate through the postmodern condition, what does this consist of?

I am unsure; all I can do is struggle with old dichotomies: understanding and context, theory and practice, and while Braithwaite was sweeping – 'We need a theoretical revolution in criminology to extricate us from our contemporary nihilism' (1992: 1) – my own view is that the postmodern condition can only be understood as the product of modernity, as a continuum of certain of the drives and themes of modernism itself and that a new awareness drawing upon what has gone before is required. Thus it is to a brief recapping of certain modernist themes for criminology that I now turn.

The epistemological canons of the criminological enterprise

Of the narratives which have inspired modernity, the narrative of epistemological purity most clearly defines the status of crimin-o-logos. Drawing upon ancient narratives of truth and beauty the narrative of pure knowledge could interact with specifically modernist narratives of progress, of happiness through the enjoyment of an authentic and autonomous life without secure forms of social construction, to promise an overcoming of the potentiality of chaos and internal social warfare. Criminology could come to appropriate a serious task, the control and eradication of crime, only if it could be taken seriously, and the conditions of this were that it would be scientific and not metaphysical. In the narratives of modernity logos which purified themselves of metaphysics would be essential to the construction projects, part of the structure or the inside essence of the formations of the new social order, while those which did not, such as religion, art and literature, became part of the adornments or the outside dressage, mostly decoration or entertainment, occasionally therapy. But could metaphysics be so cleansed?

Part of the postmodern condition is the understanding that it cannot. This understanding takes various forms. It is implicit, for example, in Lyotard's argument that 'one of the features that characterises more "scientific" periods of history, and most notably capitalism itself, is the relative retreat of the claims of narrative or storytelling knowledge in the face of those of the abstract, denotative, or logical and cognitive procedures generally associated with science or positivism' (Lyotard, 1984: xi) since this means that these grand-narratives or meta-narratives actually create a social space for science to work within. Thus the very enterprise of 'scientific abstraction' occurs and owes its legitimisation to the existence of such narratives. In what follows certain of the background conditions, the metaphysical terrain, which criminology sought to cleanse itself of, are discussed and treated as fundamental presuppositions. The account that we shall want to obtain in the end will have to enable us to steer a path between the recognition of the fate that a social science like criminology has come to fear (that is, its reliance upon metaphysics), and our reflexive understanding that this fear is also a denial of the necessary conditions under which social science labours.

The traditions of modernist criminology

Background, the Enlightenment and modernity

In understanding the intellectual systems of the premodern and modernity it is as well to note Weber's idea of the human 'metaphysical need for a meaningful cosmos' (Weber, 1946: 281). Without systems which impose meaning upon existence humans experience life as 'senselessness' wherein no meaning can be given to innocent suffering, chance events, death and the elements of randomness in the distribution of wealth, power and status. For Weber religion has historically satisfied this desire for meaning: 'All religions have demanded as a specific presupposition that the course of the world be somehow meaningful' (1946: 353). Modernity promised to overcome the religious-cosmological worldview with a secular (scientific-mathematical) one. But because this is counter to the religious understanding of a meaningful cosmos a new problematic is set up for the secular worldview, what Weber has called 'the cosmos of natural causality': 'In principle the empirical as well as the mathematically orientated view of the world develops refutations of every intellectual approach which in any way asks for a "meaning" of inner-worldly occurrences' (Weber, 1946: 351). Since the human experience of senselessness is a universal existential phenomenon the need for meaning persists in the modern world. The question which arises is as follows: if science cannot speak the language of meaning and if religion has lost its dominance, how are we going to account for and legitimise the seemingly random or contingent dispositions of wealth, health and power?

Criminological modernity has been dominated by two major structures, namely, classical criminology and positivism.

Classical criminology

In the introduction to his famous *On Crimes and Punishments* Beccaria (1963 [1764]) is at pains to inform his reader that he brings 'philosophy' in the tradition of the rationalist 'who from the despised obscurity of his study, had the courage to cast the first and long fruitless seeds of useful truths among the multitude!'. However, Beccaria tells us that 'we now know the proper relationships between subject and sovereign' and 'by going back to general principles' we 'destroy the errors accumulated over several centuries' and 'use the strength of recognised truth to check the unbridled course of ill-directed power'. Using these newly recognised 'moral and political principles' will 'lead to happiness in this mortal life' (1963 [1764]: 8–9).

These philosophic truisms give a foundation, a bedrock for building logical structures of social relations. The movement is both destructive and constructive, both a thesis on the self and of society. It is destructive in that it turns against the power and webs of social relationships founded on opinion, religious dogma and traditional methodology; it is constructive in that both the law itself and its enforcement would be rational and impersonal. The truth of the human self is not to be found in the relations of custom or religion, but in the requirements of reason. Under the guidance of the concept of the social contract the developing central authority of the state is given the authority to create a clear and rational legal code to override the arbitrary power and favours of local elites and to build up a strong social organisation.

Providing both a check and guide to the exercise of this power is the principle of utility, but the strategies of legitimisation and structuring of state power also serve as mechanisms enabling trust in the new formations of organisation to be engendered.

The judiciary, for example, are to be trusted to exercise the conduct of criminal trials and sentencing, not because 'they have received laws from our forefathers as a family tradition or a legacy which leaves to posterity only the task of obeying; they receive them, rather, from a living society or from the sovereign who represents it and who is the depository of the current will of all citizens'. A living social contract provides the bonds of society and ties together the diverse private interests into a functioning whole. Moreover, the exercise of judicial skill lies in the pure application of a logical system, a formal rational system of judicial logic overcomes 'uncertainty' and the multiplicity of viewpoints. Absolute certainty is something removed from the human condition since if justice was something that came out of the 'spirit of the law' contingency would result. (1963: 14–16).

Ultimately the trust which is engendered is the trust that the social contract will be kept and let us be aware that this social contract is about governing society. It is a concern with the art of government which to Beccaria was not solely the liberal notion of minimisation, of seeing law and the granting of civil rights as guarantees of non-interference by the authorities in the private affairs of the populace. Beccaria's advice to the sovereign displayed a catholic concern with totality, with a more general concern called sometimes the 'common good' and the advice he offers is in the name of knowledge: ruling is to be based on the touchstone of secure knowledge, of truth. As Beccaria specified in his later lectures, *The Elements of Political Economy* (1804), criminal justice was part of policing, where policing encompassed the widest variety of notions which served to make the society cohere and progressively powerful. The power of policing was closely related to the advance of knowledge and the creation of new 'social habits': policing encompassed 'the sciences, education, good order, security and public tranquillity, [constituting] the fifth and last object of public economy' (quoted in Burchell et al. 1991: 109).

This is a positive notion of policing and of criminal justice; it is not simply a notion of restraint, of boundaries, of control, but of growth, of developmental perceptions. However, although this is the context, the classical programme of Beccaria has set in place a mechanism which, as the development of grids of offence/punishment equations demonstrates, can be easily subtracted and divorced from the metaphysics of the social world.

Epistemologically, the fiction of the social contract serves as a master narrative of history which enables classical criminology to define the criminal act, to locate the entity of the criminal, and to give meaning to the events and acts which can now be labelled crimes and criminal. The criminal subject is a rational member of the social body, his/her prior agreement in the social contract means that the conditions of social life are not part of the internal factors which need to be analysed when questions of the identification of 'the criminal', or ascertaining intention and guilt arise. The criminal subject is thus positioned at the intersection of certain meta-narratives which locate the subject, the offender, and give his or her actions meaning. These meta-narratives, which serve to create the space of classical rationality, create 'crime' as a signifying practice, and the ascription of criminal/offender is the positive result of a social process founded in narratives, in stories. And although these narratives can be read in their suppositions of individual freedom and contractionism as part of the normative theories of philosophical liberalism, they belong to metaphysics rather than the supposed security of 'knowledge', the bedrock rationality of classicism is founded on metaphysics.

The counter tradition: positivism and the ideal of a functional natural order

The contractarian assumptions underpinning classical criminology were the result of a choice. There was an alternative reading, a formative science of man which was developing a critique of social contract theory and the holistic idealism of the catholic tradition. While the first used the principle of utility to guide the authority of the rulers the second tradition turned to a form of sociohistorical study where utility became an immanent principle of nature's operation. Positive criminology arose in the nineteenth century and was part of the various processes whereby the rationalist and individualist presuppositions of philosophical liberalism were dissected from a mixture of ideological and theoretical perspectives. The narratives which underpinned philosophical liberalism were shown to be neither an adequate theory of history nor of social reality. Although David Hume was by no means speaking for a coherent single perspective he put succinctly what the anti-contractarians would all agree upon: that contractualism relied upon a 'philosophical fiction of the state of nature', whereas in reality 'men are necessarily born in a family-society' (Hume, 1965: 195). As Voltaire put it: 'I do not think this solitary life, which our forefathers are supposed to have led, is in human nature.' Instead: 'The foundations of society ever existing, there has therefore ever been some society' (Voltaire, 1901: 177).

Opposed to the rationalistic system building Hume argues in *A Treatise on Human Nature* for a science of man based on a 'cautious observation of human life . . . where experiments . . . are judiciously collected and compared' (1978 [1739]: xix). The catch cry is experience rather than introspection. The narratives of history were either unfocused or a subjective interpretation, while contract theory simply lacked empirical foundation. Hume's methodological principles for this new science were to set the template for positive criminology: 'though we must endeavour to render all our principles as universal as possible . . . it is still certain we cannot go beyond experience'.

But one element of this experience appears as 'difference', multiplicity, variation. The solution to the dilemma of observable variation in mankind's customs and behaviour and yet the need to preserve a notion of a totality was in the metaphysics of 'nature'. As Voltaire put it:

> It is clear that everything which belongs intimately to human nature is the same from one end of the universe to the other; that everything that depends on custom is different . . . custom sheds variety on the scene of the universe; nature sheds unity there; she establishes everywhere a small number of invariable principles. (quoted in Cassirer, 1951: 219)

The epistemological model for empirical modernity is founded in the project of David Hume's *A Treatise on Human Nature*. In the *Treatise* Hume is at pains to tell us that he brings the correct methodology for establishing the truth of 'the science of man'. Upon this fundamental bedrock the construction of modernity can be founded: put another way, sciences of human nature (call them sociology or psychology) and not philosophy, were to be the discourse which could tell the truth of the human condition and ground progress.

Hume is normally taken to have established that only an empiricist methodology based on the notion of an experiencing self can succeed: 'the only solid foundation . . . must be laid on experience and observation' (1978[1739]: xvi). From Hume onwards, empirical methodology has taken on the role of usurping the fictions of classicism in the name of providing the 'truth' of the human condition and providing the framework for technical processes which will build the new society. However, in the *Treatise* Hume actually deconstructs both the security of the human self and his own use of truth into another set of pragmatic suppositions which were to render empiricism into a state where it, as much as the rationalist systems Hume abhorred, was founded on metaphysics. Hume's crucial move occurs in the last section of Book One of the *Treatise* where he pursues a sceptical challenge upon the introspection of the rationalist system builders. In its attack upon reasoning scepticism reduces certainty; in fact it is so successful that 'by this means you cut off entirely all science and philosophy'. Hume expresses his dilemma at bedrock: 'We have, therefore no choice left but betwixt a false reason and none at all' (Hume, 1978[1739]: 268). The only security becomes the empirical operation of the mind and sentiments of the human self, the bedrock of the truth of propositions and realities lies not in the objects but in our impressions.

It is this impasse, and the reflexive paradox involved in the statement that 'I can never catch *myself*', which Kant is said to have resolved for Liberalism by taking Hume as succeeding in the task of demonstrating that the self is not derivable from experience, but must be recognised as a condition of the possibility of experience. Thus the unity of consciousness is a postulate of both theoretical and practical reason, not something to present us with a cause of anxiety.

Hume's own solution had been in recourse to 'nature'. At the moment of greatest doubt, when Hume's reflexive and sceptical questioning had reduced his search for absolute knowledge to the status where all beliefs were relative, where truth appeared lost, 'Nature' intervened dispelling the tension by either weakening the intensity of the dilemma or transferring the attention to more practical concerns. Hume found himself 'absolutely and necessarily determined to live, and talk, and act like other people in the common affairs of life' (Hume, 1978[1739]: 269).

This return to the common life, and the psychologism which appears to underpin it, provides the point of departure at which Hume has been taken by many to despair finally of reason and reduce progressive effort to a hope in the current of nature; that is, to a meta-functionalism wherein the metaphysical faith in God is replaced by faith in the functionality of everyday life and the different rankings and status we find therein. One which also holds a notion of the inherent sense of everyday life.

This dilemma of Hume has never been resolved and to a large extent is rediscovered in postmodern writings. Hume engaged in a search for secure foundations, for the Archimedean point of the truth of the human self, but succeeded only in deconstruction. His apparent resort to the language and narratives of common life under the metaphysical solace of the inherent functionality of nature became, perhaps, the dominant blueprint of modernity. Kant's rationalistic reaction and the edifice of critical rationality which went forth as a result (and in which Nietzsche's creative self is the end result) presuppose the ability of the self to control narratives and sets of interpretative understandings in the name of a rational (or aesthetic) agent.

Hume's position led to the conservative ascription of human nature reflecting natural functionality. The ontology of the criminal was naturally given, criminology's goal of crime reduction and eradication achievable by aligning ourselves with the knowledge of nature's processes; criminology able to speak the language of nature.

With early criminological positivism this process was explicit. Lombroso sought to treat the categories and demarcations of the discourse of the criminal law as if they were reflections of underlying natural processes. A commensurability is established which converts the items of common sense and legality into facets of a common natural flow which lies beneath the variance of language; the criminal law thus drew from natural process and so the categories of the criminal law, the 'juridical figures', actually could stand in close connection to the categories of scientific positivism. In his writings, for example, Lombroso replaced the juridical category of incendiarism with the psychiatric figure of pyromania, homicide with homicidal monomania, theft with kleptomania, habitual drunkenness by dipsomania, rape and pederasty to sexual inversion, crimes of lust by satyriasis and nymphomania and idleness and vagabondage by neurasthenia. For Ferri science was to replace the abstractions of morality. 'Science must control' and science would bring social justice:

> justice ceases to be a coercive external and material mechanism, it will become more and more an intimate general organic sentiment, the product of a social environment which will ensure to every man the material and moral conditions of everyday existence. This means that the disappearance of penal justice as a political institution will coincide naturally and necessarily with the universal predominance of justice as a specific sentiment and force in social life. (Ferri, 1917: 568–9)

Raffaele Garofalo located the meaning of criminality in the concept of 'natural crime' wherein crime is what offends the 'norm' of the moral sense of the community:

> the injury must wound the sentiments not in their superior and finer degrees, but in the average measure in which they are possessed by a community – a measure which is indispensable for the adaptation of the individual to society. Give such a

violation of either of the sentiments, and we have what may properly be called a natural crime. (quoted in Taylor et al., 1973: 16)

The moral sense of the community is guaranteed by its form of natural law, since in Humean style, Garofalo finds two 'elementary altruistic sentiments of pity and probity'. An early critic, Gabrielle Tarde, called this thesis 'a desperate effort to attach himself at some point in this unfathomable flood of phenomena and cast an anchor exactly in what is the most fluid and evasive thing in the world, that is to say, feeling' (both quotes in Taylor et al. 1973: 17).

This was the project of modern positivism, a commitment to social advancement and human happiness and security through scientific enlightenment. The metaphysics of this is the presumption not only of the things of the world sharing a continuum, of nature as a cohesive totality, but that we can have secure knowledge of the processes, can control these and fashion a new structure, a new society.

However, we should remember that Hume returned to an acceptance of the common life because he actually found contingency, diversity and chaos, as the foundational bedrock. Hume's denial of an acultural, non-narrative, ontologically given human essence can be both conservative and radical. He actually espoused a 'mitigated scepticism' towards the common life but underneath the metaphysics of modernism optimism reigned. The postmodernist rediscovery of Hume's dilemma too easily appears to replace optimism with pessimism, mitigated scepticism with Nietzschean unmasking and deconstruction.

Criminology in the postmodern condition

Modernist criminology worked from the metaphysics of totalities, whether the 'one' of the social contract, or the 'one' of nature; postmodern criminology must live in the metaphysics of difference, plurality, multiplicity. Whereas the faults of traditional criminology/penology and also the fears of critical criminology concerned the assumption of the one, the predominance of consensus, the belief in universalism, the accepted dominance of the liberal/capitalist axis, the problematic of postmodern criminology will be how to create and sustain a social solidarity which takes pragmatism as its epistemology and plurality and contingency as its foundational ontology.

Two readings of the work of Durkheim and Weber can serve as examples. Modernist readings of Durkheim assume that he claims a 'collective conscience' actually exists as a social ontological entity and therefore the task of socialisation is to ensure that individuals come to incorporate its features into their individual psychics. This crime and punishment are a function and a defence of this collective conscience. A postmodern reading holds Durkheim as arguing for the non-existence of a stable collective conscience in late modern society while holding to the necessity of a collective conscience as a 'regulative idea'.

Weber gave a prognosis of increasing cruelty and human indifference arising out of the failure to create neo-religious all-encompassing systems in the face of an all-embracing structure of purposive rationality in modernity:

> The specific intellectual and mystical attempts at salvation in the face of these tensions succumb in the end to the world domination of unbrotherliness. . . . In the midst of a culture that is rationally organised for a vocational workaday life, there is hardly any room for the cultivation of a cosmic brotherliness. (Weber, 1946: 357)

But Weber was anticipating a modernism that is already past. The modernist calls of romantic criminology – to reduce the hold of the 'one' and to demand society free the 'other', to allow diversity in the face of the power to criminalise (Taylor et al. 1973) – have been borne out in the postmodern context. The postmodern life world cannot be reduced to a rationally and bureaucratically organised unity (Foucault's rereading of Weber was overdone), to a sphere colonised by legal-rational domination, but exists as a plurality of lived experiences within diverse life games, language games, ethnic traditions, positive ideologies and searches for 'meaningful and authentic' experiences. Experience is embedded in contexts partaking of the social but whose locality is marked by variety and specificity. Identity becomes fragmented, partaking of an irreducibly pluralist world where appreciation, granting rationality and credence to the life forms and actions of others, coexists not only with the bureaucratic surveillance which Foucault feared but also tolerance and indifference.

The possibilities of postmodernism, openness, powers and freedoms, are also the possibilities of a postmodern nightmare. Lost in the midst of a postmodern disjointedness, of processes of decentring so varied that no centre can be dreamt of, the process of ruling becomes authoritarian. The demands of a populace searching for meaning prioritises basic certainties, walls, divisions, demarcations and territories to control temporal space in the void of non-meaning. The only counter to this demand, which arises out of the impossibility of natural meaning, lies in the realm of metaphysics: the attainment of solidarity in the context of diversity and difference demands a new metaphysics, an awareness in which a generality is struggled for which embraces plurality.

But this appears unfashionable. In the main, postmodernist social theory turns away from the traditions it associates with modernism, in particular it labels the constructivist project of modernism the product of a metaphysical desire for totalities. Thus no attempt is made to theorise societies as totalities using the grand traditions of Marx, Durkheim or Weber. Instead a deconstruction of positivist and post-positivist attempts to build a science of society is entered into in the name of purity. It concentrates on producing theoretical-interpretative accounts which seek to analyse the social world through the detailed analysis of selected social texts. The outcome of the modernist metaphysics of a structural-functioning totality is labelled as terror. As Lyotard put it: 'The nineteenth and twentieth centuries have given us as much terror as we can take. We have paid a high enough price for the nostalgia of the whole and the one' (1984: 81).

On language it exhibits a shift from a modernist, rational, discursive system of representation, to a postmodern, figural, paralogical system of representation. This rejects the depicting or essential basis, the search for an answer to the question 'what a cultural text depicts or means', and prefers to focus on the pragmatic issue of what it does or achieves. Within the broad area of criminological concern the arrival of the postmodern condition brings confusion and decentring, multiple tendencies with little idea of interconnectedness. A list of tendencies would include the following, for example:

technicism
appreciation
reformed consensualism (that is, New Left Realism)
abolitionism/romanticism/left idealism
feminism
conservative and ordinary language
Just Desserts and neo-classical penology
neo-rehabilitative/anti-Just Desserts
systems management
behaviourism

Perhaps the clearest future will be technics, the giving of information to the bureaucratic power centres so that efficient mechanisms of control and preserving the authority of legal codes can be developed. But while providing such information may well aid in mechanisms of accountability, for institutions such as the police and the penal network, let us not forget that much of the context for the growth of bureaucracy has been the democratisation and institutionalisation of the nation state and after these narratives have lost their appeal, technics may well be, as in the words of critique of positivism, 'reason in the absence of reason'. These processes which modernist criminology were a movement within appeared (certainly to the criminological 'insiders') part of a progressive equalisation of social conditions. Classical criminology tried to connect both the creation of crimes through legislation and the social reaction to crime to the task of governance and legitimacy (with authority and, in the European context, sovereignty, but also the generation of sets of citizen rights). Positivism saw the search for the criminal person and the aetiology of crime as part of the management of social processes and problems (aiming for the 'health' of society). Postmodern criminology has the remnants of all these attempts but without the metaphysical support of the modernist projects. Not only does criminology in postmodernity face the cutting edge of the reversal of claims to minimum standards of living, the de-equalisation of social conditions, the deligitimising of social rights in favour of economic freedoms, but criminology in postmodernity is compromised in that it (post labelling school) realises that the identities which provide the data of criminology are founded in social processes, rather than the metaphysics of naturalness – there is no ontology of the criminal. Or, put another way, the ontology of the criminal is process itself.

Contingency and irony reign not only as the end result of scientific investigation into the composition of the social world but also as existential states of mind. Take class relations: it has become vogue to use the concept of the underclass to a new social class which commits most of the traditional street crime; most frequently in analysis in the United States (Glasgow, 1981; Auletta, 1982; Murray, 1984; Lemann, 1986; Wilson, 1987; Katz, 1989), and applied to Britain (Murray, 1990, and from the left: Dahrendorf, 1985; Field, 1989) and Japan (Schoenberger, 1990). There are two opposite sets of explanations for the underclass. To the radical right, which sees the underclass in terms of crime and ungovernability, of promiscuous self-indulgence, of a culture in which rational self-control is lacking, the underclass is a consequence of the unconditional social programmes offered by the welfare state which do not obligate beneficiaries to behave conventionally in order to receive benefits. To the right, the underclass is the ironical result of the projects of modernity designed to attain social solidarity in modern Western industrial states. This attack is also linked to wider assaults on the welfare state as economically detrimental to a market economy since they use up taxes, monies that the private sector needs for capitalisation. At the same time as the right talk of the underclass development, supply-side economic discourse justifies for the well off, middle and employed working class, substantial reductions in their direct payment tax obligations (although indirect taxation may well increase squeezing the less well off the hardest) which cuts the amount of transfer payments members of the 'underclass' are entitled to.

Radical right advocates argue that the level of tax transfer payment requires reduced profit margins and entrepreneurial incentives. Welfare demands become self-perpetrating and destroy the competitive edge of welfare states. Moreover, the welfare state demands an increasing intrusion of the state into private life, and is in effect a harbinger of totalitarianism, and is paternalistic and anti-libertarian. This argument maintains that any state which has the power to shift resources from one group to another represents a form of economic tyranny. Thus, instead of the social-democratic-liberal approach which emphasises the rights of the poor, the radical right focuses on the rights of those coerced into subsidising the poor. Furthermore, the welfare state has, in their view, lost sight of basic American values (Gilder, 1981). According to these critics, the welfare state has failed to reinforce the work ethic; the goal of self-sufficiency, self-support and self-initiative; the importance of intact families (Mead, 1986); the fiscal responsibility of the parent to the child; and the notion of reciprocity – the idea that recipients have a social obligation to perform in return for receiving assistance. In part this conservative perspective, the desire to return to traditional values, led to the electoral victories of Reagan, Bush and Thatcher.

The radical right believes that the family is the basis of correct socialisation and the focus of welfare functions and that these can only be enabled if the family is defended and strengthened as the basic institution in Western society. In the United States the Institute for Cultural Conservatism (1987) laid out a programme for defending family life. First, the traditional nuclear family must be restored and one parent, the mother, should remain in the home permanently to raise children. Second, the incidence of divorce, out-of-wedlock pregnancy, abortion and pre-marital sex must be reduced. These are part of a decline in moral standards which is identified as a major cause of social decline in the industrial nations. Third, it is necessary to reinstall certain values on which stable families depend, including responsibilities to and for offspring, disapproval of extra-marital sex, and reverence for life, both before and after birth, and the legal system can play an important role by defending the legal control of parents and presuming the reasonableness of parental action. Legislative, administrative and judicial actions which work to undermine the traditional family, must be avoided and economic conditions developed to enable stable nuclear families to be self-sufficient. In short, the government should not be indifferent to the form of family existence but actively support and recreate the traditional form. However, when the immediate, nuclear family is unable to be self-sufficient, members of the extended family, friends and neighbours are to be the preferred sources of assistance.

In part, the radical right's desire to return women to the home and recreate the nuclear family is a response to the disappearance of any pre-given ontological stability to identity in postmodernity. Put another way, for much of this century identity was closely linked to the function one performed (again this was linked to one's place within the structures of production). But where is a functional essence to be found when late modernity is characterised by an extremely high division of labour and division of occupational and social roles? A mother, for instance, may also be a lawyer, a school governor, a company director, a keen painter, a collector of antiques. The so-called nuclear family is the exception not the norm. Moreover, identity in postmodernity can be more easily seen as linked to determination through consumption patterns rather than production relations. Recast in terms of Hume's dilemma, the answer to the question 'who am I and how am I to behave?' could traditionally have been answered in terms of the narratives of everyday life – those which specified the individual's gender, work, place, family, class and past. But modernity has turned these narratives into temporal guides rather than truths, placed the burden of identity onto an abstract self to create continually anew. Thus identity is a burden as much as a refuge, providing only the weakest of ontological security and little protection against the demands of consumerism and the dialectics of angst–desire.

The left explanation of the underclass is that while modernity has rightly stripped self-identity of the psychological constraints of class, gender and subordination to irrational authority and custom, it has not kept up the process of freeing structures and creating spaces for new identities to engage in meaningful occupations and life experiences. One strand of the left's explanation concerns the role of structural changes, particularly economic changes, in employment opportunity and the lack of interventionist government policy to cope with this. The second strand is more suspicious of government policy and reads it as a deliberate redistribution of wealth from the poor sections to the richer sections of society. In the first reading the underclass is a recent phemomena caused by a lack of government policy to deal with the transformations of a postindustrial society. In Britain it is found in the works of Ralf Dahrendorf (1985) and Frank Field (1989). Field argues that four forces have brought about the underclass in the United Kingdom: unemployment; widening of class differences; exclusion of the poorest from rising living standards; and a change in public attitudes towards those who have not succeeded in Thatcher's Britain. Since the Second World War full employment brought about greater equality in income distribution but in recent years, although for those in employment this has continued, those out of work have suffered a downward mobility. In the last decade, for the first time since 1945, we have seen increasing class divisions which, Field argues, have broken up the sense of 'common citizenship, whereby each of us feels we belong to the same society' (1989: 3). This is compounded by the fact that the poor have not gained from the rising standards of living of the rest of society for benefit levels have merely been protected from rising prices. The ideology of the Thatcher years, that of individualism, has resulted in a change in attitudes towards those on the bottom rung of society. The solidarity of the working class has, according to Field, been replaced by a 'drawbridge' mentality whereby those working class people who have benefited during the last decade do not wish others to succeed as they have.

What is common to all these accounts of the underclass, however, is the implicit acceptance that the underclass is a direct result of previous government policy, whether the creation of the welfare state, the failure to develop post-industrial strategies, or rejecting social justice in favour of supply-side economic theories. The implict message given to the members of the underclass is that there is nothing natural in their position. It is a creation of society; their life and their suffering is a contingency. The message: 'You could just as well have been born the son or daughter of a white wealthy individual, but you are also being made the scapegoat for economic decline.' In the metaphysics of the postmodern condition, contingency impacts as a criminogenic factor (for why should the present rules of the game be played with, that is, lawful conduct be regarded as a necessity for underclass life, if the arrangements have no legitimacy or naturalness?). The experience of deep inequalities, bereft of the security of naturalness and cast in the light of contingency, create not alienation (for what is there to be alienated from?) but resentment. As Nietzsche warned, the emotion of the repressed in the postmodern condition cannot be seen in the rationality of meaningful dialectical engagement, but as the absence of meaningfulness. The rage of the deprived is vengeance on anything which links to the excesses of the advantaged. How can there be a way to make people content or to reconcile them to either the advantage of others or the disadvantage of themselves when the narratives of legitimacy have become subjected to the trope of irony and one's position in the seemingly arbitrary and chaotic array of life chances, sacrifices, rewards and benefits, understood as just that, arbitrary and contingent?

What is the response of criminology to the underclass? Or indeed to the experience of contingency and existential freedom/indifference? It does not appear to have impacted in the theoretical debate but we know the practical response. Some appreciation (that is, discourse which seeks to articulate the experience of the members of the underclass and communicate this to us superclass members), but also target hardening and differential policing. With the demise of projects of universalism and incorporation, aided by the rhetoric of postmodern pluralism, soon, no doubt, the underclass will live in their areas, kept under surveillance, their journeys into our housing areas registered and neutralised, while 'we' get community policing. We, after all, need fewer forms of formal social control for we are seduced into playing the multitudinous life games of the superclass – we know that if we play these games they will give us rewards, pleasures, the circle of stimulation, boredom, stimulation/simulation.

Furthermore, instead of facing up to the postmodern condition criminal justice policy has avoided tactics of connectedness. Take, for example, just deserts. Just deserts gives a system of partial rationality, of particularised regulation – chains of equivalence which enable an image of predictability and coherence, a framework for sentencing on the basis of desert but where the rationality of this desert is closely contained in the reciprocity of the penal equation. Just deserts has no role of communicating or interpreting social actions, but acts as a formula of regulation. While we can explain just deserts, tell the story of its arrival and explain why it exists, we cannot legitimise it. Instead we have a mechanism divorced from the sets of narratives which gave a totality to classicism. But it does not seem to matter because legitimacy is not a central concern in postmodernity. In a strange way this feature was recognised by Habermas (1976) when he referred to the continual tendency of modern capitalism to have crises of legitimacy. The paradox is that while present societies are illegitimate on the basis of those narratives which served to provide legitimacy (after all we know that present societies are radically unjust, that capitalism works for the West at the expense of the Third World, that racism and exploitation are features of our productive systems) those who took the issue of legitimacy seriously, you and I who now constitute the superclass, are seduced into playing the games of postmodern existence, while the others, the underclass, are kept in check by techniques of discipline and repression and the creation of political and social apathy.

By way of contrast, one current response to just deserts is the Not Just Deserts scheme of Braithwaite and Pettit's search for a philosophy of

republicanism as a foundation for criminal justice policy (1990). Here we can
see a desire for foundationalism, for a framework to grant coherence and
interconnectedness to the diverse strands of policy and labelling of crime.

Such an attempt appears out of tune with the populist strand of
postmodernism where law and order politics appeal to ordinary experience
and ordinary language as foundations against modernism. This is explicit in
the recent scheme of the 'general theory' of Gottfredson and Hirschi (1990)
where the recourse to the notion of 'self-control' as the universal concept to
found a general theory upon is most notable for the absence of any general
theory of society being openly espoused (a consensual one is implicitly
presupposed) even though, as we have seen at the beginning of this chapter,
they acknowledge that 'a general theory of crime must be a general theory of
the social order'! Not only is there a rather crass reliance upon positivist data
but nowhere is the whole movement of modernity which creates the
self-activating, self-reliant, self-controlling individual encountered. The
resulting work is not only ahistorical, it is atheoretical. Moreover, even on
its own terms it suffers from abstraction from the cutting edge of modern
social theory. Namely, while social determination no longer is a viable
notion, neither is self-determination since the basis of individual autonomy
and freedom of choice is social contextuality and the social provision of
ideas, of symbols, of identifications, of all those things by which the self
would make decisions and be autonomous.

Conclusion

Criminology began within the claims of the philosophical and then scientific
perspectives to tell the truth of the human condition. Assuming the
metaphysics of wholeness, of natural totalities, criminology carved out
processes of social control as its area of concern and although much of this
concern was mundane and constraining, a matter of working on understanding and reinforcing the restraint mechanisms of society, it was also positive.
For this knowledge of social control was to be aligned to greater paradigms,
and modern projects. The demise of those projects and the deconstruction of
those paradigms, the demise of foundationalism, the arrival of the
postmodern condition, threatens to push criminology into nihilism and
melancholy.

In this condition there is need for a new awareness, for little in our
previous structures of thought has prepared us for life in societies which do
not have overreaching master narratives. As a criminological factor there is
little to prepare individuals for life in the midst of great inequalities and
static economies after the stories of social progress and building just societies
have exhausted themselves. Without work being done to compose new
dreams, new projects, new senses of solidarity there is nothing to lend
theoretical support to the patterns of distribution of late modernity:
legitimacy vanishes. The absence of legitimacy coincides in postmodernity

with the rise of apathy and the decline of dialectics. Alienation, and the dialectics of class struggle, of the desire to make whole (to rehabilitate), are lost in the experience of resentment, apathy and localised anarchy. The future will be one of scepticism, of playing localised games and denying the need to think socially, but it may also contain elements of an energetic underclass who act out of resentment, understanding the contingency and irony of the postmodern world. The members of the superclass will not be able to understand the underclass, for without a social metaphysic that defines why they are the advantaged and in what social evolution their advantages are to be put, they are morally unskilled to possess such advantages and turn with perversity to demand of criminology strategies of control and discipline of the others. These measures may gain popular support, for in the chaotic plurality of the postmodern condition the call to authority asserts itself, but all that authority can do outside legitimacy, outside systems of meaning, is engage in stratagems of desperation, the terror of repressive intervention side by side with occasional therapy and to turn away from intellectual strategies of interconnectedness for that way appears to lie the weakness of self-doubt.

Rejecting the conservatism of the postmodern condition I have called part of our need the need for a new metaphysics. We need new formulas, based not on models of the past but on the results of the uncompromising search for foundations and the pragmatism modernity uncovered. One thing is certain, to the extent that the purpose of social theory was to tell the truth of the human condition the old methodologies stand discredited but on false grounds. Their claims to tell the truth were, after all only pragmatic – their truths consequent to their narratives and their suppositions. The post-modern awareness of pragmatism and contingency, of irony and metaphor underlying description, need not lead to a sense of nihilism. Nor to the denial of any sense of purpose and agency as to social development, but to a consciousness of the limits of analysis and of the interdependency of processes. Criminology has a viable task – it is to read crime, penality and victimology in such a way that it alerts us to aspects of the human condition otherwise suppressed in the name of normalcy. This role puts our modernity on trial in the name of the social; to represent the truths of the human condition as it is lived out and labelled as deviant or caught in the binary opposites, both in locality and in generality. Caught in the task of observing and articulating, of engaging the projects of human solidarity in the postmodern condition, criminology must stand still in the terrain of modernity, using the knowledge of the past to understand the dilemmas of the future, turning its back upon the seductions of melancholy. Straddling always the two sides of reason, hopes and dreams against the sceptical, condemned to a belief in a perpetual motion towards a goal and the realisation that the goal can never be effectively reached. Understanding that the notion that the goal is either already here or attainable in a master stroke gives power to the forms of totalitarianism, whereas the unchallenged domination of the sceptical spirit condemns us either to a hopeless hyperstagnation or a restless toing-and-froing dissipating humanity. Perhaps Nietzsche said it 100 years ago:

> Ultimately man discovers in the universe nothing but what he has himself instilled: the rediscovery is called science, the instilling – art, religion, love, pride. One ought to continue in good spirit in both activities, even if they should turn out to be only a kind of game; some ought to continue in rediscovery, others, we others, in the instilling. (Nietzsche, 1967: Aph. 606)

In the postmodern condition criminology must do both.

References

Auletta, K. (1982) *The Underclass*. New York: Random House.

Baudrillard, J. (1984) 'On nihilism', *On the Beach*, 6 (spring): 38–9.

Beccaria, C. (1804) *Elementi di Economia Pubblica*. Milan.

Beccaria, C. (1963 [1764]) *On Crimes and Punishments*, trans. by Henry Paolucci. Indianapolis: Bobbs-Merrill.

Braithwaite, J. (1992) 'Reducing the crime problem: a not so dismal criminology', *Australian and New Zealand Journal of Criminology*, 25.

Braithwaite, J. and Pettit, P. (1990) *Not Just Desserts: A Republican Theory of Criminal Justice*. Oxford: Clarendon Press.

Burchell, G., Gordon, C. and Miller, P. (eds) (1991) *The Foucault Effect: Studies in Governmentality*. Hemel Hempstead: Harvester Wheatsheaf.

Cassirer, E. (1951) *The Philosophy of the Enlightenment*. Princeton, NJ: Princeton University Press.

Dahrendorf, R. (1985) *Law and Order*. London: Stevens & Sons.

Ferri, E. (1917) Criminal Sociology, American edn, trans. by J. Kelly and J. Lisle. Boston, reprinted Agathan Press, New York, 1967.

Field, F. (1989) *Losing Out: The Emergence of Britain's Underclass*. Oxford: Blackwell.

Foucault, M. (1977) *Discipline and Punish*. Harmondsworth: Allen Lane.

Glasgow, D. (1981) *The Black Underclass*. New York: Vintage.

Gilder, G. (1981) *Wealth and Poverty*. London: Buchan and Enright.

Gottfredson, M. and Hirschi, T. (1990) *A General Theory of Crime*. Stanford, CA: Stanford University Press.

Habermas, J. (1976) *Legitimation Crisis*. London: Heinemann.

Hume, D. (1978 [1739]) *A Treatise of Human Nature*. Oxford: Oxford University Press.

Hume, D. (1965) *Essential Works*, R. Cohen (ed.). New York: Bantam Books.

Institute for Cultural Conservatism (1987) *Cultural Conservatism: Toward a New National Agenda*. Washington, DC.

Katz, M. (1989) *The Undeserving Poor: From the War on Poverty to the War on Welfare*. New York: Pantheon Books.

Lemann, N. (1986) 'The origins of the underclass', *Atlantic Monthly*, June/July: 31–68.

Lyotard, Jean-François (1984) *The Postmodern Condition: A Report on Knowledge*. Manchester: Manchester University Press.

Mead, L. (1986) *Beyond Entitlement: The Social Obligations of Citizenship*. New York: Free Press.

Murray, C. (1984) *Losing Ground*. New York: Basic Books.

Murray, C. (1990) 'The British underclass', *The Public Interest*, 99: 4–28.

Nietzsche, F. (1967) *Will to Power* (tr. by Walter Kaupman). New York: Vintage Books.

Schoenberger, K. (1990) 'In Japan's worst slum, angry underclass feels a nation's prejudice', *Los Angeles Times*, 30 October.

Taylor, I., Walton, J. and Young, J. (1973) *The New Criminology: For A Social Theory of Deviance*. London: Harper Torchbooks, Harper & Row.

Voltaire, F.M.A. De. (1901) *Works, Vols 1–42*. New York: E.R. Dumont.
Weber, M. (1946) *From Max Weber: Essays in Sociology*. New York: Oxford University Press.
Wilson, W. (1987) *The Truly Disadvantaged*. Chicago, IL: University of Chicago Press.

7

The Law of Victimage in Urbane Realism: Thinking Through Inscriptions of Violence

Alison Young and Peter Rush

Deviance is the freedom made possible in a crowded city of lightly engaged people.

Sennett (1990)

It is not the 'Thin Blue Line', but the social bricks and mortar of civil society which are the major bulwark against crime.

Young (1992)

In the early hours of 30 August 1974, local residents in Station Road, Gloucester called the police to make a complaint about noise in the street. Just over three months later, on 6 December, Henson George Venna was convicted in the Gloucester Crown Court of threatening behaviour contrary to s.5 of the Public Order Act 1936 and of an assault occasioning actual bodily harm. Venna appealed against conviction to the Criminal Division of the Court of Appeal. The judgment of the Court was read by Lord Justice James and was reported in the All England Law Reports.[1] According to the judgment, Venna and four other men were 'creating a disturbance in the public street by shouting and singing and dancing. At one stage there was a banging of dustbin lids' (p. 790). After 'at least one complaint' (p. 790) was made by the local residents to the police, a police officer named Leach was sent to investigate the disturbance. Three taxi drivers described the subsequent events which they witnessed. The court said that 'Leach patiently and tactfully tried to persuade the four youths to be quiet and to go home' (p. 790). The result is described tersely as 'a remark by [one of Venna's companions] Robinson, "Fuck off"' (p. 790). The singing and dancing then continued. Leach informed them of the complaint about noise, whereupon Robinson ceased singing and dancing and stood apart quietly. The others, however, 'continued a sort of war dance and went on singing' (p. 790). Leach warned Venna and the others that arrest was imminent if they did not stop making the disturbance. One, Allison, sat down 'in defiance' on the pavement. The police officer placed his hand on Allison's shoulder and announced that all five men were thereupon under arrest.

Allison began struggling to free himself, while Venna and the others tried to pull him from Leach's grip. Leach, meanwhile, called for help on his radio. A scuffling fight began. According to the report, the 'scene' was such that 'the taxi drivers were about to intervene' (p. 790). In fact, one passer-by, 'referred to as " the fat man"' (p. 790), did intervene on the officer's behalf.[2] Other police officers arrived and assisted Leach in overpowering Venna and his comrades. Venna 'fought so violently that four officers were required to restrain him' (p. 790). While two police officers held his arms, he kicked another police officer; Venna is described by the court as 'lashing out wildly with his legs' causing 'a facture of a bone' in the hand of the officer (p. 790). This kick and its injury constituted the assault with which he was charged and convicted.

Venna's defence was that he was never informed that he had been creating a disturbance and that he had been trying to tell Leach that he should not arrest Allison (p. 790). He said that he had been struck on the chin and knocked to the ground and had not been 'lashing out' with his feet in order to kick anyone, but merely attempting to stand up. Thus, in the doctrines of criminal law, his defence was that he did not have the necessary mental state to commit an assault, namely, intention or recklessness. His appeal failed. In the judgment, Lord Justice James, stated: 'the whole incident leading to the charges was, unfortunately, a very ordinary and all too common one. On any view the appellant and his friends were behaving in an unruly and disgraceful anti-social manner, but it was not a very grave or serious incident' (p. 790).

The primary concern of the legal judgment is with the character of the criminal engaged in this 'very ordinary and all too common' event. As an all-too-common event, however, the selection of Venna for criminalisation has the effect that he becomes a surrogate for the punishment of all the others who participate in rowdiness. In short, as a criminal, Venna is a victim. But in conventional terminology, the victims of the assault are those in whose name Venna is held responsible: first, the police officer who suffered a broken bone, and second, the local residents whom the judgment describes as being 'disturbed' (p. 790). The concern of this chapter is with the crimino-legal representation of the victim. To that extent, our interest is coincident with the increasingly prominent theme of victimisation in contemporary criminological writing.[3] One of the most notable exponents of this theme is the (Left) Realist genre of criminology.[4] For Realist criminology, the central object to be investigated is 'crime' – an object which takes the Realist not so much to the figure of the criminal but to a portrait of the victim. Nevertheless, as in *Venna*, the all-too-common crime will have been street assault and the all-too-common victim will have been the local residents. The tranquillity and quiet of the home in the early hours of the morning was shattered by the rowdy, masculine activity of the public street. The solid walls of the houses were breached by the singing, dancing and banging of Venna and his comrades. Such a breach of boundaries becomes paradigmatic of criminal victimisation in the modern city. The first section of the chapter follows the contours of the victim as assembled in Realist criminological writings. We then juxtapose the Realist programme of victimage with the event of conjugal violence represented in the case of Kiranjit Ahluwalia. Such a juxtaposition forestalls the current and all-too-easy vanguardism of the victim. The remainder of the chapter describes the strategy of universalisation through which the city (as global space) and the victim (as sovereign subject) are linked in the reiteration of the sacrificial dynamic which constitutes conjugal violence.

Systematising the real

Criminology must be authentic to itself and to its object. Such is the overriding imperative of the Realist programme. What is promised by Realism to criminology is the ability to capture, once and for all, the criminal process in its totality. Jones et al. write: 'criminology must embrace the totality of the criminal process: it must be true to its *reality*' (1986: 3). What is crucial here is not so much the investment in the real, but the desire to constitute the real as a total, continuous and homogeneous system. In short, it is not the real of the criminal process which is at issue in the programme, but the real*ism* of the criminal process. Such a displacement of the real by Realism is done for good reason. It makes possible an isomorphic relation between the criminal process and criminology. Of course, such isomorphism is impossible but nevertheless extremely powerful.

This should come as no surprise given the structuralism of the so-called Realist 'deconstruction' of crime (Young, 1992: 27). As Young notes, Realism constructs 'a square of crime' which formally 'consists of two dyads, a *victim* and an *offender*, and of *actions* and *reactions*: of crime and its control. This deconstruction gives us four definitional elements of crime: a victim, an offender, formal control and informal control' (1992: 27).[5] All four elements constitute the systematised reality of the criminal process which is then grouped and subdivided into two sets of opposing couples, namely, the couplet of crime (offender and victim) and the couplet of control (state and informal social control).[6] This, then, is all there is and all that can be said. The criminologist *must not* say any more, because the criminologist *cannot* say any more. It is such a doubled prohibition which accounts for the now-familiar claustrophobia of structuralism. However, the Realist programme *does* say more. There is always an excess to structuralism and that excess is represented in the Realist programme by the injunction to remember the victim.

The crime couplet involves an opposition between the offender and the victim. But against the overriding focus on the criminal in traditional criminology, the Realist programme grants a privilege to the victim. Thus 'we must never forget, however, the other half of the dyad of crime: the victim' (Young, 1992: 47). Married to the criminal (its 'other half'), the victim – and not the criminal – is the sign through which the couplet of crime can be read. Such a reversal no doubt reveals the interests – political and axiological – of traditional criminology. It does not, however, displace the hierarchical structure which makes possible the reversal of offender and victim.[7] That structure is what Young refers to as a 'developing system' which traces an unbroken line from the causes of crime to the effects of crime: 'our approach then views crime as a developing system, from its initial causes to the impact on the victim' (1992: 47). Such a developing system works as a hall of mirrors, in which the identities of victim and criminal can only be represented as the reflection of each in the other. But this is no more than to point out the already mentioned claustrophobia of structuralism. Without something more, the Realist programme cannot ground the privilege and importance of the victim. It requires a necessary supplement and that supplement is the experiences recounted by victims. For all its emphasis on the totality of the criminal process, the reader of Realist criminology is insistently reminded that to be true to the reality of crime, it is necessary to posit the experiences of victims as the a priori of the criminological enterprise, albeit an a priori which is recounted by victims and surveyed by criminologists. In short, a claustrophobic structuralism which posits the systematicity of the real criminal process has as its necessary supplement an unbounded subjectivism of the victim.

The victim is present to excess. The identity of the victim is fragmented into a proliferation of archetypal categories. 'Victim' is now not only a unitary category but also, simultaneously, contains within its unity various predicates of identity. These constitute subspecies or *types* of victim. Those favoured most by Realism include: ethnic groups subject to racist harassment; residents troubled by burglars (whether of the 'professional' type or the opportunistic type performed by the 'young lad' [Young, 1992: 40]); the working class exploited by corrupt employers and corrupt police officers; the inner-city dweller confronted by drug dealers; females victimised by violent men (Lea and Young, 1984: 262; Young, 1992: 50). Thus any particular event is understood in terms of a plethora of typical victims. The exemplary event, however, is street assault, which the Realist understands as the minimal unit for the offender–victim dyad. In the situation of Venna's case, the local residents are victims of late-night rowdiness, while the police officer whose hand is crushed is the victim of an assault. In fact, *Venna* is exemplary for the Realist in as much as assault in a public place operates as the archetypal instance of the offender–victim dyad.[8] But more than this, the proliferation of types of crimes – and hence victimisation – is interminable. Assault is not 'domestic violence' (Young, 1992: 30). Assault is 'a purely coercive act' which may occur 'in the street, in a public house, or in some other public venue' (Young, 1992: 29, 30), whereas 'domestic violence' can only occur in the home. 'Domestic violence' is also unlike opiate use and burglary, in as much as it has its own 'variety of sub-species, each with its own life cycle' (1992: 40–1). These are no more than illustrations of the impetus of the Realist programme as it parades the experiences of the victim – namely, the more the experiences of the victim are taken into account, the more the identity of the victim is fractured into proliferating types.

The proliferation does not, however, result in the loss of identity. Rather, all the types are unified as instantiations of the universal category of Victim; the Realist proliferation of types becomes a reiteration of identities across the totalised criminal process. In short, then, victimisation is the name by which Realism systematically references the real.

The visibility of the victim

There is no doubt then that the victim is accorded a determining, if not determinate, place within the Realist pantheon of criminology. If there is a 'square of crime', it is from the victim's corner that the square is constituted. The victim is the filter through which the criminal process – offender, informal social control and state social control – is described and analysed. But if the victim provides a portrait of the total criminal process, the Realist programme also provides a portrait of the victim. It is to this latter portrayal that we now turn.

As a preliminary point, we note the peculiar position of the so-called 'victimless' crime within an enterprise devoted solely to the victim. A crime without a victim is one in which the immediate participants are consenting, and in which the transaction occurs in private. Thus, Young notes that 'certain crimes are more difficult to control than others (particularly if they are consensual and in private)' (1992: 45). While this is made as a general point, his discussion of drug use is illustrative. At all levels of drug use, the interpersonal interactions – between importer and dealer, between dealer and user – are held to be consensual. The only point at which a victim appears in the pyramidal portrait of drug use is at the level of dealer–user (Young, 1992: 29). The problem here is not the consent between the dealer and the user, but the fact that the dealing takes place on the street. As such, a third character – the public – is introduced as an index of victimisation.[9] It is the consent of the public to the dealing that is lacking. The victim is thus the local resident or the passer-by, both of which, it is implied, do not consent to dealing on the streets (Young, 1992: 30). In short, there are only victims where the event takes place in public (not private) and there is no consent. In the post-Wolfenden era of neo-liberalism, privacy and consent have become familiar crimino-legal categories. What is important about this neo-liberal strategy is that the categories of privacy and consent are always-already articulated with each other.[10] Thus if a situation is held to be private, then consent, whether implied or explicit, is a necessary consequence. According to this logic, if, as Young states, domestic violence is a private affair (1992: 30), then it is also consensual and there is no victim. As such, for the Realist enterprise, domestic violence is a victimless crime. No wonder, then, that an enterprise that is devoted to the victim is rendered inarticulate in the face of so-called domestic violence. Moreover, such silence is an effect of the more general strategy of cognising the real, a strategy which sacrifices the ethical demand for justice in favour of the moral response of legality. We will return to this ethical failure as we elaborate an account of conjugal violence. For now, we follow Realism's abandonment of 'victimless' crimes and turn to their portrait of the victim. For the purposes of this chapter, three features frame the victim as Realism oscillates between a rigid structuralism and a limitless subjectivism.

We're all victims, OK!

Crime is the great leveller. It gives us all a sense of community and belonging; 'crime [is] a unifier' (Young, 1992: 58). But our belonging comes not from the fact that we are all criminals – or, as a *soi-disant* new criminology once put it, we are all deviants now – but rather, that we are all victims. It is through our victimage that we come to belong to the socius. To be a victim is to be a citizen. Thus, Young states: 'crime, like illness, is a universal problem' and as such 'rates very highly in people's assessment of problems of their area' (1992: 53). In short, a citizen has self-understanding and understands him- or herself to be a victim. Moreover, crime 'affects all classes, ages, races; men and women' (1992: 53). For Realism, one of the great virtues of crime is that it does not discriminate: first and foremost, the victim is unmarked, neutral. Class, age, race, gender are, for Realism, only secondary characteristics of the victim in as much as they arise from the differing distributions of crime across the socius.[11]

Crime as analogy

In portraying the citizen as a victim, Realism deploys a series of metaphors, the most prominent of which is an analogy between crime and illness. Crime is said to resemble illness in several respects. As already quoted, both crime and illness are universal problems. The victim of crime is therefore ill. Illness, like victimage, is also unevenly distributed in its effects as experienced by the citizen. Young writes: 'ill-health is a universal human problem, but ill-health focuses more on certain sectors of the population than it does on others'. The analogy is elaborated even further when the talk gets around to what is to be done about crime. If crime is a universal problem then the objective of social control becomes 'to reduce crime in general. In this it [crime policy] is like a community health project'.[12] Moreover, since crime, like illness, is unevenly distributed across the socius, and since the justice system, like the health system, has scarce resources, so Young proposes that crime control must 'target our resources . . . to those in greatest need'. Finally, the success of such a crime control programme is measured in the same way as that of a community health project: 'not . . . by the extent to which the well-off can purchase vaccines, private health care and medicines, but the degree to which such indicators as the levels of infectious diseases are reduced, infant mortality in general curtailed, overall lifespan increased, etc.' (Young, 1992: 53).

Analogies, in asserting resemblances between disparate things, displace the invisible by the visible. Crime is put to one side and in its place comes the concept-metaphor of illness.[13] What is to be noted here is not so much the fact that Realism uses analogies – after all, analogy is the time-honoured mechanism of legal reasoning – but rather that analogies have productive force.[14] By virtue of this creative force, the category of crime is laminated with new meanings. Every time Realist criminology uses the word 'crime', the reader is compelled to substitute 'victimisation'. The distinctiveness of this substitution becomes clearer when we juxtapose it to the conventional medicalising comparison in which crime is likened to disease. In the traditional analogy between crime and disease, crime comes to evoke the 'sick' criminal. As such, the gaze is directed towards the criminal whereas, in the Realist programme, the gaze is turned squarely on the victim. In an analogy, however, something is always beyond the pale of vision. The visibility of the victim has displaced the criminal, so that he or she becomes a shadowy figure, little more than a blurred reflection in the eyes of the victim. Thus the slippage of terminology between 'crime survey' and 'victim survey' has more than a casual importance; it in fact describes a reorientation in criminological enquiry from the causes of crime to the effects of crime, from criminality and criminalisation to victimage and victimisation. Whereas positivism had searched for the 'causes of crime' in order to identify the criminal, Realism searches for the effects of crime in order to identify the victim. The price of the victim's visibility is the invisibility of the criminal.

Such at least is one cost of drawing an analogy between crime and illness. A further consequence of the analogy is not so much in respect of the offender–victim relation, but in terms of the question of crime control. Crime control becomes a matter of minimizing the risk of victimisation and the taking of remedial steps once victimisation has occurred. Just as the person who becomes ill is encouraged to respond by eliciting the help of the health care system and by following their advice as to treatment, so the victim of crime is enjoined to call on the criminal justice system to respond with a cure, a panacea or a placebo. Passivity (for the victim) is an essential aspect of the crime–illness analogy, in that crime, like illness, happens to the citizen, with all the forcefulness of circumstance.[15] The citizen is then incited to assume the role of an active social agent, fitting locks and bolts to doors and windows, avoiding dark streets and purchasing alarm systems. If everyone is a victim, then everyone has a part to play in the struggle against crime. Even more strongly, everyone has a *duty*: it is part of the offices of the citizen to minimise the risk of becoming a victim (see Beck, 1992). Just as now we are invited to look after the health of our bodies, by choosing to eat the right foods, do the right exercise, avoid the wrong drugs, so too the citizen is incited to participate in his or her de-victimisation. The suspicion here is that Realism's talk of risk leads to a mode of self-government, or, more polemically, self-interest. Thus the victim may escape the strictures of his or her tutelage to the unknowable 'other' that is the criminal, by focusing on the effort to escape the identity of victim. It is an act of self-assertion, an act of will – with, of course, a little help from the police, friends and neighbourhood watch.

Crime is elsewhere

The crime survey is one of the most distinctive elements in the Realist arsenal.[16] As suggested above, the importance awarded to victimisation renders the offender invisible with the consequent effect that Realism devolves into a programme which maps not so much the causes of crime as the effects of crime. These effects are registered in the crime survey as the incidence of victimisation. It is the crime survey which plots this incidence. While the results of such surveys have been useful in debunking the authority of official crime statistics, what has received less comment is the fact that the incidence of victimisation is not simply a statistical but also a geographical phenomenon (see Harvey, 1973; Smith, 1986; Soja, 1988; Jackson, 1989). Thus, for our purposes it is not so much the numbers of victims which concern us, but rather the portrayal of these victims against the backdrop of a map.[17] In short, victimisation refers to the distribution of victims across urban space. Young writes: 'if we were to draw a map of the city outlining areas of high infant mortality, bad housing, unemployment, poor nutrition, etc., we would find that all these maps would coincide and that further, the outline traced would correspond to those areas of high criminal victimization' (1992: 52).

The portrait of the victim in urban space has as its corollary a portrait of the criminologist. Just as the 'other half' of the offender is the victim, so Young's marital metaphorics elaborates a topography of the criminologist. He writes:

> Theory is divorced from practice; theoreticians are divorced not just from practitioners, but from those who are the objects of their study. This is particularly true in criminology; criminologists live in different areas than criminals, they work in an academic milieu: the world of street crime or corporate crime, for that matter, is socially distant from them. (1992: 60)

Crime is elsewhere. But here, just as the victim is a unitary category divided into subcategories, so the city is a unitary space divided into discrete institutional spaces, each of which is occupied by a different subjectivity: the academy by the theorist, the Home Office by the practitioner, the street by Venna, his comrades and the police, and so on. Locked in his institutional space, no direct knowledge of crime can be gleaned by the criminologist. Thus, whether he is 'the most armchair radical theorist or the establishment criminologist . . . all are cocooned from reality by their social distance from their subjects, their obdurate preconceptions and myopia and, above all, by their political impotence' (Young, 1992: 60). However, his saving grace as far as the pursuit of criminological knowledge is concerned comes from the fact that he, like anyone else, can be the victim. As Young states, 'the exterior world always penetrates the academic interior' (1992: 60). Crime may be elsewhere, but it becomes immediate in the experience of victimisation. The criminologist may not live near a burglar, but may well have experienced burglary or know someone who has.[18] Such a doctrine of separate spheres, in as much as it draws a portrait of the criminologist, has no place for the feminist critic. The feminist critic never has been and never could be an armchair theorist. As feminist analyses of victimisation, risk and fear have demonstrated all too often, women are assailed and insulted in their everyday lives: by the images on advertising hoardings that line the streets on their way to work, by the images on noticeboards at work, by the fear of walking home at night and by watching sexual violence on television when they get home.[19] There is therefore no 'outside' for women. Further, the doctrine of separate spheres can say nothing about conjugal violence and child abuse.[20] To focus on conjugal violence: the woman criminologist may well be living with an abusive partner. She is then not at all 'divorced' from the object of study; rather, she may well be married to it.

The world of the Realist then is a world composed of disparate subjectivities defined by discrete spaces. It is here that the crime survey resonates. The crime survey is addressed to capturing the disparate spaces of the city. A survey is concerned with spatialisation; once the spatial dimension is captured, the Realist gains access to subjectivities. In short, Realism creates a cartography of the modern subject. To be a subject, as has been suggested above, is to be a victim, and to be a victim precisely because it is only as a victim that the subject can be incited to engage in self-government. That self-government has a spatial quality; it takes place at nodal points in the city: for example, the entrance door to one's house must be strengthened and the windows locked; the dark city street must be avoided for the safety of the well-lit one; multistorey car parks avoided after dark.[21] In short, the government of the self demanded by Realism is a government of one's movements across and through the city space. No wonder, then, that the typical Realist instantiation of victimage is the street assault, taking place in the city's circulatory arteries – at the crossroads, on the streets and, as in *Venna*, obstructing the pavements. By a discipline of motion, then, the subject as universal victim asserts him- or herself as a citizen of the city.

In this section, we have been concerned to delineate the representation of the victim in Realist criminology. Representation has a double meaning: one in which representation acts as a proxy (stands *for* the victim); the second in which representation performs as a portrait *of* the victim. Such a double reading has displayed: the universality of victimage, the shift from criminalisation to victimisation and from criminal to victim, and finally the spatialisation of victimage. The archetypal situation of victimisation is thus represented as street assault. The victim that is portrayed is neither the abused woman nor child, but rather the citizen-subject assaulted or threatened by a stranger in the public thoroughfare. To this extent, the Realist programme is entirely coincident with the legal problematisation of Venna and his comrades. Furthermore, Realism excludes itself from thinking through the event of sexual violence except by way of an analogy with street assault. Thus, noting the extent of harassment that women experience in public places (verbal abuse, innuendo, 'wolfwhistling'),

Young writes that: 'the *equivalent* experience for men would be if every time they walked *out of doors* they were met with catcalls asking if they would like a fight' (1992: 50, emphasis added). To this extent, conjugal violence is rendered unintelligible in and for Realism.

In stating this, we do not wish to be read as suggesting that Realism should be criticised simply because it is silent about conjugal violence. We have not ignored the fact that a Realist crime survey does include questions on domestic violence, nor that its proponents comment on domestic violence in their texts, nor that since its inception Realist criminology has announced its indebtedness to feminism (and particularly feminist work on male violence against women) (Lea and Young, 1984: 21; Jones et al., 1986: 2–3; Young, 1992: 25). Rather we are referring, and not without a degree of irony, to the deeply embedded rhetorical structures that direct the ambit and argument of Realist criminology. Our question has been: what structure of reference motivates the Realist programme? Our response has been that, at the level of its referential structure, conjugal violence is the constitutive absence or silence of Realist criminology. Thus we have opened up a reading which can trace the *itinerary* of silencing in the crimino-legal enterprise. We begin thus with the event-as-violation translated as *R* v *Ahluwalia*.[22]

Conjugal sacrifice

In the midst of the media debate on abused women who have killed their abusive partners, one case has proffered hope for the gloomy prospects of legal reform.[23] On 9 May 1989, Kiranjit Ahluwalia threw petrol over her husband's bed, while he slept, and set it alight. He died six days later, from burn injuries. On 7 December 1989, Ahluwalia was convicted of murder and sentenced to life imprisonment. In July 1992, her appeal against conviction was heard by the Court of Appeal. The conviction for murder was quashed and she was granted a new trial. At the retrial, in September 1992, she was convicted of manslaughter by reason of diminished responsibility.

Before the law can come to a decision, it must represent to itself the event of conjugal violence. In more conventional terminology, that self-representation is a description of the facts. Let us then follow the facts. Kiranjit Ahluwalia had suffered years of violence at her husband's hands; a variety of his assaults is described in the case report. These include hitting her several times on the head with a telephone; throwing hot tea over her; threatening her with a knife while gripping her throat. Twice she obtained injunctions against her husband; twice she attempted to commit suicide. And then, we are told, from January 1989, his violence intensified.

In the four months leading up to his death in May 1989, Ahluwalia sustained a battery of physical injuries. Her doctor and her work supervisor both reported on the injuries she sustained: bruising to her face and wrist on 18 April; fresh bruising on the cheek, temple and arm on 24 April; knocked unconscious at Easter, with a broken tooth and swollen lips. She missed work through these injuries and her supervisor described her as having lost weight, nervous and distressed. Around this time, Ahluwalia discovered that her husband was having an affair. He is said to have 'taunted' her with this relationship. He left her for three days in April 1989 and Ahluwalia wrote to him, begging him to return. The letter is quoted in the judgment:

> Deepak, if you come back I promise you – I won't touch black coffee again, I won't go town every week, I won't eat green chilli, I ready to leave Chandikah and all my friends, I won't go near Der Goodie Mohan's house again, Even I am not going to attend Bully's wedding, I eat too much or all the time so I can get fat, I won't laugh if you don't like, I won't dye my hair even, I don't go to my neighbour's house, I won't ask you for any help. (p. 892)

Lord Chief Justice Taylor describes this letter as containing 'self-denying promises of the most abject kind' and as evidencing the 'state of humiliation and loss of self-esteem' to which her husband's behaviour had reduced her. Her wish to remain with this violent man is attributed by Lord Taylor to 'her sense of duty as a wife' and 'for the sake of the children' (p. 892).

The case report then goes on to scrutinise in detail what it calls the 'events of 8–9 May'. Deepak Ahluwalia returned home from work late in the evening of 8 May and informed his wife that their relationship was over and that she should leave. He demanded money from her; threatened to beat her and to burn her face with a hot iron. When Kiranjit Ahluwalia went to bed, she was unable to sleep. The judgment describes her as 'brooding on the deceased's refusal to speak to her and his threat to beat her the next morning'. Two and a half hours later, she got up and fetched the caustic soda and petrol she had bought some days earlier. The judgment states that these had been purchased 'with a view to using them on the deceased'. Such evidence of intention, while played down in the judgment, is further developed in the account of her subsequent actions: downstairs, she 'poured about two pints of the petrol into a bucket (to make it easier to throw), lit a candle on the gas cooker and carried these things upstairs. She also took an oven glove for self-protection and a stick' (p. 893). Such a description is in stark contrast to the hyperbolic legal description of Venna as 'unruly', 'anti-social' and engaging in a 'war dance' and to the detailed documenting of Deepak Ahluwalia's brutalities towards his wife. The neutral, technical description is the way in which the case report finesses the question of intention to kill or cause really serious harm (necessary to convict of murder).

The description continues in the calm, measured tones of law. Kiranjit Ahluwalia went upstairs to her husband's bedroom. She threw in the petrol and the candle. She then went to dress her son. Her husband, on fire, tried to immerse himself in the bath, and then ran outside. He screamed 'I'll kill you'. Neighbours rushed up to him to offer assistance. Kiranjit Ahluwalia was standing at the window, clutching her son. Other neighbours raced to the house, but the door had been locked. The house was now on fire. The case report describes Ahluwalia as 'just staring and looking calm' and 'with a glazed expression'. When encouraged to leave the blazing house, she is reported to have opened the window and said 'I am waiting for my husband'.

Later, she wrote to her mother-in-law that her husband had committed so many sins 'so I gave him a fire bath to wash away his sins' (p. 893).[24] After neighbours remonstrated with her, she was, however, convinced to leave the house with her son. Deepak Ahluwalia died six days later.

At trial, Kiranjit Ahluwalia was accused of the murder of her husband. Her primary defence was that she did not intend to kill or cause really serious bodily harm. A second line of defence was provocation, which, if successful, would reduce a conviction of murder to manslaughter. She did not testify and no medical evidence was given on her behalf. She argued that she intended to inflict 'some pain' on her husband and relied on the history of the marital relation in seeking a verdict of manslaughter (p. 893–4). She was convicted of murder. On appeal, the judgment of the court clearly identifies Kiranjit Ahluwalia as the one who experiences the pathos of the victim. She is called 'slight', in contrast to her husband who is 'a big man'. She is 'abject' and in a 'state of humiliation and loss of self-esteem' (p. 892).[25] Moreover, it is out of this pathos that she acts, a pathos constituted by the law as the duty of a wife towards her husband and of a mother towards her children (p. 892). It is to this pathos that the law responds in judging. Thus the Court of Appeal finds her behaviour 'strange' rather than violent and her mental state is characterised as 'endogenous depression' rather than wilful (p. 900). In sum, as Lord Taylor puts it in his opening sentence, 'This is a tragic case which has aroused much public attention' (p. 891).

Tragedy is always a question of representation.[26] The scene of representation is the scene of law and its crimes. As Derrida has argued, 'a trial may be impossible, for by the simple fact of their articulation the proceedings and the verdict unceasingly reiterate the crime' (1987: 35). What must thus be rendered intelligible is the structure of reference within which the law portrays and betrays the pathos of Kiranjit Ahluwalia. At her first trial, she is represented as the criminal. On appeal and at her second trial, she is represented as the victim. In both trials, she is a scapegoat – a proxy for the crime of law.

Legal discourse reiterates a sacrificial dynamic which structures human relationships. The human species, according to Girard, originates in the aleatory selection of a scapegoat whose elimination puts an end to the chaos of random violence. The scapegoat – or, in more modern language, the victim – thus tells a story of community and belonging. The violence of all against all translates into the violence of all against one, where one member of the community is arbitrarily singled out for destruction. Upon this act of violence, the community writes its social contract. Thus 'the victim is held responsible for the renewed calm in the community and for the disorder that preceded this return. It is even believed to have brought about its own death' (Girard, 1987: 26). The victim represents the violence of the community and its subsequent peace as coming from outside, as absolutely other. But this is impossible: in representing the other, the community reiterates both the violence and the victimage. It is this reiteration which accounts for the way in which the victim is both revered and reviled: the ambiguity of the law's response to Ahluwalia as both criminal and victim, and the way in which public attention has been – in Lord Taylor's fortuitous phrase – 'aroused'. In sacralising the victim, the community is founded on a metalepsis, namely, the effect of violence is represented as the cause of violence; crime means victimisation.

While following the general outline of Girard's argument, here we consider that the question of sexual difference requires us to note that the selection of a victim is less arbitrary than he claims.[27] The victim is always already Woman; her sacrifice is inevitable and necessary for an economy of representation, which produces the (illusion of the) social contract. Further, the portrait of the abused woman as victim is a signifier of the violence of the marriage relation. The crime of the marriage contract lies at its heart – in its representation as a union between man and woman. To regard Woman as victim, and thus as signifier, is to testify to the violence which underlies this contractual meeting of hearts and minds. When the object of desire is located in marriage, we have two violently mimetic rivals.[28] As such, the crime of the marriage contract pre-exists any violence suffered by the abused woman, or the homicide she may commit. As surrogate, the abused woman is the matrix of the difference between good and bad, true and false, which is at work in the law's judging of good and bad women, true and false victims. In the moment of judgment, law reveals itself as the heir to sacrifice and its paradoxes (the violent expulsion of violence). In a community which obtains its cohesion from the sacrifice of Woman, the legal system's refusal to manifest disapproval of or to enact effective measures against conjugal violence is simply a local strategy that sustains the sacrificial dynamic. To this extent, 'conjugal violence' is a product of a crimino-legal practice which stands in as proxy for the violence of the marriage relation. There is then a legal culture of violence in which conjugal homicide takes place. Violence resides in the house of law, the house of marriage. The violence that takes place in the city streets is only ever a pale reflection and prolongation of that which has already been sacrificed in the law of marriage. Once we attend to representation, it is the sacrificial dimension of criminal legal practice that occupies the place of the unpresentable in representation, the place of silence in Realist criminology.

The deep structure of reference which founds crimino-legal representation is best described as a sacrificial structure of simulation. In the remainder of the chapter, our attention devolves upon two features of the structure: first, the way in which the reverence *and* revulsion towards the victim renders intelligible the contemporary universalisation of victimage; and second, the way in which the victim is a representation which narrates a story of belonging in the city.

The bricks and mortar of civil society

As described above, Realist criminology focuses on the urban space and the experiences of city dwellers. In doing so, it provides a portrait of urban life, the main terms of which are civility, decency and tolerance, which moreover promote the cohesion of community against criminogenesis. Thus crime is 'lack of respect for humanity and for fundamental human decency' (Lea and Young, 1984: 55). One of the many major aims of criminal justice policy elaborated by Realism, therefore, is to determine the 'changes in what is tolerable behaviour and what could be done to achieve a more civilized society' (Young, 1992: 25). It is the 'quality of life' which becomes the predominant concern of the Realist: 'what can be more central to the quality of life than the ability to walk down the street at night without fear, to feel safe in one's home, to be free of harassment and incivilities in the day-to-day experience of urban life?' (Young, 1992: 49–50). Given this, it is not the formal institutions of social control which act as a guarantor of social order and cohesion, but rather what Young, in a curious metaphor, calls 'the social bricks and mortar of civil society' (1992: 45). These values are sought within the space of the modern city.

The city is full of individuals who are not connected to each other and of social groups which do not mix. Within the geographical area covered by a city, the Realist does not find a real *community*; rather, a highly populated area in which crime thrives. Crime is

> the run-down council estate where music blares out of windows early in the morning; it is the graffiti on the walls; it is aggression in the shops; it is bins that are never emptied; oil stains across the streets; it is kids that show no respect; it is large trucks racing through your roads; it is streets you do not dare walk down at night; it is always being careful; it is a symbol of a world falling apart. (Lea and Young, 1984: 55)

Such a millennial vision of the apocalyptic city recalls Rousseau, who found the city horrifying and threatening. For Rousseau, a concentration of individuals in a limited space, far from enhancing the social bond, destroys it; civil liberty, far from flourishing, founders and is nullified. Rousseau writes: 'It is [in the city] that men commit, in the midst of their kind, what no other species does among itself: they turn against themselves; they devour one another' (1959a: 114). City dwellers live by exploiting each other, seeking to maximise their own interests. A legal system is thus required which orients the war of all against all towards the war of all against one, or, in more Platonic terms, towards the common good. The telos of law and crime control is to enhance city life by promoting safety (from being, in Rousseau's terms, devoured) and in promoting civic-mindedness (through localised community crime prevention schemes). Individuals would then each possess knowledge and law, and become full citizens of the city with respect and compassion for each other, transcending the reality of urban crowding and excess in the modern age.

Such nostalgia is unavoidable. The Realist vision of the urban space deploys a dichotomous polarisation of two conceptions of the city.[29] No doubt one cannot avoid positing oppositions; but what is important is how they are used. The 'city' has very different traditions: one is *urbs*, the stones of the city, its layout, its accession to the needs of shelter, warfare and commerce; that is, its planning. The other is *civitas*, the emotions, rituals and convictions that take shape within a city; that is, its community. The *urbs* is simply a pattern of stones, asphalt, wood, concrete, street names, buildings, opaque boundaries. *Civitas*, on the other hand, connotes a neighbourhood, a collective, a shared enterprise of living, a community of homes with common values, a grouping of workplaces organised around mutual goals, lucidity and transparency.[30] The crime survey, such as those which took place in Islington (Jones et al., 1986; Crawford et al., 1990), collapse these two notions of the city into one – or more correctly, metaphorises *civitas* in terms of the *urbs*, thinks of civility as a matter of bricks and mortar. The Islington crime surveys provide a map of behaviour derided as anti-social and analysed against the topography of individuals' hopes, desires and fears. That is, the emotions and anxieties of *civitas* are being examined as if they were immediately comparable with the layout of the *urbs*. The modern urban space has thus already been constructed as the space of excess, of devouring, of criminality; the place where civic ideals have failed, where individual morality has been lost. As Rousseau said: 'a capital is an abyss where nearly the entire nation goes to lose its morals, its laws, its courage and its freedom' (1959b: 911). So the Realists view the city as the place of excess and loss: excess of individualism, loss of civic spirit. Such a nostalgic impetus sends the Realists out onto the street searching for civic spirit among the stones of urban space. Hence the prevention advice resonates with the demands of planning. In short, the passion of civility is sacrificed to the urbane planning of Realism.

The victim as universal subject

As bearer of the lost civic spirit, Realist criminology seeks a human subject who will resist the depradations of city life. Parallel to its fascination with the city, Realism is fascinated by the victim. Moreover, it is a fascination which, we have suggested, produces a victim that is universalised. Why is this so?

In a situation of ultramodernity, where we are experiencing the loss of horizons, the loss of certainties and limits, the victim stands out as a *liminal* figure.[31] That is, the victim offers a certainty, that of the experience of pain or fear or frustration, the certainty of the passionate body. Against the loss of horizon achieved by the accelerating instrumentalisation of late twentieth century culture,[32] the victim promises an end. The victim assures us that there *is* a limit to the loss of faith, that there is a point beyond which nihilism cannot go because it must not go. The victim represents the finality of reality. The victim's certainty, definitiveness and liminality result from its constitution within Realist criminology as a figure representing *total reality*. In short, the universalisation of the victim is an effect of the systematisation of the real. The victim is thus faceless; it has no marks of identity other than its victimage. Indeed, it is essential that it has none, in order for it to be successfully universal. We are all victims. And what could be more masculine than that. The privilege of masculinity has been asserted through an opposition with femininity, in which masculinity is always-already the unmarked term. Unremarked, the smooth surface of the universal victim is first and foremost masculine. In short, the universalisation of victimage sacrifices femininity in the interests of securing masculinity against the loss of limits that marks the late twentieth century. The feminine is constituted as the horizon of men. The first victim of universal victimage is thus the feminine. The ethical particularities of woman as victim are elided and obscured. The response to the demand for justice takes the moral form of law: cognised as criteria of individual difference, the *details* of her victimisation – sex, marital status, form of abuse suffered – are secondary features.

In short, then, the victim as universal subject is a transcendental signifier which holds in place a series of substitutions in Realist criminology. It stands in for crime, for theory. It simulates subjectivity; it is a proxy that creates a sense of lost community for the individual. Knowledge of the sharedness of victimisation reunites us all. It stands in for the real, as much as for the urbanity of modern life. Urbanity takes the Realist to street crime, which functions as the exemplary mode of victimisation. And if at the end of this series of substitutions, we arrive at its beginning, this is because the universal victim is both the subject and the object of criminological investigation. For the criminologist understands crime because he or she, like all of us, is victimised. The horizon then that is constructed as a bulwark against the nihilistic loss of faith is, after all, the Realist criminologist.

Conclusion

The business in which Realist criminology is engaged is the building of a horizon which will contain, which will lock up, the loss of faith which characterises ultramodernity. But no horizon is a continuous line, without aporias, without fractures. In this chapter, then, we have been concerned to trace the itinerary of conjugal violence as the unpresentable within the Realist representation of victimisation. This task has required not so much a critique or denunciation – although there has been a little of that – but rather that we think through the *failure* of Realism. In such a way, it is possible yet again to hear the ethical demand for justice that resounds in the contemporary culture of conjugal violence. In as much as there has been critique, Realism has been characterised as a programme which sacrifices the real for reality, the feminine for the masculine, passion for planning, *civitas* for *urbs*. In such a way is violence inscribed and reiterated in Realist criminology. The ethical particularities of the scapegoat are sacrificed to the universal law of victimage.

Notes

1 The case report is at [1975] *All England Law Reports* 788. All subsequent page references to this report will be in the main text.

2 A fact that is interesting in the light of the recent debate on citizens 'having-a-go'; and see the acquittal, by reason of self-defence, of Elliott, who stabbed a self-styled vigilante intervening to prevent Elliott from slashing car tyres. See also recent articles in the press: for example, in *The Guardian*, 20 July 1993.

3 For example, as the focus of reflective debates in Maguire and Pointing (1988) and Walklate (1989).

4 As exemplary, see Lea and Young (1984); Jones et al. (1986); Kinsey et al. (1986); Young (1987); Painter (1989); Painter et al. (1989); Crawford et al. (1990); Young and Matthews (1992).

5 The 'square of crime' should be compared here to the 'semantic rectangle' of the structuralist semiotician, as to which see Greimas (1970).

6 On the couple generally, see Cixous (1981).

7 For the suggestion that the binary structure of an opposition is always-already subtended by the Man/Woman couple, see Cixous (1981) and further with Clement (1986).

8 Refer to Figure 2.2 in Young (1992: 29).

9 On the public as third term in socio-legal regulation, see Rush (forthcoming a).

10 For the best description of the neo-liberal strategy of moral-legal regulation in the post-Wolfenden era, and in particular with respect to its uses of the private, see Brown (1980).

11 'Race' and 'gender' are marked as signifiers in *R.* v. *Ahluwalia*; neither gender nor race are deemed remarkable in *R.* v. *Venna*.

12 For a radically different view of a community health project, see Johnstone (1991) on a community treatment programme for habitual drunken offenders.

13 On the allegorical matrix of health and medicine, see Sontag (1978, 1989).

14 On metaphor's productive qualities, see MacCannell (1986: 98, 103, 105).

15 Occasionally, discourses of illnesses and criminality merge as in the case of HIV; see Shilts' representation of 'Patient Zero' in Shilts (1987).

16 Realist criminology came to prominence with the Islington Crime Survey; subsequent crime surveys include Painter et al. (1989) and Painter et al. (1990).

17 Note the prevalence of cartographic maps in Realist texts. For example, in Jones et al. (1986).

18 Lea and Young, in their foreword to *What Is To Be Done About Law and Order?*, describe how one of the manuscript's chapters was stolen, on two separate occasions, from a parked car (1984: 7).

19 See Cameron and Frazer (1987); Caputi (1988), Wilson (1988), Caputi and Russell (1992), and more generally, the feminist concern with the 'everyday' as site of oppression and insult.

20 For an analysis of the portrait of the victim in child (sexual) abuse, see Rush (forthcoming a).

21 On one of the nodal points of city living, see Matthews (1992); and on the minimisation of risk in general, see Smith (1986: Ch. 8).

22 The case report is at [1992] 4 *All England Law Reports* 889. All subsequent page references to this report will be included in the text.

23 In the last few years, national campaigns were organised by Justice For Women, and Southall Black Sisters, to demand legal reform and to support imprisoned women who had killed their abusers. Ahluwalia was one of the women whose case received media attention thanks to these campaigns. Sara Thornton's appeal had failed and her subsequent hunger strike increased media interest in conjugal violence. A number of men who had killed their wives received comparatively lenient sentences: see especially, Joseph McGrail who received a suspended sentence for manslaughter when he strangled his wife for putting the mustard pot in the wrong place on the kitchen table.

24 The event and the legal response must here be articulated with the tradition of suttee. More generally, we take this occasion to remark the question of race, which we do not address in this chapter. The report states that the marriage was an arranged marriage. Kiranjit was born in India to a middle-class family. She did an arts degree and started a law degree. Deepak was from a Kenyan Asian family 'who emigrated in 1971'. The trial judge's direction to the jury on

the question of provocation is instructive: 'she is an Asian woman, married, incidentally to an Asian man, the deceased, living in this country. You may think she is an educated woman, she has a university degree. If you find these characteristics relevant to your considerations of course you will bear them in mind' (p. 897).

25 On abjection, see Kristeva who writes 'Abjection is . . . a friend who stabs you'. And 'Any crime, because it draws attention to the fragility of the law, is abject' (1982: 4).

26 On tragedy and the law, see Douzinas and McVeigh (1992).

27 This has been extensively argued in the context of Thornton's case of conjugal homicide by one of us: see A. Young (1994).

28 See Kristeva (1987); especially the chapter 'Romeo and Juliet: love-hatred in the couple'.

29 Sennett describes the studies of St Isidore, who wrote *The Etymologies* and who thus discovered the two separate traditions of the city (Sennett, 1990: 11).

30 In common with Rousseau, who longed for transparency and lucidity, the Realists offer lighting in a pedestrian effort to challenge the dark opacity of the city streets. See especially, Painter (1989).

31 For an account of another liminal figure which also acts as a moment of universal subjectivity, see A. Young (1993).

32 See Toulmin (1990) for an innovative and accessible charting of ultramodernity against the background of the Enlightenment. For an account of crime in ultramodernity, see Young (forthcoming).

References

Beck, U. (1992) *Risk Society*. London: Sage.

Brown, B. (1980) 'Private faces in public places', *Ideology and Consciousness*, 7: 3–16.

Cameron, D. and Frazer, E. (1987) *The Lust To Kill*. Cambridge: Polity Press.

Caputi, J. (1988) *The Age of Sex Crime*. London: Women's Press.

Caputi, J. and Russell, D.E.H. (1992) 'Femicide: sexist terrorism against women', in J. Radford and D.E.H. Russell (eds), *Femicide*. Milton Keynes: Open University Press.

Cixous, H. (1981) 'Castration or decapitation?', *Signs*, 7(1): 44–55.

Cixous, H. and Clément, C. (1986) *The Newly-Born Woman*. Manchester: Manchester University Press.

Crawford, A., Jones, T., Woodhouse, T. and Young, J. (1990) *Second Islington Crime Survey*. Middlesex Polytechnic; Centre for Criminology.

Derrida, J. (1987) *The Post-Card*. Chicago: Chicago University Press.

Douzinas, C. and McVeigh, S. (1992) 'The tragic body: the inscription of autonomy in medical ethics and law', in S. McVeigh and S. Wheeler (eds), *Law, Health and Medical Regulation*. Aldershot: Dartmouth.

Girard, R. (1987) *Things Hidden Since The Foundation of the World*. Stanford, CA: Stanford University Press.

Greimas, A.J. (1970) *Du Sens*. Paris: Editions du Seuil.

Harvey, D. (1973) *Social Justice and The City*. London: Edward Arnold.

Jackson, P. (1989) *Maps of Meaning*. London: Unwin Hyman.

Johnstone, G. (1991) 'Between permissiveness and control: community treatment and penal supervision', *Law & Critique*, 2(1): 37–61.

Jones, T., MacLean, B. and Young, J. (1986) *The Islington Crime Survey*. Aldershot: Gower.

Kinsey, R., Lea, J. and Young, J. (1986) *Losing The Fight Against Crime*. Oxford: Blackwell.

Kristeva, J. (1982) *Powers of Horror*. New York: Columbia University Press.

Kristeva, J. (1987) *Tales of Love*. New York: Columbia University Press.

Lea, J. and Young, J. (1984) *What is To Be Done About Law and Order?* Harmondsworth: Penguin.

MacCannell, J.F. (1986) *Figuring Lacan*. London: Croom Helm.

Maguire, M. and Pointing, J. (eds) (1988) *Victims of Crime: A New Deal?* Milton Keynes: Open University Press.

Matthews, R. (1992) 'Replacing "broken windows": crime, incivilities and urban change', in R. Matthews and J. Young (eds), *Issues in Realist Criminology*. London: Sage.

Painter, K. (1989) *Lighting and Crime: the Edmonton Project*. Middlesex Polytechnic; Centre for Criminology.

Painter, K., Lea, J., Woodhouse, T. and Young, J. (1989) *The Hammersmith and Fulham Crime and Policing Survey*. Middlesex Polytechnic, Centre for Criminology.

Painter, K., Woodhouse, T. and Young, J. (1990) *The Ladywood Crime and Community Safety Survey*. Middlesex Polytechnic, Centre for Criminology.

Rousseau, J.-J. (1959a) 'Essai sur l'origine des langues', in *Oeuvres Complètes*. Paris: Gallimard.

Rousseau, J.-J. (1959b) 'Emile', in *Oeuvres Complètes*. Paris: Gallimard.

Rush, P. (forthcoming a) *The Trials of Sex*. London: Routledge.

Rush, P. (forthcoming b) 'The desire of criminal legal practices: an indecent event', in S. McVeigh, P. Rush and A. Young (eds), *Criminal Legal Practices*. Oxford: Oxford University Press.

Sennett, R. (1990) *The Conscience of the Eye*. London: Faber and Faber.

Shilts, R. (1987) *And The Band Played On*. Harmondsworth: Penguin.

Smith, S.J. (1986) *Crime, Space and Society*. Cambridge: Cambridge University Press.

Soja, E. (1988) *Postmodern Geographies*. London: Verso.

Sontag, S. (1978) *Illness as Metaphor*. New York: Farrar, Straus & Giroux.

Sontag, S. (1989) *Aids and its Metaphors*. New York: Farrar, Straus & Giroux.

Toulmin, S. (1990) *Cosmopolis*. Chicago: Chicago University Press.

Walklate, S. (1989) *Victimology* London: Unwin Hyman.

Wilson, E. (1988) 'Death City', in E. Wilson, *Hallucinations: Life in the Postmodern City*. London: Radius.

Young, A. (1993) 'Decapitation or feticide: the fetal laws of the universal subject', *Women: A Cultural Review*, 3–4.

Young, A. (1994) '*Caveat Sponsa*: violence and the body in law', in J. Brettle and S. Rice (eds), *Public Bodies/Private States*. Manchester: Manchester University Press.

Young, A. (forthcoming) *Postmodern Criminology*. London: Sage.

Young, J. (1987) 'The tasks of a realist criminology', *Contemporary Crises*, 11: 337–56.

Young, J. (1992) 'Ten points of realism', in J. Young and R. Matthews (eds), *Rethinking Criminology: The Realist Debate*. London: Sage.

Young, J. and Matthews, R. (eds) (1992) *Rethinking Criminology: The Realist Debate*. London: Sage.

8

Actuarial Justice: the Emerging New Criminal Law

Malcolm Feeley and Jonathan Simon

Introduction

In a recent article we argued that there is a paradigm shift taking place in the criminal process. Focusing on selected issues of penology, we examined what we termed the Old Penology and the New Penology (Feeley and Simon, 1992: 449). In this chapter we broaden this argument, and outline the features of this new development, which we term *actuarial justice*. In the earlier paper we argued that the Old Penology is rooted in a concern for individuals, and preoccupied with such concepts as guilt, responsibility and obligation, as well as diagnosis, intervention and treatment of the individual offender. It views committing a crime a deviant or antisocial act which is deserving of a response, and one of its central aims is to ascertain the nature of the responsibility of the accused and hold the guilty accountable.

In contrast the New Penology has a radically different orientation.[1] It is actuarial. It is concerned with techniques for identifying, classifying and managing groups assorted by levels of dangerousness. It takes crime for granted. It accepts deviance as normal. It is sceptical that liberal interventionist crime control strategies do or can make a difference. Thus its aim is not to intervene in individuals' lives for the purpose of ascertaining responsibility, making the guilty 'pay for their crime' or changing them. Rather it seeks to regulate groups as part of a strategy of managing danger.

In our article (Feeley and Simon, 1992) we addressed the general logic of the New Penology in terms of discourses, techniques and objectives. Here in our more general enquiry we explore how 'actuarial justice', is being institutionalised and survey the broader intellectual, political and social contexts which have facilitated its emergence. This shift, we believe, is shaping and will continue to shape the agenda of criminology. Indeed, as we show here, and in our earlier article, a new actuarial criminology has already emerged and made itself felt.

In the first part of this chapter, the basic characteristics of actuarial justice are analysed. We begin with an examination of three practices that most clearly exemplify the qualities of actuarial justice: incapacitation, preventive detention and drug courier profiles. These are far from the only locations where actuarial justice is present, but an examination of these forms reveals

important features they have in common. Next, we look at some examples of
how traditional practices in the criminal justice system are being reshaped by
the imperatives of actuarial justice. Finally, we explore how the logic of
actuarial justice is influencing the application of constitutional norms which
might have acted as a constraint on its expansion.

The second part of this chapter is an exploration of the intellectual,
political, and social contexts of actuarial justice. This falls far short of a
causal explanation, but by linking actuarial justice to emerging practices
elsewhere we can identify some of the forces that are facilitating the growth
of actuarial justice.

THE ELEMENTS OF ACTUARIAL JUSTICE

Actuarial justice is nebulous, but it is significant. Actuarial justice involves
how we conceive of and talk about crime policy, but it is not an ideology in
the narrow sense of a set of beliefs and ideas which constrain action. It
involves practices, but is not reducible to a specific technology or set of
behaviours. Indeed it is powerful and significant precisely because it lacks a
well-articulated ideology and identification with a specific technology. Its
very amorphousness contributes to its power. Below we outline an account
of actual practices and discourses which are giving shape to this emerging
formation in the criminal process.[2] Following that we abstract some of the
critical features of these developments. However, it is important to keep in
mind that what we describe is not a mentality or a blueprint that can be
cleanly separated from the material it analyses.

New practices

It is somewhat misleading to speak of new practices, since the practices we
discuss are, in fact, partial practices which have had long and varied
histories. Their newness lies in their particular combinations and the
particular micropractices they are embedded in and the functions which they
perform.

Incapacitation

Possibly the clearest indication of actuarial justice is found in the new theory
of incapacitation, which has perhaps become the predominant model of
punishment (see Greenwood, 1982; Moore et al., 1984). Incapacitation
promises to reduce the effects of crime in society not by altering either
offender or social context, but by rearranging the distribution of offenders in
society. If the prison can do nothing else, incapacitation theory holds, it can
detain offenders for a time and thus delay their resumption of criminal
activity in society.

According to the theory, if such delays are sustained for enough time and for enough people, significant aggregate effects in crime can take place although individual destinies are only marginally altered. In this sense, incapacitation is to penology what arbitration is to investments, a method of capitalising on minute displacements in time; and like arbitration it has a diminished relationship to the normative goal of enhancing the value of its objects.

These aggregate effects can be further intensified by a strategy of *selective* incapacitation. This approach proposes a sentencing scheme in which lengths of sentence depend not upon the nature of the criminal offence or upon an assessment of the character of the offender, but upon risk profiles. Its objects are to identify high-risk offenders and to maintain long-term control over them while investing in shorter terms and less intrusive control and surveillance over lower risk offenders.

First articulated as a coherent scheme for punishing in a report by the RAND Corporation (Greenwood, 1982), an operations research-oriented R&D organisation, it was quickly embraced and self-consciously promoted as a new justification for punishment by a team of scholars at Harvard University (Moore et al., 1984), who were keenly aware that it constituted a paradigm shift in the underlying rationale for imposing criminal sanctions.[3]

The focus on the group rather than the individual is not, of course, completely new. The 'group' has been an organising unit in many societies from time immemorial, and in Western liberal society since the eighteenth century thinkers have been concerned with the general preventive effects of criminal punishment, sometimes called general deterrence (Andenaes, 1974). But general deterrence is essentially a theory of communication. Through punishment the political sovereign is able to communicate to the public as such and signal the degree of prohibition to be associated with various forms of proscribed conduct. The broadcast is general, but the receivers are individuals who will presumably integrate the information in their rational management of their own lives. In contrast, incapacitation (selective or otherwise) attempts to manipulate the public as a demographic mass or aggregate, bypassing the *res cogitans* of individuals altogether. The aim is not to induce altered behaviour as a result of rational calculations by individuals, but the management-through-custody of that segment of the population that is dangerous. Length of custody is determined by calculated risk factors not seriousness of offence.

Preventive detention

Pre-trial decision making in the United States has always made evident a concern for preventive detention as well as for the task of assuring the presence of the accused at trial. Both concerns were pursued on an individual basis, albeit one which embodied plenty of collective stereotypes. The new logic of pre-trial detention operates in a manner similar to selective incapacitation. Preselected categories of information about an arrestee are collected and run through a collective algorithm.

The origins of this development are found in the bail reform efforts of the early 1960s, when liberal reformers and the courts rejected a constitutional 'rights strategy' for bail reform in preference to an 'administrative strategy'. The rights strategy called for clarification of the Eighth Amendment's prohibition against 'excessive bail'. Arguing that the purpose of bail was to assure appearance at trial, it called for clarification and expansion of the standard of 'least restrictive conditions' and assurances that bail would not be used as a form of preventive detention or summary punishment. It saw the right to bail as an undeveloped constitutional issue in need of development, and called upon the courts to clarify it. In the United States, this strategy was set forth in a series of path-breaking articles by Caleb Foote in the 1950s who foresaw a 'coming constitutional crisis in bail' and set forth its agenda. However, liberal reformers and judges rejected the constitutional revolution and the rights strategy that Foote advocated, and instead developed an alternative administrative strategy. Agreeing with Foote that the purpose of pre-trial release was to assure presence at trial (as opposed to detaining 'dangerous individuals' or imposing summary punishment), they conceived of pre-trial release as an administrative matter to be handled by scientific not legal expertise. The alternative administrative strategy sought to base conditions of pre-trial release on models of 'predictors' of appearance and non-appearance. The US Department of Justice vigorously promoted the establishment of specialised pre-trial release agencies which developed multivariate models to predict appearance and non-appearance at trial and report their findings to the courts. These developments stunted constitutional clarification of the *right* to bail.[4] As one of the authors noted a decade ago:

> Professor Caleb Foote's hope that a crisis in bail would be resolved through constitutional law reform has not been fulfilled. . . . [L]egal challenges to current bail practices have met with . . . numbing defeats. Perhaps these defeats have been conditioned by the conservative tenor of the Burger Court, but they may also be due to a sense of complacency about the administrative approach to bail reform as reflected in pretrial release programs. (Feeley, 1983: 77)

Once established 'pre-trial release agencies' developed a life of their own. What began as a reform calling attention to the problems of unnecessary pre-trial detention, quickly became 'part of that problem'. Seemingly without effort the pre-trial release agencies moved from developing actuarial-like models to predict appearance at trial to developing models to predict dangerousness and on to models to predict the consequences of testing dirty to various types of drugs (Feeley, 1983: 79). Once a rights strategy had given way to an administrative strategy, each of these moves was but a small step along the path of actuarial justice.

The conventional explanation for shifts in pre-trial release policy in the United States and Western Europe from the 1960s to the 1990s is that due process-oriented liberals were displaced by law-and-order conservatives. But this explanation is incomplete if not altogether wrong. Pre-trial release policies do not divide neatly along these lines. Indeed it was well-known liberal reformers who were responsible for first promoting actuarial justice in the form of administrative strategy of pre-trial release agencies. They set aside issues of rights, and once having claimed the ability to predict appearance at trial, it was a small step to applying their risk assessment models to the issue of dangerousness, the consequences of testing dirty, and the like. In hindsight one can trace the development of actuarial justice in this area and see how it cuts across traditional liberal-conservative lines.

Drug courier profiles

Over the last two decades law enforcement has utilised a variety of objective and quasi-objective 'profiles' to identify suspected criminals in specific settings. The first such profile to be widely used was for hijackers at airports. Developed in 1969 by a federal task force, the profile includes 24 to 30 characteristics which the task force concluded could be used in selected combinations to differentiate potential hijackers from other air travellers (Cloud, 1985: 874).[5] In 1974, the federal Drug Enforcement Agency developed a 'drug courier profile' which contained a list of behavioural factors which in combination were believed to differentiate individuals transporting illegal narcotics by air from other air travellers. The profile and variants have been widely used to identify suspects for further surveillance or brief detentions and interrogations (Cloud, 1985: 844–5). Similar profiles have also been used to identify drivers transporting drugs on the nation's highways and illegal aliens across the border (Cloud, 1985: 854).

The drug courier profiles that have been revealed in court proceedings provide evidence of the form of actuarial prediction, but lack the substantive data and methods which generally support their use. Factors such as the city the suspect is travelling from, his or her type of luggage, order of departure from the plane, and nervousness and many other factors have been included in such profiles. While government agents have often defended the relevancy of these factors on the witness stand, they have never presented systematic statistical analyses of their individual association or aggregate efficiency as predictors.

Despite these shortcomings, their popularity suggests that actuarial justice fits well with prevailing ideologies of what makes the exercise of power rational although its actual use may be riddled with subjectivity and prejudice. In the future we may expect pressure both to validate the profiles statistically, refine them and to expand their use.

Analysis of actuarial justice

What these forms have in common is not the repetition of a singular structure but a set of overlapping features.

The population itself, in its biological and demographic sense, is taken as the target of power The emergence of criminological positivism in the late nineteenth century divided between those who focused on crime as a set of prohibited acts (whether understood economically or morally) and those who focused on criminals as a set of dangerous individuals (embodied in both classicism and moral philosophies of punishment). As late as the 1970s it seemed as if the central tensions in criminal justice policy could be understood as a dialectic between these positions.[6] We argue that the new practices radically reframe the issues, and target something very different, that is, the crime rate, understood as the *distribution* of behaviours in the population as a whole. In this sense actuarial justice should be seen as a part of the general movement noted by a number of scholars towards the exercise of state power as 'governmentality'.[7]

This does not mean that individuals disappear in criminal justice. They remain, but increasingly they are grasped not as coherent subjects, whether understood as moral, psychological or economic agents, but as members of particular subpopulations and the intersection of various categorical indicators.

Power is aimed at prevention and risk minimisation Rather than seeking to respond to past offences, these techniques are mainly aimed at preventing future offences. Prevention has always been a concern of the criminal process and a justification of punishment. Some of the new techniques – selective incapacitation and pre-trial detention – present a possibly purer form of prevention. More important, however, prevention is aimed less at halting proscribed activities than reducing the likelihood and seriousness of offending.

Justice is increasingly understood not as a rational system but through the rationality of the system Criminal justice has always been concerned with how to distribute its own considerable powers. The classic theorists, such as Beccaria and Bentham, worried about the distribution between legislators, prosecutors and juries. Positivists defined the scientifically trained expert as the obvious repository of power. Until recently our debates on sentencing and other topics have operated as if this was still the fundamental set of choices. The new techniques discussed here suggest the rise of formal systems of internal rules, analogous in many respects to computer programs.

The new techniques we discussed above are a small subset of all criminal justice practices. They are attached to institutions that seem largely to operate in 'the old fashioned way', that is, responding reactively and often brutally to crime. Yet, while these measures are all in varying degrees defined as new and controversial, an examination of how the logic of actuarial justice has penetrated more venerable practices in criminal justice suggests that the future is already here.

New functions for old forms

New formations rarely grow on ground totally cleared of the past. They develop alongside practices created at various times which have accrued social and political weight against the demands of coherence and reform. The significance of actuarial justice is not only to be found in the development of the new practices described in the preceding section, but as well in the reorientation and redefinition of older practices. Below we explore several of the new functions for old forms.

Recidivism

Although the term 'recidivism' is used in penology and continues to be used in actuarial justice, its function has undergone an important metamorphosis. Once used extensively as an indicator of programme effectiveness (such as, 'Did the programme reduce recidivism, and if so, by how much?'), now it is much more likely to be used as an 'indicator' of another sort, as data to be considered along with still other indicators to make judgements about risk classification, incarceration and surveillance.

Drug testing

The traditional aim of drug tests was to identify deviance, self-destructive behaviour – in itself an individual failure that should trigger a concern for intervention. In actuarial justice, such tests are data in a flow of information for assessing risk. To the extent that drug use (and type, frequency and amount – all of which can be roughly calibrated by the tests) is an indicator of social dangerousness, information revealed by drug tests can be folded into the decision-making algorithms of the system. Drug use – like other indicators which once were more easily obtainable, such as residency, marital status, employment status, criminal record, education and the like – can also be systematically included in developing profiles of dangerousness.

Prison, probation and parole

Actuarial justice invites new justifications for, and hence new forms of, custody and surveillance. Increasingly imprisonment and 'supervision' assume new functions and forms. Actuarial rationales for imprisonment and supervision are not anchored in aspirations to obtain restitution, rehabilitate, reintegrate, train and the like. Rather they are justified in more blunt terms: variable detention and surveillance depending upon level of risk assessment. They invite low-cost, no-frills prisons – custody centres – without education and vocational training services. And they invite expanded and variable use of detention, and especially greater reliance on short-term detention with little or no accompanying educational or training opportunities.[8]

The small boom in private prisons in the United States has largely been aimed at providing such no-frills, short-term 'custody centres', institutions whose value is in the aggregate, as institutions for marginally reducing danger in society by detaining high-risk offenders.

Similarly, probation and parole have assumed new functions. Once conceived of as 'half-way' stages whose aim was to reintegrate offenders back into their communities, parole and probation are now simply alternatives to custody for lower-risk offenders. 'Supervision' consists of monitoring levels of risk as determined by several indicators, most prominently drug testing. Moreover, with large portions of the non-incarcerated population in some of the poorest and most crime victimised communities in the country, probation, parole or some form of community supervision are becoming a lower cost alternative to traditional justice (Simon, 1993).

For instance procedures for revoking parole and probation in most American states and the UK are far lower than those for criminal conviction. Given that in many American states a substantial proportion of all new inmates entering prison are people whose probation or parole has been revoked, a new, managerial process of incarceration already has been established and is functioning. And even here revocation hearings are often waived as part of a rapidly expanding new form of plea bargaining where even truncated revocation hearings are waived (and the probationer returns to custody voluntarily) in exchange for dropping new charges (Greenspan, 1991).

Adoption of new models of rationality in judicial review

The courts are one force that could do much to slow the development of actuarial justice. The criminal jurisprudence embodied in the Constitution and the Bill of Rights is loaded with values of individual autonomy and social equality which clash with the logic of actuarial justice. And indeed many of the landmarks of American constitutional criminal procedure throughout the 1960s elaborate this social vision. However, an analysis of more recent Supreme Court decisions suggests that this development has been reversed. The Court is engaged in rethinking the values of constitutional criminal jurisprudence from an orientation deeply informed by actuarial justice. This has, we believe, even more profound implications than the appointment of more conservative, 'law and order' federal judges that has been the object of so much concern among the liberal community. An actuarial social vision, clothed in familiar language, is powerful precisely because it subtly restructures concepts and language. In the long run, we suspect that it will be more powerful than the 'law and order' political movement precisely because it will be more deeply ingrained in the law.

Preventive detention

In *United States* v. *Salerno* (1987) the Supreme Court upheld preventive detention provisions of the Bail Reform Act of 1984 which permitted pre-trial detention to protect the 'safety of the community' based on a set of prescribed factors including the seriousness of the charge, the extent of the evidence and the nature of the threat posed. Then Associate Justice William Rehnquist, the author of the Court's opinion, argued that preventive detention does not trigger the same level of protection as other penal detention decisions because pre-trial release is intended to manage risks rather than punish.[9] So long as Congress intended to regulate (and hence subject its provisions to review by the traditional rationality test), rather than punish dangerous people, due process standards were not offended (*Salerno*, 1987: 748).

While the Court's distinction may appear disingenuous to some, it does have the virtue of openly acknowledging that the Court is constructing a new way of thinking about criminal justice. The risk factors considered by the trial court in *Salerno* were different from the purely actuarial associations employed in selective incapacitation, or even in the quasi-actuarial methods of the drug courier profile. In *Salerno* the government claimed that Mr Salerno was the boss of the Genovese family of the New York ' Cosa Nostra' (*Salerno*, 1987: 743). The Court's analysis does not dwell on methodology in its rush to affirm confinement based on dangerousness. Actuarial factors may even be fairer bases. The important point is that the Court openly and explicitly recognised a regulatory exercise of power operating in and through the criminal justice process that aims at *managing* a population of dangerous people at an appropriate level of control. This decision stands in stark contrast with the social vision informing its earlier pre-trial release rulings (see, for example, *Stack* v. *Boyle*, 1951).

Mass surveillance and probable cause

The line between regulatory power and punishment has been further blurred in the Court's Fourth Amendment jurisprudence. Where the Court once treated probable cause to believe that a suspect has committed or is committing a crime as a prerequisite to police intervention, more recently it has described a broader area of police intervention as falling outside the protections of the Fourth Amendment or requiring only general rationales. Indeed it has come close to turning the Fourth Amendment on its head and treating it as an affirmative grant of power to the police (Wasserstrom, 1984).

Normalising a surveillance society   One way of accomplishing this is by treating less formal encounters between police and citizens as consensual rather than detentions. The Court has described as 'consensual' and increasingly coercive set of encounters – airport stops where individuals are asked for their ticket and identification, sweeps of factories, random inspections of intercity buses, and the like. Thus in *Florida* v. *Bostick* (1991) the Court held that a person was *not* detained by the police even though it was reasonable for him to believe that he was not free to terminate the encounter.

The border is everywhere   Similarly the Court has enlarged the border 'exception' to expand the power of the police to stop and search people. In

Michigan State Police v. *Sitz* (1991) the Supreme Court approved a sobriety checkpoint set up by police. The case was the first to approve a police stop without any individualised suspicion in a non-specialised setting. Prior cases had limited such stops to airports, and at or very near international borders. These special settings, most especially the border, represent those liminal spaces of the political community where its democratic internal life comes into contact with its quite different ethos as a sovereign subject seeking to minimise its risk in international affairs. The recognition that anyone who enters these spaces is operating within a domain of generalised suspicion is justifiable because of this liminality. In contrast, *Sitz* represents the expansion of the mentality of the border to virtually *all* the interior spaces of the United States.[10]

Profiles in suspicion   And as mentioned earlier, the Court has embraced the use of 'profiles' as the basis for detaining persons. In a series of 1980s cases,[11] often employing the language of a 'war against drugs', the Supreme Court endorsed the use by the Federal Drug Enforcement Agency (DEA) of drug courier profiles, and in so doing greatly enhanced the capacity to detain and search people. In *Reid* v. *Georgia*, the US Supreme Court reversed a state high court ruling upholding a stop made on the basis of a drug courier profile. In so doing the US Supreme Court rejected detention based upon factors such as 'drug source city departure, early-morning arrival, no luggage other than shoulder bag', and the like (*Reid*, 1980: 441) as an acceptable basis for detaining persons because these factors 'describe[ed] a very large category of presumably innocent travellers'.

However, in *Sokolow* (1989) a majority on the Supreme Court changed course, and upheld a stop based on the same sort of information. While *Reid* suggested that the Court was at least sensitive to the special nature of actuarial knowledge, *Sokolow* took the path of avoiding any explicit analysis of the significance of this knowledge, treating it instead as an ordinary instance of inevitably probabilistic evaluation. In declining to even engage a lower court's strongly argued concern about the implications of using actuarial-like profiles, it signalled a new willingness to allow the expansion of search and seizure powers of the police without any corresponding adjustment of constitutional protections to the individual. In short it represents a significant expansion of what we call actuarial justice.

The particulars of the case are revealing, especially when contrasted with the lower appellate court's ruling to the contrary, and the Court's earlier case attempting to define carefully the conditions under which police can stop and frisk someone in the absence of probable cause. Because *Sokolow* represents a significant endorsement of a powerful actuarial technique, it is worth reviewing them at some length.

In *Sokolow* a traveller had been detained in the Honolulu airport by DEA agents who had been alerted to him by the following factors which matched their current drug courier profile:

(1) he paid $2,100 for two airplane tickets from a roll of $20 bills; (2) he traveled under a name that did not match the name under which his telephone number was listed; (3) his original destination was Miami, a source city for illicit drugs; (4) he stayed in Miami for only 48 hours, even though a round-trip flight from Honolulu to Miami takes 20 hours; (5) he appeared nervous during his trip; and (6) he checked none of his luggage. (*Sokolow*, 1989: 3)

A lower appellate court rejected this use of actuarial justice, arguing that the relationship between the knowledge and police action in *Sokolow* were distinct from a narrow test of suspiciousness that would justify detention enunciated by the Supreme Court in *Terry* v. *Ohio* (1968) itself. Rejecting the theory that the profile elements were fragments of a larger picture assembled by the government of crime in action, the lower appellate court characterised the information as forming: 'a vaguer shape resulting from the improper attempt to define not ongoing criminal activity but a class of people that is predominantly criminal' (*Sokolow*, 1987: 1419). This lower court went on to acknowledge that some information used in the profile might bear independently on the likelihood of a criminal activity being afoot, but went on to argue that other elements only identified a population which might be deemed more likely to be involved in crime. The Supreme Court swept such reasoning aside, and allowed the type of categoric information used in *Sokolow*, failing to note that in its earlier decision in *Terry*, it had treated as crucial the fact that the officer had observed the behaviour of a particular individual which led him, because of his training and experience, to believe that a robbery might be unfolding. It had not allowed the stop and frisk merely because Terry and his cohorts 'looked like' robbers, but because they acted like robbers. In contrast they upheld the detention of Sokolow simply because he possessed some of the character-istics contained in the profile of risky persons (*Sokolow*, 1987: 1419).

Reversing the lower appellate court, Chief Justice Rehnquist declined to acknowledge any significant difference between actuarial information which identifies a class of people more likely to be involved in drug trafficking, and evidence of trafficking itself. Indeed, from his perspective all information in the criminal process is 'probabilistic'. In the light of this, he regarded the lower court's effort to separate different kinds of information as an exercise in 'unnecessary difficulty in dealing with one of the relatively simple concepts embodied in the Fourth Amendment' (*Sokolow*, 1989: 8–9). The fact that information here was part of a drug courier profile was irrelevant to his (and the majority's) analysis (*Sokolow*, 1989: 10).

Justice Brennan's dissent in *Sokolow* characterised the distinction between actuarial information and more individualised forms of suspicion in strong terms.

In my view, a law enforcement officer's mechanistic application of a formula or personal and behavioral traits in deciding whom to detain can only dull the officer's ability and determination to make sensitive and fact-specific inferences 'in light of his experience.' . . . Reflexive reliance on a profile of drug courier characteristics runs a far greater risk than does ordinary, case-by-case police work of subjecting innocent individuals to unwarranted police harassment and detention. (*Sokolow*, 1989: 13)

Unfortunately none of the opinions succeeded in specifying the concrete effects of the use of actuarial knowledge in defining targets for police investigation. Both the lower appellate court and Justice Brennan saw the use of the profile as creating an unreasonable risk of innocent persons being subject to police intrusion. If this is true it is surely no more than a matter of degree since many indicia of suspicion will end up touching on innocent individuals. Moreover, neither makes an effort to wrestle with the claim that a profile at least places some restraints on what is as likely to be subjective prejudice as 'sensitive and fact-specific inferences'.

A comparison of *Terry* with *Sokolow* reveals one important difference. In the former, the arresting officer observed Terry and his compatriots repeatedly walking in front of a store and then conferring with each other. As the Supreme Court recognised, the suspicious behaviour in *Terry* fits the 'hypothesis' of a burglary in progress. But because a pattern of behaviour was at issue, there are imaginable actions that could have disproved the hypothesis. For example, had a young woman come running out of the shop and said to Terry, 'I'm sorry dad, I was trying on a dress', Officer MacFadden would have shifted his attention elsewhere. In contrast, there was nothing Sokolow or anyone else could do that would throw off the suspicion (other than the police search itself).

Rehnquist's opinion in *Sokolow* also illustrates the features of the pervasive private security networks that increasingly provide the background for public justice. The Chief Justice noted the fact that Sokolow paid for his ticket in cash from a roll of bills as especially probative: 'Most business travelers, we feel confident, purchase airline tickets by credit card or check so as to have a record for tax or business purposes' (*Sokolow*, 1989: 8–9). Thus, to fail to already be part of the practices of private security and scrutiny is itself a mark of dangerousness.

Sokolow stands for the Court's unwillingness to recognise the special features of actuarial knowledge. The majority's unwillingness to directly confront the issue is disappointing for two reasons. First, it is far from clear that the sinister view of actuarial knowledge and the glowing view of individualised expert judgment drawn by Justice Brennan is accurate. Brennan noted with approval the *Terry* Court's concern about 'police conduct carried out solely on the basis of imprecise stereotypes of what criminals look like' (*Sokolow*, 1989: 12). But what if actuarial profiles turn out to be more precise stereotypes than those of the ordinary officer's working assumptions. The opinion might have provided a real analysis of the relative merits of both kinds of knowledge in the criminal process.

Second, the lower appellate court's opinion, far from offering a 'luddite' rejection of actuarial technology just because it is new and different, actually sought to define new forms of evaluation, including having the government provide empirical proof of the associations drawn in the profiles. While these devices take the form of actuarial prediction, their actual statistical validity has rarely been confirmed. The Supreme Court, by avoiding any recognition of the special features of actuarial knowledge, permits the exercise of power on the basis of such knowledge to go forward with no adjustment in constitutional protection.

As this extended examination of the *Sokolow* case reveals, criminal procedure, influenced by the absorption of administrative law rationales, is becoming a jurisprudence of actuarial justice. Government action against criminal activity, even when mixed with traditional punitive functions, is increasingly subject to a different constitutional standard because instead of emphasising the goals of public justice, it emphasises the goals of risk management. It is preventive rather than responsive. It seeks not to punish but to exclude those with criminal proclivities. It is directed not at a general public norm but at security within a specialized and functionally defined arena.

THE CONTEXT OF ACTUARIAL JUSTICE

Our claims about the emerging constellation of discourses and practices, knowledge and power, in the criminal process can be further illuminated by looking briefly at the intellectual, political and social contexts in which that constellation has emerged. Such an examination helps clarify the importance of this emerging constellation and distinguish it from less important developments. This enquiry, if developed, may offer the basis of a causal account of the emergence of actuarial justice, but at present this is premature. Here we simply attempt to locate the emergence of actuarial justice in a broader intellectual and social context. It remains to be seen, how far these connections can be developed.

The intellectual origins

Foucault's (1977) study of the emergence of the prison, *Discipline and Punish*, was really about the rise of a technology of power, the disciplines.[12] The historical transformation in the practices of punishment represented not only an opportune site to explore the disciplines in general, but also a significant social locus wherein the practices of discipline were forged. There is nothing in Foucault's account, however, to lead us to the conclusion that punishment must always be the site where new technologies of power develop.

In fact it appears to us that the factors accounting for the rise of actuarial justice in the criminal process have their origins in technologies developed elsewhere. We see three factors as especially important: the emergence of a concern for managing risks in other fields of law, particularly torts; the practical application of systems engineering to manufacturing and warfare; and the rise of the law and economics movement.

Legal theory

Although social utility analysis or actuarial thinking is commonplace enough in modern life – it frames policy considerations of all sorts – in recent years this mode of thinking has gained ascendancy in legal discourse, a system of reasoning that traditionally has employed the language of morality and focused on individuals (Simon, 1987, 1988). The new mode of reasoning is now commonplace in the law.

Thus, for instance, it is by now the conventional mode of reasoning in tort law. Traditional concerns with fault and negligence standards – which require a focus on the individual and concern with closely contextual causality – have given way to strict liability and no-fault. One sees this in both doctrines, and even more clearly in the social vision that constitutes the discourse about modern torts. The new doctrines ask, how do we 'manage' accidents and public safety. They employ the language of social utility and management, not individual responsibility.

This development was noted in the early years of the century by visionary legal academics such as Young B. Smith and William O. Douglas (Simon, 1987). More recently, in an enterprise which seeks to trace the shifts in modern tort law, and the 'social vision' that underlies them, Professor Henry Steiner has observed:

> [Judges employing modern tort doctrines] visualize the parties before them less as individual persons or discrete organizations and more as representatives of groups with identifiable common characteristics. They understand accidents and the social losses that accidents entail less as unique events and more as statistically predictable events. Modern social vision tends then toward the systemic-group-statistical in contrast with the vision more characteristic of the fault system, the dyadic-individual-unique. (Steiner, 1987: 8)

In developing this theme, Steiner traces shifts in the doctrine, justification and the social vision and in so doing provides a conceptual framework for understanding the 'dynamics of change that informs other bodies of law [as well as torts]' (Steiner, 1987: 1).

Although Steiner's analysis of developments in torts focuses almost exclusively on shifts in discourse, and the social vision underlying it, he as well as other commentators on recent developments in torts are not unmindful of social processes that have affected this transformation. In particular, they all emphasise the importance of insurance, and high transaction costs in determination of fault in accidents. If injured parties are covered by insurance and as well if the cost of assessing blame under traditional fault doctrines is high (relative to the injuries caused), modern tort lawyers hold, it makes little sense to employ these doctrines. Thus they advocate an accident-management policy, and in some places, for example New Zealand, have replaced tort coverage with mandatory accident insurance schemes (Sugarman, 1989).

The practice of tort law, in fact, remains much more messy. Efforts to intensify the risk management rationality of tort law through reforms have met with mixed success in the face of fearsome resistance by trial laywers and the recent successes of individual responsibility discourse in political life. Yet, as Steiner has shown, actuarial discourse has become *the* language of tort law and is likely to endure and push practice further along when less enduring political contingencies shift.[13]

Systems analysis and operations research

By systems analysis we mean the application of operations research techniques and approaches which conceive of the criminal process as a 'system' which can be analysed as such for purposes of policy analysis and management, and to which overarching and integrated goals can be assigned. Systems analysis posits a synoptic (even if hypothetical) vantage point for assessing goals and efficiency. When the history of twentieth century American criminal justice is written, the rise of 'criminal justice system-thinking' may be regarded as the single most important contribution of criminology and criminal justice policy discourse.[14]

Although there is nothing inherently antithetical to traditional conceptions of individual justice in the techniques employed by systems analysis, the latter is fundamentally concerned with rational management and the regulation of aggregates, and the former with individual-focused justice. Indeed the distinct claim of operations research is that it offers generic insights and techniques for managing seemingly different phenomena – systemic processes – airports, communications, manufacturing, criminal justice.

Systems theory evolved out of the fields of mathematics, physics and electrical engineering during the 1950s and early 1960s (Ruberti, 1984: xi). It was first introduced into the practice of government in the early 1960s by US Secretary of Defense, Robert McNamera, to rationalise Pentagon procurement practices. It was quickly applied to a host of other areas, including the criminal process. This step was bold and deliberate; a group of 'whiz kid' consultants to the Department of Defense were appointed to staff a Task Force for the President's Commission on Law Enforcement and Administration of Justice, and subsequently published the *Task Force Report: Science and Technology* (1967b), which became one of the Commission's most widely read reports. In the midst of an escalating war on crime, modern systems analysis, the latest Defense Department technique, gained instant credibility and appeal.

The most stunning symbol of this rapid and dramatic addition to modern American criminology is the near instant and widespread acceptance of the 'funnel of justice' flow chart published in the Report of the President's Commission on Law Enforcement and Administration of Justice (1967b: 8–9). This chart, no doubt the most frequently reprinted and distributed 'chart' in modern American criminology, captures the essence of the new criminology, a shift away from concern with individual-focused justice to a concern with the efficient management of danger.[15] It constitutes the new symbol of justice in the newly announced criminal justice *system*.[16]

The chart does much more than provide a pictorial overview of the criminal process. The 'funnel of justice' fosters a perspective that invites us to think about the elimination of bottlenecks, pre-trial diversion, 'early case assessment' bureaux to weed out 'junk cases', 'fast track' prosecution bureaux to go after 'career criminals', use of probation and parole revocations to avoid the 'trial loop', 'selective incapacitation' to deploy limited prison space more efficiently, and the like. It suggests new forms of plea bargaining; drop new charges if the arrestee agrees to return a revocation of parole or probation and a return to custody (Greenspan, 1991). It invites the creation of categories and the specification and rationalisation of goals, ideally reduced into a single metric scale, which we suggest is the 'management of danger'. Thus it is possible to weigh the relative benefits of, say, increased investment pre-trial diversion for low risk offenders and expanded use of selective incapacitation for high risk offenders.

Contrast the implications of the chart depicting the 'funnel of justice', the new symbol of (actuarial) justice with another traditional symbol, which represents Justice as a blindfolded woman holding scales. This earlier symbol captures the aspirations if not the reality of individual-focused justice. Justice is a woman to represent mercy; the blindfold symbolises disinterest and impartiality, and the scales suggest carefully weighed individualised assessment. As Curtis and Resnik (1987) have noted, such iconography is no longer in fashion. In criminal justice it appears to have been replaced by the flow chart of systems analysis.

Law and economics

An important movement in contemporary jurisprudence with possible links to actuarial justice is law and economics. Economic thinking has a powerful influence on contemporary scholarship in a variety of substantive law fields, especially torts, contracts, environmental law and anti-trust, and in turn this has influenced the courts.[17] Some scholars have also applied it to the analysis of criminal law and procedure (Becker, 1968; Posner, 1985; Shavell, 1985). Economic analysis and actuarial justice share several important features. They both emphasise utilitarian purposes of punishment over moral considerations. They both prefer quantitative analysis over qualitative analysis. They both focus on the performance of the criminal process as a *system* in which the effects of various stages have implications for each other and for the overall operation of the criminal law.

However, these similarities hide important differences. To say that they are both hyperutilitarian highlights certain similarities, but to contrast utilitarianism against morality-based analysis obscures a great deal. Indeed in our view the superficial similarities of economic analysis and actuarial justice obscures crucial differences.

However useful the contrast between utilitarian and moral reasoning may have been in the eighteenth century when utilitarianism was first introduced as a system of reasoning, today it embraces such a range of considerations, that it can no longer be easily contrasted to 'moral' reasoning. Indeed the systemic logic of economic analysis and actuarial justice is a good example of the inability to make such simple comparisons. The differences can be illustrated by contrasting the deterrent (economic) and incapacitative (actuarial) approaches to punishment. Although both are utilitarian, they are also quite different. Deterrence is economic analysis par excellence since it focuses on the behaviour of individuals as rational actors responding to socially broadcast pricing signals.[18] It treats the offender as a rational economic actor to be influenced by the pricing system of punishments. Incapacitation, in contrast, treats the offender as *inert* from the point of view of influencing decision making. Thus deterrence theory views criminal punishment as only one end of a broad spectrum of incentive signals produced by government and various markets to influence individual decision making (as well as the aggregation of these individual decisions). In contrast, incapacitation theory marks punishment off as a special form of power appropriate to specific categories of people. Its aim is not to influence the decisions of individual would-be criminals, but simply to identify and incapacitate a designated high-risk population.

As Posner recognises, the criminal law's deterrence capacity is a power intended to be deployed largely on a special portion of the population – the poor. The affluent in contrast, he argues, are kept in line adequately by tort sanctions (1985: 1205). Since the poor have too little available wealth to be adequately deterred through the traditional monetary sanctions of the tort law system, imprisonment and the stigma of punishment have a special role to play in their social control. Posner does not pursue this analysis too far because it would seem to undermine his insistence that the criminal process is best understood as a system aimed at attaining efficiency. Since efficiency only has meaning in relation to value in economic theory, and since value is only measurable by willingness to pay, it follows that those outside the cash economy are outside of the efficiency maximisation process.

This suggests that the rise of incapacitation and the other instruments of actuarial justice as a reflection of social forces are pushing a larger portion of the population out of the range of normal economic signals. Deterrence in the end relies on the existence of alternatives for the population being deterred. Posner's major hypothesis is that the criminal law is aimed at preventing forced transactions outside the marketplace (1985: 1195). Ultimately deterrence can only do so to the extent that the people being deterred have basic access to market allocation through participation in the labour market and the cash economy.

Despite these crucial differences, however, economic analysis still may facilitate actuarial justice in two ways: its emphasis on collective goods (rather than individual rights) is deeply compatible with the normative assumption of actuarial justice. And, by undermining the claims of traditional moral (individual-focused) analysis of crime and punishment as forming the basis of the criminal process, it weakens a source of resistance to actuarial justice.

The pendulum swings of crime politics

At first impression there appears to be a strong and obvious connection between the rise of conservative political stances and towards crime actuarial justice, and liberal stances and a traditional due-process focus. Although there may be some connection, it is neither obvious nor strong, and it is our contention that actuarial thinking represents deeper 'pre-political' thought that cannot easily be associated with conventional political labels. As a new technology, no doubt it can be employed somewhat differently by those with any number of different political perspectives. For instance, it was the due-process-oriented liberals of the Great Society era who provided much of the impetus to bring operations research into criminal justice, and it was the reports of the liberal-oriented members of the President's Commission which did much to promote this view. In contrast the 'lock-'em up' conservatives who held sway in the 1980s often employed traditional, individual-focused discourse (although their propensity to increase imprisonment placed such strains on prisons that it no doubt contributed pressures to expand actuarial rationalisation of the criminal process) (Feeley and Simon, 1992). In the long run, however, the implications of actuarial justice are much more far-reaching than are the periodic pendulum-like shifts in emphasis between liberal and conservative policies.

Liberal due-process values and the emergence of actuarial justice

The 1967a report of the President's Commission reveals the connection between liberal values and actuarial justice. The tone of the report, especially its sections on corrections, drugs and crime, was overwhelmingly liberal. Indeed, from a 25-year perspective, the Commission's report must be seen as one of the high water marks of postwar liberalism, and a reminder of what federal policy might have looked like in the 1970s and 1980s had contingent political events played out differently. But at the same time the President's Crime Commission provided the launching pad for the operations research discourse discussed above. The central statement of this innovative approach was found in the volume authored by the Commission's Task Force on Science and Technology (1967b), but it was more pervasive. In turn the Science and Technology Task Force had significant influences on each of the several other volumes produced by the Commission. The new discourse modelled on the operations research paradigm it introduced permeated the entire work of the Commission and its staff.

Another important sector of liberal criminal policy formation was through the constitutional jurisprudence of the federal courts. During the 1960s and

1970s the courts specified reforms in law enforcement, courts and corrections. In a way which was hard to see contemporaneously, judicial mandates to regularise procedures contributed to the effort to systematise the criminal process and rationalise the system. The exclusionary rule required major investments in monitoring and training police conduct, the right to counsel spurred the formation of bureaucratically organised public defender services in some (but by no means all) localities, and prison suits compelled the state to monitor population and coordinate the flow of arrestees and prisoners in jails. While each of these developments spawned effects that cannot be catalogued here, it is important to recognise how much they stimulated the formation of a professional class of criminal justice managers and the adoption of technologies that would permit greater coordination.

Conservative crime control policies seal the deal

As we suggested earlier, despite a 'lock-'em up' stance, conservative crime policies appear to repudiate much of the logic of actuarial justice. Yet there are features of the conservative policies that have also facilitated the expansion of actuarial justice. Two of the most conspicuous are support for the death penalty and enthusiasm for imprisonment. Both have increased reliance on actuarial techniques.

The consequences of these policies on the system are only now being taken stock of (Blumstein, 1993). In the short run the propounders of the get-tough approach are being blamed with distending the system for uncertain gains. In the long run, however, the conservative build-up in the 1980s has facilitated the dependence upon actuarial justice. Distention when it does not truly result in the collapse of a system forces important adaptations, which in the case of the criminal process has meant greater systemic thinking and planning. The swollen size of the process has facilitated institutionalisation of actuarial solutions. By creating an enormous population of persons under criminal custody,[19] the conservative policies of the 1980s in the United States and some European countries has made 'system' perspective all but inevitable as governments struggle to deal with consequences. One sees these developments in any number of new penal policies, which increasingly are designed to manage risks rather than punish or rehabilitate (Feeley and Simon, 1992).

Another indication of the consequences of expanded reliance on systemic thinking is the developing link between civil and criminal processes. For instance Section 5101 of the Anti-Drug Abuse Act of 1988 requires that leases in federally funded public housing contain a provision providing that 'criminal activity, including drug-related criminal activity, on or near public housing premises' by 'a public housing tenant, any member of the tenant's household, or another person under tenant's control . . . shall be cause for termination of tenancy.'[20]

When taken together, these and other actions provide an impressive arsenal not for identifying the guilty and holding them accountable, but for 'managing' populations, the 'dangerous class'.

Social factors: the discovery of the 'underclass'

An old term, 'underclass', has been revived to characterise a segment of society that is increasingly viewed as permanently excluded from social mobility and economic integration.[21] It refers to a largely black and Hispanic population living in concentrated zones of poverty in the centre of US cities, separated physically and institutionally from mainstream American social and economic life. In contrast to others who may be poor and unemployed, the underclass is a permanently dysfunctional population, without literacy, without skills and without hope; a self-perpetuating and pathological segment of society that is not integratable into the larger whole, and whose culture fosters violence.[22] Actuarial justice invites it to be treated as a high-risk group that must be managed for the protection of the larger society.[23]

The underclass and crime

Building on Wilson's (1987) book, *The Truly Disadvantaged*, and the earlier ecological studies of juvenile delinquency by Chicago sociologists Clifford Shaw and Henry McKay (1969), Sampson and Wilson (1993: 24) have developed a theory of race, crime and urban inequality, which links persistent high crime among black youth to both structural and cultural concepts. They conclude that community-level social disorganisation may go a long way towards explaining how current patterns of crime have been shaped by rapid social change in the macrostructural context of inner-city ghetto poverty. 'In our view', they comment, 'the unique value of this community-level perspective is that it leads away from a simple "kinds of people" analysis to a focus on how changing social characteristics of collectivities foster violence' (Sampson and Wilson, 1993: 11).

They portray the 'concentration effects' of an urban underclass which sustains and reinforces a 'culture of violence' through 'structural social disorganization and cultural social isolation that stem from the concentration of poverty, family disruption, and residential instability', and which associates an increasingly entrenched urban underclass with violence (Sampson and Wilson, 1993: 14). To the extent that the underclass is understood as a permanent feature of modern urban society, and that it sustains a culture of violence and social disorganisation, it resonates with the discourse of actuarial justice, which is couched in terms of collectives.[24]

The underclass and criminal justice

But if the emergence of the term underclass reinforces the salience of actuarial justice, the links to practice are even more significant. Sampson and Laub (1992) argue that intervention by criminal justice officials is differentially applied to various segments of the youth population as determined by their position in the social structure. Members of the black underclass are, Sampson and Laub show, 'managed' more stringently than others accused of the same offences. Although they react to this as a demonstration of the 'inequalities' in the juvenile courts, their own conceptual framework leads to an even more chilling conclusion: when framed in terms of their own theory of the culture of violence of the black underclass, *and* seen in the light of actuarial concerns of danger-management, the pattern reveals a new and different social logic – danger management, not individualised criminal justice.

It is not that officials are 'merely' violating traditional ideals of equality when dealing with or intervening in underclass communities, it is that they are animated by a powerful new social logic, risk management. When married with the emerging conception of actuarial justice, the concept 'underclass' sets concerns with individualised justice, and its correlates of equality and inequality, to one side. In this new and emerging formulation, the emphasis is on groups and aggregates and danger management, not individualised justice.[25]

The concept of an underclass, with its connotation of a permanent marginality for entire portions of the population, has rendered the traditional goal of reintegration of offenders incoherent, and laid the groundwork for a strategy that emphasises efficient management of dangerous populations.[26] Imagine for instance how ludicruous it is to think of a parole officer attempting to 'integrate' an offender back into his or her community. One can work through any of several other institutions in the criminal process and come to much the same pessimistic conclusion: likelihood to appear at 'trial' versus risk of dangerousness, adjudication of guilt versus risk management, punishment versus population control, and the like (Irwin, 1986; Doyle, 1992).

Conclusion: some notes on crime and civil war from the *intifada* to South Central Los Angeles

It may seem odd to conclude an examination of developments of largely American (and European)[27] criminal processes with a digression on an international problem, the *intifada*, the Palestinian uprising in the Israeli occupied territories (Judea and Samaria and Gaza). Yet, as we will attempt to show, the metaphoric discussion of 'two societies' that often goes on in the United States is illuminated by looking at a situation where there is nothing metaphoric about it.

In responding to violence and illegality, in both the United States and in the territories held by Israel since the 1967 war, the language of rights is employed. But in both settings, this discourse is commingled with another language, that of actuarial justice. In the United States it is muted; the rhetoric of liberal legal discourse still predominates; actuarial discourse is found only at the margins. In contrast in Israel in reference to the territories, the language of the danger-management is as prominent, if not more so, than the rhetoric of rights.

Although when confronted with criticism of preventive detention, collective punishment, aggressive interrogation, extensive surveillance, street sweeps for weapons and law-breakers, truncated procedure, extensive road blocks, a system of passes, use of colour-coded licence plates, and pressed for clarification of long-term objectives, Israeli officials struggle to characterise policies in the familiar language of rights and judicial officials oblige. But such efforts are seen as the charades they are. Everyone – Palestinians and Israelis, hawks and doves – acknowledges that what is taking place is a war, 'a war that is not a war' in the words of one prominent official, and that the overwhelming task at hand is the management of danger and not the identification and sanctioning of guilty individuals.

Thus despite a facade of the language of rights, there exists another more powerful discourse in which the conflict is described: it is group conflict. It employs actuarial language: preventive detention, aggressive surveillance, mass arrests, collective punishments, curfews, censorship, mass deportation, identification papers and passes, decisions based upon profiles and symbols are all justified in terms of the management of 'danger'. The techniques to pursue these aims include decision making based upon profiles, constructs pieced together from partial bits of information and designed to provide assessment as to a person's – and a group's – risk; extensive surveillance; preventive detention; mass detention; aggressive interrogation. For instance age is, at times, an important variable. And so too is employment. Young unemployed males are high risks and their mobility – as opposed to older employed males and women – may be more severely restricted. A variety of identity cards indicating one's status as defined by these and other characteristics facilitates regulation of movement.

All of this is, of course, commonplace to war. After all, war is conducted between groups and not individuals. And 'offence' is about belonging, belonging to the 'enemy' group, and not individualised conduct. Furthermore, it is young men who constitute the main combatants in war. And although there are emerging 'rules of war', no one argues that it is to be conducted according to due process.

The Israeli dilemma is, of course, that although the *intifada* is a sort of war, it is also 'not a war'. Control in the territories has become a sort of permanent struggle woven into the fabric of civil existence (but not quite a civil war which could signal a prospect of a resolution). This precarious situation no doubt accounts for the effort to normalise policies by employing the rhetoric of rights. But such an effort is widely acknowledged for what it is, a veneer on the effort to manage a permanently dangerous population.

This comparison obviously invites more careful consideration of the metaphors being used in America today, such as 'war on crime' and 'war on drugs', than is usually given. But it also does more. The readily apparent actuarial considerations in Israel unwittingly provide a basis for appreciating how actuarial American criminal processes have become. Apart from the frequency with which the metaphor war is used in both societies, a comparison also reveals that many of the policies employed by the Israelis in managing danger in the territories have their counterparts in the American criminal process as well. And it reveals a similarity in rhetoric as the new aims and techniques of actuarial justice are described and justified.

In recent years both the Israeli and the American governments have endorsed 'preventive detention', and (in at least selected areas of organised crime and drug sales in the United States) collective sanctioning. Both have come to rely extensively on 'profiles' and 'associations' as predictors of dangerousness, and employed 'sweeps', 'checkpoints' and other technologies to target entire populations. And both employ 'balancing' tests and 'reasonable-under-the-circumstances' standards to justify aggressive patrolling, and frequent questioning searches in the absence of probable cause (the new 'reasonableness' standard), and expanding reliance on preventive detention.

Of course, one can press this comparison too far. After all, Israel must control an alien population which no one wishes to be integrated into the larger society and which aspires to national self-determination. Under the circumstances, it is hardly surprising that a risk management strategy crowds out liberal legal principles in shaping policy. However, before we discard the comparison because of the vast difference in political situations, it is interesting to reflect on just how similar – in certain respects relevant to this chapter – the American situation is to the Israeli situation. Both the Palestinian population in the territories and the American urban underclass (although for profoundly different reasons) are alienated and cut off from the larger dominant society and social institutions, and both present seemingly intractable problems of violence for this order. In fact violence by (both within the group and against others) the black underclass population in the United States is much greater than violence in (again, both within and against others) Palestinian communities in the territories. Per capita there are more deaths of young black males in American cities than there are of young Palestinians. And at any given time a higher proportion of young black American males are in custody than are Palestinian males of the same age group from the territories. After the April 1992 civil disorders in Los Angeles, few can doubt the potential for much more overt forms of urban warfare. Indeed, Los Angeles already strikes some observers as embodying much of the urban form and social structure of Third World cities (Davis, 1990; Cooper, 1993).

Many defend the Israeli policy of aggressive danger management as necessary 'under the circumstances'. We need not enter into this debate about the propriety of Israeli policy here, but we do wish to note that the 'circumstances' in the United States are in some important respects much worse. Indeed by itself the Israeli policy on violence in the territories might be understood as an ad hoc response to a distinctive and complicated international dilemma, an ill-defined military matter. But juxtaposed against even greater American violence, these policies may also be seen as a harbinger of things to come in the criminal process of Western societies more generally. Danger management may be the wave of the future, and the Israeli experience, admittedly wrenched out of context here, may provide a glimpse of that future. In other countries the 'recalcitrant population' may be an underclass. Although indigenous and formally part of an inclusive national community, it nevertheless still may be perceived as unintegratable and dangerous to the dominant communities.

Indeed the internal status of the underclass may mean that solution to the American dilemma is even less tractable than the Israeli issue which at least everyone agrees requires a 'political solution' to foster normality and reduce danger. In contrast the 'dangerous class' in America is indigenous; and neither expulsion nor divestiture nor any form of separation and autonomy nor any other political solutions appear viable. The very term 'underclass' comes close to suggesting that it is a permanent condition to be managed rather than solved or eliminated.

To the extent that this pessimistic assessment is accurate, actuarial justice may be regarded by a growing number of people as an obvious and practical – the only – response to an intractable problem involving at least certain types of dangerous people. Actuarial justice may be seen not as an emergency policy to deal with an anomalous situation, but an effort to normalise the situation. It may become an integral part of – rather than an embarrassing adjunct to – the process of justice. If this is true, ironically we may now see the future in a setting where in the future it may not be present.

Notes

An earlier version of sections of this chapter was presented by Professor Feeley at the Drapkin Lecture, Hebrew University, 5 December 1992, and a subsequent faculty workshop at the School of Law, Hebrew University in March 1993. The authors wish to acknowledge the helpful comments of a number of people, including Stanley Cohen, Alon Harel, Menachem Horowitz, Mordechi Kremnitzer, Michael Maltz, David Nelken, Robert J. Sampson, Yoram Shachar. They also wish to express their gratitude for support from the Daniel and Florence Guggenheim Foundation and the UC Berkeley Committee on Research.

1 Both European and North American scholars have noted the recent rising trend within criminal justice agencies to target categories and subpopulations rather than individuals, and for scholars to formulate analyses which follow suit (Bottoms, 1983; Matthiesen, 1983; Cohen, 1985; Ewald, 1986; Reichman, 1986).

2 We acknowledge that the term actuarial justice is nebulous, and that our analysis lacks sufficient analytic clarity. But the phenomenon is relatively new, not well developed and is emerging. Writing a 'history of the present' is always dangerous. However it is real, growing and, we maintain, significant. The general form of our thesis is readily apparent to anyone familiar with Marxist theories of law. Like us, they too assert that the criminal process does not provide liberal, individual-oriented justice, but is best understood as one element in a scheme of class repression. There are, of course, many variations to this theme. Although our analysis has some affinity with this perspective, we reject the notion of any 'grand theory' of society or any master plan for the criminal process. This, of course, makes actuarial justice more nebulous,

but in our view also more convincing. In addition, we argue that we are witnessing a decline of liberal legalism, that is a shift away from individual-oriented jurisprudence to one that is oriented towards aggregate considerations. This is not the place to put forward the theoretical bases which inspire our perspective. However, our debt to Michel Foucault will be obvious to the reader, and he or she should note that one of Foucault's enduring contributions will be his insistence that we treat knowledge and power as inextricably bound up in complex relations of reciprocal expansion (so that one might simply speak of 'knowledge/power' or a specific complex of 'knowledge/power' like medicine) (Foucault, 1977, 1980). And, like him, we note that discourse and knowledge emerge in decentralised, not directed ways, but nevertheless can congeal in ways that exert powerful 'strategies', though these strategies are not master plans (Simon, 1992).

3 Selective incapacitation is still largely an 'idea', and is not widely incorporated in sentencing laws. Some may regard it as a bad memory from the 1980s but we suspect it will continue to reappear in more subtle forms within sentencing systems that do not highlight the centrality of selectivity. The United States Sentencing Commission, *Supplementary Report on the Initial Sentencing Guidelines and Policy Statements* (Washington DC: United States Sentencing Commission, 1987, 197–8), emphasised the predictive powers of the criminal history score in the guidelines and suggested that further research would improve its selectivity.

4 For an account of this see Chapter 2, 'Bail reform', in Feeley (1983: 40–80).

5 The task force drew upon social science methodologies, but the specific analysis and the specific factors are classified secrets (Cloud, 1985: 879).

6 Herbert Packer's (1968) two models of the criminal process – the due process model and the crime control model, and the tension between them – continue to dominate discussion of the underlying social vision that shapes crime policy.

7 In this respect criminal justice is not leading but following trends laid down in health care, employment policy and social welfare. See generally the essays in Burchell et al. (1991).

8 In the American states, state prisons are designed for housing the more serious offenders who are serving sentences of one year or longer. Less serious offenders serve their time in local jails. Yet in recent years, an increasing proportion of inmates in state prisons are there for short periods, of six months or less. These inmates have been returned to custody after revocation of parole or probation.

9 Then Associate Justice Rehnquist made this distinction in *Salerno*. Although critics scoffed at this distinction and the reasoning in this case, it does reveal an acknowledgement of the shift in objectives we have emphasised and openly redefines rights more narrowly accordingly.

10 The immigration context has long been one of policing 'masses' rather than individuals (Auchincloss-Lorr, 1993: 111). The Court has recognised that limiting enforcement by individualised suspicion would make much of the immigration function impossible. Increasingly the Court seems to be recognising and endorsing the shift of regular law enforcement towards mass surveillance. Sweeps, checkpoints and airport stops are the police forms of actuarial justice. The Court has not only upheld these measures but diluted the strength of Fourth Amendment protections in order to do so.

11 *United States* v. *Mendenhall* (1980), *Reid* v. *Georgia* (1980), *Florida* v. *Royer*, (1983), *Florida* v. *Rodriguez*, (1984) and *United States* v. *Sokolow* (1989).

12 A similar perspective has also been put forward by David Garland in his book *Punishment and Modern Society* (1990).

13 Parallel developments are taking place in other legal fields including business associations, employment rights relations and environmental law.

14 Indeed, that history is already being written. Samuel Walker has painstakingly charted the first steps of this 'innovation' in thinking (1992, 1993).

15 Both authors can attest to seeing copies of the chart in the offices of an astounding variety of criminal justice operatives from judges to parole officers, a perception shared by many other researchers we have spoken to about this.

16 We are not the first to note shifts in iconography about the criminal process (see, for example, Curtis and Resnik, 1987).

17 The seminal statement of the contemporary variety of law and economics remains Posner (4th edn, 1992).

18 Posner (1985) recognises that deterrence is insufficient to account for the system of criminal punishments in use. He suggests that the place of incapacitative sanctions, which seek to suppress certain individuals altogether rather than alter their calculations is understandable when it is recognised that unlike the treatment of accidents by tort law, the criminal law seeks to attain complete suppression (1985: 1215). According to Posner this has an overall economic logic since unlike behaviour that leads to accidents crime has no overall social benefit (1985: 1215).

19 An accumulation that will endure and even widen as the effects of over arrest, prosecution and imprisonment have their effects on future sentencing, detection of crime through surveillance of known offenders, and the reproduction of criminal life styles through the loss of fathering for another generation of male children.

20 Anti-Drug Abuse Act of 1988, Pub. L. No. 100–690, Section 510:, 102 Stat. 4181, 4300 (codified as amended at 42 U.S.C. Section 2437d(1)(5) (1988)).

21 William Julius Wilson first began talking about 'the underclass' in the late 1970s. The term was popularised first by journalist Ken Auletta (1982), and later presented in its most influential form by Wilson himself (1987). Wilson is Professor of Sociology at the University of Chicago and a recent President of the American Sociological Association. His book provoked immense and intense comment, precisely because it was read to suggest that there was a segment of American society that has all but been written out of the social contract, a permanent 'underclass'. Although in subsequent writings Professor Wilson has expressed some regret about using the term because of the permanence and hopelessness that it conveys, it is nevertheless powerful precisely because it does convey such profound problems.

The term, of course, has a much longer history, and some variation of it has long been used by Marxists. In German, the term *untermenchen* has long been used to characterise a segment of the population that is in but not really of the community because of deprivations and depravity. The term 'dangerous classes' was widely used in the late eighteenth and early twentieth centuries to convey that portion of the population that is 'rabble' and inherently dangerous (Irwin, 1986). Indeed discussion of crime in late-eighteenth-century England may closely parallel recent developments in actuarial justice, a period when criminal justice administration was largely privatised.

22 There is by now considerable criticism of the political assumptions behind the 'underclass' talk, much of which we agree with. Here we use this term mainly because it is the talk as such that we want to highlight.

23 A recent study estimated that on any given day in 1988 roughly one in every four young (between ages 20 and 29) black males was under some form of correctional custody in the United States (Mauer, 1990). More recently, a similar study calculated that on a randomly selected day in 1990, some 42 per cent of all young black males in Washington, DC, were in custody (reported in Terry, 1992). The growing visibility of the link between criminal management and race is likely to reinforce the sense that crime is the product of a pathological subpopulation that cannot be integrated into the society at large, as well as the perception that the penal system can do no better than maintain custody over a large segment of this population. See also, Austin (1992: 1782).

24 This formulation of issues is hardly new to us. Wilson himself has expressed reservations about his use of the term 'underclass' precisely because it tends to imply hopelessness and permanence, something that as a committed social reformer he rejects (1991: 475).

25 Our characterisation of law enforcement tactics in the black community is hardly distinctive. We draw on the standard field work studies on urban neighbourhoods, the drug culture and gangs, which routinely describe mass arrests, frequent street sweeps for drugs, weapons and violators. See, for example, Austin (1992) and Davis (1990) – matter of fact descriptions of massive gang crackdowns by Los Angeles Police Department; Jankowski (1991) – describing routine anti-gang sweeps in South-Central Los Angeles.

26 The underclass is not the only feature of the contemporary social scene that seems linked to actuarial justice. One powerful influence is the growth of illegal immigration into the United

States and the techniques that have been deployed against it by the Immigration and Naturalisation Service (INS). Katharine Auchincloss-Lorr (1993) worries that the Supreme Court has been influenced by the use of techniques of mass control ('sweeps' and 'surveys') by the INS in accepting their increasing use in the criminal process. Another important source of new technologies and ideologies for the criminal process is the problem of regulating organisational behaviour. The spectre of elite criminality in the form of white-collar crime invites assimilation of regulatory methods to detecting and prosecuting criminal acts. The emergence of civil forfeiture and the panoply of prosecutorial devices under the federal Racketeering and Corrupt Organizations Act are examples. We do not have space here to discuss these sources further but plan on addressing them in a future article.

27 Our discussion here has been overwhelmingly American but see the citations in note 1.

References

Andenaes, Johannes (1974) *Punishment and Deterrence*. Ann Arbor: University of Michigan Press.

Auchincloss-Lorr, Katharine (1993) 'Police encounters of the third kind: the role of immigration law and policy in pre-seizure interrogation strategies', *Search and Seizure Law Reporter*, 20: 105–12.

Auletta, Ken (1982) *The Underclass*. New York: Random House.

Austin, Regina (1992) ' "The Black Community", its lawbreakers, and a politics of identification', *Southern California Law Review*, 65: 1769–1817.

Becker, Gary (1968) 'Crime and punishment: an economic approach', *Journal of Political Economy*, 76: 169–87.

Blumstein, Alfred (1993) 'Making rationality relevant – the American Society of Criminology 1992 Presidential Address', *Criminology*, 31: 1–16.

Bottoms, Anthony (1983) 'Neglected trends in contemporary punishment', in David Garland and Peter Young (eds), *The Power to Punish*. London: Heinemann.

Burchell, Graham, Gordon, Colin and Miller, Peter (eds) (1991) *The Foucault Effect: Studies in Governmentality*. Chicago, IL: University of Chicago Press.

Cloud, Morgan (1985) 'Search and seizure by the numbers: the drug courier profile and judicial review of investigative formulas', *Boston University Law Review*. 65: 843–921.

Cohen, Stanley (1985) *Visions of Social Control*. New York: Oxford University Press.

Cooper, Marc (1993) 'Falling Down', *Village Voice*, 23 March: 24–9.

Curtis, Dennis E. and Resnik, Judith (1987) 'Images of Justice', *Yale Law Journal*, 96: 1727.

Davis, Mike (1990) *City of Quartz: Excavating the Future of L.A.* New York: Vintage.

Doyle, James M. (1992) ' "It's the Third World down there!": the colonialist vocation and American criminal justice', *Harvard Civil Rights – Civil Liberties Law Review*, 27: 71–126.

Ewald, François (1986) *L'etat Providence*. Paris: Grasset.

Feeley, Malcolm M. (1983) *Court Reform on Trial: Why Simple Solutions Fail*. New York: Basic Books.

Feeley, Malcolm M. and Simon, Jonathan (1992) 'The new penology: notes on the emerging strategy of corrections and its implications', *Criminology*, 30: 449–74.

Foote, Caleb (1965) 'The Coming Constitutional Crisis in Bail', *University of Pennsylvania Law Review*. 113: 959–1185.

Foucault, Michel (1977) *Discipline and Punish: The Birth of the Prison*. New York: Pantheon.

Foucault, Michel (1980) 'Truth and Power', in Colin Gordon (ed.), *Power/Knowledge: Selected Interviews and Other Writings 1972–1977*. New York: Pantheon.

Garland, David (1990) *Punishment and Modern Society*. Oxford: Oxford University Press.

Greenspan, Rosann (1991) *The Transformation of Criminal Due Process in the Administrative State*. PhD thesis, University of California at Berkeley.

Greenwood, Peter (1982) *Selective Incapacitation* (with Alan Abrahmse). Santa Monica, CA: Rand.

Irwin, John (1986) *The Jail: Managing the Underclass in American Society*. Chicago, IL: University of Chicago Press.

Jankowski, Martin Sanchez (1991) *Islands in the Street: Gangs in American Urban Society*. Berkeley: University of California Press.

Matthiesen, Thomas (1983) 'The future of control systems – the case of Norway', in David Garland and Peter Young (eds), *The Power to Punish*. London: Heinemann.

Mauer, Marc (1990) *Young Black Men and the Criminal Justice System*. Washington, DC: The Sentencing Project.

Moore, Mark H., Estrich, Susan R., McGillis, Daniel and Spelman, William (1984) *Dangerous Offenders: The Elusive Target of Justice*. Cambridge, MA: Harvard University Press.

Packer, Herbert (1968) *The Limits of the Criminal Sanction*. Palo Alto, CA: Stanford University Press.

Posner, Richard A. (1985) 'An economic theory of the criminal law', *Columbia Law Review*, 85: 1193–1231.

Posner, Richard (1992) *Economic Analysis of Law* (4th edn). Boston, MA: Little Brown.

President's Commission on Law Enforcement and Administration of Justice (1967a) *The Challenge of Crime in a Free Society*. Washington, DC: US Government Printing Office.

President's Commission on Law Enforcement and Administration of Justice (1967b) *Task Force Report: Science and Technology*. Washington, DC: US Government Printing Office.

Reichman, Nancy (1986) 'Managing crime risks: toward an insurance based model of social control', *Research in Law and Social Control*, 8: 151–72.

Ruberti, A. (1984) 'Introduction', in A. Ruberti (ed.), *Systems Sciences and Modelling*. Boston, MA: Reidel Publishing.

Sampson, Robert J. and Laub, John H. (1992) 'Crime and deviance in the life course', *Annual Review of Sociology*, 18: 63–89.

Sampson, Robert J. and Wilson, William Julius (1993) 'Toward a theory of race, crime, and urban inequality', in John Hagan and Ruth Peterson (eds), *Crime and Inequality*. Stanford, CA: Stanford University Press.

Shavell, Steven (1985) 'Criminal law and the optimal use of nonmonetary sanctions as a deterrent,' *Columbia Law Review*, 85: 1232–61.

Shaw, Clifford and Henry McKay (1942; rev. edn 1969), *Juvenile Delinquency and Urban Areas*. Chicago, IL: University of Chicago Press.

Simon, Jonathan (1987) 'The emergence of a risk society: insurance, law, and the state', *Socialist Review*, 95: 93–108.

Simon, Jonathan (1988) 'The ideological effects of actuarial practices', *Law & Society Review*, 22: 772.

Simon, Jonathan (1992) ' "In another kind of wood": Michel Foucault and socio-legal studies', *Law & Social Inquiry*, 17: 49–55.

Simon, Jonathan (1993) *Poor Discipline: Parole and the Social Control of the Underclass, 1890–1990*. Chicago, IL: University of Chicago Press.

Steiner, Henry (1987) *Moral Argument and Social Vision in the Courts: A Study of Tort Accident Law*. Madison: University of Wisconsin Press.

Sugarman, Stephen D. (1989) *Doing Away with Personal Injury Law: New Compensation Mechanisms for Victims, Consumers, & Business*. Westport, CA: Greenwood.

Terry, Don (1992) 'More familiar, life in a cell seems less terrible', *The New York Times*, 13 September.

Walker, Samuel (1992) 'Origins of the contemporary criminal justice paradigm: the American Bar Foundation Survey, 1953–1969', *Justice Quarterly*, 9: 47–76.

Walker, Samuel (1993) *Taming the System: The Control of Discretion in Criminal Justice, 1950–1990*. New York: Oxford University Press.

Wasserstrom, Silas (1984) 'The incredible shrinking Fourth Amendment', *American Criminal Law Review*, 21: 257–401.

Wilson, William J. (1987) *The Truly Disadvantaged: The Inner City, the Underclass, and Public Policy*. Chicago, IL: University of Chicago Press.

Wilson, William J. (1991) 'Public policy research and the truly disadvantaged', in Christopher Jencks and Paul E. Peterson (eds), *The Urban Underclass*. Washington, DC: Brookings.

Table of cases

Florida v. *Bostick*, (1991)
Florida v. *Rodriguez*, (1984) 469 U.S. 1
Florida v. *Royer* (1983) 460 U.S. 491
Michigan State Police v. *Sitz* (1991) 469 U.S. 444
Reid v. *Georgia* (1980) 448 U.S. 438
Stack v. *Boyle* (1951) 342 U.S. 1
Terry v. *Ohio* (1968) 391 U.S. 1
U.S. v. *Mendenhall* (1980) 446 U.S. 544
U.S. v. *Sokolow* (9th Cir. 1987) 831 F.2d 1413
U.S. v. *Sokolow* (1989) 490 U.S. 1

9

The 'Economy' of Illegalities: Normal Crimes, Elites and Social Control in Comparative Analysis

Dario Melossi

In the last 20 years, the United States has witnessed a 'great confinement' that has come to rival in scope the seventeenth-century confinement immortalised by Michel Foucault in his *Madness and Civilization* (1965: 38–64). A deep change in criminological rhetoric in the same period has certainly contributed to this dramatic increase in penal severity (Melossi, 1993). That rhetoric change was connected to an understanding of social control as a totalising, all-inclusive feature of social reality, opposite to which the individual was conceived as the source of more or less freely-willed deviations. A practical consequence of this view has been the idea that by increasing the amount of social pressure on those individuals who seem to be somehow bearers of deviation, society will become better, and the symptoms of social malaise, such as violence and organised crime, will decrease if not disappear.

In this chapter I wish to argue against this concept of social control as the property of a social system, and go back instead to a previous idea of individual maladjustment – one more fully sociological, according to which a plural and processual concept of social control is at the roots also of deviance. The heyday of this latter concept was in the sociology of deviance of the 1960s and early 1970s – a sociology, however, that failed in studying the connection between social processes of labelling and social structures (Melossi, 1985). I want to propose instead that we should consider 'deviance' and 'crime' within an overall 'economy' of social control, by focusing on the efforts, by specific individuals and groups in society, to get their 'audiences' to 'conform' (Shibutani, 1962). Therefore, crime should not be seen as a negative 'measure' of social control, as it is usually seen, but as a dependent variable in the definitional battle among various social forces. This is a perspective inspired by George Herbert Mead's work, who saw crime and especially the criminal as instruments through which a 'social object' is constituted in society and a large audience is symbolically cemented against the 'common enemy' (Mead, 1917–18, 1925; Melossi, 1993). From the standpoint of social elites, in fact, social control means the reproduction of the type of society that they identify with the basis of their hegemony – reproduction, therefore, also of the appropriate rates of deviance and crime (Durkheim, 1895). As the American idiom says, such rates literally 'come with the territory'.

Starting from this premise, it is impossible to claim anything about crime, without spelling out the specific social position one is speaking from. It is impossible to claim that crime is a threat for social order without knowing of which order we are talking about, in the same way in which it is impossible to claim that crime is a path to 'liberation' – as in some recurring apologies of crime *anarchisant* – if we do not know what is meant by such liberation. It is possible, on the other hand, to claim that crime *may* be used in order to shore up social order – once we know something more about that order. The perspective that I am adopting here, and which is particularly useful for comparative research, is one informed by Edwin Sutherland's emphasis on the 'cultural consistency' between crime, and especially social reaction to crime, and the main features of the cultural environment in which that reaction is produced. As summarised by Sutherland and Cressey, '[t]he societal reactions to lawbreaking and the methods used to implement or express those reactions show a general tendency to be consistent with other ways of behaving in the society' (1978: 348).

In particular, in this chapter I intend to consider the nexus crime–social control with regard to some features of 'the criminal question' in the United States and Italy. In this connection, I want to suggest: first, that a concept of social control as an active and plural process is more useful in order to account for the actual practices of social control that we witness in these societies; and second, that from such a 'realistic' perspective one can understand how social control may be obtained also through the management of crime and deviance, indeed through the most 'corrupt' tolerance of crime and deviance.

Social control: constitutive, plural, conflictual

As anticipated above, the two basic ways of conceiving the emergence of deviance are grounded in as many ways of conceiving social control. The first, the concept of social control that I intend to develop in this chapter, is tributary to a sociological tradition started by German social theorist Georg Simmel and then furthered at Chicago and elsewhere by a sociological criminology oriented towards interactionism. It is the idea that the human individual finds him- or herself at the intersection of 'social circles' (Simmel, 1922), circles that control the individual through his or her orientation towards the audiences, reference groups or vocabularies that correspond to, and are typical of, those circles (Mills, 1940; Shibutani, 1962). Individuals usually belong in a number of different circles, more or less overlapping. Most of the time this does not constitute a problem. At times, however, these multiple belongings may originate what has been variously defined as a dilemma, an antinomy, or a normative conflict (Baratta, 1963; Cressey, 1968). This situation is typically and famously represented in the myth of

Antigone, taken between fidelity to the traditional religious value of piety, with the social circles of family and traditional community supporting that value – and the positive law of King Creon, with the social circle of the political community supporting his command. In the eyes of Creon, Antigone was a deviant, indeed the most dangerous type of deviant, a subversive who wanted to bury the body of her brother, the rebel Polynices, against the express prohibition of the King.

Antigone's deviance was not the result of faulty genetic or social make-up, even if we cannot exclude that she might have been endowed with exceptional stamina and moral temper. Certainly, she did not suffer from a low degree of self-control. On the contrary: her deviance derived from an excess of socialisation, even if of a kind disliked by Creon, as well as, probably, by those criminologists of the time who were Creon's advisers, intent on legitimising the superior wisdom of his rule. Indeed the control of her conscience on her self arrived at the point of making her disregard the laws of the state, that she deemed repugnant, at the cost of her own life. Such was Antigone's self-control that it brought her to the very annihilation of herself. In this view, deviance is the product of an antinomy between the laws of the two (or more) circles, or audiences, one belongs to. What is the norm for one, is deviance for the other, and vice versa.

Another sociological view sees, instead, deviance as the result of something which is at fault with the individual, something that is amiss either in his or her genetic make-up or in the socialisation process. This latter view depends on a concept of society that is monistic and all-inclusive. Social control will, therefore, consist of 'fixing' deviance – a 'homeostatic' concept of social control (Mayhew, 1982: 59–60). Canonized by Parsons in the footsteps of Durkheim and Freud, this has become the *Vulgata* of contemporary criminologists' social control, especially of those who are advisers to today's Creons, for whom it is very important to state that Leviathan's perspective is the perspective of societies in general, and the conflict is not between different concepts of the good, but is instead between good and evil.

This monistic concept of social control, and of deviance as a kind of want, are to be found in intellectual tendencies very different from each other. If, on the one hand, we have the already mentioned conservative tendency of mainstream criminology (Gottfredson and Hirschi, 1990: 85–120), a type of criminology that reminds one of Svend Ranulf's classic work on *Moral Indignation and Middle Class Psychology* (1938), on the other hand, we have a 'left-wing' tendency, of radical/Marxist derivation, that focuses on a *1984* 'Big Brother' type of social control. The heyday of this position was of course in the late 1960s – early 1970s, but we can still find it, for instance, in a characteristic statement by Cloward and Piven that I took from John Hagan's *Structural Criminology* (1988: 239), 'the dialectic between social control and resistance is at the core of all social life' (Cloward and Piven, 1986: 2). Consider, by the way, that the two tendencies are not all that different conceptually, at least in the sense that they are both mainly state-

or at least law-driven, and that they tend to see social control as a monolith, whether to praise it or to condemn it.

In my reconstruction of the active and plural tradition of social control and deviance (Melossi, 1990: 97–186), I focused on the way this concept was used by authors such as Mead and Dewey, and the young Mills and Lemert. In this view, social control is the process, or set of processes, through which a group (and therefore those in a group who have the most power) secures a conforming orientation among its members. In contemporary social theory one is accustomed to attribute a somewhat similar view to Michel Foucault, with his notion of power as 'constitutive' as opposed to 'repressive' (Foucault, 1976; Lacombe, 1993). The contribution of the type of social science inspired by Mead's and Dewey's pragmatism, however, is all but forgotten. As Rorty puts it, 'On my view, James and Dewey . . . are waiting at the end of the road which Foucault and Deleuze are currently traveling' (1982: xviii).

The struggle around the definition of crime and deviance is located within the field of action constituted by plural and conflicting efforts at producing social control. What counts from an 'active' perspective, in other words, is the social activity (by elites, as well as by common members of society, and 'criminals') directed to exert influence in accordance with historically situated (but not necessarily 'rational') goals. Definitions of crime and deviance, as well as social control in the traditional sense of the word, should merely be seen as by-products of such efforts. The successful application of a criminal label is not the product of a quasi-automatic societal reaction, but the result of action by given groups in society oriented towards specific ends. Their action might also consist of withdrawing the application of the label or its enforcement. What is important for social control is the consistency between the given ends of the social controllers, and the actual outcome of the social situation, in a way which is completely independent from any 'objective' 'measure' of social control (such as, say, the murder rate).

An aspect of the same problem is that both right- and left-wing 'critics' take for granted that the goal of 'the state' is to enforce the law, that is, in the case of criminal law, 'to suppress crime'. The right-wing praises such a goal in the name of law and order, and the left wing condemns it in the name of fighting repression, inequality and discrimination. It is surprising that the lesson of legal realism may have been forgotten so easily. In fact, I would like to advance the 'realistic' hypothesis that 'crime', at least in the abstract and rather stultified way in which it can be 'found' 'on the books' of law, is not very high on the elites' list of priorities, except of course when it can be used to mobilise energies in pursuit of some overarching political goal (Edelman, 1988). A more likely hypothesis is that power elites, if they are to be such, care first and foremost about the preservation of the kind of society they cherish. I see the type of 'social control' pursued by societal elites, in other words, quite literally as the control of society, in the sense of the reproduction of the most fundamental social relations that belong in that society. From the perspective of elites the reproduction of society and of themselves as elites is one and the same thing. They by definition fully identify with the social relations they are trying to protect. Whereas it may appear reasonable to hypothesise that there is an interest of groups in power to guarantee basic values of life, work, property, etc., that such is the case in specific instances and/or sociohistorical circumstances has to be empirically shown.

Social control: turning 'illegalities' into 'normal crimes'

At least in Western societies, law is certainly not ignored, usually, but functions more as a rhetorical device. Law in this sense is the vocabulary used in order to give a public account of what is done, an account which, in societies hegemonised by formal rationality (Weber, 1956: 36, 215), and in the ordinary course of events, is quite prestigious. As far as criminal law is concerned, for instance, according to David Sudnow in his article on plea bargaining (1965), *normal crimes* are legally defined, but socially produced and administered, categories of crime. They are instantly recognisable as occurrences that belong to a familiar phenomenology of criminal behaviour and are taken care of by competent members of the criminal justice system by means of a standard inventory of established linguistic and procedural routines. These crimes are normal, I would add, also in the sense that they are expected criminal occurrences of the type of society one lives in, as that society is interpreted by its elites. In spite of the fact that they *have* to be *legally* defined, normal crimes are not normal in any *legal* sense, but in the sense that the characteristics of the crime, the people who are involved, the circumstances, the situation, the victims, are 'normal', from the practical standpoints of the members of the Public Defender and District Attorney offices. When that kind of situation obtains, it is very easy to reach an agreement, about the plea for instance, between the Public Defender and the District Attorney. It is just a matter of routine.

There are, of course, exceptions. Political crimes represent a common exception. When the Chicago police and the FBI chose to deal with the Chicago Black Panther Party in 1969, for instance – which resulted, among other things, in the killing of Fred Hampton and another member of the Chicago Black Panther Party, and the wounding of seven people – those crimes, if there was actually *any* crime involved *before* its repression, were not 'normal' in any way (Carson et al., 1991: 500–38). When a 'crime wave' is constructed, that is not at all a normal crime, a lot of resources are funnelled into the public management of these crimes. For instance, a few years ago American politicians loudly denounced the missing children crisis (Joe, 1991) or drinking and driving (Gusfield, 1981). If there is a lot of public attention then the police will have to pay more attention too. They have to do so often unwillingly or begrudgingly, because they have to do something in which they might not believe. They have to do it, however, in order to avoid political consequences.

How are these distinctions between normal and exceptional crimes constructed? Once again, the role of elites and of conflict among different elite groups seems to be central. In fact, competing discourses should be seen as competing proposals for organising society, or specific sectors of society. The emergence of conflicting ideological projects corresponds to divisions among various elite groups, each with its own constituency. The literature on social control has shown the connection between the range of given forms of communication, and the 'others', 'audiences', or 'reference groups', towards which these forms are directed (Shibutani, 1962; Melossi, 1990: 140–5). The actions by 'moral' elites defining situations as critical and calling for specific remedies, are 'projects' launched towards society, projects whose fate rests with the exits of the 'distant roar of battle' to which Foucault referred in his conclusion of *Discipline and Punish* (1975: 308), and which I would dare call the battle for hegemony.

In fact, after having devoted about 250 pages of *Discipline and Punish* (1975) to reconstructing the origins of discipline based on penal reformers' blueprints, Foucault had to acknowledge that, from its inception, the project of the prison 'was denounced . . . as the great failure of penal justice' (1975: 264). Not only have prisons never accomplished the task of reforming criminals, but they have made them tougher, smarter, and more hopeless, giving birth to the cliché of the 'Universities of crime'! At the end of *Discipline and Punish*, therefore, Foucault chose to shift from a narration based mainly on a view of imprisonment as training for discipline, to one according to which the social function of imprisonment has been from the beginning to transform 'illegalities' into 'delinquency':

> one would be forced to suppose that the prison, and no doubt punishment in general, is not intended to eliminate offences, but rather to distinguish them, to distribute them, to use them; that it is not so much that they render docile those who are liable to transgress the law, but that they tend to assimilate the transgression of the laws in a general tactics of subjection. Penality would then appear a way of handling illegalities, of laying down the limits of tolerance, of giving free rein to some, of putting pressure on others, of excluding a particular section, of making another useful, of neutralizing certain individuals and of profiting from others. In short, penality does not simply 'check' illegalities; it 'differentiates' them, it provides them with a general 'economy'. . . . The 'failure' of the prison may be understood on this basis. (Foucault, 1975: 272)

This position can hardly be reduced to a new instrumental and intended function, the control of the working class (Garland, 1990: 6). Rather, it reminds one of Durkheim's famous chapter in *The Rules of Sociological Method* dedicated to the distinction between the normal and the pathological, according to which a society without crime would be inconceivable because it would be a society without norms (1895: 47–75). The main purpose of penality would then be its symbolic social use as a sort of mystery play, indeed, as I have called it, as an official gazette of morality (Melossi, 1993). Foucault shares with other social thinkers, chiefly Marx and Weber, the insight that the control of large masses of people in contemporary societies cannot be meaningfully separated from the sustenance of the moral and ideological universe to which the power elites appeal as legitimating grounds for their rule.

In other words, those emotions, those 'outbursts of common sentiment', as Garland refers to them in his summary of Durkheim's position on punishment (1990: 8–9), are socially produced, both in their amount and their direction. They express outrage at certain behaviours and not at others. As we have learned from the sociology of deviance and social control (Becker, 1963; Erikson, 1966; Cohen, 1972; Gusfield, 1981), the symbolic character of the social reaction, on the one hand, may be distinguished from an intended and instrumental reaction, and on the other hand depends on precisely located class and political sensibilities, socially hegemonic in given historical and social circumstances.

What Foucault terms turning illegalities into delinquency, would appear to be, in sociological language, the day-to-day mode of operation of a criminal justice system whose members by and large share the ideologies, biases and preferences of the larger society, and who essentially operate not so much with the goal of eliminating crime – as any criminal justice officer will readily acknowledge – but with the goal of 'containing' it within limits that are somehow 'acceptable', or 'normal' in a given society at a given time. Police and criminal justice system officers, in other words, cannot help but be an integral part of a structure of power and ideology, by which I mean that their way of understanding what fighting crime is all about is steeped in their more general understanding of what their society is all about – and therefore also what their relationship to it is all about. This does not mean that they 'instrumentally' 'intend' to transform illegalities into delinquency. It simply means that in their day-to-day activities, they will have to make practical choices about an array of behaviours which may be socially defined as crimes, and they will have to make these choices from the perspective of the society, as well as the professional and institutional structures, of which they are a part. Basically their job is one of maintaining a volatile compromise between the social production of activities which are usually identified as or connected with 'crime' (drugs, gangs, prostitution, gambling, corruption, occasionally white-collar crime, etc.) and the containment of these activities within limits which, at least ideally, avoid a type of 'innovation' (in the Durkheimian sense) which would be deemed undesirable from an hegemonic perspective (in the way in which such a perspective is constructed within the specific circumstances of their profession).

Indeed, without being too aware of it Foucault (1974) developed a theme that runs throughout the sociology of deviance, from Durkheim's 'pathology' (1895), to Mead's 'common enemy' (1917–18), to Stanley Cohen's 'amplification of deviance' (1972). Cohen in particular showed that the 1960s British youth gangs of 'Mods' and 'Rockers' had been socially controlled through a reconstruction of their images by the combined action of official agencies of control and the media, a reconstruction that eventually had consequences for the self-image of these groups (Cohen, 1972). This reconstruction took place through the amplification and the increasing criminalisation of deviance, a social process that one can find *in nuce* in the time-honoured police practice of using undercover agents and *agents provocateurs* (Marx, 1988).

If Cohen's analysis concerned groups that were on the boundary between the 'delinquent' and the 'Bohemian' 'subterranean traditions of youth' (Matza, 1961), the same type of analysis could be applied to the ways in which, in the 1960s and 1970s, hegemonic social control was able to neutralise the third type of tradition identified by Matza, 'political radicalism'. This has happened in a number of Western democratic countries in similar fashion, even if through the use of different means. Whereas the main ingredient was certainly the naivety of political radicals, the use of mass media, undercover policing, *agents provocateurs*, character assassinations, and outright terrorism, were all used, to different extents in different countries, in order to transform mass democratic social movements into the kinds of movements that could be publicly represented by the media as the perfect impersonation of 'the public enemy'. In different ways, this was the case for J. Edgar Hoover's COINTELPRO operations, connected to such cases as the already mentioned killing of Fred Hampton (Carson et al., 1991: 517–38), the American media's treatment of 'Students for a Democratic Society' (Gitlin, 1980), or the political utilisation of terrorism in order to reestablish a conservative hegemony throughout Western Europe, in the late 1970s and 1980s (Hess et al. 1988; Catanzaro, 1991; Trenz and Zaitch, 1991).

Uses of violence: the case of the United States

If 'normal' crimes are part of the reproduction of 'normal' social relations, then normal crimes will be akin to each society's 'normality'. They will be related, in other words, to the cultural, political and economic specificity of each society. If one looks at contemporary United States, for instance, with its very high rates of violent crime, it is hard to avoid seeing a 'cycle of violence' at work here, between 'crime' and official agencies of 'social control'.

After the arrest and brutal beating of the black motorist Rodney King on 3 March 1991, in Los Angeles, a reality was unveiled that was unknown to the average American but not to the average African-American, especially in Los Angeles (Skolnick and Fyfe, 1993: 1–22). The Los Angeles Police Department (LAPD) was at the time the big city department in the United States which had the highest number of killings per officer (Dunne, 1991: 66). For years, it had conducted 'search and destroy' actions into minority neighbourhoods mimicking the behaviour of its rivals, the gangs, to the point of spray-painting its own slogan, 'LAPD RULES', on the 'searched' dwellings (Davis, 1990: 276; Dunne, 1991: 67). Its social composition, mainly white, suburban and low middle class, was basically foreign to the people it was to police (Dunne, 1991: 66), a fact that became painfully obvious when the California state trial of the four police officers charged with the beating was moved to Simi Valley, one of the favourite suburban residences of LAPD members. Even more revealing was the substantial suspicion with which members of the LAPD seemed to receive the first news of 'the truce' among gangs that followed the turmoil in Los Angeles in spring 1992, after the acquittal of the four police officers in the State trial. The notion of the truce in fact could be seen as conferring a measure of human dignity and responsibility upon the members of the gangs, that run directly opposite the portrayal of brutish savagery with which they had traditionally been depicted by the LAPD and its political allies (Davis, 1990: 221–322).[1]

The Rodney King incident took place right at the end of the Gulf War. At the same time, then President George Bush was urging the Congress '[to] bring that same sense of self-discipline, that same urgency', of the Gulf War, 'to the way we meet challenges here at home' (1991b: 260). In an atmosphere of cheers and flag-waving, Bush added, 'If our forces could win the ground war in 100 hours, then surely the Congress can pass this legislation in 100 days' (1991b: 260). This call for military-style *élan* in the disciplining of the nation had been more carefully specified in a previous speech at an 'anti-crime conference' convened by then Attorney General Richard Thornburgh, where Bush 'linked' the war *tout-court* with the war on crime, by calling on Congress to pass new 'anti-crime' legislation and encouraging the audience to 'seize the day' and employ 'the kind of moral force and national will that freed Kuwait city from abuse' to 'free America's cities from crime' (Bush, 1991a: 255). In that same speech Bush hailed Chief Daryl Gates as an 'all-American hero'.

Indeed, one cannot help but wonder whether urgency, discipline and force might not have been germane to the type of attitude displayed by the 'thin blue line' at about the same time in Los Angeles in the King incident and others. As Patrick Buchanan, the conservative journalist, Presidential candidate, and finally prominent backer of the Bush candidacy, commented at the time, 'If the police beat [King] brutally, many will say that even though the cops went too far, they are our troops' (Dunne, 1991: 27).

There are authors who have suggested that we may want to look at the relationship between crime and punishment, not as linked by the supposedly negative effect of deterrence but rather by a positive correlation, due to what has been called the 'brutalisation' effect: the one who lives in a society where violent resolution of conflicts is emphasised, will be more likely to use violence in order to achieve his or her ends than the one who lives in a society where tolerance and compromise are rewarded. So, it indeed makes sense, in a comparative framework, to do what Dane Archer and Rosemary Gartner have done, following in the steps of Bowers and Pierce (1980). Bowers and Pierce had found that, in New York State, over the period 1907 to 1963, capital executions tended to be statistically associated with subsequent higher murder rates. Archer and Gartner tried to see, in a cross-national study, whether there had been historically a correlation between governments' official sponsorship of violence (measured by countries' engagements in wars and use of the death penalty), and their violent crime rates (1984: 63–97, 118–39). Indeed Archer and Gartner found that, with few exceptions, the homicide rates of postwar periods are higher than the homicide rates of prewar periods, in a way that extends to all age groups and that has nothing to do, therefore, with the so-called 'violent veteran' syndrome (1984: 63–97). Likewise, they found that those societies that abolished the death penalty – Italy being one case in point – tended to have lower homicide rates after the abolition of the death penalty than before.

If criminal behaviour is connected to the values and lifestyles that are dominant in a given society, the domestic and foreign policy actions of the main agency in society, that is government, are likely to have an exemplary effect throughout society. One may ask oneself: what is the message that a child is going to receive about the best way to solve problems when confronted with what appears to be some limitation on his or her rights? Is it the use of rational conversation and debate? Is it avoidance? Is it force? The chances are that a child raised in the United States will be exposed to a number of recommendations to use force and violence more often than a child raised in Europe, or Japan, or indeed many other countries. Consider the amount of violence it is possible to watch on the media, consider the easy availability of weapons, consider the war rhetoric coming from the high echelons of society, be these drug warriors or Gulf warriors, with the President of a supposedly 'kinder and gentler' nation who wanted to 'kick ass' and not be considered a 'wimp' anymore. Consider, finally, the emphatic positive role that is attributed to violence in the very United States Bill of Rights.[2]

One of the very few United States Representatives unwaveringly opposed to the Gulf War, Honorable Henry Gonzalez of San Antonio, Texas, expressed this point very effectively in his request to impeach President Bush for a number of reasons related to his decision to go to war with Iraq, the last one being 'that the President has generally, and in every way, breached the peace by his unwarranted commitment to violence'. Gonzalez argued,

> We have violence in our streets – San Antonio's murder rate is soaring, as is the murder rate in our nation's capitol and other cities around the nation. How can we preach to our children and our adult citizens that violence is not the way to solve conflicts when our nation is engaging in violence of such magnitude?[3]

One is obliged to comment: if indeed 'our leaders' need to be ready to have a society capable of using violence, because they want to lead us to war, how serious are they really when they talk against violence in the streets? Consider Merton's (1938) perspective: if violence is often defined as a legitimate means to achieve social goals (as in wars), it will be very difficult to keep the taboo on it in relation to situations where we do *not* want to consider violence as a legitimate way of accomplishing one's ends. And so the leadership of society, through the law, through wars, basically sends the message that there is something good about violence, that violence can be useful and helpful.

Social control through 'tolerance': the case of Italy

This 'tactic of subjection', to use Foucault's expression, does not necessarily work, however, only in the direction of severity. Exactly because the pre-occupations and sensibilities of political elites are associated with the control of government – even if in the rather general sense of 'il tenere lo stato',[4] as Machiavelli ([1573]1977) poignantly described it – such preoccupations may be better expressed, under certain historical and cultural circumstances, through leniency, understatement, and 'tolerance'. In the case of Italy, for instance, such tolerance is linked to a specific Roman Catholic tradition, a tradition that persists in Italian culture, in spite of the process of secularis-ation. The Catholic tendency to limit religious experience and interpretation to a priesthood rigidly separated from the rest of 'the herd', was reinforced in Italy by the century-long temporal power of the Papacy, against which Italian aspirations to nationhood had to fight harshly. One of the results of this specific Italian brand of Catholicism was the tendency to be extremely tolerant in individual moral and social issues, but very firm against any actual open challenge to political and religious hierarchies. This attitude was transferred from the Church to the lay Catholic political nomenklatura, the nomenklatura that has dominated Italian politics since 1947, probably the most stable in the world until its current and most serious crisis. The secret of this elite is in fact its ability to rule amidst conflict, giving that external impression of instability of which the columnists of newspapers in the English language so naively used to write.

What I mean to say is that the preoccupation with law and order is a typically Protestant, especially English and most particularly North-American, obsession (for a somewhat similar comparison of Mexican and North-American cultures, see Paz, 1979). No wonder that authors like Kai Erickson, Howard Becker, David Matza, or Joseph Gusfield, have written such wonderful pieces on these topics. It is the New England, Puritanic obsession with good and evil, it is a neurotic obsession for method and sharpness, that is behind these works. This is certainly not the Italian obsession.

One of the innumerable examples that could be brought to bear as an illustration of this point, is the public statement of then Prime Minister, Christian Democrat Giulio Andreotti, after the escalation of bloody crimes in the Italian local elections of May 1990. These involved the murders of a number of candidates for public office in the Neapolitan and Calabrian areas of Southern Italy, very probably the work of organised crime. Our ineffable (former) Prime Minister, whose party happened to gain in those elections and in those areas, commented on these events as 'a few no doubt serious cases of violence' the meaning of which however should not be 'exasperated and amplified'.[5] Mr Andreotti actually said 'amplified'! How praiseworthy would his statement have been in the eyes of those 'critical criminologists' who have so much decried the creation of 'law and order' and 'moral panic' campaigns! Had Mr Andreotti read Jock Young, or Stan Cohen, on 'amplification of deviance'? I do not think so, even if some of his aids might have read some of *La questione criminale's*[6] translations of Young and Cohen. More importantly, however, Mr Andreotti was the very incarnation of that Catholic style of governance that is 'tolerant' of absolutely anything that does not challenge the bases of (its) *political* power. It used to be the temporal power of the Church. For Mr Andreotti it was the central role of the Catholic party in Italian government. This tolerance is particularly emphasised, of course, if the deviance, or the very serious crime, as in this case, happens to unfold within a social and economic situation that contributes to Mr Andreotti and friends' hegemony.

One would expect, therefore, that Mr Andreotti's position might have changed somewhat when, in the midst of the subsequent electoral campaign of 1992, the escalation of violence reached his closest friend and most powerful politician in Sicily, the Honorable Salvo Lima, a member of the European Parliament. This killing 'seemed to be metaphorically laying a corpse on the Prime Minister's doorstep' (Stille, 1993: 69), because, as the investigators theorised, Lima had eventually failed in his role of Great Mediator between the Sicilian Mafia and the central political power in Rome. Even after the killing of this close associate of his, Mr Andreotti's anger was still directed against those whom he dubbed the 'anti-Mafia professionals'.[7] Not long after that, the two main 'anti-Mafia professionals', judges Giovanni Falcone and Paolo Borsellino, were killed in two separate terrorist-style mayhems that contributed greatly to the very high level of delegitimisation reached by Italian political institutions (and especially by some of its central representatives such as Giulio Andreotti) at the end of 1992.[8]

The Mafia investigations in the South and the emergence of investigations about *Tangentopoli*, of 'Kickback City', in the North, exposed the deep interpenetration of 'organised crime' and 'political system', to a point where the boundaries between one and the other seemed to vanish:

> It seems that the relationships between mafia and politicians in Sicily have been continuous. This continuity is questioned today for the first time. We should seriously consider the possibility that the relationships between individual Sicilian politicians and Cosa Nostra families may have involved formal membership, affiliations, oaths, and corresponding obligations of fidelity to the rules of the secret society, to a much higher degree than what we already know. The same should be said for Cosa Nostra's relationships with professionals (especially attorneys but also medical doctors, public notaries, etc.) and various types of State employees. (Arlacchi, 1993: 10)

Tolerance may be considered a value when it is tolerance of the ideas and deeds of a minority by a powerful majority. But in Italy, tolerance often seems to mean de facto acceptance of the arrogance of the powerful. In the same way civil libertarianism, called in Italy *garantismo*, may at times have happened to take the form described by a former *mafioso* turned state's witness, Gaspare Mutolo, who, in his deposition before the 'Anti-Mafia' Committee of the Italian Parliament, spoke of a high judge in Rome,

Corrado Carnevale, notorious for acquitting in appeal all the *mafiosi* on grounds of technicalities, and stated that

> [for us, Corrado Carnevale was a] *marca*, a guarantee. For us *mafiosi* Corrado Carnevale was smart, cunning, a very intelligent person. Around him there was a bustle of attorneys and politicians. Attorneys *absorbed* his advice. The politicians *were able to get in touch* with Carnevale [*arrivavano a Carnevale*]. I do not know whom but it was obvious to us that the politicians were close to him'.[9]

This situation is characteristic, I believe, of an implicit general social contract between traditional Italian governments and the populace, that an English-speaking commentator would call 'corrupt', without realising that there is nothing actually 'to corrupt', since the deal has been going on, especially in the South of Italy, from time immemorial. Gramsci wrote that 'Popular "subversivism" correlates with "subversivism" at the top, i.e. with the fact of there never having existed a "rule of law", but only politics characterised by absolute power and cliques around individuals or groups' (1929–35: 275).[10] According to Gramsci's celebrated essay on 'the Southern question', repeating the central analysis of *meridionalismo*, since the time of Italian Unification in 1861, the central Roman governments have held an at best ambiguous attitude towards the presence of various forms of organised crime in the South. This presence, in fact, has traditionally been functional to the preservation of a national balance of power able to offset the more progressive social and political composition of Northern and Central Italy (Gramsci, 1926; Salvemini, 1963; Salamini, 1989, 1992). This would appear to be an excellent textbook case for Foucault's argument, according to which social apparatuses of crime management and punishment are usually geared to channelling 'popular illegalism' into a politically useful 'delinquency' (Foucault, 1975: 273–92).[11]

For a reflexive criminology: social analysis of the uses of crime

In conclusion, in both Italy and the United States, there seems to be a rather comfortable fit between the core cultural values of a society and its elites, and the main characteristics of crime in that society, that is a pervasive, decentred, individualistic criminal violence in the United States, and a 'politically' organised crime in Italy. This is not at all contradictory to notions of social control exercised by power elites, even if it may certainly be contradictory to notions of social control advocated by competing or aspiring elites (such as those, for example, who might want to work towards the regeneration of democracy in these two countries, or those who position themselves from the perspective of 'the whole of society' or 'the social system').

The apparent contradiction between emphasis on the imposition of disciplinary practices, that is the usual image connected to social control, and the actual reality of a universe of deviance and crime that unfolds in symbiotic unity with the structures of control, may be resolved once we understand that we should abandon any notion of a monistic social control.

We should adopt instead the pluralist and conflictual stance that actually allows us to ask: social control for what, for whom, by whom? The members of a ruling elite in a given society are the ones, by definition, who are able, among other things, to bring social conflict under control. In other words, social control should be seen as the successful reproduction of a system of social relations, from the perspective of those who have a stake in those relations. This simply means society's ability to reproduce itself without implying any ideal standard of social peace. What is in fact reproduced is a complex 'social package', that includes a rough amount of 'crime and punishment'.

For instance, I would claim that in the United States, with the high and pervasive rates of violent crime – exemplified in the murder rate, many times higher than that of any other developed country – there is a high degree of social control. What I mean by this is that the hold on society of a power elite and of the value system that elite seems to cherish – not least the possibility of using violence in the management of human affairs – is very strong. Something substantially different, yet formally similar, could be said of the traditional relationship between Italian 'Roman' politics and organised crime: not only have they traditionally reflected each other, but they have also overlapped, especially in the South (Arlacchi, 1983). In the richer North, instead, where there is a lesser tradition of violence and opposition to politics, the structure of illegal procurement of affairs overlapped exactly with the structure of the political system through a very intricate and well-organised system of payoffs.[12]

In sum, the task of a reflexive criminology is the study of the overall complexity of the social attributions of criminal label and punishment. Social control is always social control from one perspective, and even there where it is presented as social control from the standpoint of a Meadian 'generalised other', such is the standpoint that was erected in (the given) history (of a given society) as hegemonic. Because this hegemonic picture is the one that we have often been presented with, the view that sees social control as an attribute of 'society' in general is well understandable, as is the other common idea of seeing Leviathan at its centre. Anybody who has witnessed periods of deep social unrest, however, like, for my generation, the world-wide movements around the year 1968, or the European turmoil begun in 1989, has learned that this totalising authoritarian-patriarchal myth – one is reminded of the head of the primal horde in Freud's *Totem and Taboo* (1913) – very often not only has no clothes on, but has hurriedly left town altogether. It then becomes easy, as Foucault suggested (1976: 88), to complete the job by beheading his image in our theories.

That very reflexivity that applies to concepts of crime and social control applies to the concept of the state as well (Melossi, 1990). It will not do, therefore, to beg the question by moving the problem from 'crime' and 'social control' to 'the state', as David Matza proposed in one of the main texts of the 1960s sociology of deviance, where he announced that the deviant 'concretely realizes that he is a *subject of Leviathan*' (Matza,

1969: 177). Rather, the production of a criminal label and its further processing within the machine of criminal justice, are the result of given historical, social and cultural conditions. Social control and deviance cannot be understood outside of those conditions. Nowhere, as in the field of social control and deviance, is the uprooting from their cultural soil more lethal to a thorough understanding of the phenomena studied. Whereas this may be a common 'professional' mistake among social scientists, it is instead a rare mistake among members of power elites, who are forced to express hegemonic claims to leadership in the moral vocabulary specific to the society and culture that they intend to lead.

Notes

This is the much revised version of a paper presented at the 'State-of-the-Art Conference' on 'Inequality, Crime and Social Control', 10–12 April 1992, The University of Georgia, Athens.

1 See 'Rival Gangs Picnic in L.A., Despite Weekend Killings', *San Francisco Chronicle*, 18 May 1992, p. A3. This scepticism was repeated, in the media as well as by police officers, when, about a year later, several hundred representatives of 'gangs' and community activists convened at a 'National Urban Peace and Justice Summit' in Kansas City (see 'From weapons to words: Gangs to talk peace', *USA Today*, 30 April p. 3A). Possibly one of the reasons for police aversion is what happened after the 1965 Watts riots truce. It led to a politicisation of the black youth and a massive presence of the Black Panthers in Southcentral Los Angeles, to be ended only in 1970 by the LAPD's newly created Special Weapons and Tactics (SWAT) team's day-long siege of the Panthers' headquarters (Davis, 1990: 297–8).

2 And rightly so, because the Second Amendment 'right of the people to keep and bear arms', is not only a justification for National Rifle Association politics but also a sober reminder to those holding positions of power, of the Lockeian right of resistance, the only real ultimate guarantee of civil liberties. It was so invoked by Huey P. Newton and his comrades of the Black Panther Party when, on 2 May 1967, they carried rifles into the California capitol in Sacramento, an act that would have been deemed 'subversive' in any European society, but that could be presented as simply an exercise of right in the United States – which does not mean, of course, that the members of the Black Panther Party did not have to pay dearly for that kind of reminder later.

3 From an informative letter by Representative Henry B. Gonzalez.

4 For the meaning of this expression, see Melossi (1990: 12–17).

5 From the statement of Prime Minister Giulio Andreotti on 25 May 1990, at the Italian House of Representatives, as reported by the newspaper *Il popolo*, organ of the Christian Democratic Party, on 26 May 1990, p. 32.

6 *La questione criminale* was the title of a journal published in Italy from 1975 to 1981, representing the positions of an Italian critical school of criminology and criminal law.

7 See *La Repubblica*, 14 March 1992, for Mr Andreotti's reactions to the killing of Lima (*I professionisti dell' anti-mafia* was a label coined by the Sicilian writer Leonardo Sciascia (*Corriere della Sera*, 1 January 1988)). Thereafter, see *La Repubblica* of 22 October of the same year about the political background of the murder according to the investigation of the prosecuting magistrates.

8 Of course, the very serious charges brought against Mr Andreotti himself at the time of writing this chapter, according to which he was in collusion with the leadership of the Mafia in Sicily, charges based on testimony rendered by *mafiosi* turned state's evidence, would shed quite a different light on Andreotti's tolerant propensities. According to such charges, a trade-off situation existed between Mr Andreotti, who gave the *mafiosi* political protection, and the *mafiosi*, who, in exchange, would have taken care of the dirty work of high politics for

him. The most serious charge would be the alleged instigation of the murder on 20 March 1979 of the journalist Mino Pecorelli, who would have 'known too much' about certain circumstances of the kidnapping of the Christian Democrat leader Aldo Moro and his murder by the Red Brigades in 1978 (see 'E Andreotti disse: Fermate Pecorelli', *La Repubblica*, 11 June 1993; see also other articles, ibid.). Whatever the judicial truth will turn out to be, if it ever will, the fact is that an attitude of complicitous tolerance is very widespread in Italian culture and is the best protective cover under which powerful criminals, whether *mafiosi*, industrialists or politicians, have been allowed to prosper.

9 From *La Repubblica*, 11 February 1993, italics in the original.

10 The situation of Italy today is certainly different from that at the time when Gramsci was writing, also thanks to the work of people like him, given that probably the most memorable contribution to a contemporary Italian civil tradition was the Resistance against the Fascists and the German occupation in the period 1943–5. However, this took place only in the North, and much more sporadically in some areas of the Centre and the South, a fact that certainly emphasised the traditional differences between North and South (Banfield, 1958; Putnam, 1993).

11 It should be noted in passing that the public management of the terrorist crisis of the 1970s, especially in relation to the Moro affair, had been quite different; then, the political/social controllers had indeed chosen to amplify deviance! (Lumley and Schlesinger, 1982; Wagner-Pacifici, 1986; Hess et al., 1988; Catanzaro, 1991; Trenz and Zaitch, 1991).

12 This certainly does not imply that such precarious balances should last forever; indeed, the waning of the Cold War anti-Communist blackmail is showing the increasing loss of legitimacy of governmental regimes for which one voted, as Italians used to say, while holding one's nose.

References

Archer, Dane and Gartner, Rosemary (1984) *Violence and Crime in Cross-National Perspective*. New Haven, CT: Yale University Press.

Arlacchi, Pino ([1983] 1986) *Mafia Business: The Mafia Ethic and the Spirit of Capitalism*. London: Verso.

Arlacchi, Pino (1993) 'Mafia, Cosa Nostra, ed istituzioni nell'Italia di oggi', paper presented at the International Symposium 'Deconstructing Italy? Emerging Issues in Italian Society, Culture and Politics', 29–30 March, Berkeley.

Banfield, Edward C. (1958) *The Moral Basis of a Backward Society*. New York: The Free Press.

Baratta, Alessandro (1963) *Antinomie giuridiche e conflitti di coscienza*. Milano: Giuffré.

Becker, Howard S. (1963) *Outsiders: Studies in the Sociology of Deviance*. New York: The Free Press.

Bowers, William J. and Pierce, Glenn L. (1980) 'Deterrence or brutalization: what is the effect of executions?', *Crime and Delinquency*, 26: 453–84.

Bush, George (1991a) 'Address Before a Joint Session of the Congress on the Cessation of the Persian Gulf Conflict', 6 March 1991, Weekly Compilation of Presidential Documents 27: 257–61.

Bush, George (1991b) 'Remarks at the Attorney General's Crime Summit', 5 March 1991, Weekly Compilation of Presidential Documents 27: 254–56.

Carson, Clayborne, Garron, David, Hill, Gerald, Harding, Vincent and Clark Hine, Darlene (1991) *The Eyes on the Prize Civil Rights Reader*. New York: Penguin.

Catanzaro, Raimondo (1991) *The Red Brigades and Left-wing Terrorism in Italy*. London: Pinter.

Childs, John Brown (1993) 'Straight from the "Hood: Urban Peace and Justice"', *The Nation*.

Cloward, Richard A. and Piven, Frances F. (1986) 'Challenge and control as sociology's core', paper presented at the ASA Meetings, August, New York.

Cohen, Stanley ([1972] 1980) *Folk Devils and Moral Panic: The Creation of the Mods and Rockers*. New York: St. Martin's Press.

Cressey, Donald R. (1968) 'Culture conflict, differential association and normative conflict', in M. E. Wolfgang (ed.), *Crime and Culture*. New York: Wiley.

Davis, Mike (1990) *City of Quartz: Excavating the Future in Los Angeles*. London: Verso.

Dunne, John G. (1991) 'Law and disorder in Los Angeles', *New York Review of Books*, 38(16): 23–9 and 38(17): 62–70.

Durkheim, Emile ([1895] 1930) *The Rules of Sociological Method*. New York: Free Press.

Edelman, Murray J. (1988) *Constructing the Political Spectacle*. Chicago, IL: University of Chicago Press.

Erickson, Kai (1966) *Wayward Puritans*. New York: Wiley.

Foucault, Michel ([1965] 1973) *Madness and Civilization: A History of Insanity in the Age of Reason*. New York: Vintage.

Foucault, Michel ([1974] 1991) 'Michel Foucault on Attica: an interview', *Social Justice*, 18(3): 26–34.

Foucault, Michel ([1975] 1977) *Discipline and Punish*. New York: Pantheon.

Foucault, Michel ([1976] 1978) *The History of Sexuality. Volume 1: An Introduction*. New York: Random House.

Freud, Sigmund ([1913] 1955) *Totem and Taboo*, in *The Standard Edition, vol. 13*. London: Hogarth.

Garland, David (1990) 'Frameworks of inquiry in the sociology of punishment', *British Journal of Sociology*, 41: 1–15.

Gitlin, Todd (1980) *The Whole World is Watching*. Berkeley: University of California Press.

Gottfredson, Michael R. and Hirschi, Travis (1990) *A General Theory of Crime*. Stanford, CA: Stanford University Press.

Gramsci, Antonio ([1926] 1978) 'Some aspects of the Southern question', in *Selections from Political Writings (1921–1926)*. New York: International Publishers.

Gramsci, Antonio ([1929–1935] 1971) *Selections from the Prison Notebooks*. New York: International Publishers.

Gusfield, Joseph (1981) *The Culture of Public Problems. Drinking-Driving and the Symbolic Order*. Chicago, IL: University of Chicago Press.

Hagan, John ([1988] 1989) *Structural Criminology*. New Brunswick, NJ: Rutgers University Press.

Hess, Henner, Moerings, Martin, Pass, Dieter, Scheerer, Sebastian and Steinert, Heinz (1988) *Angriff auf das Herz des Staates: Soziale Entwicklung und Terrorismus*. Frankfurt: Suhrkamp.

Joe, Karen, A. (1991) *Milk Carton Madness: The Heart of the Missing Children's Crisis*. PhD Thesis in Sociology, University of California, Davis.

Lacombe, Dany (1993) 'Les liaisons dangereuses: Foucault et la criminologie', *Criminologie*, 26(1): 51–72.

Lumley, Bob and Schlesinger, Philip (1982) 'The press, the state and its enemies: the Italian case', *The Sociological Review*, 30: 603–26.

Machiavelli, Niccolò ([1513] 1977) *The Prince*. New York: W.W. Norton.

Marx, Gary (1988) *Undercover: Police Surveillance in America*. Berkeley: University of California Press.

Matza, David (1961) 'Subterranean traditions of youth', *The Annals of the American Academy of Political and Social Science*, 338: 102–18.

Matza, David (1969) *Becoming Deviant*. Englewood Cliffs, NJ: Prentice-Hall.

Mayhew, Leon H. (1982) 'Introduction' to T. Parsons, *On Institutions and Social Evolution: Selected Writings*. Chicago, IL: University of Chicago Press.

Mead, George H. ([1917–18] 1964) 'The psychology of punitive justice', in G.H. Mead, *Selected Writings*. Indianapolis: Bobbs-Merrill.

Mead, George H. ([1925] 1964) 'The genesis of the self and social control', in G.H. Mead, *Selected Writings*. Indianapolis: Bobbs-Merrill.

Melossi, Dario (1985) 'Overcoming the crisis in critical criminology: toward a grounded labeling theory', *Criminology*, 23: 193–208.

Melossi, Dario (1990) *The State of Social Control: A Sociological Study of Concepts of State and Social Control in the Making of Democracy*. Cambridge: Polity Press; New York: St Martin's Press.

Melossi, Dario (1993) 'Gazette of morality and social whip: punishment, hegemony, and the case of the USA, 1970–1992', *Social and Legal Studies: An International Journal*, 2: 259–79.

Merton, Robert K. (1938) 'Social structure and anomie', *American Sociological Review*, 3: 672–82.

Mills, C. Wright ([1940] 1963) 'Situated actions and vocabularies of motive', in C.W. Mills, *Power Politics and People*. New York: Oxford University Press.

Paz, Octavio ([1979] 1985) *The Labyrinth of Solitude*. New York: Grove Press.

Putnam, Robert D. (1993) *Making Democracy Work: Civic Traditions in Modern Italy*. Princeton: Princeton University Press.

Ranulf, Svend (1938) *Moral Indignation and Middle Class Psychology*. Copenhagen: Levin and Munskgaard.

Rorty, Richard (1982) *Consequences of Pragmatism*. Minneapolis: University of Minnesotta Press.

Salamini, Leonardo (1989) 'Capitalism and Southern Italian underdevelopment: the historical roots of the "Southern Question"', *International Journal of Contemporary Sociology*, 26: 39–54.

Salamini, Leonardo (1992) 'Southern Italian underdevelopment in the post-war period: some observations on state policies and the Mafia', *International Journal of Contemporary Sociology*, 29: 201–15.

Salvemini, Gaetano (1963) *Movimento socialista e questione meridionale*. Milan: Feltrinelli.

Shibutani, Tamotsu (1962) 'Reference groups and social control', in A.M. Rose (ed.), *Human Behavior and Social Processes*. Boston, MA: Houghton Mifflin.

Simmel, Georg ([1922] 1955) 'The web of group-affiliations', in *Conflict and the Web of Group-Affiliations*. New York: The Free Press.

Skolnick, Jerome H. and Fyfe, James J. (1993) *Above the Law: Police and the Excessive Use of Force*. New York: The Free Press.

Stille, Alexander (1993) 'Letter from Palermo: The Mafia's Biggest Mistake', *New Yorker*, 1 March.

Sudnow, David (1965) 'Normal crimes', *Social Problems*, 12: 255–76.

Sutherland, Edwin H. and Cressey, Donald R. (1978) *Criminology*. Philadelphia, PA: Lippincott.

Trenz, Hans J. and Zaitch, Damián (1991) 'Terrorismo y Control Social: Estrategias, Funciones y Conflicto Simbólico', paper presented at the Workshop on 'Sociology of Criminal Law and Punishment', 3–4 July, Onati International Institute for the Sociology of Law, Onati, Spain.

Wagner-Pacifici, Robin E. (1986) *The Moro Morality Play: Terrorism as Social Drama*. Chicago, IL: The University of Chicago Press.

Weber, Max ([1956] 1968) *Economy and Society*. New York: Bedminster.

10

Whom can you Trust? The Future of Comparative Criminology

David Nelken

Systematic research on the variability of trust in human societies is one of the biggest challenges for contemporary sociology.

(Roniger, 1992: 47)

Trusting is good but not trusting is better.

(Fourteenth century Tuscan proverb)

What is the point of doing research in comparative criminology? What are the problems of such investigations and how should they be overcome? In the first part of this chapter I shall consider some of the answers that can be given to these large demands and review a few examples of work in the field. I shall then go on to offer an illustration of how these questions may be tackled in the course of empirical research by drawing on a current project that has led me to examine the possible relationships between types of trust and different systems of criminal justice in Europe. The two parts of the chapter are united by a search for an adequate framework in which to pose questions concerning similarities and differences in forms of crime and crime control. My goal throughout is also to find ways in which comparative enquiry may be used to broaden our approach to the study of crime.

Why do research in comparative criminology?

There are, obviously, many possible motives for engaging in any intellectual enquiry and the reasons which justify it cannot always be specified from the outset. I shall underline here only a few of the considerations which suggest the increasing importance of this subject. Even if the future of criminology cannot be reduced simply to the success with which it faces the challenge of comparative criminology there are both practical and theoretical arguments which suggest that an awareness of the comparative dimension of crime is becoming increasingly essential.

At the practical and policy making level there is mounting evidence of serious and costly transnational and cross-border crimes. Those involved include organised and professional criminals occupied in the smuggling of drugs, arms and other contraband as well as white-collar criminals, often acting in collaboration with other types of criminals, who may be involved in fiscal crimes such as fraud, money laundering and tax evasion. There are also international aspects to crimes against the environment such as the illegal dumping of waste. The weakness of national and international efforts to combat these crimes is no secret. Historical and policy-oriented comparisons of criminal justice systems offer important background knowledge (Mawby, 1990; Muncie and Sparks, 1991). But they provide only limited insight into the mixture of cultural differences, practical difficulties and political factors (including turning a blind eye or even colluding with crime) which inhibit collaboration between states. One important obstacle derives from the defence of political sovereignty which is very much identified with independent national systems of criminal law and procedure. Even within the European Union this reluctance to cede criminal jurisdiction means that there are crimes, such as fraud against its system of agricultural subsidies, which thrive precisely because of the contrast between regulation organised at supranational level and enforcement which is limited to the national level (Passas and Nelken, 1991, 1993).

Major changes in political systems and boundaries, in particular those connected with the enormous changes taking place in the ex-Soviet Union and the ex-Soviet bloc, also have consequences such as the large increase in organised crime, which need to be better understood. Some of the most important current political trends and projects have to do with the attempt to construct new forms of social order and social control. Will the countries of Eastern Europe succeed in creating new political and judicial institutions able to secure some version of the rule of law despite the apparently inhospitable social conditions which presently characterise them? Will the European Union develop into a 'fortress' using all manner of sanctions to keep out the expected influx of immigrants from less economically favoured countries? Less dramatically, comparative work is indicated (though often not undertaken) when countries seek to 'borrow' other states' penal laws, procedures or initiatives in the course of reforming their own systems. This is likely to become more common as information about other countries' practices becomes more available and as continuing dissatisfaction with the existing functioning of criminal justice prompts the introduction of radical change.

The reason for doing comparative research may have as much to do with understanding one's own country better as it has with understanding anyone else's. Comparative enquiry has as one of its chief concerns the effort to identify the way a country's types of crime and of crime control resonate with other aspects of its culture. Many claims about crime causation or about crime control which purport to be universal in fact take their sense and limits of applicability from such cultural connections. I shall take two examples of question-begging assumptions about crime control which can be easily seen when comparing criminal justice in Britain and Italy, the countries I know best.

Much British writing on the police takes it for granted that nothing could be more ill advised than for the police to risk losing touch with the public by relying too much on military, technological or other impersonal methods of crime control. The results of this, it is claimed, could only be a spiral of alienation which would spell the end of 'policing by consent' (see, for example, Lea and Young, 1984; Kinsey et al., 1986; Maclean, 1993.) In Italy, however, two of the main police forces are still part of the military and in a recent opinion poll in a news magazine, one of these – the *carabinieri* – was recently voted the legal institution in which people had most confidence.[1] Another case of differences in enforcement lies in the approach taken to business and regulatory crime. Britain, like most English speaking countries, adopts a style of responding to many of these offences in a sufficiently different way to be characterised as a system of 'compliance' as compared with punishment (Nelken, 1993). If the principal goals of the punishment of ordinary crime are to deter and stigmatise, the aim of this form of enforcement, which is entrusted to special agencies and inspectorates rather than to the regular police, is to negotiate or induce the end of law-breaking behaviour by constant pressure to improve standards. The use of the courts is kept as a last resort and treated virtually as a sign of failure. In Italy such a contrast is much less noticeable. Enforcement is guided by an activist judiciary and ordinary judges (especially those particularly highly motivated to combat such behaviour) do their best to combat pollution, neglect of safety at work, etc., using the normal techniques of criminal law and punishment.

These contrasts reflect consistent differences in legal culture; in both examples the Italian style is the more bureaucratic and impersonal (Nelken, 1991). This, in turn, can be related to the Italian inheritance of a particular mix of Bourbon and Austrian forms of imperial rule as well as more generally to the historical factors responsible for shaping the continental state and legal tradition differently from that of the (English) common law (see Dyson, 1980). For sociological purposes, however, we also need to ask how and why these inherited patterns come to persist. We may be able to answer these questions in terms of the framework which I shall be setting out in the second half of this chapter. Enforcement styles in Italy and Britain can be related, I would argue, to differences in the patterns of trust and distrust in each country. For example, an emphasis on impersonal enforcement in Italy came to be justified as a protection against favouritism and corruption because the society is divided into numerous competing groups and even the political parties could not be sure whose interests the legal system would serve (Nelken, 1991, 1992a). A discretionary or compliance style of law enforcement would be seen as too easy an excuse for corruption. In Italy this attitude continues to be sustained both by the judiciary and by important sections of political opinion although there are also other voices which stress the extent to which this approach actually encourages hidden discretion and may have negative side-effects on the organisation and coordination of enforcement (Nelken, 1992b). In Britain, by contrast, the identification of the criminal justice system with the interests of government is much more marked as is the perceived coincidence of interest between regulators and the interests of business. Whatever arguments in terms of effectiveness may be offered for the compliance style of regulatory enforcement used in Britain so much more than in Italy it also reflects the extent to which the British system of criminal justice is willing to trust some groups more than others (as well as the meaning and priority given to 'effectiveness' in different kinds of law enforcement).

The discovery of such policy contrasts certainly helps to overcome ethnocentrism. Could it not be argued, however, that each country has the system it requires? The answer cannot be given a priori and depends on evaluations which I will not enter into here, but there can be little doubt that comparative work raises or sharpens some awkward questions. Would it necessarily be so counterproductive for Italy to try to make its police forces more approachable? What is it that really prevents the adoption in Britain of methods to deal with business crime more similar to those used against ordinary crime?

Even apart from its immediate practical or policy relevance comparative criminology can also contribute to the theoretical development of criminology itself. The introduction of a comparative aspect can help in the reformulation of central problems in criminological theory. For example, as I have just illustrated, it may be easier to pursue the important question of the relationship between crime and social reaction where both are seen as expressions of the wider culture (see Melossi, Chapter 9 in this volume). Comparative work can also breathe new life into the sociology of deviance (now rather out of fashion) because it poses the problem of how to understand the 'other' without either resorting to stereotypes or denying 'difference'.[2] Since comparative criminology usually concentrates on describing other countries' systems of criminal justice it often leads to rival accounts proposed by criminologists of the countries concerned.[3] The debates that follow, painful and replete with misunderstanding as they sometimes tend to be, are fundamentally healthy for limiting the pretensions of a discipline which too often studies the powerless. Studies in comparative criminology should help make criminologists become more reflexive concerning the way their concerns already form part of their own culture. The danger of the growth of a community of comparative criminologists with shared reference to American or English language criminology is that it might actually hinder such debate.[4] Because comparative criminology poses the need to understand different cultures it requires confronting the anti-positivist or post-positivist methodologies required for such a task. Comparative work therefore provides a way for criminology to go beyond a stress on crime and social structure towards the study of the relationship between crime and culture, ideology and discourse. 'Culture' would then be seen not simply as another factor or variable to be added into the explanatory equation but more as the name for the context in which such causes operate and which supplies them with their sense. But this of course begs the controversial question of what is the best way of doing comparative criminology.

Ways of doing comparative criminology

If it is clear that there is much to be gained from attempts to develop this subject it is also true that there is considerable disagreement and uncertainty about how best to go about it. The methodological difficulties commonly cited range from the differing reliability of criminal statistics to the lack of shared concepts. But the more fundamental questions to be asked are: what is the goal of our comparisons and what should we be comparing?

The answers to these questions are bound to reflect wider disagreements over theory and methodology in the social sciences (though the level of debate within comparative criminology does not always reflect this). While some scholars see comparative criminology as constituting no obstacle to criminology's traditional enquiry into the causes of crime others see it as the best demonstration of the futility of such a mandate. For example, Gottfredson and Hirschi (among the most widely cited of mainstream American criminologists) and Beirne (one of the most theoretically open minded) agree that comparative work quickly reveals the culture-bound quality of much national criminology. Curiously, they both use the example of the alleged inappropriateness of Cohen's subcultural theory of juvenile delinquency when translated to the context of a South American slum. But the conclusions they draw from this are radically different. For Gottfredson and Hirschi (1990) this serves as justification for their attempt to build a culture-free theory of crime.[5] They see evidence about comparative variation as a secondary aspect of criminological theorising because they argue that cultural variability only affects the opportunity for crime and not the nature of crime itself. But the paradoxical result of this commitment to universal theorising can be the reinforcement of an ethnocentric view of crime.[6] Beirne (1983a, 1983b), on the other hand, discusses the implications of what he describes as methodological and epistemological relativism in relation to comparative work. He criticises the attempt to bring cases under a master theory whether this involves what he calls the 'method of agreement' or 'the method of difference'. For him neither method succeeds in overcoming the disabling problem of determining the conceptual equivalence of what is to be compared because crime in different cultures can be compared only if the definitions and meanings of criminal behaviour in these cultures is the same (Beirne, 1983b). To get round this methodological obstacle he recommends focusing on the relationship between controllers and controlled in different countries rather than on crimes themselves (Robertson and Taylor, 1973). But this argument seems to err in the other direction from that of Gottfredson and Hirschi. It is surely part of the task of comparative criminology, rather than one of its presuppositions, to seek to establish to what extent the meaning of crime in different countries is in fact comparable. Even if positivist methodologies are not well suited for this task interpretative approaches may yield better results.[7]

It may be helpful to distinguish three of the interrelated issues which tend to get mixed together in disagreements concerning the best way to do comparative criminology. Should we be looking for similarities or differences? Should we try to provide explanations or understanding? Should we be looking at culture as a means of explaining variations in crime and its control, or instead be examining crime and control as clues for making sense of culture? It is easy to see why the alternative answers to these questions tend to come ready packaged. If the goal of research is to discover (or to test for) similarities the appropriate research approach would be to explain the effects of similar factors in different situations or to conduct a search for the 'functional equivalents' used in various societies to resolve common problems. Using these approaches comparative criminology becomes nothing other than the application of normal sociological methods to new contexts. Differences in culture are reduced to little more than further explanatory variables which can be used to explain why similar causes or problems lead to different outcomes in different societies. Where, on the other hand, the goal is to understand difference, in the sense of culture as a unique constellation of meaning, more attention will need to be paid to interpretative strategies. Comparative investigation turns into the hermeneutic exercise of trying to use evidence about crime and its control to resolve puzzles about culture.

The choice between these alternative strategies is partly a matter of what is to be achieved. How far must a comparative study satisfy us that it has offered a comprehensive account of each of the societies under investigation? It is quite possible to come away from a reading of Clinard's classic study of 'cities with low crime', for example, without feeling much wiser about the nature of Swiss Protestant culture and the way it discourages (certain kinds of) crime (Clinard, 1978). To this Clinard could reply that his object was not to provide such insight but rather to develop and partly test a universal theory concerning which social factors go together with a low crime rate. Yet it is reasonable to think that greater discussion of these matters would have enriched his study.

But how far is it possible to combine different strategies of comparison? The question is discussed in a valuable recent overview of theoretical approaches to comparative sociology by Ptor Sztompka (Sztompka,1990: 54 ff.). Sztompka contrasts two alternative projects. The aim of the first type, which he calls comparison in an extensive direction, is 'to widen the scope of applicability (of a concept) or the scope of objects or predicates; the attempt is to seek for commonalities and uniformities among variety'. The consequence of such a strategy is that 'we know more, but we know less in the sense of detail, concreteness and specificity'. The second strategy, of intensive enquiry, on the other hand, is 'to narrow down the scope of applicability, or the scope of objects, or the scope of predicates'. The result is 'the opposite of the former approach. The gain in informational content (interpreting power) is paid by the loss of comprehensiveness (systematising power). We know more, but about less.' Sztompka insists, virtually by definition, that these strategies are mutually inconsistent, 'unfortunately, as so often in life, one can't have it both ways'. But he goes on to offer two arguments in favour of the second strategy. The first is that the so-called 'soft' methodologies of interpretation and hermeneutics are more appropriate than the search for positivist generalisations when it comes to unlocking the secrets of culture. In addition, the increased opportunities for cultural contact and the (presumed) consequent growth in cultural uniformity means that it is now the continued existence of cultural diversity which is worthy of investigation. We should, therefore, 'seek for divergences, uniqueness amongst uniformity' which should be understood as the results of past divergences and unique chains of historical traditions (Sztompka, 1990: 54 ff.).

Much as I am sympathetic to Sztompka's analysis, there is some danger of his presenting us with false dichotomies. The task of comparison is likely to lead us to employ both extensive and intensive strategies at different stages and for different purposes. Sztompka is right to argue that positivistic methodologies are not the best way to clarify the sense of a concept. But any such investigation will nevertheless need to be placed within the context of extensive comparisons if only because the attempt to grasp the meaning of a concept in another culture always parts from and returns to ideas derived from one's own culture. An account of another culture is therefore never a 'view from nowhere'[8] but is the particular product of this process of shifting between meanings in the culture under consideration and those of the observer. 'Difference' or even 'uniqueness' is always relative. Rather than facing a choice between advancing general laws or specific interpretations we are in fact constrained to offer specific perspectives on an implicitly generalisable problematic.

What is undeniable is that much existing work in comparative criminology errs on the side of over-reliance on positivistic methodologies. In fact, correctionalist and positivist approaches are particularly well entrenched in comparative criminology even in the contributions of scholars who are sceptical about these approaches in their other work.[9] By contrast, there has been little attempt to 'appreciate' the perspective of deviants in a comparative perspective. Nor, despite its obvious potential, has much been written which applies the social construction approach to the construction of crime problems in different countries.[10] (It is easy to find examples of striking contrasts, even in the countries with which I am most familiar, which cry out for such analysis. Why is there hardly any discussion, let alone moral panic, about juvenile delinquency in Italy? Why is there so little exposure of corruption in Britain?) Those on the outside of a society may feel safer with approaches such as behaviourism, positivism, or functionalism (including Marxist varieties), which rely on an 'external' point of view. If the issue pursued is the relationship between crime and modernisation, for example, the observer may well feel that what is being explained is a process which goes on behind the backs of the members of the society affected so that it is unnecessary to understand how matters are seen by the members of the country concerned. But the security of the external point of view is largely an illusion; as soon as we get beyond the most superficial comparison of crime rates there are few topics in comparative criminology on which progress can be made without the possibility of being able to interpret the significance of crime and control in relation to other social and cultural phenomena.[11] For this to be possible it is essential to have first-hand familiarity with daily life in the societies to be compared. The under achievements of comparative criminology so far are therefore largely the result of over-ambition: the search for universal theories of crime: the effort to compare too many countries over too many features. More progress could be made through more modest but more focused efforts to investigate specific examples of crime and control in two or three countries.

Two recent collections illustrate the strengths and weaknesses of existing work. *Crime and Control in Comparative Perspectives* (Heiland et al., 1992) is an official production of the International Sociological Association which can perhaps be taken as representative of much mainstream comparative criminology. It contains a series of single-country studies of levels of crime and the response of the criminal justice system together with some introductory and closing chapters which attempt to provide theoretical direction. Despite declaring themselves in favour of a variety of different approaches and interdisciplinary synthesis the editors' own approach is strongly positivistic.[12] For them the point of comparative criminology is the search for general scientific laws since 'each explanation can only be convincing when it is not designed for certain countries (e.g. Japan or the USA) but drawn up comparatively' (Heiland and Shelley, 1992: vi). A guiding question set for the contributors to their volume is 'How is one to explain the increasing lack of discipline and the lack of civilised behaviour of the offender, on the one hand, and the growing caution, personalisation and individualisation of bodies of social control?' (Heiland and Shelley, 1992: viii).

The editors elaborate a framework for comparative investigation based, on the one hand, on the effects of modernisation and industrialisation and, on the other, on what following Elias they call 'the civilising process' – seen as a long-term shift from external controls to internal controls. The attempt to apply these bodies of theory to such a diversity of cultures with different histories is in principle open to doubt. In any event, as is not unusual, only some of the contributors (such as Joutsen, 1992) accepted the editors' invitation to examine the data concerning their societies in the light of these general hypotheses. In some cases the authors avoided these questions because they were less concerned with the explanation of crime than with other matters such as the need for certain penal reforms or the valiant achievements of state socialism in reducing the crime problem (for example, Binsong, 1992). More interestingly, however, some contributors more or less openly rebelled at the editors' approach to comparative work. Shrivastava, for example, in a careful account of the complexities of studying crime in India, insists that 'the assessment of the relationship between crime and development can be made only with reference to the specific and sometimes unique, social and cultural context'. As he goes on to explain 'the meaning of specific conditions such as poverty is determined for people within their social and cultural context. Tradition, social institutions and cultural values are crucial variables in determining the containment and growth of crime in a modernizing society' (Shrivastava, 1992: 189).

The collection thus raises important questions of methodology. With so many widely different countries and cultures to consider (the United States, Nordic countries, Nigeria, West Germany, Venezuela, India, China, Hungary, Caribbean countries and Japan) it may be said that only general questions were possible. But the well-tried tactic of putting together studies written by representatives from the countries concerned is not well suited to furthering comparative work. There are really no short cuts which can dispense with the need for individual or collaborative immersion in different realities. Only in this way can something be done to reduce the twin dangers that afflict comparative research. For we need to be concerned not only that an 'outsider' may ask inappropriate questions of a society he or she has not learned to understand but also that the 'insider', just because of this familiarity, may fail to appreciate what is most singular about the society seen from a comparative point of view. It takes a Briton or American, for example, to be puzzled by the Continental 'principle of legality' in prosecution decision making which in its extreme form – as in Italy – refuses to authorise any use of discretion in enforcement or prosecution by police or prosecutor. Conversely, it is only from the viewpoint of Continental Europe that it becomes pertinent to discuss the ingrained 'pragmatism' (a term which is not intended as a compliment) of many British and American criminal justice procedures and practices.

Crime in Europe (Heidensohn and Farrell, 1991) looks at fewer countries but in some ways offers a greater variety of topics and approaches. As before, this collection too sets out to address criminological issues which transcend single countries so as to highlight broader trends in crime and ways of responding to it. It discusses the growth in crime rates in Europe and examines police cooperation (or the lack of it) in the international responses to drug trafficking and other crimes. Attention is drawn to the continuing uniformly low rate of female criminality and the disproportionately high number of apprehended offenders from ethnic minorities. There is also an attempt to provide an overview of differences in criminological traditions in various European countries. Of particular interest, however, are the attempts to compare and contrast different countries. The collection includes, for example, a comparison of the introduction of new methods of diversion from prosecution in Germany and Austria as well as of the rules and practice of prison discipline in four European countries.

There is much to be said for these more focused studies particularly when they are based on genuine first-hand familiarity with the countries con-cerned (which is practical only if the number of countries is limited). In the second part of this chapter I shall be setting out a framework for just such comparative investigation of certain features of crime and its control in Britain and Italy. But there are problems even in the case of two-country comparisons. What is the goal of the comparison? How are the countries or other units to be chosen (should they be chosen for similarity or difference)? Is the issue one which is equally salient in both countries (does it need to be)? A risk of concentrating on a limited number of countries is the temptation to assume that the countries or cultures concerned represent polar opposites or, at least, the full range of possible contrasts in a given phenomenon, when they may be no more than two points on a continuum. Often it is only after shifting to a perspective anchored in a third reality that the factors which the countries actually have in common emerge clearly. To some extent such problems may be overcome by resorting to the Weberian methodology of 'ideal types' (see, for example, Damaska, 1986) though this is not without its own drawbacks. More generally they underline the importance of interlinking intensive and extensive comparison; even close comparisons of a limited number of countries must be placed within a framework which is in principle open to wider application.

To summarise: it would be unwise to select only one of the strategies of comparison indicated by Sztompka if it would also be possible to incorporate elements from the other. Without pretending to resolve basic dilemmas in social theory the most useful way forward in comparative criminology is one which seeks to combine approaches seeking explanation as well as understanding (without forgetting that it is the latter which is most commonly neglected). But the search for understanding carries a number of implications for comparative work. It is necessary to abandon global comparisons and concentrate on no more than two or three countries at a time. Any attempt to synthesise different strategies of comparison will inevitably have to handle a variety of tensions. These include that between external and internal conceptions of crime and crime relevant phenomena and the need to develop concepts which are apt for the particular countries being compared but are also capable of wider application. The search for understanding also involves a shift between crime and culture as independent and dependent variables. In addition to looking for social and cultural factors capable of explaining such familiar criminological topics as variations in crime rates or differences in the practices of control institutions we also need to read data about crime and its control as a clue to the culture of the countries under consideration.[13] Contrary to the arguments of some influential criminologists[14] this wider remit requires reaching out to sister disciplines including some criminology often tends to neglect.[15] Both the findings and the methods (and the debates over method) of these other approaches may pose problems for the boundaries of criminology as a discipline. But the insights which they make possible offer the only hope of ending the artificiality of many discussions of crime and the marginalisation of criminology itself.[16]

Trust, crime and criminal justice in Italy and the United Kingdom

In order to illustrate the application of these protocols, and in particular the last of these recommendations, I now want to propose a tentative framework for comparative examination of crime and criminal justice systems in different societies in terms of the level and types of trust they mobilise. The framework was developed for a specific purpose and arises out of empirical research into frauds against the European Union's agricultural subsidy programmes and the somewhat vain efforts so far to control them. It was therefore intended to make sense of a particular form of criminality and its control in relation to wider social and cultural patterns of behaviour and to be of use mainly in comparing Italy and the United Kingdom. But it should also have wider implications and applicability.

An enquiry into structures of trust and distrust is particularly appropriate for explaining fraud since this may be seen, almost by definition, as the result of misplaced trust. It is also interesting that previous discussions of the connection between crime and trust have also been in the general area of white-collar crime, as in the contributions of Sutherland (1949) or Shapiro (1989).[17] But the significance of trust for criminology is not limited to this type of crime. Rather, it offers the possibility of building the type of theory which could integrate concepts relevant to both the genesis and handling of many other kinds of criminal behaviour. It is even relevant to criminology's fundamental methodological problem regarding the varying reliability of crime statistics in so far as it can easily be shown that the level of reporting crime itself depends on the degree of trust in the authorities (Birkbeck, 1992; Ellis, 1992; Shrivastava, 1992).

Recent writing in social theory provides a rich source of ideas about trust and its importance in social life (see, for example, Luhmann, 1979, 1988; Barber, 1983; Mutti, 1987; Gambetta, 1988; Roniger, 1989, 1992).[18] Obviously, not all these authors speak with one voice. The significance, purposes and functions ascribed to trust varies with the theoretical position of each writer, depending for example on whether the problem is examined from the point of view of individuals and groups (Barber, 1983) or from that of the social system (Luhmann, 1979). Likewise, different disciplines tend to interpret trust in competing ways (Gambetta, 1988). Questions typically focused around the concept of trust – Are there different kinds of trust? Is trust a limited resource? How can it be increased? – themselves depend on and lead back to wider discussions of social, economic and political structure and culture. [19] But for this reason the effort to examine crime and criminal justice in these terms may be particularly fruitful for opening criminology to the approaches and findings of other disciplines.

A brief recapitulation of some of the contributions to the discussion of trust will provide us with some bearings. The definition adopted by many of these writers is that trust is involved if faith (and not just hope) is placed in a person or institution where something serious is at stake if such reliance turns out to be misplaced. In an extensive discussion of trust and in more recent writing on the topic Luhmann examines the way trust relates to the functional requirements of predictability of social expectations. From the point of view of the social system trust serves, like money, as a generalised means of exchange. An insightful point which we will return to is his claim that, whatever their differences, trust and distrust should not be seen as opposites but rather as functional equivalents. This is because both responses serve to eliminate uncertainty and allow a system to take action. A drawback of Luhmann's work for our purposes, however, is the impression he gives that all modern societies are similarly reliant on system trust. For example, he asserts categorically that 'Trust remains vital in interpersonal relations, but participation in functional systems like the economy or politics is no longer a matter of personal relations. It requires confidence but not trust' (Luhmann, 1979: 102). As we shall see, this would be a very misleading guide to the place of trust in Italian public life.

Luhmann's concentration on the supposedly universal needs of modern societies to reduce complexity can be balanced by two recent contributions to a leading Italian sociological journal which helped move the debate onto more comparative ground. Mutti (1987) writes of trust as a concept insufficiently well formulated in sociology but a solid reality in social life. He discussed the favourable conditions for the flourishing of trust and its particularities in different spheres of life such as work relations, organisational coordination or political legitimacy. He also distinguished personal from system trust. Roniger (1989) responded to this article with one entitled 'Trust . . . a no less fragile reality'. Drawing on his well-known previous work on the persistence of clientelism and patronage in many societies (Eisenstadt and Roniger, 1984) he stressed the difficulties they faced in establishing trust in institutions as opposed to the personal trust reposed in groups or individuals. He then developed his ideas further in a fuller presentation explicitly directed at the comparative study of trust. Here he broke down the concepts of personal and system trust into four sub-types of trust. Between the extremes of 'total focalisation of trust' and 'total generalised trust' he added 'selective generalisation of interpersonal trust' (for example, where you only trust other members of your ethnic group) and selective generalisation of institutional trust (for example, where people do trust their own political parties but not the political system as a whole). Roniger's interest was in the problem of extending trust from the immediate, specific and interpersonal sphere into more generalised trust as well as the factors that lead to the breakdown of system trust. But it can equally well be adapted to asking questions about the symbiosis between forms of trust and distrust in any given society.

These differences between interpersonal and system trust (and their varieties) can provide the basis for a variety of comparative enquiries between societies. They could be used, for example, to investigate the role of trust in a series of different vertical and horizontal relationships. We could consider the relationship of trust *between* government (and enforcement staff) and those being controlled; citizens, potential or actual offenders. In addition we could ask about relationships *among* controllers and *among* the controlled. A comparison of the type, manner and level of trust in each of these cases should provide important clues to the shape and success of both enforcement and criminal activities. However, in examining these relationships it may also be useful to distinguish different aspects of trust. For analytical purposes we can ask about the *decision* to trust (whom can you trust?); the *manner* of trusting (how, when and why do you trust?); and the *degree* of trusting (how much do you trust?). Using these headings the following brief discussion will attempt to show some ways in which differences in the construction and maintenance of trust may throw light on characteristics of crime and criminal justice in Italy and the United Kingdom.

Whom can you trust?

In all societies some groups and individuals, for example, certain professionals, are more trusted than others (Barber, 1983). On the other hand, there will be those, second-hand car salesmen, for example, who will be deemed to be less trustworthy than the average; and they may find that they have to behave accordingly (Leonard and Weber, 1970). Trust may be self-reinforcing because it leads to fewer examples of misbehaviour becoming known, such as when regulation has been delegated to the group concerned. The opposite is also true; the more control that is exercised over less trusted groups or individuals the more this leads to the discovery of rule breaking which confirms initial suspicion.

These ideas find ready application in a comparative context. It would be easy to show that different societies do not necessarily see the same groups and individuals as trustworthy (likewise some countries are seen as more reliable than others). For example, the weakness of institutional trust in Italy is such that professionals are rarely trusted on impersonal criteria. Italians talk, rather, of their doctor or dentist '*di fiducia*', a title gained on the basis of special qualities, ties or obligations. Personal trust has to be brought in to supplement whatever trustworthiness is supposed to derive from merely being a member of a learned profession.

The most interesting question regards the fundamental relationship of trust between a state and its citizens. The solutions proposed for the control of official discretion may be seen as a measure of such trust (Bankowski and Nelken, 1982). In my present research I have found the differences between administrative and legal practices between Italy and the United Kingdom so stark that it is tempting to apply Luhmann's ideas about trust so as to say that while the British political and administrative system seeks to respond to citizens on a basis of trust the Italian, on the other hand, does so on the basis of distrust. Each system would then find its predictability in operationalising this choice to trust or to distrust paying the price for the inevitable mistakes (those who could have been trusted or should have been distrusted). Something like this is indeed the explanation offered by Gambetta, an acute observer of the two countries, in an important recent collection of essays on the subject of trust. According to Gambetta:

> Some of the cumbersome aspects of Italian vis-à-vis British bureaucracy can be explained by the fact that the former invariably starts from the assumption that the general public are an untrustworthy lot whose every step must be carefully

checked. Quite apart from the likely effect of self-fulfilment, there is the suspicion that the cost of running such a system may far outweigh the cost of even a large amount of cheating. (Gambetta, 1988: 221)

By contrast, the English legal system, as seen by a French observer, does indeed give the impression of being based on trust, on knowing the limits, on implicit conventions. In so far as this extends beyond the establishment or middle class this is attributed less to open hearted collaboration than to the residues of a culture of deference: 'even when they feel overwhelmed by the coalition between their prosecutors, defenders and judges; petty criminals – ever the submissive sons of paternalism – are more inclined to trust in the equity of their superiors, than they would in that of their equals' (Daudy, 1992: 253). Even if some of this (and this is precisely the point) may be no more than appearance management, it is not without important effects. If we adapt Roniger's distinction between generalised and focalised trust (Roniger, 1992) so as to look at trust from the point of view of the system doing the trusting rather than, as his presentation tends to do, at the viewpoint from below, we could say that, whereas the Italian legal and administrative systems appear to operate on the basis of a *generalised* distrust (with some exceptions for the 'favoured' few), the English tend towards a *focused* distrust (against a general presumption of trust-worthiness).

On the other hand we must avoid the dangers of an oversimplification so radical that it ignores the more subtle distinctions which each system makes in addressing itself to different populations. Offenders are not equal before the law; some are more trusted than others. For example, the ambivalent status of white-collar criminals (far more a feature of Britain than Italy) can be seen as testimony to the difficulty of reconciling the idea of criminality and presumed general trustworthiness (Nelken, 1993). The opposite claim that ordinary businessmen should be seen as 'amoral calculators' willing to commit crime wherever this is feasible (or perhaps whenever they are obliged to do so by the logic of the capitalist system) has, therefore, become central to arguments over the sense, justice and efficiency of the compliance systems of enforcement characteristically used in Britain and the United States (see Hawkins, 1990, 1991; Pearce and Tombs, 1990, 1991). Even for comparable forms of criminal behaviour, such as defrauding social security, groups may be treated differently in terms of the basis on which they are deemed trustworthy (Cook, 1989).

As we have noted, trust is also a relevant factor in regulating the relationship between government and controllers (and among controllers) themselves. Thus the importance of the various stages of appeal in Italy, as in other Continental systems, originally had less to do with the rights of the accused than with ensuring the control of the central administration over the outcomes of important cases (Shapiro, 1981; Damaska, 1986). Even now the relationship between political control and the judiciary is much more sensitive in some Continental countries than in England and in Italy reciprocal lack of trust between politicians and judges is particularly acute.

Police and other enforcement agents who have to collaborate in the pursuit of crimes which have transnational implications (such as EU fraud) also have to develop networks of trust with their opposite numbers in other countries. The apparently banal, practical, difficulties in the way of such cooperation ('why can't the prosecutors in ———— just give us their telephone numbers?' complained some English prosecutors engaged in EU fraud cases) conceal more fundamental rivalries and difficulties of communication arising from different legal and professional cultures. Attempts to overcome these on an ad hoc basis and create informal forms of mutual trust goes against established national procedures and may offend the susceptibilities of Interpol which may seek to discourage such free floating cooperation.

Trust can also provide the key to the relative success of criminals in their attempts to avoid control. Precisely because they act outside the law all cooperation between criminals is ultimately on the basis of 'trust' [20] even if this is typically reinforced by other bonds, incentives and threats. In the case of organised criminal groups, there is the further factor of quasi-familial identification and alliance. Where the law of the 'state' is not seen to guarantee basic protections then organised criminals come to offer this as one of their principal services (Gambetta, 1988, 1992). Trust is also essential between criminals and those whose assistance they require such as corrupt politicians, administrators, policemen as well as experts and professionals or even other groups of criminals (although it is often just such connections which can prove a weak link).

How do you trust?

The way trust is gained (and lost) casts a particularly sharp light on the distribution and maintenance of power and authority in different societies. Both in Italy and in the United Kingdom to a greater or lesser degree 'who you know' is often more important than 'what you know' and much could be written about the differences between these countries in terms of who it is important to know and how such links are consolidated. If the United Kingdom still has its 'Establishment' and 'the old school tie', in Italy, political, social and family groups tend to count more than institutions; there is difficulty in formulating 'the public interest', and institutions are often exploited for the material and ideal interests of the groups to which individuals are affiliated. In the United Kingdom the circuits of power are relatively hidden and the trading of favours indirect and well camouflaged; in Italy 'power' is palpable and the exchange of favours and obligations virtually formalised.

In considering the when, how and why of trust one of the most promising and underexplored hypothesis for the comparative study of social control has to do with the point at which trust is gained and the implications of this. An overall contrast can be drawn between two types of groups, institutions and societies. In the one it is difficult to gain trust (or, what is often the same thing) to become a member but, afterwards, once gained, little further control is exercised. In the other it is relatively easy to become a member but surveillance thereafter is continuous.[21] The relevance of this to criminal justice in general, and the control of fraud in particular, is not far to seek. A priori those groups, or those societies, such as Italy, which stress control beforehand ought to be less prone to fraud. But all depends on who is doing the controlling, when, and for what purpose. We can see this if we try to explain Italy's apparently high level of EU fraud.[22] We could simply say that the national or local politicians (and in part also the controllers) are not really committed to suppressing these crimes and are often even in collusion with the organised crime groups who commit the most lucrative frauds. The political lack of interest in prevention is particularly demonstrated by their failure to exercise effective controls over the way the national body (known as AIMA) which is responsible for providing EU and national agricultural subsidies actually dispenses its funds. But any explanation of the level of EU fraud in Italy as a result of too little control provides only part of the story. It is at least as important to appreciate that the access to the funds distributed by AIMA is made to depend on intermediary associations who grant membership on the basis of quite rigorous political and other criteria of affiliation. Though denounced regularly by the national Court of Auditors, and by the Partito Democratica della Sinistra (PDS) (formerly communist) opposition in parliament, the government continues to rely on these associations both for providing the lists of entitlement and controlling the honesty of applications for subsidies. Thus, strong systems of trust are in operation, at least to determine who is to receive subsidies if not what is done with them, but the function of such trust is to reinforce clientelistic links rather than to facilitate the control of fraud (Chubb, 1982).

A further key element here concerns the methods controllers use to bestow and monitor trust. Italy, when compared with the United Kingdom, exhibits a striking divide between the methods used in personal life for the establishment of trust and that used for official purposes. Social trust depends on face-to-face and telephonic exchanges, preferably mediated at the outset by a third party known to both parties (letters have a rather formal feel and suggest lack of trust). But official life proceeds on the basis of written documents which have to satisfy complicated and often tortuous requirements. Unlike the methods which would be used in private transactions, presentation of the appropriate documentation can easily come to be taken as sufficient proof of reliability, as a 'performative action' rather than as merely a defeasible sign of trustworthiness (Nelken, 1991). This divide between public and private ways of establishing trustworthiness may help to explain why the major method of fraud in Italy involves the use of false or inflated receipts and other documentation presented for (merely) formal control to public authorities. In the United Kingdom or the United States, by contrast, frauds are more likely to flourish by exploiting the initial presumption of trust – and hence initial lack of control – in both the private and public sector. Indeed, one way of interpreting the 'compliance' systems used for regulating business crime is in terms of a deliberate effort to delay the point at which distrust must replace trust.

As this suggests, the real differences in the reasons why personal or impersonal trust is granted also have implications for the way crime is controlled. Only personal trust reflects and reinforces a variety of obligations deriving from a continuing relationship of some kind. In many countries of Continental Europe it would be seen as inconsistent with the impersonal idea of the state for officials to seek to create such a relationship with those they have responsibility for controlling (Dyson, 1980). In turn the licence given in some countries to police or inspectorates to negotiate agreements with offenders represents a measure of the trust bestowed on them by central government.

How much can you trust?

Some authors claim that risk is in the eye of the beholder and that perceived levels of given threats depend on the 'cultural bias' of the group to which the observer belongs (Douglas and Wildavsky, 1982). With still more reason it could be argued that trusting is in some sense constitutive of the trustworthiness of the person or group to be trusted. The level of trust is a variable which therefore depends both on cultural patterns of disposition to trust as well as on any objective differences in the extent to which some individuals and groups can be trusted.

Much of the explanation of the relative economic underdevelopment of Southern Italy has been attributed to the scarcity of this resource. As Walston (an experienced commentator on the politics of Southern Italy) says of one of its regions: 'The first quality that strikes an observer in Calabria is diffidence, not just diffidence towards the outsider, but also within the community, even in small villages. Trust is not a commodity in great supply' (Walston 1988: 98; cf. the classic version of this thesis and the consequent debate in Banfield, 1958, 1976). Is it possible to increase the amount of trust in a society? Is trust a zero-sum game? The answer depends on the type of trust in question. Personal trust essentially rests on a dyadic involvement which is backed up by the exchange of favours over the long term; impersonal trust, on the other hand, is more linked to a willingness to trust in the universalistic operations of economic, financial, political and technical institutions. While the first sort of trust is extended at the implicit expense of those not party to the relationship, the second sort of trust feeds on itself (as in the way confidence in a bank allows it to expand the proportion of its loans which are unsecured at any time by actual cash deposits in its vaults). In a sense it is true that Italy is characterised by both more and less trust; there is more interpersonal trust but less impersonal trust. As a generalisation we could assume that in Italy friends need to, and are willing to, do much more for you than could be expected in Britain. But the very search for trust which so characterises Southern Italy in particular only reinforces the sense of insecurity and lack of a larger background on which to rely. Each time that one individual or group increases the extent to which it can trust others, those outside that pact must face yet another area in which they can trust less.[23] This does not mean, on the other hand, that those who rely on impersonal trust are always right to do so. If the goal for Southern Italy is to learn to trust in trust (Gambetta, 1988) it is also possible as perhaps the British case shows, to put too much trust in financial, political and legal institutions without paying sufficient attention to whose interests they actually represent.[24]

It is widely argued (and this seems also to be Roniger's assumption) that the way to increase trust in modern societies is to attempt to make it more impersonal. Certainly this is true of a certain kind of trust which both makes possible and is itself spread by the growth of the economic forms of reliance of the marketplace. Similarly, the development of impersonal institutions and 'the rule of law' apparently leaves the ordinary citizen freer to pursue his or her activities without having to worry about securing the alliances necessary to create a stable public order (this is not to deny, of course, that impersonal structures of trust benefit some particular groups or interests rather than others). If the Mafia is seen as 'the price of distrust' (Gambetta, 1988) it has also been described as doing its best to ensure that trust remains low (Catanzaro, 1988). On the other hand, the growth of impersonal trust also represents an opportunity which can be exploited by criminals of all kinds. Hence those difficult choices, highlighted by students of white-collar crime, between whether or not to increase economic specialisation which depends on trusting agents (Shapiro, 1989) or how far banks should be allowed to trust their customers as not being engaged in recycling the profits of illicit deals (Levi, 1991). It should also be remembered that a common 'excuse' for crime relates it to the merely impersonal ownership of the goods harmed or stolen and that it is the theft of this form of property which has witnessed the greatest increase over recent years (Heiland et al., 1992).

Crime may be as much a result of too little trust as of too much. A general lack of trust in politicians and leaders can reinforce their tendency to be untrustworthy as they feel forced to surround themselves and reward only those they can really trust (Theobald, 1990). Where trust is low attempts to increase it can often be counterproductive. In the United Kingdom the overwhelming majority of criminal cases are decided at first hearing; it is only as a result of a series of miscarriages of justice (involving in the main those accused of IRA outrages) that thought is now being given to automatic procedures for review. In Italy, on the other hand, many criminal cases pass through two levels of appeal and almost all criminal cases have two trials on the 'facts'. But the benefits in trust and legitimacy that are gained from ensuring everyone 'a second bite at the cherry' are counterbalanced by the loss of trust in the system that comes from the delay which is its consequence. Complicated cases of organised and white-collar crime take an average of 8–10 years to be finally decided. Even fraud can be a result of too little trust and not just a matter of trusting too much or too easily. The complicated procedures which need to be satisfied in order to make claims for EU subsidies help reinforce the dominance of those large organisations – including criminal ones – which have the expertise to deal with them.

Asking questions about the decision to trust and the manner and level of such trusting in different societies therefore allows us to trace out the implications for criminology of different forms of trust. But what then of our original methodological problem of similarity and difference? On the one hand it is important not to identify typifications of trust with given societies or cultures. Even in the same society different and carefully differentiated logics of trust and distrust may be at work contemporaneously among different actors, in different institutions, at different moments, or in response to different phenomena (Bardach and Kagan, 1982). Indeed in the case of Italy understanding the form taken by both crime and criminal justice depends on discovering the complex relationship between both of the two major types of trust we have discussed. For example, the Mafia may be said to flourish in part because it offers a way of securing interpersonal trust where trust is in short supply, in part because many of its criminal enterprises (such as EU fraud) are able to take advantage of ineffective systems of impersonal trust, and in part because the methods used to combat the loyalties on which its solidarity is based tend to rely on unconvincing appeals to have impersonal trust in the 'state' (see Gambetta, 1992).

On the other hand, in order to grasp the characteristic cultural patterns of a given society it will not be sufficient to rely only on 'external' approaches to explanation. As we have seen, the question which would seem to best lend itself to such transcultural operationalising and measurement is that which concerns *the level* of trust.[25] But even this bristles with difficulties. There is certainly empirical evidence about at least some trust relationships, such as the opinion surveys of the level of trust that citizens have in their legal systems, or their politicians. But can such surveys be used to examine the difference between cultures of personal and impersonal trust? Both the United Kingdom and the United States have revealed astonishingly high levels of political disinterest and alienation (see, for example, Held, 1984). Such lack of interest and participation has even been (controversially) argued to be functional for the operation of stable democratic institutions. But whatever the truth of this it does seem as if the institutions of these countries operate 'as if' the level of impersonal trust were greater than it is. What can attitude sampling do to clarify these points? They do show some higher level of institutional trust in the United Kingdom than in Italy though the difference is much less than we might expect (Ashford and Timms, 1992).[26] But what is the significance of even a 'significant' difference? We cannot be sure that the questions and answers mean the same against different cultural backgrounds. At the least (in order to clarify the issue that most concerns us) we would need to be certain whether the meaning given to the concept is personal or impersonal. And this is an issue which surveys up until now have singularly failed to address. We also do not have any guarantee that the responses in favour of trusting carry the same practical implications in different societies. Cultural differences even shape the degree to which coherence between words and actions is considered mandatory. (Our subjects can hardly be expected to adopt a 'view from nowhere' so as to make their replies commensurable.) The answers to such surveys turn out to be raw data which have to be interpreted hermeneutically in the light of wider knowledge of the relevant culture. Fortunately in this task of 'thick description', as Geertz (1973) termed the goal of cultural interpretation, it is not hard to find relevant clues all around, even if they do not allow for mathematical certainties. It is not for nothing, for example, that the entry for trust in a leading Italian dictionary is accompanied by illustrative phrases in which trust always seems to be betrayed.[27] Similarly, an ingenious publicity campaign for wine currently announces 'you can trust what you see', actually playing on the still tempting desire to bestow (impersonal) trust even in a world of often misleading appearances. The title 'Can you trust in trust?', which Gambetta gives the paper in his edited collection, is not just a clever invitation to comparative reflections on the paradoxes of trust; it also offers us valuable insight into the reflexive logic of culture.

Notes

1 Continental criminologists too are more favourable than might be expected to military policing and find the views of their British colleagues less than self-evident. See, for example, the response of German and French commentators to Tony Jefferson's critique of the use of specialised military police forces in Britain in the *débat* published in *Déviance et Sociéte* (1992).

2 In these and in other ways there is a clear link with the agenda of some feminist and postmodern criminologists (see Chapter 1 in this volume).

3 See, for example, Clinard, 1978; Balvig, 1988; Downes, 1988, 1990; Killian, 1989; Franke, 1990).

4 I am therefore less worried by Shapland's finding that criminologists in different European countries are 'not working with a common universe of discourse and addressing common concerns' (Heidensohn and Farrell, 1991: 10) than I would be by the growth of a homogeneous European Criminology.

5 Hirschi and Gottfredson see crime as a universal propensity towards low self-control associated with a tendency to seek quick and risky gratifications (this propensity is itself correlated to other universals relating to age, race, etc.).

6 Their emphasis on deferred gratification is curiously close to the Protestant ethic. Nor is it even true, as they argue, that societies always assume that rigorous defence of the criminal law is essential to social order. This can be seen in the many societies in which the same elites that make the laws simultaneously engage in large scale theft and corruption.

7 While it is certainly a helpful idea to compare the relationship between controllers and controlled in different societies this does not entirely eliminate the need for checking the comparability of the behaviour being controlled.

8 This raises the question of the intended audience for the findings of comparative research. Of Henry James' attempts to write about Americans while living in England, it has been observed that 'James knew that exile from his native country would deprive him not so much of material, as of a world in which his material could resonate' (Gooder, 1988: vii).

9 See for example the contribution of Heidensohn to Heidensohn and Farrell (1991) where she praises the use of comparative data because it provides 'an automatic control group'.

10 For an exception, but one hardly cited in the criminological literature, see Wagner-Pacifici (1986).

11 Eva Halevy-Etzioni (1990), in her excellent study of corruption in Australia and England, shows that even in countries so similar in language, law and culture, as well as having close historical connections, the important issue was whether behaviour was regarded as corruption not just the extent of it.

12 Although the final chapter is preceded by the intriguing heading 'The interpretative turn: a second look' (Haferkampf and Ellis, 1992), it contains in fact no attempt to understand the meaning of crime for the members of the countries concerned but rather an attempt to explain changes in crime rates and sanctions in the United States, Western Europe, Japan and Jamaica on the basis of a somewhat eclectic mix of theories of the levelling out of power (Western Europe), excessive individualism (United States), the weakness of politicians (Jamaica), and the strength of informal controls (Japan).

13 It is interesting to note that Peter Just concludes his review of recent work in anthropology of law by saying that 'it is time to stop looking at culture to illuminate law and start looking at law to illuminate culture' (Just, 1992: 408). But once again we need to avoid taking such dichotomies too seriously – our task must be to tack backwards and forwards so as to use one to illuminate the other.

14 Gottfredson and Hirschi claim that 'criminology shows that interdisciplinary attention is the road to theoretical and practical obscurity' (1990: xiii).

15 Such disciplines and subdisciplines include sociology of law, comparative law, comparative criminal procedure, dispute-processing, social theory, political science, economics, comparative studies of regulation, anthropology, cultural sciences and even cultural psychology.

16 As shown for penology by Garland (1990).

17 Sutherland argued that, if left unchecked, the growth of white-collar crime would lead to the growth of social distrust and the erosion of political legitimacy. Shapiro emphasises the way trust in agents is a necessity of modern economic life but at the same time creates the opportunities for white-collar crime. More generally she argues that all systems of control are subject to necessary limits: eventually *someone* has to be trusted.

18 Italians, who have been well represented among contributors to these debates over trust, have often had a particular concern with explaining why the South has not followed the same road to modernisation as the North of the country.

19 Nor is it easy to isolate the issue of trust from other questions. Indeed trust is so fundamental to social organisation that, as Gellner has warned, unless care is taken an enquiry into its forms can easily come to absorb all questions regarding social order (Gellner, 1988).

20 'You have to trust me. Trust all the way: that's the bottom line when you're smuggling' (Nicholl, 1989: 252).

21 A more comprehensive typology for other purposes might also include those groups (for example, fan clubs) which exercise little control either before or after membership, and those (like organised crime groups) which control carefully both before and after.

22 Annual figures published by the European Commission consistently show Italy declaring much larger value of frauds.

23 This characterisation has been challenged by Mutti (1991) who argues – not entirely convincingly – that clientelistic methods succeed in canalising loyalty towards institutions and that (with the Mafia somehow marginalised) they could be built up so as to produce a distinctively Southern Italian model of development. This would no more presume a background of Protestant social relations and culture than did the successful economic breakthroughs in Japan or other countries of South Asia.

24 It would take us too far from the topic of the present chapter to speculate on the relationship between the strength of impersonal trust in Britain and, as compared with Italy, the relative weakness of personal trust as in family relationships.

25 Other difficulties in actually operationalising trust or distrust as a causal explanation of some feature of crime or criminal justice include deciding where and why to stop the chain of causation. How is the factor of low trust in institutions to be isolated from broader factors (still part of cultural consciousness) such as the late centralisation of the Italian state or the enforced integration of the South? There are also problems of deciding which is cause and which effect. Is

impersonal trust low because of extensive clientelism and corruption or is clientelism and corruption the only way to gain loyalty and some sort of legitimacy in the absence of impersonal trust?

26 Sixty-eight per cent of Italians did not trust their legal institutions – but the same was true for 46 per cent of British respondents (Ashford and Timms, 1992: 16, Table 2.5).

27 *Il Nuovo Ragazzini* (1984) entry for 'fidare'.

References

Ashford, S. and Timms, N. (1992) *What Europe Thinks: A study of Western European Values*. Aldershot: Dartmouth.

Balvig, F. (1988) *The Snow White Image: The Hidden Reality of Crime in Switzerland*. Scandinavian Studies in Criminology 17 Oslo, Norwegian University Press, Scandinavian Research Council for Criminology.

Banfield, E. (1958) *The Moral Basis of a Backward Society*. Glencoe, IL: Free Press.

Banfield, E. (1976) *Le Basi Morali di una Società Arretrata*. Bologna: Il Mulino. (Italian translation of the above which also reprints a range of Italian articles commenting on the author's thesis.)

Bankowski, Z. and Nelken, D. (1982) 'Discretion as a social problem', in M. Adler and S. Asquith (eds), *Discretion and Welfare*. London: Heinmann.

Barber, B. (1983) *The Logic and Limits of Trust*. New Brunswick, NJ: Rutgers University Press.

Bardach, E. and Kagan, R.A. (1982) *Going by the Book: The Problem of Regulatory Unreasonableness*. Philadelphia, PA: Temple University Press.

Beirne, P. (1983a) 'Generalisation and its discontents' in E. Johnson and I. Barak-Glantz (eds), *Comparative Criminology*. Beverly Hills, CA: Sage.

Beirne, P. (1983b) 'Cultural relativism and comparative criminology', *Contemporary Crises*, 7: 371–91.

Binsong, H. (1992) 'Crime and control in China', in H.G. Heiland, L.I. Shelley and H. Katoh (eds), *Crime and Control in Comparative Perspectives*. Berlin and New York: De Gruyter.

Birkbeck, C. (1992) 'Crime and control in Venezuala' in H.G. Heiland, L.I. Shelley and H. Katoh (eds), *Crime and Control in Comparative Perspectives*. Berlin and New York: De Gruyter.

Catanzaro, R. (1988) *Il delitto come impresa*. Padua: Lavinia.

Chubb, J. (1982) *Patronage, Power, and Poverty in Southern Italy: A Tale of Two Cities*. Cambridge: Cambridge University Press.

Clinard, M.B. (1978) *Cities with Little Crime*. Cambridge: Cambridge University Press.

Cook, D. (1989) *Rich Law, Poor Law*. Milton Keynes: Open University Press.

Damaska, M.R. (1986) *The Faces of Justice and State Authority*. New Haven, CT: Yale University Press.

Daudy, P. (1992) *Les Anglais: Portrait of a People*. London: Headline.

Déviance et Sociéte (1992) (Débat) 16, 4: 377–405.

Douglas, M. and Wildavsky, A. (1982) *Culture and Risk*. Berkeley: University of California Press.

Downes, D. (1988) *Contrasts in Tolerance*. Oxford: Oxford University Press.

Downes, D. (1990) 'Response to H. Franke', *British Journal of Criminology*, 30(1): 94–6.

Dyson, K. (1980) *The State Tradition in Western Europe*. Oxford: Martin Robertson.

Eisenstadt, S.N. and Roniger, L. (1984) *Patrons, Clients and Friends*. Cambridge: Cambridge University Press.

Ellis, H. (1992) 'Crime and control in the English-speaking Caribbean: a comparative study of Jamaica, Trinidad, Tobago and Barbados 1960–1980', in H.G. Heiland, L.I. Shelley and H. Katoh (eds), *Crime and Control in Comparative Perspectives*. Berlin and New York: De Gruyter.

Franke, H. (1990) 'Dutch tolerance: facts and fallacies', *British Journal of Criminology*, 30(1) 81–93.

Gambetta, D. (ed.) (1988) *Trust*. Cambridge: Cambridge University Press.

Gambetta, D. (1992) *La Mafia Siciliana: Un Industria di Protezione Privata*. Turin: Enaudi.

Garland, D. (1990) *Punishment and Modern Society*. Oxford: Clarendon Press.

Geertz, C. (1973) *The Interpretation of Cultures*. New York: Basic Books.

Gellner, E. (1988) 'Trust, cohesion and social order' in D. Gambetta (ed.), *Trust*. Cambridge: Cambridge University Press.

Gooder, R.D. (1988) 'Introduction' to Henry James *The Bostonians*. Oxford: Oxford University Press.

Gottfredson, M. and Hirschi, T. (1990) *A General Theory of Crime*. Stanford, CA: Stanford University Press.

Haferkampf, H. and Ellis, H. (1992) 'Power, individualism and the sanctity of human life: development of criminality and punishment in four cultures' in H.G. Heiland, L.I. Shelley and H. Katoh (eds), *Crime and Control in Comparative Perspectives*. Berlin and New York: De Gruyter.

Halevy-Etzioni, E. (1990) 'Comparing semi-corruption among parliamentarians in Britain and Australia', in E. Oyen (ed.), *Comparative Methodology*. London: Sage.

Hawkins, K. (1990) 'Compliance strategy, prosecution policy and Aunt Sally: a comment on Pearce and Tombs', *British Journal of Criminology*, 30: 444–66.

Hawkins, K. (1991) 'Enforcing regulation: more of the same from Pearce and Tombs', *British Journal of Criminology*, 31: 427–30.

Heidensohn, F. and Farrell, M. (1991) *Crime in Europe*, London: Routledge.

Heiland, H.G. and Shelley, L. (1992) 'Civilization, modernization and the development of crime and control', in H.G. Heiland, L.I. Shelley and H. Katoh (eds), *Crime and Control in Comparative Perspectives*. Berlin and New York: De Gruyter.

Heiland, H.G., Shelley, L.I. and Katoh, H. (eds) (1992) *Crime and Control in Comparative Perspectives*. Berlin and New York: De Gruyter.

Held, D. (1984) 'Power and legitimacy in contemporary Britain', in G. Mclennan, D. Held and S. Hall (eds), *State and Society in Contemporary Britain*. Cambridge: Polity Press.

Il Nuovo Ragazzini (1984) (2nd edn). Bologna: Zanichelli.

Joutsen, M. (1992) 'Developments in delinquency and criminal justice; a Nordic perspective', in H.G. Heiland, L.I. Shelley and H. Katoh (eds), *Crime and Control in Comparative Perspectives*. Berlin and New York: De Gruyter.

Just, P. (1992) 'Review essay – History, power, ideology, and culture: current directions in the anthropology of law', *Law and Society Review*, 26(2): 373–411.

Killian, M. (1989) Book review (of Balvig) in *British Journal of Criminology*, 29: 300–5.

Kinsey, R., Lea, J. and Young, J. (1986) *Losing the Fight Against Crime*. Oxford: Blackwell.

Lea, J. and Young, J. (1984) *What is to be done about Law and Order*. Harmondsworth: Penguin.

Leonard, W.N. and Weber, M.G. (1970) 'Automakers and dealers: a study of criminogenic market forces', *Law and Society Review*, 4: 407–24.

Levi, M. (1991) 'Regulating money laundering', *British Journal of Criminology*, 31: 109–25.

Luhmann, N. (1979) *Trust and Power*. New York: Wiley.

Luhmann, N. (1988) 'Familiarity, confidence and trust: problems and alternatives', in D. Gambetta (ed.), *Trust*. Cambridge: Cambridge University Press.

Maclean, B.D. (1993) 'Left realism: local crime surveys and policing of racial minorities', *Law, Crime and Social Change*, 19: 51–87.

Mawby, R. (1990) *Comparative Policing Issues*. London: Unwin Hyman.

Muncie, J. and Sparks, R. (1991) *Imprisonment: European Perspectives*. Milton Keynes: Open University Press.

Mutti, A. (1987) 'La fiducia. Un concetto fragile, una solida realtà, *Rassegna Italiana di Sociologia*, 1: 223–47.

Mutti, A. (1991) 'Sociologia dello svillupo e questione meridionale oggi', *Rassegna Italiana di Sociologia*, 5: 155–79.

Nelken, D. (1991) 'Some problems with the impersonal rule of law in Italy', Paper presented and distributed at the International Conference of the Law and Society Association, Amsterdam, 28 June.

Nelken, D. (1992a) 'The impersonal rule of law in Italy – a study in comparative sociology of law', Paper presented and distributed at the colloquium on The Rule of Law in Western and Eastern Europe, New York University, 30 March.

Nelken, D. (1992b) 'The judicialisation of politics in Italy: some notes on the relationship between the academic and the political debate', Paper presented and distributed at the Interim Meeting of the Research Committee on Comparative Judicial Studies, Forli, Italy, 14 June.

Nelken, D. (1993) 'White-collar crime', in M. Maguire, R. Morgan and R. Reiner, (eds), *Oxford Handbook of Criminology*. Oxford: Oxford University Press.

Nicholl, C. (1989) *The Fruit Palace*. London: Picador.

Passas, N. and Nelken, D. (1991) 'The fight against fraud in the European Community: cacophony rather than harmony', *Corruption and Reform*, 6: 237–66.

Passas, N. and Nelken, D. (1993) 'The thin line between legitimate and criminal enterprises: subsidy frauds in the European Community', *Crime, Law and Social Change*, 19: 223–43.

Pearce, F. and Tombs, S. (1990) 'Ideology, hegemony and empiricism: compliance theories of regulation', *British Journal of Criminology*, 30: 423–43.

Pearce, F. and Tombs, S. (1991) 'Policing corporate "Skid Rows"', *British Journal of Criminology*, 31: 415–26.

Robertson, R. and Taylor, L. (1973) *Deviance, Crime and Socio-Legal Control*. Oxford: Martin Robertson.

Roniger, L. (1989) 'La fiducia. Un concetto fragile, una non meno fragile realtà', *Rassegna Italiana di Sociologia*, 3: 383–402.

Roniger, L. (1992) *La Fiducia nella società moderna: Un approccio comparato*. Rubbetino: Messina.

Shapiro, M. (1981) *Courts*. Chicago, IL: University of Chicago Press.

Shapiro, S. (1989) 'Collaring the crime, not the criminal: reconsidering "white-collar crime"', *American Sociological Review*, 55: 346–65.

Shrivastava, R.S. (1992) 'Crime and control in comparative perspective: the case of India', in H.G. Heiland, L.I. Shelley and H. Katoh (eds), *Crime and Control in Comparative Perspectives*. Berlin and New York: De Gruyter.

Sutherland, E.H. (1949) *White Collar Crime*. New York: Holt, Rinehart and Winston.

Sztompka, P. (1990) 'Conceptual frameworks in comparative inquiry: divergent or convergent', in M. Albrow and E. King (eds), *Globalization, Knowledge and Society*. London: Sage.

Theobald, (1990) *Corruption, Development and Underdevelopment*. London: Macmillan.

Wagner-Pacifici, R.E. (1986) *The Moro Morality Play*. Chicago, IL: Chicago University Press.

Walston, J. (1988) *The Mafia and Clientelism*. London: Routledge.

Index